THE SHAPING OF WESTERN CIVILIZATION

THE SHAPING OF WESTERN CIVILIZATION

VOLUME II: FROM THE REFORMATION TO THE PRESENT

MICHAEL BURGER

UNIVERSITY OF TORONTO PRESS

Library and Archives Canada Cataloguing in Publication

Burger, Michael, 1962–, author
    The shaping of western civilization / Michael Burger.

Also published in a single volume.
Includes bibliographical references and indexes.
Contents: v. I. From antiquity to the mid-eighteenth century—v. II. From the Reformation to the present.
Issued in print and electronic formats.
ISBN 978-1-4426-0756-9 (v. 1 : pbk.).—ISBN 978-1-4426-0759-0 (v. 2 : pbk.).
—ISBN 978-1-4426-0757-6 (v. 1 : pdf).—ISBN 978-1-4426-0758-3 (v. 1 : epub).
—ISBN 978-1-4426-0760-6 (v. 2 : pdf).—ISBN 978-1-4426-0761-3 (v. 2 : epub)

    1. Civilization, Western—History. I. Title.

CB69.B87 2013   909'.09821   C2013-906149-5
C2013-906150-9

We welcome comments and suggestions regarding any aspect of our publications—please feel free to contact us at news@utphighereducation.com or visit our Internet site at www.utppublishing.com.

North America
5201 Dufferin Street
North York, Ontario, Canada, M3H 5T8

2250 Military Road
Tonawanda, New York, USA, 14150

ORDERS PHONE: 1–800–565–9523
ORDERS FAX: 1–800–221–9985
ORDERS E-MAIL: utpbooks@utpress.utoronto.ca

UK, Ireland, and continental Europe
NBN International
Estover Road, Plymouth, PL6 7PY, UK
ORDERS PHONE: 44 (0) 1752 202301
ORDERS FAX: 44 (0) 1752 202333
ORDERS E-MAIL: enquiries@nbninternational.com

Every effort has been made to contact copyright holders; in the event of an error or omission, please notify the publisher.

The University of Toronto Press acknowledges the financial support for its publishing activities of the Government of Canada through the Canada Book Fund.

For Hal Drake, for debts that can't be paid

CONTENTS

FIGURES

MAPS

PREFACE

... that putrefying corpse of historical thought, the "information" to be found in text-books.

—R.G. Collingwood[1]

No picture is exactly like the original; nor is a picture good in proportion as it is like the original. When Sir Thomas Lawrence paints a handsome peeress, he does not contemplate her through a powerful microscope, and translate to the canvas the pores of the skin, the blood-vessels of the eye, and all the other beauties which Gulliver discovered among the Brobdingnagian maids of honor. If he were to do this, the effect would not merely be unpleasant, but, unless the scale of the picture were proportionately enlarged, would be absolutely false.... No picture, then, and no history can present us with the whole truth: but those are the best pictures and the best histories which exhibit such parts of the truth as most nearly produce the effect of the whole.

—Thomas Babington Macaulay[2]

R.G. Collingwood was hard on textbooks. To him, as to most academic historians, real history is history written in support of a thesis, a thesis that itself answers some question in the historian's mind. The work of reasoning from the detritus left by the past—primary sources, such as letters, buildings or shards of pottery—in order to get those answers is an interpretative art. This book attempts such an account of the West from the Protestant Reformation to, roughly, the present. Its goal is to put readers in a position to ask fruitful questions of primary sources. I have a particular collection of sources in mind,[3] but the book will likely work with others as well. Because readers would better spend their time with the primary sources than with this book, it is short. I hope to provide just enough of what Collingwood did not like—a simple conveyance of information—that readers will be able to follow the larger developments presented here.

Interpretation inevitably involves selection, as Macaulay implies. Even textbook writers do it, although they may seek an encyclopedic inclusiveness. Rather than avoid this necessity, I have embraced it in order to give shape to the enormous landscape this book seeks to present, and to do so succinctly. This approach means ruthlessly ignoring exceptions to sweeping generalizations. Moreover, many, many developments fail to appear at all. Some will decide that I have made wrong decisions. Perhaps they will be right. I can only

---

1 *An Autobiography* (Oxford: Oxford University Press, 1939), 75.

2 "The Romance of History," in *The Varieties of History, From Voltaire to the Present,* ed. Fritz Stern, 2nd ed. (New York: Vintage Books, 1972), 76.

3 *Sources for the History of Western Civilization,* ed. Michael Burger (Toronto: University of Toronto Press, 2002), I-II.

hope that the developments rendered here appear with reasonable accuracy, and that most readers will agree that some sort of selection is necessary. It will, however, come as no surprise to receive correction regarding both accuracy and selection, for which I shall be grateful. Perhaps, too, a book by a single author, rather than the teams of historians who usually write these books, will mean a greater overall coherence to compensate for the greater expertise a group of historians can supply.

Decisions about what to discuss have also been guided by a desire to explain the West's present by reference to its often alien past. This aim inevitably means departing from how people in the past viewed their own time. A good example is the space devoted to early modern English political history. This attention is less a matter of Anglophilia than a recognition of the importance of the accidents that made the English Parliament, rather than, say, the Castilian Cortes or the imperial Diet, the "mother of parliaments." I have also written in recognition that most readers of this book will inhabit the West's North American branch.

Another goal has been to give those new to historical study a sampling of different kinds of history. Hence, intellectual, cultural, social, political, gender, and other forms of history appear here in, I hope, coherent union. Again, this approach requires selection. For example, detailed political narrative, like that appearing here on the French Revolution would have produced a very long book if systematically provided throughout.

Interpretation does not mean originality. This book began in the classroom, and it is written primarily for it. Teaching history is also an interpretative art, but one in some ways closer to performing music than to writing history. Musicians select what to play and enjoy some latitude in how to play it; that is why any musical performance is an interpretation. But the notes on the page impose restrictions. Teaching history is like playing works of history, pieces written by people who have done the larger creative work. The history instructor's creativity lies in deciding what to play and how to play it in a way that carries conviction. In this book, cadenzas are rare.

Other classroom imperatives mold this book. One is to give readers a sense of how historians go about using evidence to reconstruct the past. Doing so systematically would be impossible in a book of this scope. Occasional discussion of evidence, along with occasional discussion of historians' disagreements, will have to suffice to provide a glimpse of the world practicing historians inhabit. I have also avoided direct discussion of primary sources that appear in the reader for which this book was written. Hence, some sources that scream for discussion, such as the *Communist Manifesto*, do not get it here; the aim is to leave plenty of room for students to analyze these texts on their own. More mundanely, I hope instructors will find that the division of chapters into numbered subchapters eases assigning parts of chapters for different days. These divisions will also make it easier to drop certain sections altogether without losing overall coherence. Some people and terms have been used in relation to more than one point both to give readers the greater familiarity repeated exposure provides and to create a pool of people and terms more richly significant for "identification" sections on examinations.

I have many people to thank. A number of friends, colleagues, and strangers put their expertise—historical, stylistic, or pedagogical—to my use by criticizing individual chapters: Hal Drake, Will Glass, Paul Harvey, Donald Redford, Barbara Shapiro, Ken Vickers, and Scott Waugh. I benefited from similar careful reading by Broadview Press's panel of anonymous readers. Ginger Hitt generously read all the chapters, as did Miriam Davis, multiplying my benefits and debts. I have also profited very greatly from discussing the course for years with Miriam Davis as we both taught it. Gary Gibbs kindly advised me regarding Ovid's reception in the Middle Ages, and Adam Lynde similarly guided me on aspects of military history. J. Sears McGee graciously talked over with me some large points of early modern history. All this criticism and advice will not, however, have prevented my falling into error, for which I alone am responsible. I am grateful for institutional support from Mississippi University for Women, and in particular to Sheila Adams, Bridget Pieschel, and MUW's president, Claudia Limbert, for approving that support. A grant from MUW's Southern Women's Institute helped finance some of the research in the literature from which this book benefits. As MUW's interlibrary loan librarian, Gail Gunter has, as usual, been my essential link to scholarly collections hither and yon. M.A. Claussen, Robin Fleming, Katherine French, and J. Sears McGee gave me helpful advice when I started to consider this project. This book would not have been written without Mical Moser's persistence in pursuing the idea of a book to accompany *Sources for the History of Western Civilization*, or completed without Martin Boyne, Judith Earnshaw, Natalie Fingerhut, Michael Harrison, and Tara Lowes, who carried the project through to completion. Jennifer Berryman and Carol Morgan also afforded last-minute help. And, finally, I am thankful for the hospitality of the Bean Counter, where some chapters were roughed out.

Musicians learn their craft from other musicians, some of them distinguished composers in their own right. So, too, I have learned much about what to play and how to play it from my own teachers, in particular from Sharon Farmer, J. Sears McGee, Richard Sullivan, and Emily Tabuteau. But those acquainted with Hal Drake's History 4A will recognize his imprint on this book more than anyone else's, and wish it were deeper than it is. I dedicate what follows to him, with gratitude.

In addition to those thanked above, I am grateful to Natalie Fingerhut for suggesting a new edition of this book, one that would take the story from the Enlightenment down to the present and revise and correct the previous discussion. She and others have made the University of Toronto Press a congenial new home for the book. I am especially indebted for improvements wrought by Karen Taylor. Again, Miriam Davis has much improved the book in various ways, especially in critiquing the new chapters. I am also indebted to the University of Toronto Press's team of readers who vigorously identified errors and lacunae. On my end Amanda Moss smoothed the text's passage between me and the press, and Rachel Phillips identified errors. All deficiencies that remain are my responsibility.

NOTES ON REFERENCES, FURTHER READING, AND DATES

All biblical quotations are to the *Revised Standard Version*. In keeping with textbook convention, only direct quotations receive citations. The readings suggested at the end of the chapters scratch the surface of this book's dependence on original scholarship. These lists are not meant to be systematic. The suggestions consist largely of general surveys (often textbooks), source collections (especially ones with extensive introductions and notes), biographies, and more specialized studies. I have favored recent works in part because of the recent bibliographies they offer, but have included the occasional older classic. In all cases, the chief aim is to direct readers to some rewarding books, whether they concur with the lines of interpretation taken here or not. Annotations are minimal. Students may also want to follow up the sources cited in the notes.

Nearly all people named in the text appear with their dates (if known) when first mentioned. Monarchs and popes receive the dates of their rule rather than their lifetimes.

INTRODUCTION

This book is about the history of Western civilization from the end of the Middle Ages (ca. 500–ca. 1500) to the present. It may seem odd that most people in the West ca. 1500 did not think of their civilization as "Western." They instead thought they lived in "Christendom," a seamless union of society and religion. The inhabitants of Christendom were convinced that there was only one true form of Christianity: theirs. These Christians also saw their society as united. Hearkening back to a biblical image, they described their society as "the body of Christ." Different groups in society formed different parts of that body, but were also united like the body's different organs. In a more secular way, this image was sometimes described as "the body politic." Christendom stretched from Western to parts of Eastern Europe, from Spain to Poland.

To the east of Christendom lay another Christian society, one that Western Christians regarded as heretical. The Orthodox, sometimes called the Eastern Orthodox, Church did not recognize the authority of the pope, as Western Christians did. Some of the East's theology and ceremony were different and their priests, unlike Western priests, married. This division between two Christian societies sprang from an older division. Many centuries before, the Roman Empire had been divided into Eastern and Western halves, each assigned an emperor. The Latin-speaking Western Roman Empire's capital continued to be the city of Rome. In the Greek-speaking East, a "New Rome" was founded to serve as the capital: at Constantinople in what is today Turkey. Christendom, at least Western Christendom, was the descendant of the Western half of the empire. Historians have called the Eastern half of the empire "Byzantium" or the "Byzantine Empire," although the Byzantines continued to call themselves Romans. From Byzantine civilization derive the societies that look to the Orthodox Church, such as modern Greece and Russia.

My description of the medieval West as Christendom may, however, deceive. Yes, medieval people did not tolerate non-Christians (with the exception of the barely tolerated Jews) or, for that matter, forms of Christianity other than their own. But Christendom ca. 1500 was not a monolithic civilization. Instead, various authorities coexisted in a sometimes uneasy truce.

First, there was church and state. Most people were ruled by some sort of monarch, the king of France, or the king of England, and so on. Such monarchs, however, were far from all powerful. Nobles everywhere limited their authority. Everywhere, too, the authority of the Church was recognized, headed by the pope. Indeed, the Church seemed to be a kind of state, with its own courts that heard matters ranging from marital infidelity to disputes over wills. Moreover, from the city of Rome, the pope ruled over a portion of central Italy, raising and paying armies to defend his lands or conquer new ones; Pope Julius II (1503–1515), wearing armor, even led his forces in person. Popes also had grand claims to wield the ultimate authority in Christendom, supreme over kings as well as bishops. But such claims did not reflect reality. Kings, although limited by noble power, still exercised much more effective control over their kingdoms than the pope. Rather than insist on bishops loyal to Rome, popes often simply appointed bishops that kings wanted rather than force the issue of who really controlled such appointments. Royal courts readily curbed church courts, and popes accepted such limits more than they protested them. The pope's very need to deploy his own forces to defend his territory in Italy indicates that kings were not at his beck and call. In practice, popes and kings preferred compromise to conflict by ca. 1500, with kings getting the better part of the bargain.

Papacy and crown were, however, just two of a multitude of authorities to which people looked for guidance at the close of the Middle Ages. The clergy, although often subject to criticism on moral grounds, played a leading role in the salvation of individual Christians. They were the channels through which God's forgiveness flowed when Christians confessed their sins and priests performed the transformation of bread and wine into the body and blood of Christ, a ritual central to Christian worship. At the same time, individuals turned inward, seeing their own interior, spiritual lives as of essential importance, looking to themselves, not just the clergy, as authorities.

And there were exterior authorities other than clergy or crown. Women regarded, or at least were expected to regard, men, specifically husbands and fathers, as authorities. Yet some holy women, embracing bodily suffering as Christ did, exercised a special authority respected by men, whereas others escaped fathers and marriage by entering the monastic life. Then there were written authorities. Ancient Greece and Rome spoke through texts such as those of the Greek Aristotle (384–322 BC) or the Roman Virgil (70–19 BC). The literate looked to such works for guidance, believing that, except for religious matters, such pagan writers had known all that could be known. The eyes of the humanists of the Renaissance were as fixed on such works as their predecessors and, indeed, humanists themselves as reviving a lost past through restoring such works. Reason, too, was an authority, often thought to have been perfectly exercised—except where it conflicted with Christian teaching—by Aristotle. Indeed, ideally, Christian faith (another authority) was expected to agree with reason, as represented by ancient pagan philosophy, although this view was under challenge in the last centuries of the medieval period. A major project of medieval intellectuals, known as "scholastics," was to reconcile the truths of Christian faith, as revealed in the Bible, with those of reason, as revealed by Aristotle. The Middle Ages had seen periodic efforts to reform the Church, generally led by clergy. The unity of religion and society in Christendom had meant that these movements had shaken society as well as the Church. In the Middle Ages, reformers and their opponents ultimately compromised. What would happen if new reformers refused to do so?

THE EARLY MODERN WEST I

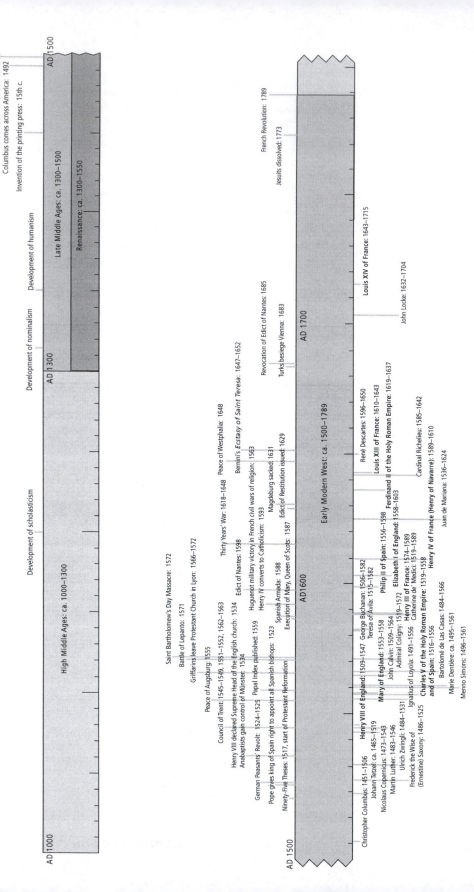

SIX

THE EARLY MODERN WEST I: THE REFORMATION, THE GREAT CONSOLIDATION, AND THE END OF CHRISTENDOM

6.0 INTRODUCTION

The sixteenth century saw a massive effort to reform Christendom yet again: the Protestant Reformation. The result was the West's division into two broad religious camps. One was composed of Protestants, those people who attempted (in their view) to reform the medieval church and, dissatisfied with the unwillingness of that church to reform, broke from it. The other was composed of those who have since come to be identified as "Catholics," those who remained loyal to the remains of the medieval church.

Christendom had vast consequences for the Reformation, and the Reformation had vast consequences for Christendom. Christendom's lack of distinction between religion and society meant that the attempt to reform religion ultimately touched just about every aspect of Western society, from high politics to family life. Thus, a thorough discussion of the Reformation means a discussion of just about everything in the sixteenth century. But the Reformation also ultimately helped bring about the end of Christendom itself. Most obviously, the permanent division between Catholic and Protestant meant that the West could no longer see itself as a single Christian society. By ca. 1600, most of northern Germany, Scandinavia, part of Switzerland, parts of France (especially in the south), and the kingdoms of England and Scotland were Protestant. Italy, Spain, most of France, and southern Germany were Catholic, and the newly conquered lands of Latin America were in the long process of becoming so (see Map 6.2). The Netherlands was divided, the southern and Catholic portion remaining under Habsburg rule (centuries later to become the kingdom of Belgium), the north, Protestant, retaining its identity as the Netherlands. It was not until ca. 1650 that the allegiance of Poland to Catholicism would be clear. Setting aside French Protestantism, these divisions remain. Just as critically, however, the conflicts brought by the Reformation in the long run fostered moves to separate religion from society and politics, to see religious belief as a private matter. Thus, the Reformation helped end the fusion of religion and society that was Christendom. This development explains part of the title of this chapter. Those historians dissatisfied with the notion of the Renaissance as the fundamental break between medieval and modern Western history have increasingly tended to see the Reformation of the sixteenth century as marking the start of a new period of Western history, "early modern," running from ca. 1500 to ca. 1789 (the beginning of the French Revolution).

Finally, the Reformation brought about a consolidation of authority in various senses. Yet, at the same time, it contributed to a crisis of authority in the West by ca. 1600.

6.1 FUNDAMENTALS: PROTESTANT DOCTRINE AND THE MIDDLE AGES

Historians often root the Reformation in various social, economic, and political conflicts, seeing people's decisions to become Protestant or remain Catholic as expressions of other, non-religious considerations. (There are good reasons for this approach. For some of them, see 6.5.) When all is said and done, however, the Reformation was a battle over Christian doctrine. And so it is necessary to begin there.

Starting with theology means starting with a monk and theology professor, Martin Luther (1483–1546). Luther sparked what would become the Protestant Reformation at Wittenberg in Germany when, in 1517, he posted "Ninety-Five Theses," or statements of belief, on a church door. This rather public move had been prompted by particularly crude measures of the papacy and some bishops to raise money by distributing indulgences. Johann Tetzel (ca. 1465–1519), the agent charged with issuing indulgences in Germany, had, it was said, told prospective donors that "As soon as the coin in the coffer rings / The soul into heaven springs."[1] Technically, an indulgence was not effective if the recipient did not truly repent. Moreover, indulgences were not sold; they simply certified a good deed in the form of a donation to the church. Indeed, the pope directed that the poor were to have them for nothing. But these technicalities were easily lost on recipients and glossed over by men like Tetzel who had financial targets to meet. Anyone who has entered

---

1   Hans J. Hillerbrand, ed., *The Reformation in Its Own Words* (London: SCM Press, 1964), 42.

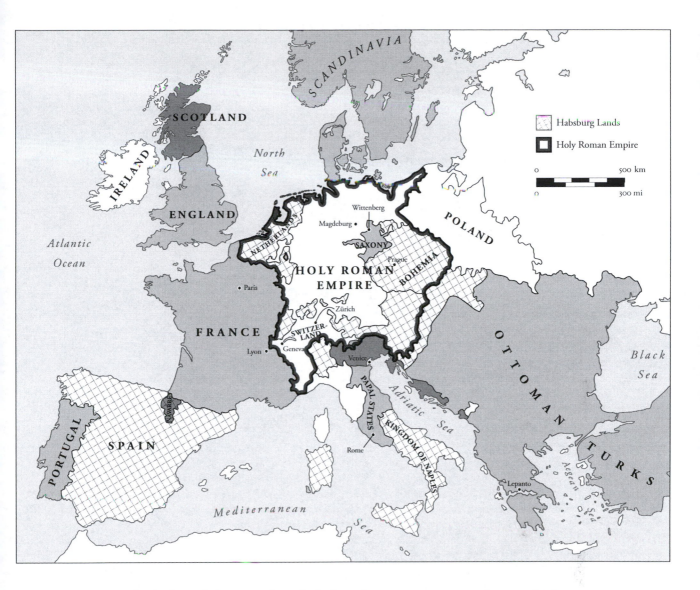

Map 6.1: Europe ca. 1500

a museum that is free of charge, and yet finds that admission requires a ticket on which a "donation" of a certain amount is listed, will see how practice can mask theory. Entry does not feel free, and the museum has good reason for it not to. The fact that Tetzel's task was to raise money to recover costs associated with the archbishop of Mainz's dispensation for pluralism only added insult to injury.

But in attacking indulgences, Luther found himself taking theological positions that the church would not accept. In a manner reminiscent of the doctrinal battles of the early church, the conflict led Luther and his opponents to refine their thinking, widening the conflict. What ideas did Luther end up spelling out?

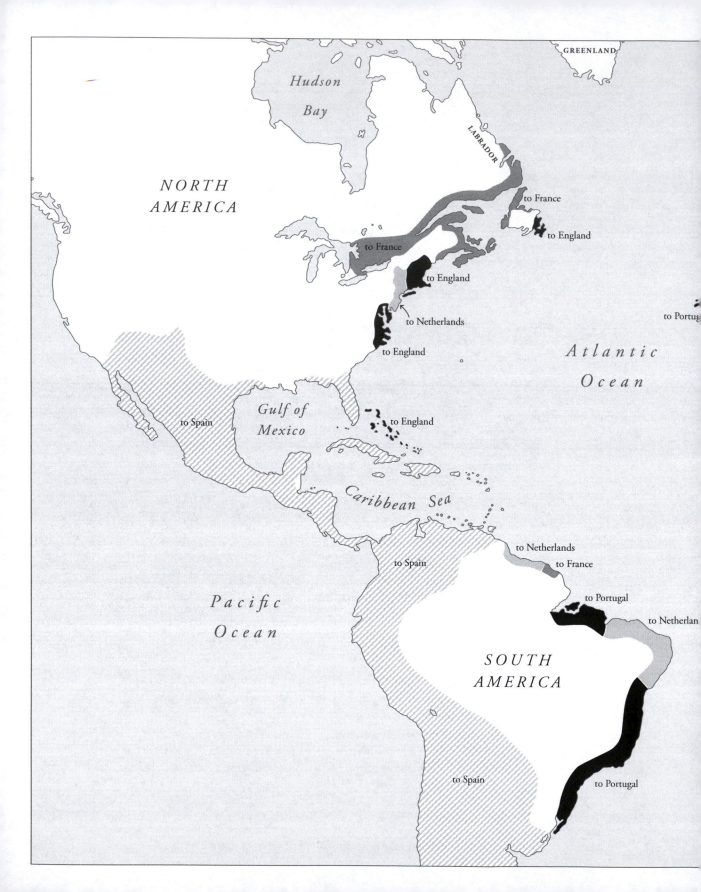

GREENLAND

Hudson
Bay

LABRADOR

NORTH
AMERICA

to France

to England

to France

to England

to Netherlands

to England

Atlantic

Ocean

to Portug

Gulf of
Mexico

to Spain

to England

Caribbean Sea

to Netherlands

to France

to Spain

to Portugal

to Netherlan

Pacific

Ocean

SOUTH
AMERICA

to Spain

to Portugal

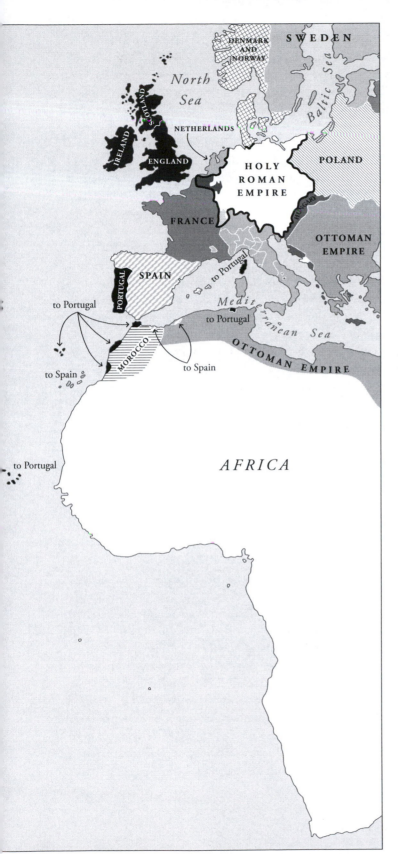

Map 6.2: The West and the Americas ca. 1648

First among them was "solifidianism," salvation by faith alone. The medieval church had long held that faith in the Christian god could, by itself, gain one entry into heaven. But the church had also allowed the doing of good deeds, or "works," an additional, supplementary role. Such works could range from caring for the poor and the sick to embracing perpetual poverty, chastity, and obedience in a monastery, from endowing a priest to say masses for the good of one's soul (or those of one's parents and friends) to a donation to the church (on the occasion of receiving an indulgence, for example). Works could count with the Christians' god. In attacking indulgences, however, Luther denied that his god had any interest in works whatsoever. Faith, and only faith, could please him. To use Luther's language, the Christian god cared only about the "inner man" not the "outer man."

Luther's championing of faith had another side to it. Medieval scholastics had been interested in allowing reason some role in religion; in particular, they wanted to reconcile faith and reason. Luther rejected such moves. For him, authority in religious matters stemmed from two sources only: a plain, literal reading of the Bible and the simple Christian faith that made such a plain and literal approach possible. The rational speculations of philosophers led only to hell.

Both aspects of Luther's stress on faith are evident in his account of the communion. The church had long held that the bread and wine consumed in that ritual became Jesus's actual flesh and blood, citing the New Testament in which Jesus said, "This is my body.... This is my blood."[2] In the High Middle Ages, this miracle increasingly highlighted the special authority of the clergy, for it was the priest's utterance of those words that made it happen. Yet how was it that Jesus's blood could still taste like wine, his flesh like bread? Scholastic theologians deployed the ancient philosopher Aristotle's distinction between "substance" and "accident" to argue that, although the bread and wine themselves changed into flesh and blood (i.e., their "substance" changed), the outward characteristics of bread and wine (their "accidents") remained unchanged. So reason and faith could be reconciled in this, the theory of transubstantiation.

To Luther, transubstantiation was nonsense, in two respects. First, Luther contended that it was not the priest who led God to produce Christ's flesh and blood in the bread and wine; it was the faith of the individual believer receiving the bread and wine that did so. Yes, communion was important to a Christian's salvation, but it was the Christian's faith, not the action of some third party (such as a priest), that made communion happen. Second, although Luther accepted the physical appearance of Christ's flesh and blood in the communion—to him, a simple and literal reading of the Bible left no choice but to do so—that did not justify fouling faith and scripture with rational, Aristotelian analysis. Of course, this position, known as that of the "Real Presence," left Luther vulnerable to just the sort of objection the theory of transubstantiation had been designed to answer: how can the bread and wine become flesh and blood but not taste, smell, or look like flesh and blood? Luther's answer reveals his attitude toward rational analysis: "I will, for one,

---

2 New Testament, Matthew 26.26–28.

take my understanding prisoner."[3] To do otherwise was to challenge faith and scripture. The farthest he would go was that Christ's flesh and blood coexisted with the bread and wine of communion.

Luther's solifidianism and stress on the authority of the Bible read literally became hallmarks of Protestantism. Other characteristics of the Protestant movement flowed from them. The stress on individual faith as the only means of salvation left individual Christians to face their god alone. Nothing but their own faith—and their god's mercy— could save them: not the prayers of friends and family, not the prayers of monks and nuns. Monasticism and asceticism in general, built as they were on works, became, at best, irrelevant to Protestants. The cult of the saints, those dead holy people who could call on God to help the living and the dead, was pointless. Moreover, Protestant theology sapped the distinction between clergy and laity and thus the clergy's special position. Luther signaled this change by speaking of the "priesthood of all believers." After all, if those who have faith convert bread and wine into Christ's body and blood in the communion, they were, in medieval (and modern Catholic) terms, exercising the power of priests. Indeed, Protestants avoided the term "priest" for their clergy, calling them "ministers" (i.e., "servants") instead to stress their lack of special authority. Similarly, Protestant clergy married, denouncing celibacy both as one of those works for which God did not care and as a meaningless distinction between clergy and laity. Moreover, if individual Christians faced their god alone and if a simple and literal reading of scripture was the only religious authority a Christian should accept, then individuals should read and understand the Bible for themselves rather than rely on clergy to do that critical work for them.

Their stress on the Bible's authority, particularly that of the New Testament, and their conclusion that the church in their own time failed to live up to that authority led Protestants to an historical explanation for the gap between the early church and their own time. Protestants concluded that the first Christians had known what they did, which explained why the New Testament said what it said and could be taken simply and literally. But subsequent generations, they held, had corrupted that early vision. Led by sin and the devil, those later Christians had based Christian teaching and practice on slowly evolving tradition, shaped by clerical ambition and an untoward reliance on rational philosophy. Now, however, with the New Testament's light piercing the mists of time, Christians could return to the early, uncorrupted church.

If Luther began the Protestant movement, John Calvin (1509–1564) turned out to be its second founder. Beyond Germany, Calvinism became the dominant, but not the only, form of Protestantism. (The largest modern Calvinist denomination is that of the Presbyterians, stemming from Scotland.) Calvin, like other Protestants, stood in broad agreement with Luther on the issues already discussed, with the partial exception of the communion (see 6.4). He also clarified an important element in Luther's theology: a belief in predestination. Calvin, a good Protestant, held that faith and faith alone determines one's

---

3 Martin Luther, "The Pagan Servitude of the Church," in *Martin Luther: A Selection from His Writings*, ed. John H. Dillinberger (Garden City, NJ: Doubleday & Company, 1961), 260.

salvation. Yet, he asked, what decides whether one will have that faith? Luther had already answered this question. Following Augustine as well as some medieval theologians (but basing his ideas on scripture), Luther had concluded that human beings alone were incapable of willing themselves to have the faith necessary for salvation. They required God's help when they could not help themselves. Over the years, however, Calvin put the case even more boldly. He considered carefully the omnipotence of the Christian god. If the individual could decide to have faith, that took away from the power of a god who was supposed to be all-powerful. After all, a truly omnipotent god could not be faced with a believer's chit for salvation: "Here I am: I believe; you must admit me to heaven." So, Calvin concluded, it must be God alone who decrees who has faith and thus decides both who will be saved and who will be damned, hence the doctrine of "double predestination," to heaven or hell. And, naturally, the works that individuals do cannot lead God to decide who will have faith and be saved; to think that would be both to undermine the role of faith in salvation and, again, to leave individuals able to exercise power over God by doing deeds that force his hand. So God decided who will have faith, and so be saved, and who will not, and so burn, at the beginning of time, for no reason. (This emphasis on an incomprehensible deity might have found sympathy among ancient Hebrews.) The Christian god has thus predestined everyone to heaven or damnation, regardless of one's action or merits. Calvin remarked, quoting Augustine, that God did not save the damned because "he did not want to, and why he did not want to is his own business."[4]

The drive to stress biblical authority and to erase intermediaries between individuals and their god produced a Protestant style of worship distinct from that of the traditional church, a style that was apparent even to people who did not fully follow the twists and turns of a professorial theology. With Protestant clergy no longer endowed with the power of communion, what was left for them to do? To educate. Preaching had been an occasional activity of medieval clergy, and some orders, such as the Franciscans, that aimed particularly to combat the heresies of the High Middle Ages, had specialized in it. But Protestants took up preaching—a call to faith and scripture—with a vengeance. The management of schools to ensure that all Christians received the education necessary for a proper Christian (ideally Bible-reading) life became a clerical mission. Protestants' greater stress on lay participation led to Latin being dropped from church services, to be replaced by the language of everyday speech. The stress on hearing the "Word of God" changed the physical setting in which Protestants often worshipped. Although a church full of stained glass, painting, and sculpture served well the needs of the tactile religion produced by the High and Late Middle Ages, to Protestants, such a church was full of distractions from the sermon. Worse, it was a church that appealed to the bodily senses—to the "outer man"—rather than to the spirit—the "inner man." Protestants stressed the gulf between these two aspects of human beings, whereas earlier medieval people had seen Jesus as forming a bridge between them. Calvinists, in particular, purged churches

---

4 Quoted in Jaroslav Pelikan, *The Christian Tradition: A History of the Development of Doctrine*, vol. 4, *Reformation of Church and Dogma, 1300–1700* (Chicago: University of Chicago Press, 1984), 222.

of centuries of accumulated art and decoration, harkening back to Hebrew denunciations of idolatry. Julius II's ceiling of the Sistine Chapel perfectly summed up much of what many Protestants felt was wrong about the church: not only was it built by a secular-minded pope, no doubt with the proceeds of indulgences, but its walls were covered by magnificent paintings of biblical scenes. The stress on equality between clergy and laity was made visible in church by having laity as well as clergy consume the wine that the medieval church had reserved for clergy alone. More radical Protestants demanded that clergy discard their vestments, that is, the special robes distinguishing them from laity. The tonsure (the shaving of the head required of medieval clergy), too, was abandoned by Protestant clergy.

Protestantism was, in many respects, a natural development of the High (ca. 1000–ca. 1300) and Late (ca. 1300–ca. 1500) Middle Ages. Protestant solifidianism assertively expressed the importance of the interior religious life, on felt religion as opposed to physical action, an idea that had flourished in the High and Late Middle Ages. Moreover, the Late Middle Ages had seen a large-scale assault on the authority of reason in general and on scholastic theology in particular. Calvin's predestinarian god, moreover, harmonized with the god depicted by some late-medieval scholastics: a god of will rather than of intellect, an incomprehensible god who hands out reward and punishment for no particular reason. When Protestants attacked the special standing of priests, they attacked an order whose power over and independence from lay authority had been on the decline for at least two centuries. And, in so doing, they picked up one of the tools that had long been used to criticize that order, not least by reform-minded clergy themselves. Echoing medieval protests, Protestant propaganda complained bitterly about greedy and immoral priests. The higher up they were, the worse they behaved. Men such as the pope, whose claim to lead the world was based on being above it, had long been open to the criticism that they exhibited the sort of worldliness that leading the world requires. Protestant calls to read the Bible directly echoed the humanists' call to return to an unmediated reading of old texts and, in particular, the Christian humanists' emphasis on the study of scripture. And just as humanists had come to see themselves as using texts to return to a past from which they were separated by an intervening "middle age," Protestants discovered a sense of historical distance from the early church, one to be overcome by immersion in the New Testament with faith, not reason or tradition, as a guide.

In all this, one can see a kind of consolidation going on. Protestants narrowed the number of authorities in religious matters—faith, reason, scripture, the clergy, fathers of the church—to two: faith and scripture. This sort of consolidation was to be characteristic of the Reformation.

But if so much of Protestant thought was rooted in the past, why did it shake up the West like no other reform movement since the Gregorian Reform of the eleventh century? The question is hard to answer, but it seems that two important conditions played a part. The first is the printing press. Based on methods introduced into Europe from China in the mid-fifteenth century, the printing press made books cheap. For example, in 1483 the Ripoli Press produced 1,025 copies of a translation of Plato's works for three florins a section, relying on the labor of a few men printing the work on paper (made from rags, and so a less expensive material than parchment). A typical scribe would have charged only one florin for the same portion of text—but to produce only a single copy. Printers could thus radically undercut the fees charged by scribes. The printing press meant that Protestant propaganda could spread fast before the movement could be squelched. Within weeks of their posting, thousands of copies of Luther's Ninety-Five Theses were all over Germany. One Lutheran said it was as though angels had brought them before the people. Moreover, a religion of the Book demanded that bibles be easily available. The printing press put bibles within the reach of more people. And to extend that reach further, Protestants worked to make translations available in the vernacular languages read by the less educated, in particular, by lay people. Luther took the lead, producing his own German-language Bible. Where people did not read, reformers printed cartoons illustrating Protestant talking points.

The other condition was political. The West ca. 1500 had seen a long development of overlapping and competing political authorities. Germany was a particularly extreme case, where a Holy Roman Emperor exercised limited authority over the territorial princes of the empire, who were always suspicious of imperial power. That suspicion was only sharpened by the situation when the Reformation began. Accidents of marriage and inheritance had made the emperor, Charles V (Holy Roman Emperor 1519–1558, king of Spain 1516–1556), head of the house of Habsburg, king of Spain, and ruler of the Netherlands and much of Italy. He was also rapidly becoming master of most of Latin America, then being conquered by Spain. He was, in other words, the most powerful man in the West, and German princes had reason to think that this Spanish prince might now try to make his claim to rule Germany effective in more than name. When Charles attempted to stop Luther and his heresy, Luther found protection with the prince of Ernestine Saxony, Duke Frederick the Wise (1486–1525).

Frederick was no Protestant. An enthusiastic cultivator of the saints, he had collected 19,000 of their relics in his castle (rebuilt to hold them), and he maintained both these and an endowment to support nearly 10,000 masses a year for his soul even after Luther's break with the church. Frederick's motives for protecting Luther are unclear. Perhaps he simply wanted to protect the university he had founded at Wittenberg, where Luther taught. Or perhaps he felt that emperors should know their place and respect the rights of the princes to manage their internal affairs. Other princes likely agreed. In addition, the Turks threatened a Muslim conquest from the east; Charles, as the most powerful man in Christendom, was obliged to divert resources to meet them. And so Luther's movement survived and found room to grow in a divided Germany. When Luther stood before papal agents sent to examine him under the sponsorship of the emperor and refused to recant (he was remembered as saying, "Here I stand, I can do no other"), he did so with a ready refuge in Saxony, although he may not have known it. Calvin enjoyed a similar situation when he moved from France to what is today Switzerland, then a land where cities, now city states, had largely won the competition for government authority in the High and

Late Middle Ages.[5] His new home, the city of Geneva, like Luther's refuge of Saxony, was positioned to give him safety from hostile higher powers and so fostered Calvin's and Calvinism's survival. For both men, the protection was precarious. But it was enough.

6.2 A CATHOLIC REFORMATION?

The sixteenth century also saw the remains of the old medieval church reform itself. Traditionally, these reforms have been described as the "Counter-Reformation," that is, as simply a negative reaction against the Protestant Reformation. More recently, historians have seen such efforts as a "Catholic Reformation," a reform movement stemming from concerns on the agenda before Luther's break with the church. I incline to the former view, for it seems that the church's efforts were made very much with an eye on Protestantism. The great Council of Trent (1545–1549, 1551–1552, 1562–1563), which undertook to define doctrine and reform the church, was summoned by the pope to deal with the Protestant threat. The Society of Jesus (also known as the Jesuits), a new church order that spearheaded reform, quickly channeled its energies to the same purpose. Yet it is also undeniable that reformers who remained within the church, like Protestants themselves, drew on currents running before the Protestant Reformation began. As a result, by 1700 the Catholic Church, in some ways, had more in common with the new Protestant churches than with its medieval predecessor. By the same token, in some ways, it had come closer than its predecessor to achieving what medieval reformers had aimed at.

In many respects, the Catholic Church reaffirmed what Protestants attacked. Transubstantiation, long taught but never officially adopted by the church in its technical Aristotelian guise, was made official Catholic doctrine by the Council of Trent. More broadly, the reconciliation of Aristotelian philosophy and the truths of the faith propounded by the scholastic Thomas Aquinas in the thirteenth century became official church teaching. In this way, the Catholic Church now rooted its doctrine more firmly in scholastic attempts to join faith and reason than it had ca. 1500. The role of works in salvation also received its first explicit definition in official church teaching. Catholic churches embraced the tactile religion that Calvinists denounced from their whitewashed churches. The bodily aspects of Jesus's suffering and the appeal to the senses both received stress in Catholic churches, giving birth to a new, especially sensuous style ca. 1600, the baroque. Consider the example of Bernini's *Ecstasy of Saint Teresa*, found in the church of Santa Maria della Vittoria in Rome (Figure 6.1). It captures Teresa of Ávila's (1515–1582) own description of one of her visions:

> It pleased the Lord that I should sometimes see the following vision. I would see beside me, on my left hand, an angel in bodily form.... It pleased the Lord that I should see this

---

5   Calvin moved to the city of Geneva, then not part of Switzerland but nonetheless an independent city that would join that country.

angel in the following way. He was not tall, but very short, and very beautiful, his face so aflame that he appeared to be one of the highest types of angel who seem to be all afire.... In his hands I saw a long golden spear and at the end of the iron tip I seemed to see a point of fire. With this he seemed to pierce my heart several times so that it penetrated to my entrails. When he drew it out, I thought he was drawing them out with it and he left me completely afire with a great love for God. The pain was so sharp that it made me utter several moans; and so excessive was the sweetness caused me by this intense pain that one can never wish to lose it, nor will one's soul be content with anything less than God. It is not bodily pain, but spiritual, though the body has a share in it—indeed, a great share.[6]

Although the Catholic Church gave no ground to Protestantism regarding the authority of the clergy, it did address Protestant complaints about their moral lapses, lapses that the church itself had been attempting to root out since the Gregorian Reform. A more effective clergy would dampen Protestantism's appeal. The sixteenth century saw renewed efforts to enforce clerical celibacy, to insist on monastic observance of monastic vows, and to limit the church's fiscal orientation. It also moved to create an educated clergy capable of going head to head with Protestants arguing from biblical authority. Rather than simply laying down educational requirements for clergy as in earlier centuries, the church went further, creating schools specifically designed to prepare clergy for their work: the first seminaries. These new schools offered not only a Thomist (for Thomas Aquinas) education but also a humanist one, including biblical study in a style that might have appealed to Erasmus.

Indeed, the Catholic and Protestant churches lived in a common world, so, in some ways, they came to look alike. The Catholic work of education went further than training clergy, for one way to inoculate lay Catholics against Protestantism was to make sure they had a good grasp of Catholic teaching. Catholic clergy took to preaching just as Protestants did. The pulpit, from which the priest preached, became a feature of both Catholic and Protestant churches. Following medieval precedent, both Protestant and Catholic authorities also drew up catechisms, summaries of important points of doctrine to be memorized by the faithful, and these catechisms were inculcated with greater determination. With education also went observation. In both Catholic and Protestant countries, the danger of heresy from the other side led authorities, especially clergy, to monitor people's beliefs more closely in order to correct wrong doctrine or, if necessary, erase wrong believers altogether. In Italy, the papacy revived the medieval Inquisition courts to try accusations of heresy. Another step was to prevent exposure to unorthodox belief altogether. In 1559 the pope issued the "Roman Index [or list] of Prohibited Books," which would be added to from time to time. Catholics were not to read these books, and Catholic printers were not to print them. The issues raised by Protestants ensured that vernacular bibles made the index.

Figure 6.1 (facing page): Bernini, *Ecstasy of Saint Teresa* (1647–1652)

---

6   *The Complete Works of Saint Teresa of Jesus* [Ávila], trans. E. Allison Peers (New York: Sheed and Ward, 1949), 1: 192–93.

The church sought not just to defend the souls it had but to save those it had lost. The forefront of this effort was taken by new religious orders, in particular the Society of Jesus. Its founder, Ignatius of Loyola (1491–1556), wanted to create a religious order more active in the world than the medieval orders had been. The order was to be strictly centralized for greater effectiveness and entirely responsive to the pope. The Jesuits, as they became known, quickly found their vocation in the battle with Protestantism. Part of this mission meant covert operations to bring comfort and Catholic services, such as the mass, to Catholics stranded in Protestant countries, where such services were illegal. Another part meant more direct reconversion, by preaching. The creation of Jesuit schools for lay people also aimed at reconversion. The schools were some of the best in the West, offering the finest humanist education available—indeed, they drew on examples of humanist Protestant schools—and offering it free of charge. Jesuit schools produced Catholics well versed in Catholic doctrine: both laity and clergy and, of course, more Jesuits (the 1,000 Jesuits in 1556 increased to 15,500 by 1626). In those parts of the West where Protestant and Catholic still mixed, Protestant children sent to Jesuit schools because of their quality found themselves exposed to Catholic doctrine.

But this effort at conversion was also soon directed at targets other than Protestant Europe. In 1492, Christopher Columbus (1451–1506), in Spain's employ, had sailed to find a new, westerly route to Asia. He failed, but, in the course of the next century, the Spanish and Portuguese conquered an immense area, now known as Latin America. The conquest was made possible by the highly communicable diseases, such as smallpox, carried by the conquerors. Aboriginal populations (called "Indians" because Columbus had thought he had reached the Indies, in Asia) had no previous exposure and therefore little resistance. It is estimated, for example, that the population of central Mexico, about 30 million in 1492, had fallen to about 3 million by 1568—and by almost 50 percent again by 1620. The Spanish and Portuguese thought of this conquest as simply a continuation of the *reconquista* of the Spanish peninsula from the Muslims (the last Muslim stronghold there, Granada, fell to Christians in the same year Columbus set sail). Christendom itself had expanded, but while the bodies of pagan Indians had been subdued, what of their souls? By 1600, the Jesuits were spearheading efforts at their conversion, characteristically setting up schools as part of that program. Indeed, the Jesuits went farther afield, sending missions to Ethiopia, India, China, Japan, and the Philippines.

At home, however, such efforts saw only partial success. The division of Christendom remained permanent.

6.3 THE SEXES AND THE FAMILY

One should not take the Protestant return to Christianity's earliest days at face value. Each generation lacks a full understanding of the past and a full awareness of the present; sixteenth-century Protestants were no different. Like the Renaissance humanists who adopted Carolingian minuscule in the mistaken belief that it had been the script used by the ancients, Protestants did not achieve the full resurrection of the past they thought they had. In one respect, however, Protestants did, perhaps without realizing it, revive a tradition of very early Christianity: a reliance on the energy and leadership of women. The equality of all in Christ, clergy and laity, suggested the equality of the sexes, at least in religious matters. True, in the Middle Ages, holy women might exercise authority by proclaiming their humility in a physical agony that made them Christlike. But, among Protestants, the stress on biblical authority allowed less unusual women, the merely literate, such authority through direct access to the divine word, without the mediation of priests or saints. And male Protestant leaders had good reason to encourage them. Such women served as examples of how even the simple, armed with only scripture, could confound priests. Moreover, like the early church, the early Protestant movement was a movement on the run. A largely male leadership needed support from almost any quarter. Women with disposable wealth—widows and heiresses—and influential married ladies could help even if they were not effective public debaters. And, it should not be forgotten, women's souls needed saving as much as men's.

The analogy between women's position in the early church and their position in the Protestant movement also holds, however, when one considers that movement's greater maturity. As the early church achieved growth and greater security, Christians accommodated themselves to the world as it was and thus to the expectation that men should rule and women submit. Protestantism underwent a similar evolution. From the start, Protestant clergy were ambivalent about Protestant women setting themselves up to preach or write about religion. It was good, but dangerous, propaganda. By the end of the sixteenth century, however, greater security brought greater certainty that this was men's work. The Protestant Marie Dentière (ca. 1495–1561) wrote on religious matters, but her *Defense of Women* (which argued that the Bible spoke to both sexes directly) was the last work by a woman to be published in Geneva in the sixteenth century. Moreover, a less tactile religion did not foster the authority through bodiliness that some extraordinary women had achieved in the Middle Ages and continued to achieve in lands that remained Catholic.

As always, most people in the West married, so the relations between wives and husbands shaped most people's lives. In the broadest sense, the Reformation did not fundamentally change those relationships. For centuries before the Reformation, husbands and fathers had been expected to rule their wives and children, and they would be expected to do so for centuries after. Nonetheless, Protestantism modified relations between husbands and their families by removing an external authority available to earlier women and children: the priest. This move produced a Protestant model of family life in which fathers and husbands served as the spiritual guides for their households, leading them in prayer. Catholic women continued to have the alternative authority of the priest available to them, a fact recognized by the Protestant husbands (few in number) of Catholic women in the city of Venice. Some of these men were in the habit of beating their wives returning from confession.

If Protestant women lost one means of modifying their husbands' authority over them, they also largely lost the only respected alternative to marriage and male company: the monastic life. Celibate asceticism had offered women greater independence from the obligations of family since Christianity's early days. For Protestants, however, the ascetic life was a life dedicated to works. Where they triumphed, Protestants generally closed down the monasteries. To committed Protestants, this was liberation, freedom from a demonic treadmill of works that led nowhere. Further, Protestant rejection of the celibate life disabled one engine of Western misogyny that had run especially strong since the eleventh century; indeed, without the foil of the monastic virgin, the role of wife and mother could be seen to have greater dignity, no longer a second best. Moreover, Protestants were quick to point out what was in fact true: that many people had entered the monastic life not from choice but because they had been sent there as unwanted or unmarriageable children by parents or guardians. With the Reformation, many nuns as well as monks happily left the monastery. But many were determined to remain. Marie Dentière, herself a former abbess, once announced to some nuns that they should follow her own example and marry. A modern historian sums up their response: they "spat at her."[7] Indeed, in parts of Germany, Lutherans left female monasteries alone, especially if their inhabitants were willing to convert. The fact that such nuns—now called "canonesses"—chose to keep to the common life apart from men over remaining Catholic shows how important that common life was to them.

As will be seen, Protestants attempted to reform society at large, to make it a truly Christian one (see 6.4). One element of that program had special repercussions for women, namely, the abolition of the legalized prostitution inherited from the Middle Ages. This development obviously also closed off another option for women, although it does not seem to have been one that women easily embraced when they had other choices. The authorities had regarded medieval prostitutes as necessary professionals, but not as respectable ones. But when Protestants closed the brothels (see 6.4), prostitution went underground, with repercussions for respectable wives and daughters. Long regarded as more driven by bodily desires than men, all women now became more vulnerable to the suspicion that they were clandestine whores.

As in matters of authority (see 6.1), for most Protestant women, the Reformation meant an across-the-board consolidation of the lives they had lived before the Reformation. Their choices were (usually) reduced from marriage or monastery to marriage alone. As wives, women had the most important human authorities in their lives reduced from husband and priest to husband. And—although one cannot say this direction was universally the case—the reputations they might have, as harlot or chaste wife, became blurred into one, that of potential prostitute.

For Catholic women, the Reformation saw in many ways a reenactment of developments of the High and Late Middle Ages. As the experience of Saint Teresa suggests

---

7   Natalie Zemon Davis, *Society and Culture in Early Modern France: Eight Essays* (Stanford, CA: Stanford University Press, 1975), 89.

(see 6.2), women continued to gain authority through mystical union with Christ. At the same time, the Catholic Reformation's enforcement of clerical celibacy fed worries about women's sexuality, as had been the case in the Gregorian Reform. This concern led to a replay of attempts to enforce the claustration of nuns. But some orders resisted these efforts, none with more success than the Ursulines, founded in the 1530s. Their mission quickly focused on the education of girls. But such activity now had to be under closer male direction, leaving such women less independent than some of their medieval predecessors. The Ursulines became a sort of junior partner to the Jesuits. And, ultimately, the Ursulines and the other new women's orders of the Catholic Reformation entered the cloister.

6.4 FRAGMENTATION AND FURTHER REFORM

Central to the Protestant message was a reduction, at least in religious matters, of the plurality of authorities that had held such respect in the High Middle Ages—reason and faith, the Bible and custom, early Christian writers and Greek philosophers, the self and the clergy. Now Protestants proclaimed that all Christians should seek for themselves the truth in scripture, read not with tradition or reason as a guide but plainly, without interpretation, in simple faith. True, Luther and others believed that some early theologians, particularly Augustine, had come to the right conclusions about the faith, but that was because those early thinkers had read the Bible right; their views held no independent authority.

What Luther does not seem to have anticipated was how many contrary conclusions the Bible read in simple faith would produce. For him, the one truth was so self-evident in the very words of the Bible that honest readers could come only to the same positions he had. Very quickly, however, different Protestants failed to do so. This divergence is most evident in a flashpoint of conflict in the sixteenth century: the communion. Recall that Luther's reading of the New Testament led him to advocate Christ's "real presence" in the mass: the physical presence of Christ's flesh and blood was, for him, a miracle not to be understood but to be accepted in the same faith that made it happen. Calvin, however, argued that the same words in the New Testament obviously meant not that there was a physical change but rather that Christ became spiritually present in the bread and wine. The disagreement produced a major division between Lutherans and Calvinists. And that was not the end of the matter. Ulrich Zwingli (1484–1531), an influential reformer in the Swiss city of Zürich, had adopted yet another position even before Calvin had: that Christ was only symbolically present in the bread and wine. (The fact that this was not the same as Calvin's "spiritual presence" theory serves to remind moderns that, for sixteenth-century people, the spirit was as fully real as a table or a chair.)

Particular theological positions can cease to play a central role in religion and yet never be officially discarded. The doctrine of hell is an example. For some Christian denominations, it plays little practical role today in teaching or worship, although it has never, as far as I know, been officially repudiated by any mainline Christian church. It has become a fossil, present but inactive. These various positions on the communion are another example, which is why modern Christians can have trouble seeing what all the fuss was about. In the sixteenth century, however, the communion was worth killing over. It not only severed Protestants from Catholics but also helped fragment the Protestant movement itself.

This tendency to splinter became another hallmark of Protestantism; disagreement over the communion was only one instance of its operation. And that characteristic in turn stemmed directly from Protestantism's radical reduction of the authorities permissible in religious matters to one: the Bible read by individuals without interpretation. Interpretation of some sort, however, turned out to be inseparable from the very act of reading. Protestants lacked a pope to judge among conflicting views or to determine what conflicts would have to remain unresolved. They sometimes delicately papered over differences. After all, a movement under constant Catholic threat could little afford internal division. Yet compromise over essential doctrine was difficult and ultimately impossible. For God's truth should not be compromised.

The modern West is a religiously pluralist society. A walk through any major Western city can lead to synagogues, mosques, Hindu temples, and other non-Christian houses of religious worship. In even greater numbers are various churches representing various Christian sects: Catholic, Presbyterian, Lutheran, Methodist, Anglican/Episcopalian, Baptist (in various subgroups), Seventh-Day Adventist, and on and on. But this is not the world that sixteenth-century Protestants expected. They set out not to divide Christendom, but (in their view) to reform it. All the early reformers and their opponents had grown up in a society that saw itself as a seamless union of society and right religion, an inheritance from Christianity's triumph in the Roman Empire. That vision remained. Moreover, those reformers also defined right religion in terms of correct doctrine, a tendency rooted in Christianity's confrontation with classical philosophy in Roman times. Permanent toleration of differences over critical Christian doctrine in one society was not an option.

Luther's displeasure with Zwingli and Calvin for failing to see the obvious (and their displeasure with him and each other on the same grounds) was not the limit of Protestant disappointments. German peasants were under special pressures in the early sixteenth century. Landlords, bolstered by the recovery of population since the Black Death, were attempting to reimpose serfdom. Into this volatile situation came Protestant demands that all Christians find their own guidance in the Bible. The message peasants found there was that they should resist their landlords' demands. The German Peasants' Revolt erupted in 1524. Around Bamberg, the rebels' fury leveled 200 castles and, characteristic of the Protestant message, monasteries. Rebel demands show the power of the Protestant focus on biblical authority: "Disobedience to authority was never taught by God[;] instead he says that we should be humble to those above us and to every one . . . we assume, therefore, that you will release us from serfdom unless someone can prove to us from the Bible that we, true Christians, are serfs."[8] Luther, horrified by such conclusions, wrote a pamphlet calling on the German nobility to suppress the rebellion. The title sums up much of what Luther had to say: *Against the Robbing and Murdering Hordes of Peasants*. Spiritual and social equality were two very different things and so, Luther wrote, rebels should be put down like mad dogs.

If the peasants' revolt appalled Luther and his colleagues, so did what historians have come to call the "Radical Reformation," small groups of Protestants who took the Protestant message in what most Protestants regarded as hideously absurd directions. The Anabaptists, who found no biblical justification for infant baptism, were chief among these radical groups. They argued that only adults could receive valid baptism (hence the term "anabaptist," or "re-baptizer," for the first Anabaptists had, of course, been baptized at birth). They bolstered this conclusion with a classic solifidian argument: if faith is required of true Christians and if the true church is simply the community of Christians, then only adults can be members of that community (and so baptized) because only adults are capable of knowing whether they have faith. Hence baptism should be restricted to adults.

This doctrine helps explain why so few people became Anabaptists in the sixteenth century. For a millennium, Western society had regarded itself as a Christian one, and that conception had required the baptism of all members of that society. If being a Christian was a purely voluntary decision, as the Anabaptists held, then the body of Christians could be only a subset of society as a whole. In other words, Anabaptists challenged the very notion of Christendom itself. The fact that Anabaptists read the Bible to prohibit the taking of oaths made this threat even clearer, for many social obligations in the sixteenth century were sealed with an oath. That some Anabaptists advocated communal ownership of property—a sort of Christian communism—only added to their unpleasantly spicy reputation. Their refusal to hold government office was a symptom of their readiness to reject this world in anticipation of the next, an old Christian theme.

It is a sign of Christendom's hold in the sixteenth century that Catholics and mainline Protestants could set aside their own lethal differences in order to suppress the Anabaptists. Consider the year 1534, when a group of Anabaptists gained control over the city of Münster and were soon joined by many more. Once in control of Münster, they imposed an Anabaptist program on the city (a move in tension with the Anabaptist denial of a perfect union of church and society), including polygamy and the abolition of private property. Protestant and Catholic forces converged on the city. Taking it by siege, they tortured the leading Anabaptists with red-hot irons, displaying their corpses in iron cages as a warning to others. More moderate Anabaptists remained a feared and despised group. The longest surviving branch of their movement was one of the more moderate, that founded by Menno Simons (1496–1561), for whom the modern Mennonites are named.

Christendom meant that religious reform might not have clear limits, despite Luther's attempt to draw them during the Peasants' Revolt. The attempt at Münster to abolish private property showed how Protestants might be moved to embrace a larger reform of

---

8   "Twelve Articles of the Peasants," in *Documents on the Continental Reformation*, ed. W.G. Naphy (New York: St. Martin's Press, 1996), 23.

society. Few went that far, but other Protestants moved beyond strictly solifidian considerations. In most Protestant countries, for example, legalized prostitution was abolished. Where they became dominant, Calvinists were especially likely to try to shape a more thoroughly godly society. Such attempts were embodied in the consistory, a council of leading lay and clerical citizens of the community (usually a city) that acted on the advice of Calvinist clergy. The consistory acted to stamp out violations of Christian morals, which could be defined rather broadly and could include not only traditional species of sexual immorality, such as adultery, but also immodest dress and inappropriate frivolity (raucous singing counted), anything that distracted from Christian virtue. Dancing was held to threaten Christian family life. The medieval church had, it will be recalled, long exercised jurisdiction over sexual morality. But where it had power, the consistory instituted a more rigorous supervision of daily life by the authorities than most medieval people had experienced. Medieval church courts had generally asked neighbors to report bad behavior in public gatherings, which gave the lay community some control over what got heard by the authorities. Members of the consistory, however, could be found patrolling the streets on the lookout for misbehavior; they even visited people's houses. Such vigor at times provoked complaints about new, Protestant popes. Catholic authorities, however, reinvigorated in their commitment to reform, moved in the same direction, although not with the effectiveness of the toughest of the consistories. Both sides thus attempted to fulfill the promise of a reformed Christendom, an old goal of the church in the High and Late Middle Ages. Christendom, however, had implications that not all Christians liked.

6.5 COMPLICATIONS: POLITICAL AND SOCIAL

Dedication to Christendom made blood run for more than a century. The drive to reunify a divided society brought war and massacre. From one end of the West to the other, Christians of different denominations tortured each other and burned each other at the stake.

In Germany, war between Catholic princes, led by the Emperor Charles, and the Protestant north erupted in the Schmalkaldic Wars (1546–1555), named after the Schmalkaldic League of the Protestant princes. The two sides fought to a standstill, one sealed by the Peace of Augsburg (1555). Augsburg was meant as a truce, not a permanent arrangement; Christendom could not be abandoned so easily. Even so, the treaty assumed that people and prince could not follow different religions, so it spelled out the principle "*cuius regio, eius religio*": "whose rule, his religion" (so long as the choices were confined to Lutheranism or Catholicism).

France fell into civil war between Huguenot (the term for a French Calvinist) and Catholic. The conflict began with street violence. In 1559, for example, youths set up statues of the Virgin Mary in the streets of Paris, the better to identify and harass passing Protestants who could be expected to refuse to make her a mark of reverence. Huguenots attacked Catholic churches, ripping out the "idols" that offended their god. An on-again, off-again series of civil wars broke out in 1562. But the stakes rose even higher when it became clear to all that the Catholic King Henry III of France (1574–1589) would die childless, leaving the throne occupied by his nearest male heir, the Protestant Henry of Navarre (1572–1589, king of France 1589–1610) of the Bourbon family. In this situation, the stoutly Catholic Guise family, one of the noblest in France, led those who wanted to avoid a Protestant king and maintain a thoroughly Catholic kingdom. The civil war was fought between Guise and Bourbon as well as between Catholic and Protestant.

Religion, however, was not the only consideration in these events. Although people produced by Christendom did not necessarily distinguish between religious and political motives, historians can. For the Guises, opposition to the Protestant heir to the throne also meant limits on the French monarchy's capacity to restrict noble action. Moreover, Catherine de' Medici (1519–1589), mother of the French kings Francis II (1559–1560), Charles IX (1560–1574), and Henry III, used her very great influence to allow limited toleration for the Huguenots. Her policy flowed less from a belief in religious freedom than from a fear that religious conflict would make the country ungovernable, in particular, ungovernable by the monarchy. She had reason to fear. As they were in Germany, French political conditions inherited from the Middle Ages were critical. French kings, like other rulers, lacked both an organized police and a large standing army, and they lived in a world in which nobles exercised force on their own. The king did not have much with which to suppress civil disruption when too many nobles were bent on it. Catherine's attempts to tread carefully failed, instead giving her and her sons a reputation as wishy-washy Catholics. Developments of 1572 vividly indicate how hard it was to take a moderate line. During a lull in the civil wars, Catherine had arranged a marriage between the Protestant Henry of Navarre and her daughter the Princess Margaret (1553–1615). Her goal was to bring Catholics and Protestants together. But a Catholic attempt to assassinate a leading Protestant, the Admiral Coligny (1519–1572), following the wedding led to vigorous counterthreats from the admiral, and rumors of worse. These put Catherine in a tight spot. Catholics were too powerful, especially in the capital, for her to side with Coligny. And Coligny was now bent on war. Catherine or perhaps the king (who made the decision is unclear) took what seemed the safest course, namely the swift assassination of Coligny along with the rest of the Protestant leadership. (Henry of Navarre prudently took safety in a temporary conversion to Catholicism.) What Catherine or her son seems not to have counted on was how the population of Paris would read this surgical strike against the Huguenot leadership: as proof that the government had at last recognized that the Huguenots must be expunged from Christendom. Despite royal orders to the contrary, on Saint Bartholomew's Day, nuptials were replaced by massacre. Some 2,000 Protestants died in Paris alone, and thousands more followed in other parts of the country. It was the largest single religious killing of the Reformation. France's civil wars would not come to an end until 1598.

Catherine, the Guises, and truly fervent Huguenots illustrate two contrary approaches to the political conflicts engendered by the Reformation. On the one hand, there was the position of the *doctrinaire*, that is, someone who put religious correctness above concerns for peace and stability. The Guises and their more committed opponents represent this approach. Both were quite willing to engage in bloodshed, indeed, in civil war, in the cause of right religion. On the other hand, there was the position of what came to be called the *politique*, that is, someone willing to put a concern for peace and stability above concerns for religious correctness. Catherine de' Medici serves as an example. From the start, one can find *politiques* as well as *doctrinaires* operating in the Reformation. The pope himself had turned a blind eye to Protestant power in Zwingli's Zürich in order to preserve his political alliance with that city. In today's age of religious pluralism, it is easy to condemn *doctrinaires* and sympathize with *politiques*. But, in their own time, *politiques* were accused of lacking principles, of being unwilling to defend the very foundations of their society, that is, of Christendom. Their critics had a point. It is also important to see that the designations *politique* and *doctrinaire* were relative; few politicians were absolutely *doctrinaire,* and few were willing to embrace absolute religious toleration.

The interplay of political and theological considerations was complex. The twists and turns of English developments show this. When Luther issued his Ninety-Five Theses in 1517, England was ruled by Henry VIII (1509–1547), an amateur theologian with a problem. As an amateur theologian, he replied (with, at the very least, some help) to Luther's challenge to the church by defending it with a theological treatise, *The Assertion of the Seven Sacraments* (1521). Henry thus earned from a grateful pope the designation "Defender of the Faith," held by his successors to this day. Henry's problem was that he lacked a legitimate son. He, like most people, was convinced that a man would be needed to give England competent rule upon his death. The issue grew as his wife aged. By the mid-1520s, Catherine of Aragon (1485–1536) had presented him a daughter (Mary) but was too old to bear him the desired boy. Under normal circumstances, the king would have been able to obtain from the pope an annulment. Strictly speaking, this was not a divorce (which the church had for centuries forbidden and which the Catholic Church still forbids) but a declaration that the marriage had never existed in the first place. Popes had compliantly granted secular rulers such favors for some time, and Henry had a pretext to magnify into a case for annulment. The fact that his mistress, Anne Boleyn (1507–1536), was pregnant added urgency to the matter. If she should produce a son and if Henry could marry her, the king would have his long-desired heir. But a family complication stymied Henry. Catherine's nephew was the most powerful man in Europe, Charles V, king of Spain, Holy Roman Emperor, and master of the Netherlands and the kingdom of Naples in southern Italy. Worse, the maelstrom of Italian politics led Charles to sack the city of Rome in 1527, capturing the pope in the process. He was not a man the pope could afford to alienate. The upshot of this diplomatic impasse—and the opportunity to confiscate vast amounts of church property—set Henry on a path toward Protestantism, and he had his parliament declare him the "Supreme Head" of the English church. Now the bishops, under his thumb, were compelled to declare what the pope would not. (Some refused and were ignored, hounded, or, in one case, executed.) Like other Protestants, Henry did not claim to be founding a new church; the "Defender of the Faith" was simply restoring the church in England to its original condition.

So political considerations prompted Henry's change of religious allegiance. But Henry had meant what he had written in *The Assertion of the Seven Sacraments*; at least he had meant most of it. He was a reluctant Protestant, and it showed. His Church of England retained its old structure, with the king largely filling the pope's shoes. The mass and other church services remained largely unchanged. The church continued to allow a role for works in salvation. Its clergy, to this day referred to as "priests" rather than ministers, remained distinct from the laity. Among the clergy, bishops held pride of place while most Calvinists had eliminated the position. The new Church of England even still refused to sanction divorce (as it still does); Henry procured himself an annulment rather than a divorce. He left England with a largely Catholic liturgy, canon law, and theology but with a royal pope (although not called by that name). And he was quite willing to execute Protestants as heretics.

Henry's matrimonial adventures, many of them driven by a search for a son, ultimately gave him six marriages, which were sometimes ended by judicial murder (Anne Boleyn was the first to suffer this fate). He did leave his throne to a son, a young and committed Protestant who worked under the supervision of like-minded guardians to impose his beliefs in England, only to die childless after a reign of six years. The death of Edward VI (1547–1553) resulted in Henry's nightmare scenario: a woman ruler. Catherine of Aragon's daughter Mary I (1553–1558), a doctrinaire Catholic, naturally reimposed Catholic teaching and papal authority in England. Her readiness to burn Protestants gave her the nickname "Bloody Mary." But Mary's marriage to the Catholic Philip II of Spain (1556–1598) was childless, and with her death the country's religious allegiance veered again. Henry's younger daughter, the child of Anne Boleyn, ascended the throne.

As the daughter of Anne Boleyn, Elizabeth I (1558–1603) had little political option but to be a Protestant of some sort. (To be Catholic would have meant rejecting the annulment of her father's marriage to Catherine of Aragon, which would, in turn, annul her father's marriage to Anne Boleyn, making Elizabeth illegitimate and therefore ineligible for the throne.) Moreover, the Protestant movement had attracted so many converts in England that their wishes were hard to ignore, especially when they had supported her position against Mary's. Yet there were pressures on Elizabeth not to move the Church of England, of which she was the "Supreme Governor," in a vigorously Protestant direction. One of these was political: Mary had not been universally unpopular, for, in many quarters, the old religion had its enthusiasts. Alienating these people could provoke rebellion. Another pressure was personal: Elizabeth herself sympathized with some points of traditional religion. She would have been happy, for example, to prohibit priests from marrying. The threat of civil war was a final consideration. The religious wars just across the waters in France illustrated the dangers if one side in these religious conflicts felt too threatened.

Out of these various demands, Elizabeth evolved a policy of appeasing as many people as possible. Her religious settlement has been described as a church with a Protestant, in fact, a Calvinist, theology and a Catholic liturgy (i.e., religious ritual) and structure. There is much to be said for that description. Yet there was more, and less, to Elizabeth's Church of England than that. In the liturgy—the most obvious part of religion for most people—she simply fudged some of the issues separating Catholic and Protestant. Her version of the *Book of Common Prayer* for use in all church services was studiously vague regarding what happened in the communion.

This approach was that of a classic *politique*. Notably, Elizabeth's search for political security led her to compromise her own beliefs, by, for example, allowing clergy to marry. Not surprisingly, this somewhat squirrelly approach failed to please everyone. Some fervent Catholics labored to assassinate her, noting that the unmarried Elizabeth's heir was the Catholic Mary, Queen of Scots (1542–1567, died 1587). Those who wanted a more emphatically Protestant (often Calvinist) church came to be known (at least to historians) as "Puritans," for the purification of church life they hoped Elizabeth might be pressured to carry out. Both groups, moreover, discovered that Elizabeth's toleration of religious differences had its limits, a reminder that there were only relative, not absolute, *politiques*. Those who failed to attend Church of England services were fined. Catholic priests smuggled into the country who dared perform the mass were executed. Elizabeth herself did away with two-thirds as many people for religious crimes as her notorious elder sister had, but she did so over a much longer reign. When she died at last in 1603, England had avoided civil war and disruption.

Religious division also brought international conflict. The most spectacular instance was the attempt of Philip II of Spain to remove Elizabeth from the throne and impose Catholicism on England. To carry out the invasion, he poured money into an enormous fleet. English fighting ships, smaller but more maneuverable and more suited to cannon, defeated Philip's Spanish Armada in 1588. Remarkably, however, the English were loath to take full credit for their victory. Weather troubled the Armada before its defeat, prevented it from sailing back toward England for another attempt, and sank many of Philip's ships on their way home. The English magnified those events into a story about storms defeating the Armada. This legend of a "Protestant wind" confirms that the struggle between England and Spain was not seen in simply political terms. On the Spanish side, when Philip himself exhorted one of his commanders to persist for the sake of reputation, he then thought better of it, observing that reputation was irrelevant in a cause undertaken for God. When the scale of the defeat became clear, Philip, concluding that he was being punished for his sins, prayed for death.

Indeed, Philip II's career illustrates the complexities of religion and politics on the international scene. The son of the emperor Charles V, Philip was the most powerful Western monarch of his time, despite the fact that the Holy Roman Empire had gone to his uncle. With silver from Latin America, his Spain was the superpower of the later sixteenth century. Like his father, Philip saw that with power came responsibility as the defender of Christendom. This view led him to international activity on several fronts. The Ottoman Turks to the east, having brought all that remained of the old Byzantine Empire under Islam (Constantinople itself had fallen in 1453) now threatened the West itself. Philip's defense climaxed with the victory of the Spanish fleet at the battle of Lepanto in 1571. (The West remained, however, vulnerable to the highly organized Turks. Vienna only barely resisted a siege by the Turks in 1683, after which the threat receded for good.)

Another responsibility lay closer to home. Philip's attempts to repress Protestantism in his inherited territory to the northeast of France only fed the Protestant flame, so he sent in the troops (Map 6.1). Even Philip partly failed. The southern part of the Low Countries ultimately remained Catholic (forming what has become modern Belgium). But his dedication to true religion lost him the north, which, after some struggle, achieved independence as a Protestant country, the modern Netherlands. (A measure of the Reformation's heat was that it forged one of the sixteenth century's only republics, for, when Philip lost the Netherlands, the Netherlands lost its monarch.) The attempt on England has already been mentioned. These activities and an unbending readiness to suppress the least sign of Protestantism in Spain (there were few such signs) have earned Philip a reputation as the ultimate *doctrinaire*. He is certainly a good example, dedicating himself to gloomy toil in Christendom's service from his dual monastery and palace in central Spain, the Escorial, which was also to be his tomb. Yet even Philip could let Christendom wait. He unleashed the Armada only after Elizabeth had executed her nearest heir, the Catholic Mary, Queen of Scots, who had fled to England seeking refuge from Protestant rebellion at home. Mary had been largely French in her orientation, and Philip had not wished to see England ruled by a French pawn when France, albeit a Catholic country, was his important rival in Europe. Mary's death eliminated that possibility, so it was safe to retake England for God. Once again, *doctrinaire* as well as *politique* are relative terms.

Just as religious division complicated politics and politics complicated religious division, so local social conditions and religious conflict complicated each other. Looking at one locality closely highlights this point. Consider the French city of Lyon. There, the 1550s saw Calvinism claim the allegiance of about one-third of the inhabitants. Strikingly, the new religion disproportionately attracted members of the trades that were newer at Lyon (such as printers and silk makers). People in older trades that had also lately risen in prestige (e.g., painters, jewelers, and goldsmiths) likewise tended to become Protestant. People in older businesses that had seen little change (e.g., grain merchants, vintners, butchers, bakers, and rope makers) tended to remain Catholic. So people's religious decisions seem to have been conditioned by their social situation.

Developments among the printers of Lyon show with special clarity how religious decisions were tempered by social conflict. From the early 1500s, there were labor tensions in this business. As in other cities and in other businesses at the beginning of the century, employers had fed their skilled employees, called "journeymen," at their own tables. But, early in the century, print-shop owners—"masters"—had stopped this practice. Journeymen had another grievance too; masters were turning more and more to labor supplied by unpaid apprentices and by unskilled laborers, called "Forfants," who worked for less. As a result, the journeymen formed an organization called "The Company of the Griffarins." At first sight, this company looks like a union—and, in some ways, it was. But one should probably think of it as yet another "corporation" in a society of orders and corporations.

So what has all this got to do with the Reformation? By the mid-1560s, most of the printers, masters, and journeymen were Huguenots. But, by this time also, the Huguenot consistory at Lyon was strong enough to punish Protestants who were not living up to the right standards, as the consistory defined them. The problem for the Griffarins was that the consistory, at Lyon as elsewhere, was dominated by the town's social upper crust, men who sympathized more with print masters than print journeymen. In fact, the consistory attempted to discipline the Company of the Griffarins by withholding communion from its members. The result was a change in religious allegiance by the Griffarins. Between 1566 and 1572 nearly all the print journeymen of Lyon became Catholic.

As the experience of Lyon suggests, very local conditions could influence the religious choices the Reformation made possible. But one condition was very broadly influential: the divide between city and country. Certainly, Protestantism could, in some form, inspire peasants; recall the German Peasants' Revolt. Certainly, too, many townspeople were immune to Protestantism's appeal; recall Catholic Paris. Overall, however, Protestants made their greatest and earliest gains in cities. An obvious reason is that towns had larger numbers of literate people who could become Bible readers, or at least pamphlet readers. Moreover, since the High Middle Ages town dwellers had been susceptible to exploring their interior religious lives. Peasant culture, too, in the sixteenth-century West, as in other times and places, tended to be conservative, although not unfailingly so. Finally, city and country had since civilization's earliest days been at odds.

6.6 POLITICAL RESULTS: THE CONSOLIDATION OF ROYAL AUTHORITY

In the short term, as Catherine de' Medici learned, the Reformation could undermine royal authority. In the longer term, however, religious division bolstered royal power by strengthening the control of secular rulers over the church structure in their territories. In that regard, too, the Reformation marked a continuation of the trends of the Late Middle Ages.

Why did the Reformation have this effect? The reason is most obvious regarding countries that became Protestant. Where rulers took the lead in introducing Protestantism, they looked upon themselves, and were looked upon by others, as the natural head of the (new) church. England's Henry VIII (see 6.5) is an example. In other countries, Protestant leaders looked to secular rulers for protection and support in instituting their vision of Christianity. But support and protection generally meant accepting the direction of secular rulers in church affairs. Luther was a bit reluctant about this development, preferring to acknowledge such rulers as "emergency bishops," as individuals assuming leadership only because ministers could not. In general, however, Protestant reformers, following medieval tradition but citing scripture, accepted territorial rulers as divinely appointed heads of the body politic. With the papacy now excluded, kings and princes became heads of the church, appointing higher members of the clergy, enforcing doctrine, and managing church affairs.

Perhaps surprisingly, the Reformation spurred this consolidation of royal control over the church in Catholic countries too. Of course, crown and church continued to acknowledge the pope as the vicar of Christ sent to lead his church. But the Reformation had strengthened the bargaining position of Catholic kings when it came to their seeking concessions from the pope. Catholic rulers could use the existence of a rival religious camp to extract favors from the pope. Even if they did not threaten to become Protestant themselves, the papacy desperately needed their help in the effort to roll back Protestantism, just as Protestants needed state support to further their cause. Charles V and Philip II, Catholicism's champions in the international arena, were particularly well placed in this regard. Their grip on the church in Spain tightened. In 1523, the pope conceded to the Spanish king the formal right to appoint all bishops in his kingdom and to receive the income from vacant bishoprics. Royal taxes on the clergy rose. Rights of appeal from Spanish church courts to Rome were curtailed. In the fifteenth century, the Inquisition—a special investigative court for heresy and witchcraft first instituted in the thirteenth century, which reported directly to the papacy—had been reestablished in Spain largely under royal control. Charles V snipped its last ties to the papacy. When, in 1773, Catholic kings found themselves troubled by the Jesuits, that Counter-Reformation order established as the pope's shock troops in the fight against Protestantism (see 6.2), they successfully petitioned the pope to dissolve the order. (The move turned out to be temporary.) As in other spheres of life, then, the Reformation produced a consolidation of more variegated medieval conditions.

6.7 A CRISIS OF AUTHORITY AND THE END OF CHRISTENDOM

The battle over Christendom produced devastating conflict. Yet, from ca. 1600 on, signs accumulate that the notion of Christendom was losing its hold. By the end of the seventeenth century, the *politique* concern for political stability over religious correctness was trumping *doctrinaire* desires to ensure religious correctness at any cost. This development was very slow. It took more than a century for the *politique* approach to become the dominant one in the West, and religion would never be absolutely decoupled from political life. Yet, more than at any other time since Christianity became its dominant religion, the West, at the end of the seventeenth century, was a religiously tolerant society, and one in which government was increasingly seen in secular rather than theocratic terms.

Although people may not have known it, the conclusion of the wars of religion in France was a sign of things to come. By 1593, the Huguenots, a minority, had nonetheless won victory in the field. Their leader was the same Henry of Navarre who had temporarily converted to Catholicism during the Saint Bartholomew's Day massacre (see 6.5). Now he was in a position to seize his inheritance, the French throne. Yet Henry saw that the Catholic majority was not to be easily reconciled to having a Calvinist king. The capital, whose residents had massacred 2,000 Protestants with delight on Saint Bartholomew's Day, would be especially hard to win over. Henry had to besiege Paris—unsuccessfully. And so Henry (now King Henry IV of France [1589–1610]) did the *politique* thing: he reconverted to Catholicism in 1593. His conversion produced perhaps the most famous quip of the sixteenth century: "Paris is worth a mass." Later, to reassure the Protestant minority, he issued the Edict of Nantes (1598), which guaranteed Protestants the right to public worship in certain French towns, to private worship in the rest of France, to have garrisons under Huguenot commanders in some 200 cities, to hold public office, and to gain admission to all schools and universities. Catholic masses were to be available throughout the kingdom, even in Protestant-dominated areas. This was not out-and-out toleration of Protestantism, and it was accepted, grudgingly, by the Catholic majority. That acceptance suggests that Catholics were more willing, at the close of the sixteenth century, to tolerate a religion they found obnoxious than they had been in the days of Catherine de' Medici, who had tried and failed to steer a course between Catholic and Protestant. Yet Henry IV's end points to the mood of his age: he was assassinated in 1610 by a Catholic who thought he meant to destroy the true church in France. His assassin may have been mad, yet it was a madness characteristic of his time. The edict, however, held.

The fate of the Edict of Nantes suggests Christendom's decline. In 1630, King Louis XIII (1610–1643) named Cardinal Armand-Jean du Plessis Richelieu (1585–1642) as his chief minister, the man who would set policy and run the government. Richelieu was determined to strengthen the king's control over the kingdom (more on this in section 7.4.2). An important part of their program was the elimination of military power that was not under royal command; the Huguenot garrisons had to go. Protestants were still unpopular with the rest of the country, and the king and his minister found general support for the siege of Protestant cities. What is striking is that Richelieu was not only Louis's chief minister but also a cardinal of the Catholic Church. Yet, although Richelieu was firmly persuaded of the wickedness of Protestantism, his aims were satisfied by the elimination of Protestant garrisons. He left the remainder of the Edict of Nantes untouched. Indeed, distinguished Protestants continued to perform distinguished service in the royal army.

It would be left to Louis XIII's son, Louis XIV (1643–1715), to revoke the Edict of Nantes entirely in 1685. This action was, in itself, certainly in line with those of the old days when people did not draw a clear line between society and politics, on the one hand, and religion, on the other. To Louis, a Catholic monarch should not have Protestant subjects but should drive Protestants under his rule back to the true church. Many chose to leave the country instead. As might be expected, the revocation was widely praised in Catholic circles. It also, however, provoked some criticism among the Catholic majority. Even the pope's enthusiasm was muted. Times had changed since 1500.

Ironically, the greatest religious war of the seventeenth century also points to this growing willingness to separate politics and religion. The Thirty Years' War (1618–1648) tore the Holy Roman Empire apart. It began with religious conflict. In 1618, Protestant nobles in Bohemia (the modern Czech Republic) refused to recognize as king of Bohemia the Habsburg Ferdinand, to be elected Holy Roman Emperor Ferdinand II (1619–1637) the following year. In defiance, they tossed Ferdinand's envoys out of a window at Prague; their fall was broken by dung heaps, an event grandly known as the "Defenestration of Prague." The insult must have stung, but the Catholic Ferdinand now had a pretext, finally, to attack Protestantism in Bohemia and, ultimately, in the empire. In this effort, he had support from the empire's Catholic princes. The war included the sort of horrors that conviction allied with power can produce. In 1631, Catholic forces sacked the Protestant city of Magdeburg, laying low much of the population and demolishing a city of 20,000. One Protestant soldier noted that his army, while in Catholic Bavaria, burned both castles and peasant villages to the ground, repaying "burning with burning, using the Papists at home as they used Protestants abroad . . . where we see that God the righteous judge punisheth sin with sin."[9] Pillage, atrocity, battle, and disease had killed off a third of Germany's population by the war's end. Yet, by that time, other considerations super-seded religious ones. Cardinal Richelieu, fearing that the growth of Habsburg power threatened France, intervened on the Protestant side. The war's climax also signaled the transformation of the war itself. The Catholic forces achieved a series of victories that had the Protestants on the ropes in 1629. Now that the Protestant cause in Germany seemed doomed, Ferdinand reached too far. In an Edict of Restitution (1629), he proclaimed that all lands seized from the church in Protestant territories after 1552 were to revert to the church. Calvinism was outlawed outright throughout the empire. Bishoprics that had been made into Protestant principalities would be led again by Catholic bishops. Moreover, Ferdinand moved to have those bishops appointed from members of the Habsburg family.

The Edict of Restitution unnerved the Catholic princes who had been Ferdinand's chief supporters. They had fought to spread the faith, not to mention their own influence. True, the Edict was pro-Catholic. But emperors were expected to make such sweeping decisions for the empire only in consultation with the Diet, the assembly of representatives of the greater territories that embodied constitutionalist limitations on the emperor. Ferdinand had issued the Edict of Restitution without the Diet's consent. The intrusion of Habsburgs into the restored bishoprics could only have increased the perception of an imperial grab for power.

So the Catholic cause lost steam. Maximilian, duke of Bavaria and one of the chief Catholic princes, demanded that Ferdinand cancel the edict and announced that Bavarian troops would not be used to enforce it. Swedish and French intervention on the Protestant side then gave Protestants further aid; the war dragged on until 1648, with Maximilian ultimately allying with France against the emperor. By the time the war finally ended, its religious dimension had become hopelessly compromised by people such as Maximilian and Richelieu. What had started as a war of religion ended as a war over Habsburg power in Germany. The Peace of Westphalia that concluded the war in 1648 provided protections for religious minorities within the territories of the Holy Roman Empire.

---

9   William S. Brockington Jr., ed., *Monro, His Expedition with the Worthy Scots Regiment Called Mac-Keys* (Westport, CT: Praeger, 1999), 257.

Christendom did not die; it faded away. The notion that state and society could sustain only one (true) religion remained influential into the eighteenth century. In 1701, the English legislated that a Catholic could not sit on the throne (on this law and on English conflicts over religion in the seventeenth century, see 7.4.5). But, toward 1700, religious conflict ceased to drive political conflict, as Christendom's grip slackened. Why?

One possibility was the accumulating challenges to certainty produced by the sixteenth century. Ca. 1600, the West was experiencing what one historian has called a "crisis of authority," that is, uncertainty in many quarters regarding how reliable knowledge could be had. The questions "What can I believe?" and "Why can I believe it?" seemed increasingly hard to answer. The Reformation itself fed this crisis. For decades, Catholics and Protestants of various stripes had cited the same authorities (faith and scripture) for opposing conclusions, often with murderous effect. Some observers, considering this, concluded that perhaps faith and scripture were not infallible guides to truth.

Other developments encouraged this sense of doubt. Custom had long been a worthy guide to right behavior and belief. But, in the course of the sixteenth century, Westerners confronted the very different aboriginal societies of what was, to them, the New World. The West had long been in contact with Islam. But familiarity breeds some degree of comfort. Islam, although not well understood, was not a new civilization to the West. Moreover, the two were cousins. Islam itself had grown out of the monotheistic tradition that had produced Christianity. Both Muslim and Western scholars studied classical philosophy and science.

Native Americans, however, were a shock: polytheists who did not even worship the gods of the Greeks and Romans, who (in the case of the Aztecs of central Mexico) were known to practice human sacrifice. A statement by Bartolomé de Las Casas (ca. 1484–1566), a Spanish priest who had worked to Christianize native Americans living under Spanish rule, indicates the range of Western opinion regarding these new peoples:

> [The Indians] . . . are not ignorant, inhuman, or bestial. Rather, long before they heard the word Spaniard they had properly organized states, wisely ordered by excellent laws, religion, and customs. They cultivated friendship and, bound together in common fellowship, lived in populous cities in which they wisely administered the affairs of both peace and war, justly and equitably, truly governed by laws that at very many points surpass ours, and could have won the admiration of the sages of Athens. . . .[10]

Las Casas represented minority opinion in the West; more people seem to have concluded that aboriginal Americans were barbarians and left it at that. In general, Franciscan and Jesuit missionaries worked in concert with the conquerors. But Las Casas and people like him show that the confrontation with native cultures produced division. Indeed, Charles V arranged a formal debate on the matter. In some quarters, the result was doubt about the

---

10 Bartolomé de Las Casas, *In Defense of the Indians*, trans. Stafford Poole (De Kalb: Northern Illinois University Press, 1992), 42–43.

validity of the West's own cultural tradition. After all, if native Americans rooted their beliefs and behavior in custom and Western beliefs and behavior were similarly rooted in custom, how could one be sure that Western beliefs and behavior were right? The possibility that native American culture might, in some respects, be superior to that of the West only sharpened such suspicions. So did some of the reports coming back from Jesuit missionaries in China and Japan. Some missionaries were so impressed by Chinese civilization that they argued that various Chinese customs, such as ancestor worship, were reconcilable with Christianity. Perhaps custom was not a reliable authority. The fact that Protestants had long criticized the authority of tradition in religious matters could also have weakened tradition's attraction.

What of the ancient Greeks and Romans? Classical texts had long held authority, as their frequent citation by medieval scholastics attests. Aristotle, in particular, had laid the foundations of Western physics and of some of the other sciences in the fourth century BC. Ancient geography and astronomy, with some modification in the intervening centuries, still held the field toward the end of the fifteenth century. Columbus had not set out to find new continents but to find the Western route to Asia that ancient geography implied should be there. By the end of the sixteenth century, however, the discovery of the New World had broken the grip of ancient geographical lore, which had, after all, missed two continents. The publication of a new astronomical model of the universe raised similar doubts about the ancient understanding of the structure of the universe. The Ptolemaic model—so called for the Greek astronomer Ptolemy (ca. 87–ca. 150), who had been responsible for formulating only one version of the model that bears his name—had supposed that the Earth sat still in the center of the universe, with the planets (including the sun) and the stars revolving around it. This geocentric ("earth-centered") model was challenged by the 1543 publication of Nicolaus Copernicus's (1473–1543) heliocentric ("sun-centered") model, in which the sun occupied the center of the universe, with the planets (including the Earth) revolving around it. Like Las Casas, Copernicus was in a distinct minority. But Copernicus's model was simpler to use and yet a very accurate predictor of the motions of the planets. For this reason, it presented a compelling alternative to the Ptolemaic system, disorienting for those who thought the ancients had mastered the study of nature. The early years of the seventeenth century saw the outbreak of the "Battle of the Books" between supporters of the authority of ancient texts and those who thought newer works superseded ancient knowledge.

In this situation, reason might seem a natural fallback authority. If tradition, faith, scripture, and classical learning seemed fallible, one might rely on rational inquiry to fill the breach. But reason, of course, had seemed vulnerable since the Late Middle Ages.

The lack of confidence is evident in the work of René Descartes (1596–1650). Descartes observed the absence of certain knowledge in this world. He was disturbed by the fact that even the greatest philosophers—such as Aristotle and Plato—disagreed with each other; their conclusions must therefore be uncertain. Moreover, he came to doubt common knowledge as well:

It is true that, while I spent time merely observing the customs of other men, I found hardly anything about which to be confident and that I noticed there was about as much diversity as I had found earlier among the opinions of philosophers. Thus the greatest profit I derived from this was that on realizing that many things, although they seemed very extravagant and ridiculous to us, did not cease being commonly accepted and approved by other great peoples. I learned to believe nothing very firmly concerning what I had been persuaded to believe only by example and custom....[11]

Descartes went further, noting that the senses themselves could be deceiving, an observation that went back to the Greeks. Desiring certainty and not finding it, he undertook a radical program; he would systematically doubt all that he had ever heard and seen, all that he had ever experienced or thought. His goal was to find something that could withstand such doubt, something that could not possibly be doubted—something that, being clearly true, might form the basis for an understanding of the world. Descartes even went so far as to doubt his own existence. It was a doubt that gave him the certain knowledge he sought: "*Cogito ergo sum*" ("I think, therefore I am"). Something that doubts its own existence must exist to do the doubting. From this, Descartes, at least to his own satisfaction, concluded with certainty that he must be defined as a substance that thinks (which he called "mind").

This crisis of authority undermined the fusion of right religion and society that was the basis of Christendom. From the start, the Reformation had produced *politiques*, people willing to backpedal on enforcing religious correctness for the sake of harmony and stability. But *doctrinaire* commitment to Christendom had generally trumped such approaches, with bloody results (see 6.5). Doubters, however, make poor *doctrinaires*. As the sixteenth century came to a close and the seventeenth century wore on, religious clashes tended to be followed by *politique* victory—cautious and never absolute, but victory nonetheless. The result was a tendency to decouple religion from politics, to see religious belief as a private affair, a tendency that grew over the course of the seventeenth century. In the later sixteenth century, that quintessential *politique* Elizabeth I of England had remarked of her religious settlement (see 6.5), "Let us not make windows into men's souls." Her attitude spread in the seventeenth century. In 1689, John Locke (1632–1704) argued that religion is entirely a matter for individuals, for no authority can force people to change their beliefs, even to the right ones. To compel individual faith could only undermine it.

Elizabeth's reference to the believer's inner life suggests another root of Christendom's demise: the stress on inner experience that had become increasingly important in the West since the High Middle Ages and that had helped produce the Reformation in the first place. The Reformation marked the climax of that focus on Luther's "inner man" and, with it, the climax of a religious revolution. For millennia, the divine had received worship, either

---

11 René Descartes, *Discourse on the Method for Rightly Conducting One's Reason and for Seeking Truth in the Sciences*, trans. Donald A. Cress (Indianapolis: Hackett Publishing Company, 1980), 5–6.

by priests or assembled laity or both. Starting in the ancient Near East, *cultus*—the cultivation of the divine through sacrifice or performance—had been essential to getting divine attention and favor, a point that explains why conflicts over the liturgy were so central to the Reformation. *Cultus* was visible (unlike people's thoughts), but it was also how God was pleased. And pleasing God was not just a matter of achieving heaven; it was essential to life in this world, just as it had been going back to the ancient Near East. Shortly before Saint Bartholomew's Day, a woman (perhaps a nun) had wandered the streets of Paris, announcing to its people that God would wipe out the city unless they wiped out the Huguenots first. Elizabeth I attempted to deal with the problem by creating a *cultus* that could leave the inner life of its participants opaque to others; the *Book of Common Prayer* left the communion studiously undefined. But the very stress on the inner life over *cultus* gave a handle to those who wanted to banish religious convictions to the private realm altogether. For many, they remain there. In this way, the story of the West to ca. 1700 is the story of the decline of *cultus*.

The Reformation weakened another prop of Christendom. As long as kings ruled by divine authority, they would likely see the promotion of right religion and the suppression of wrong religion as essential parts of their mission. Louis XIV's revocation of the Edict of Nantes is a reminder of that. Indeed, theocratic monarchy had a long history in the West. The ancient Hebrews had introduced an important tension into theocratic monarchy. For Hebrew kings, representing a monotheistic god who embodied the standard of right behavior had its drawbacks because wrong behavior, as even shepherds and beggars could recognize, was not backed by such a god. As the first Christian Roman emperor found, Christianity's tendency to produce heresy only made such criticisms of rulers more likely, for now these criticisms might be grounded on differences of belief as well as on royal bad conduct. The Reformation, of course, was the great generator of religious minorities: Catholics in majority Protestant countries, and Protestants of various stripes in some Catholic ones. With reluctance, such minorities drew the same conclusion that some Christian Roman emperors' Christian critics had drawn: the ruler must not be backed by God, for the ruler backs the wrong version of Christianity. The Jesuit Juan de Mariana (1536–1624), facing up to a Protestant Henry of Navarre as king of Catholic France, argued that kings have their right to rule not from God but from the community, which can remove them if need be. In Scotland, the Calvinist George Buchanan (1506–1582) had come to similar conclusions when contemplating the rule of the Catholic Mary, Queen of Scots. So many and so permanent were the religious minorities produced by the Reformation that, through much of the West, theocracy received frequent criticism and rejection.

Finally, the fading of Christendom may have been rooted in sheer exhaustion. Perhaps people are prepared to live with only so much violent disorder before they become willing to set their ideals aside.

In recent centuries, a secular public life has been a hallmark of the West, if one imperfectly observed. This feature has not been by design, something thought up by very bright people who suddenly perceived the right way to order religion and government. It was, instead, a product of historical evolution and accident carried out by people who had no such result in mind. Protestantism's founders did not advocate religious freedom. They advocated a reformed Christendom. They would not have approved of the modern West. Dig further into the past and consider the influence of the Hebrews. If one could magically transport an ancient Hebrew to the modern West, she would be appalled by many things. Among them would be the secular basis of Western government and religious pluralism. What was fundamental to the Hebrews was not religious freedom but correct religious practice.

And so a confluence of forces was producing one element of the modern West ca. 1700. Christendom had become simply the West. But, as Chistendom faded, so did the notion of community based on Christianity. With the body of Christ a less compelling basis for a sense of connection with the rest of society, the secular notion of the body politic became even more important. But for how long?

FURTHER READING

Benedict, Philip. *Christ's Churches Purely Reformed: A Social History of Calvinism*. New Haven, CT: Yale University Press, 2002.

Brady, Thomas A., James D. Tracy, and Heiko A. Oberman, eds. *Handbook of European History, 1400–1600: Late Middle Ages, Renaissance, and Reformation*. 2 vols. New York: E.J. Brill. 1994–95.

Cameron, Euan. *The European Reformation*. Oxford: Oxford University Press, 1991.

Crosby, Alfred W. *Ecological Imperialism: The Biological Expansion of Europe, 900–1900*. Cambridge: Cambridge University Press, 1986.

Davis, Natalie Zemon. *Society and Culture in Early Modern France: Eight Essays*. Stanford, CA: Stanford University Press, 1975.

Eisenstein, Elizabeth L. *The Printing Revolution in Early Modern Europe*. Cambridge: Cambridge University Press, 1983.

Hillerbrand, Hans J., ed. *The Reformation in Its Own Words*. London: SCM Press, 1964. [Primary sources.]

Holt, Mack P. *The French Wars of Religion, 1562–1629*. Cambridge: Cambridge University Press, 1995.

Hsia, R. Po-chia. *The World of Catholic Renewal, 1540–1770*. Cambridge: Cambridge University Press, 1998.

Levack, Brian P. *The Witch-Hunt in Early Modern Europe*. 3rd ed. New York: Pearson Longman, 2006.

Levin, Carol. *The Reign of Elizabeth I*. New York: Palgrave, 2002.

Lindberg, Carter, ed. *The European Reformations Sourcebook*. Oxford: Blackwell Publishers, 2000. [Primary sources.]

MacCormack, Sabine. *Religion in the Andes: Religion and Imagination in Early Colonial Peru*. Princeton, NJ: Princeton University Press, 1991.

MacCulloch, Diarmaid. *Reformation*. New York: Penguin Books, 2003. [Long and lively.]

Ozment, Steven. *Protestants: The Birth of a Revolution*. New York: Doubleday, 1993.

Rabb, Theodore K. *The Struggle for Stability in Early Modern Europe*. Oxford: Oxford University Press, 1975.

Roper, Lyndal. *The Holy Household: Women and Morals in Reformation Augsburg*. Corrected Edition. Oxford: Oxford University Press, 1991.

Skinner, Quentin. *The Foundations of Modern Political Thought*. 2 vols. Cambridge: Cambridge University Press, 1978.

Wiesner, Merry E. *Women and Gender in Early Modern Europe*. 2nd ed. Cambridge: Cambridge University Press, 2000.

Zagorin, Perez. *How the Idea of Religious Toleration Came to the West*. Princeton, NJ: Princeton University Press, 2003.

Zophy, Jonathan W. *A Short History of the Renaissance and Reformation in Europe: Dances over Fire and Water*. 3rd ed. New York: Prentice Hall, 2002. [An introductory text.]

THE EARLY MODERN WEST II

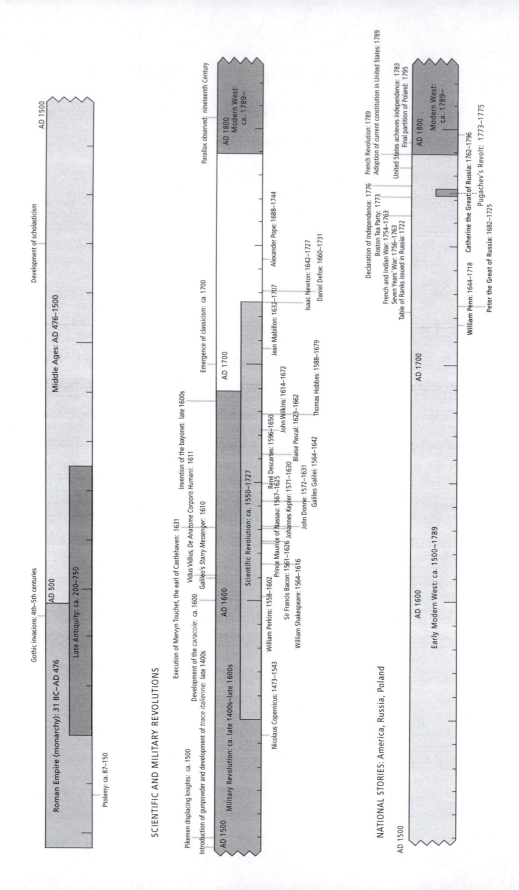

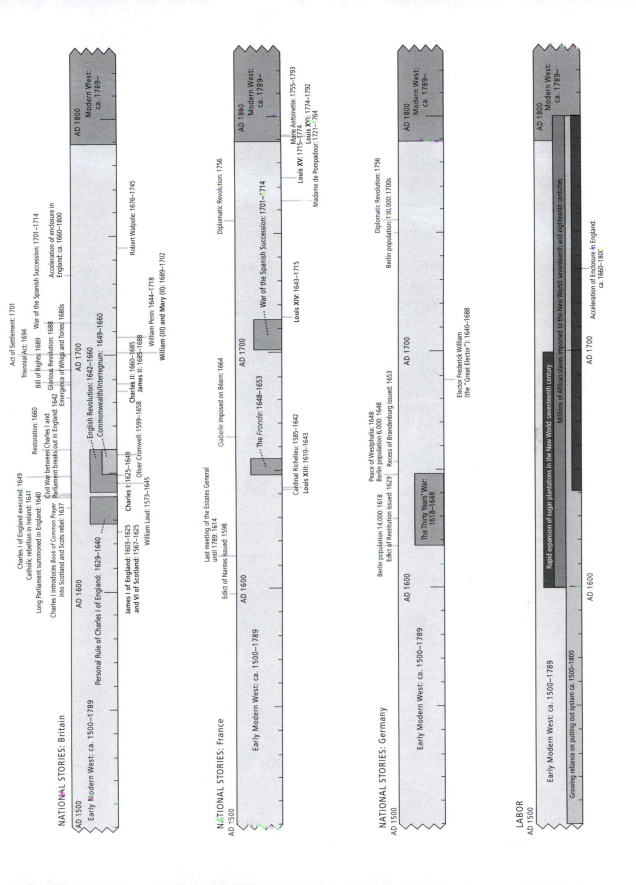

SEVEN

THE EARLY MODERN WEST II: SCIENCE, SOCIETY, AND THE STATE

7.0 INTRODUCTION

Big historical developments are not neatly divided. They overlap. So this chapter covers some of the same ground as the last, but to a different end. The chief quarry of Chapter 6 was the Reformation and its repercussions. Some of the people and events discussed there are also, however, important for an understanding of the developments discussed here, developments that overflowed into the eighteenth century. By that century's end, the West had produced much that was characteristic of its early twenty-first-century incarnation: a society tending (despite recent celebrations of diversity) toward greater standardization and equality and in which individual autonomy seems often to outweigh obligations to community. Many historians refer to Western history from ca. 1500 to the French Revolution of 1789 as "early modern," reserving the term "modern history" for the period ca. 1789–present. Yet the West's modern condition is rooted in early modern developments.

7.1 FUNDAMENTALS I: A SOCIETY OF ORDERS, ESTATES, AND CORPORATIONS

Ca. 1600, people in the West were members of one or more legally defined groups, an inheritance of the High and Late Middle Ages. In most countries, the broadest of these were known as "orders" or "estates" into which everyone throughout the country fell. In France, for example, all people were members of one of three estates: the first (the clergy), the second (the nobility), and the third (everybody else). Such orders and estates were defined by the legal rights of their members. In many countries, for instance, the nobility had the right to bear arms and to use them. But within those estates and orders, most people were also members of one or more "corporations," groups defined by their legal rights. Members of a university usually constituted a corporation. The craft gilds of many towns are examples of corporations; they often had the right to set minimum or maximum prices for goods made by their members—and to demand that all townspeople in their line of business be gild members. The citizens of a city could also constitute a corporation; they often had rights peculiar to their group; for example, some cities had the right to build or maintain defensive fortifications. Finally, to stretch the term "corporation" a little, the provinces of some countries often had rights distinct from those of other provinces.

Estates and corporations were not classes. A "class" is nowadays usually understood as an income category (e.g., the poor, working class, middle class, the rich). Rather, estates and corporations were defined by legal rights. They were often also distinguished by the degree of respect they received from others, which is why historians sometimes argue that one's status (i.e., standing derived from group membership in an estate or corporation) counted for more than class (i.e., income). The poorest noble might expect a merchant to remove his hat when he walked by, even if that merchant were richer than the noble.

Whether one talks about provinces, broad estates, or narrower corporations, throughout the West, rights and standing were defined by one's membership in a group. The rights enjoyed by such groups were sometimes described as "liberties," a term worth some examination because it reveals differences between the West of ca. 1600 and ca. 2000. Nowadays, "liberty" is used most often in the singular, to mean "freedom" (as in "Give me liberty, or give me death"). Moreover, liberty or freedom is often said to be a human right, that is, a right that all people naturally have simply by virtue of being human. But ca. 1600, as in the Middle Ages, people thought most easily in terms of liber*ties*. Not all persons had the same rights, even when these rights were understood as freedoms. The difference between modern and early-seventeenth-century usage marks the distance between modern expectations of equality and early-seventeenth-century expectations of hierarchy. Since one's rights were a matter of one's order or corporation, different people were expected to have different rights. Indeed, because rights varied from group to group, one can describe them as "privileges" as easily as "rights." It made sense, therefore, to think of rights and liberties in the plural, as the rights and liberties of orders or corporations, not of humanity. Another sign of the distance between modern and early-seventeenth-century notions about rights was that rights could be treated like property. Like property, such rights were transferable to others, and like property, they were inheritable. They were, in other words, "alienable": they could be given up. Another difference points to inequalities that contradict the modern notion of human rights. Some rights ca. 1600 were rights over others. The tithe, a tax collected by a parish priest from the people of his parish, is an example. So are the gild rights, mentioned previously.

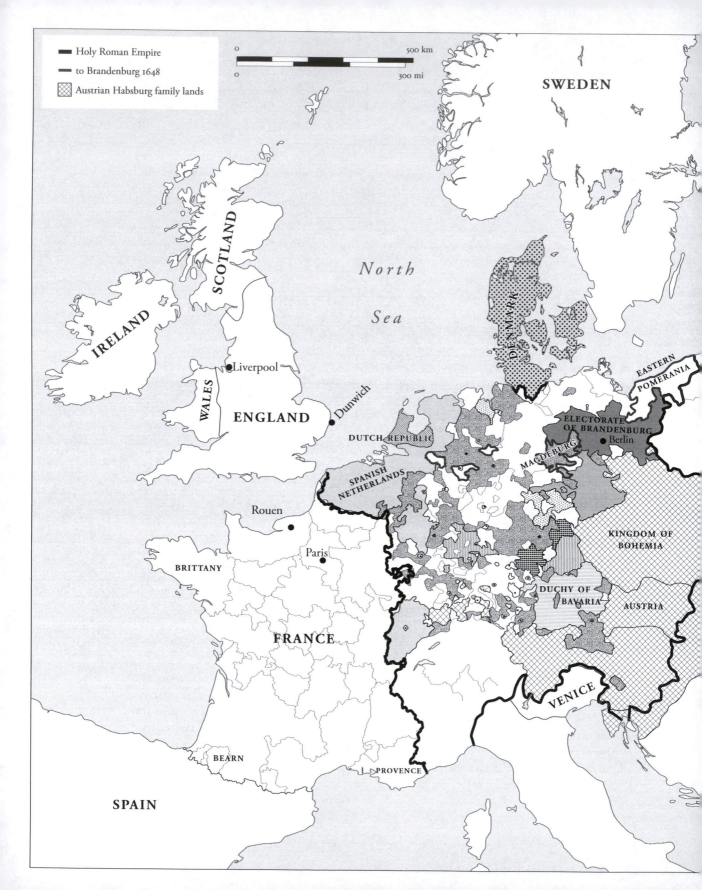

SWEDEN

North

Sea

IRELAND

SCOTLAND

WALES

Liverpool

ENGLAND

Dunwich

DUTCH REPUBLIC

DENMARK

EASTERN POMERANIA

ELECTORATE OF BRANDENBURG

Berlin

MAGDEBURG

SPANISH NETHERLANDS

KINGDOM OF BOHEMIA

Rouen

Paris

BRITTANY

FRANCE

DUCHY OF BAVARIA

AUSTRIA

VENICE

BEARN

PROVENCE

SPAIN

Map 7.1: Europe ca. 1600

Western society ca. 1600 was indeed a forest of groups, most of which had grown up in the High and Late Middle Ages. Like a forest of many different species of trees planted on uneven ground, the society of orders and corporations was very inconsistent. Moreover, these groups help account for an important political fact of the early seventeenth century, namely, the weakness (when compared with later centuries) of central political authority. Group rights hemmed in the power of kings; local independence was great. Compounding the situation was the fact that police forces were minimal and therefore unavailable to kings to enforce their will. These limitations are evident if one takes a political "tour" of parts of the West ca. 1600.

One can begin with Germany, then largely part of the Holy Roman Empire. The empire was, in theory, governed by the Holy Roman Emperor, a position held by the head of the eastern branch of the Habsburg family (the other branch ruled Spain). The empire was divided, however, into a myriad of territorial authorities, from the tiny to the large, some 1,789 in all (see Map 7.1). The greater of these territories were ruled by hereditary nobles known as princes, such as the duke of Bavaria in the south and the elector of Brandenburg in the north. The princes largely governed their territories without consulting the Holy Roman Emperor. The emperor was himself also the greatest of these princes. He ruled Austria, some other German-speaking territories within the empire, along with the kingdom of Bohemia (the modern Czech state), and, outside the empire, the part of Hungary that had not fallen to the Turks.

By 1600 the Holy Roman Emperor had little practical control over the empire. A decision of the emperor affecting the entire empire required the consent of the Diet, an assembly representing the greater territories whose rulers (the princes) wished to preserve their independence. In effect, the Diet represented and protected the rights of local authorities. Moreover, emperors were emperors by election, although, once elected, they held office for life. Characteristically, the right to elect emperors was vested not in all the empire's inhabitants but in a very small corporation—seven men called "electors," who, as princes of the larger of the territories, held this right by inheritance just as they held their territories. (The elector of Brandenburg was so called because he was one of these men.) Over time, emperors had made agreements with these electors—known as "capitulations"—in order to ensure the election of their heirs. Thus, although the Habsburgs traditionally held the throne, their power flowed more from their own hereditary lands ("the family lands," such as Austria) than from the office of emperor.

French kings, however, were kings by hereditary right and so enjoyed greater authority in their kingdom than did the emperors in the Holy Roman Empire. Yet that authority was also limited. The king could not impose new taxes throughout the kingdom without the consent of an assembly, the Estates General, which was also to be consulted about royal decisions of general concern; kings were traditionally loath to acknowledge these rights. The structure of the Estates General reveals a society structured according to estates. It was composed of representatives of the three estates, the descendants of the three orders of the Middle Ages (see above). Voting in the Estates General was not by individual member but by estate. In other words, collectively the first estate had one vote, the second estate had one vote, and the third estate had one vote. Individually, these orders also had certain rights. The first two estates, for example, were exempt from the chief tax in the kingdom, the *taille*, which was an income tax in most provinces and a land tax in some others.

French kings made law. Here too, however, their authority faced limits. These were in the form of their own courts, corporations called *parlements*. The chief parlement was that of Paris, which heard cases appealed from the lower courts scattered throughout the country. The Parlement of Paris also claimed the right to refuse to apply laws made by the king until it had formally received them, essentially a veto power. (The king could insist on their acceptance only through a rare formal procedure, the *lit de justice*, or "bed of justice," in which the king personally presided over the court.) Although the king appointed the parlements' judges, he could not so easily dismiss them. So long as they paid a tax (the *paulette*), they could keep their judgeships and, indeed, pass them on to their sons, along with the noble status that came with the office. (This situation points to how complex rights could be.) This "nobility of the robe" (for the robes worn by judges), along with the more traditional "nobility of the sword" (the old warrior class), thus limited royal power.

So did various local rights. The kings of France had stitched together their kingdom from various territories in the Middle Ages. Provinces like Brittany and Provence still maintained their own laws; some sixty different bodies of law operated ca. 1600. Some provinces had the privilege of having their own parlements or assemblies of estates, which exercised limits on royal action in the province in the same way the Parlement of Paris and Estates General did in the country at large. Other privileges came in the form of tax exemption. Béarn, for example, was exempt from the *gabelle*, a kind of tax on salt. Cities within provinces might have their own rights, such as Rouen, whose citizens did not have to pay the *taille*. (Neither did the faculty and students of universities, another corporation.) So strong were provincial identities that those moving goods between provinces sometimes paid tolls similar to the import taxes paid on goods entering a country today.

English monarchs faced a simpler situation ca. 1600. England had long been subject to a single body of law, the "Common Law," so called because it was common to the whole country. Wales, although ethnically distinct, had also been brought under this law. Ireland, although now defined as a separate kingdom ruled by the English king, was a subject territory run, in part, on lines inspired by English ones. England itself was divided into territorial districts called shires (also known as counties). Much more so than French provinces, however, the shires had identical structures (each, for example, had a figure called a sheriff and officials known as justices of the peace), and shires lacked legal rights against the king. No tolls were collected from one shire to another.

But English kings still faced limits, both when making decisions and when enforcing them. As far as decision making was concerned, the king could not legislate or impose new taxes on the realm without the agreement of Parliament, an assembly reminiscent of France's Estates General and the Holy Roman Empire's Diet. Parliament had an upper house, the House of Lords. Its membership, the peers of the realm, consisted of the heads of noble families who enjoyed the hereditary liberty of being summoned to sit there and of a smaller number of bishops, appointed by the king. In the lower house, the House of Commons, sat men who represented two different kinds of electoral districts. The first kind was the shire, into which the whole country was divided. Each shire elected members of Parliament. In addition, some towns within the shires, known as "boroughs," had the right to elect additional members of Parliament. By 1600, some boroughs were smaller than other communities that lacked borough status, but custom and a medieval royal charter granting borough status were hard to break and hard to acquire. Moreover, the right to vote varied from borough to borough. Most had some sort of property requirement.

Parliament met, however, solely when the king summoned it. If he did not want new laws or new taxes, the law did not obligate him to convene Parliament. Indeed, the right to call Parliament or not was one of the king's hereditary prerogatives or rights. He had others, such as setting foreign policy and choosing his officials. Indeed, the king of England, like other Western monarchs, can be thought of as a corporation of one, enjoying hereditary rights different from those of his subjects.

Talk of parliamentary elections should not mislead. Parliament, including the House of Commons, was not a democratic institution. The property requirements of the boroughs suggest this conclusion. Indeed, many boroughs were what would one day come to be called "pocket boroughs," districts in which a great landowner dominated the eligible voters—sometimes as their landlord—and so effectively had elections in his pocket. Tiny boroughs, mere villages, which would eventually be called "rotten boroughs," were especially liable to be pocket boroughs. One, Dunwich, was under water; it had been above sea level when it became a borough in the Middle Ages and had flooded since. Elections were not characteristic of rotten boroughs. Requirements in the shires were consistent: only men who owned land worth forty shillings a year or more could vote. These conditions resulted in the domination of the House of Commons by a group of people called "the gentry" (i.e., gentlemen). The gentry were not a legally but a socially defined group, one whose income came from the land either in the form of rent or by farming it through hired hands. Other people, today called professionals, in particular lawyers and doctors, also tended to be included among the gentry, as were the wives and daughters of gentlemen. The gentry illustrate how group identity could come from status as well as legal rights. They were the most respected group after members of the House of Lords, bowed to by their lessers. Business people—who sometimes sat for the boroughs—might be wealthy, but their status as gentry was always doubtful. (If they sold the business and invested in land, they or their children might be recognized as gentry.) Parliament, then, was a tool by which the peers and gentry might limit the king's freedom of action.

But the gentry could also limit the king in the shires. There, the king's government depended heavily on local unpaid gentlemen holding local office. The advantage for the king was that such men served without pay; after all, they had independent incomes and free time. Royal service, in turn, gave local gentlemen a chance to show their status as gentlemen, and gentlemen with connections at that. It also bolstered their influence in the shire. The justice of the peace, for example, was nearly always a local gentleman. He sat in judgment over lesser criminal charges. Lesser people would hesitate to cross such a man. So might kings. The service of gentlemen might be free, but they could be hard to control. Gentlemen officials who disliked orders coming from London might enforce them lackadaisically. Moreover, the king could not discipline unsalaried local representatives by refusing to pay them (a problem that harkens back to the Early Middle Ages. English kings got what they paid for.

Although local gentry had no legal right to control local government, locals expected that the shires be run in the customary way, in other words, by local gentlemen. In 1605, the inhabitants of Warminster refused to follow a royal order to pay the muster-master, a royally appointed official, because the local justices of the peace had not told people to pay; oddly, the people of Warminster said that, because the king's command had not come through the justices of the peace, the king had not ordered payment. Indeed, when people referred to "my country," they often meant their shire or county rather than England.

English kings faced another complication. The unmarried Elizabeth I of England (see 6.5) died in 1603, leaving as her heir King James VI of Scotland (1567–1625), who now became King James I of England (1603–1625). He inherited the right to rule both kingdoms just as his subjects inherited their own property. His kingdoms, however, remained very much separate. The Scots and the English had often been at odds in the past. Scots held that having their national church run along Presbyterian lines was one of their rights, along with having their own Scottish laws and institutions. The English felt similarly about England, although some people would have preferred a church like the Scottish church, one without bishops.

As this survey hints, in all countries, politics was monopolized by a narrow segment of society, called by some historians the "political nation." The political nation refers not to an order or corporation but, instead, simply to the people who mattered in politics, those who took part in politics and whose political views counted. The nobility was, by far, the largest component, followed by the higher members of the clergy and the more influential members of the *bourgeoisie*. (*Bourgeoisie* may require explanation. One standard definition, the "middle class," misleads because, although the bourgeoisie was, indeed, "in the middle" between the nobility and lower groups, the term more specifically refers to the business people and educated professionals of the cities, a far cry from the usual sense of the term "middle class" today. A tavern keeper was bourgeois or middle class. A banker was too. Bankers, but not usually tavern keepers, might be members of the political nation.)

This society of orders and corporations commonly makes little sense to people raised to expect equality and democracy. But it made sense ca. 1600. One justification given for these groups and their rights was custom, a notion that itself went back to the Middle Ages at least. Most of these group rights were old. But a few were not. In France, the Huguenots (i.e., Protestants), a much-hated minority, had been given rights (such as the right to worship in certain towns and to have armed forces under control independent of the king) only in 1598, when the king granted them in the Edict of Nantes (see 6.7). More fundamentally, however, the rights of estates, corporations, and provinces made sense because they fit, or at least seemed to fit, assumptions that people made about the universe as a whole.

7.2 FUNDAMENTALS II: THE UNIVERSE CA. 1600

What did people assume about the universe ca. 1600? It is best to begin concretely, with a discussion of astronomy and physics.

With a few exceptions, people with any astronomical knowledge ca. 1600 held to some version of the Ptolemaic system, named for the ancient Greek astronomer Ptolemy (ca. 87–ca.150), who had, in fact, built on earlier models. (His own views received further modifications over the centuries.) At the center of the Ptolemaic system lay Earth (see Figure 7.1). Concentric spheres carrying the planets, including the sun, rotated around Earth. These spheres and planets were made of a special substance: quintessence. The outer-most sphere carried the stars. Beyond the stars sang the angels. Beyond the angels was God.

But there was more to this geocentric, or Earth-centered, model. Quintessence means "fifth essence," as distinguished from the four elements found on Earth—earth, air, fire, and water. Earthly matter was characterized by some unstable combination of these elements, so it was corruptible; the elements themselves undermined each other. Quintessence, by contrast, was perfect matter and, therefore, incorruptible. Thus, Earth and the planets formed a simple hierarchy. The planets (and the stars) in their spheres were better than Earth, and so they were above it. But the angels, being purely spiritual beings, were better and so even higher than the stars and planets, for it had long been held that mind and spirit were higher than body and matter. And God, of course, was the Supreme Being, so he was highest of all. Thus, the cosmos was a hierarchy, running from the lowest in the center to the highest as one moved further from the center. (This structure contradicts any notion that human beings were thought to be the most important part of creation because they were at its center. The center was not a place of dignity.

Figure 7.1: Sketch of Ptolemaic universe

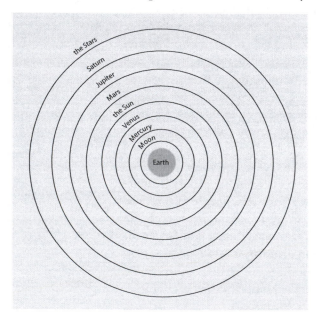

Indeed, when people imagined where the devil and the damned must be, they thought of the center of the earth, in other words, the universe's dead center.) Cosmic harmony was evident in the music made by the quintessence spheres as they carried their planets (music too perfect, alas, for human ears to hear).

This interest in perfection versus corruptibility stemmed from a preoccupation with the qualities of objects. The physics of Aristotle was still authoritative. It held that an object moves for one of two reasons: 1) because a force is applied (e.g., a hand pushing a door) or 2) because of an object's qualities (e.g., an air bubble moves up in water because air has higher qualities than water, which place it higher in the natural hierarchy than water, so it tries to move to its natural place in the hierarchy). The planets moved in circular orbits not only because the spheres carried them but because the circle was the perfect shape, an appropriate path for perfect matter. Aristotle's qualitative cause of motion also allowed the growth of animals and plants to be thought of as motion. Why does an acorn grow into an oak tree, and not into a frog? Because an acorn has certain oakish qualities that lead it to grow into (or better, "move into being") an oak tree; tadpoles, on the other hand, have the qualities that lead them to grow into frogs. This rather broad definition of motion—it really included any kind of change—meant that physics and biology were, as they had been for Aristotle himself, not the distinct branches of study they would later come to be.

The different assumptions of a world view tend to be coherent. That is, they tend to fit together and, indeed, reinforce each other. That helps explain their attraction and why they so often last a long time. When John Wilkins (1614–1672) wanted to argue in 1638 that Earth was merely a planet—and, indeed, that the moon would be habitable were human beings only able to get there—he had to argue against the assumptions built into the Ptolemaic system. He imagined an opponent voicing the obvious objection that Earth *must* be at the center of the universe because, in its "vileness," it "consists of a more sordid and base matter than any other part of the world [i.e., universe]; and therefore must be situated in the center, which is the worst place, and at the greatest distance from those purer incorruptible bodies, the heavens."[1] The universe is a hierarchy. Earth has base qualities, and the heavens pure ones. Therefore Earth must be at the center of the universe. And why is the universe hierarchical? Because it is made up of both pure and corrupt matter, with the worst matter at the center.

This discussion of physics and the Ptolemaic system exemplifies certain large assumptions about the universe in general and not just about physics and astronomy. People assumed that the universe was hierarchical; some things are placed by God and nature above others. Analysis of the universe tended to focus on its qualitative aspects over its quantitative—that is, its measurable—aspects (recall quintessence, for example). The universe was, furthermore, harmonious; the different levels of the hierarchy are supposed to work together (recall the music of the spheres). According to this view, conflict was unnatural, an offense against the divine design. The stress on harmony also fostered a sense that things functioned organically, that is, like living organisms in that each organ worked with the others. None of these assumptions was new ca. 1600. They were largely of ancient origin although modified by subsequent medieval refinements. Together, these beliefs made up the commonly held world view of the early seventeenth century.

Indeed, the Ptolemaic system was but the grandest representation of the natural hierarchy. Nested within that hierarchy was a series of smaller ones, like those Russian dolls, one hidden inside another, hidden inside another, and so on. At the level of the individual human being, spirit was supposed to rule the body as reason was to rule passion. The smallest group of human beings was organized similarly; families were governed by the head of the household, who was expected to be the husband and father (widows and, in Catholic countries, nuns, were exceptional). The term "family" is revealing. Ca. 1600

---

1   John Wilkins, *The Mathematical and Philosophical Works of the Right Reverend John Wilkins* (London: C. Whittingham, for Vernor and Hood, 1802), 1: 190 (spellings modernized).

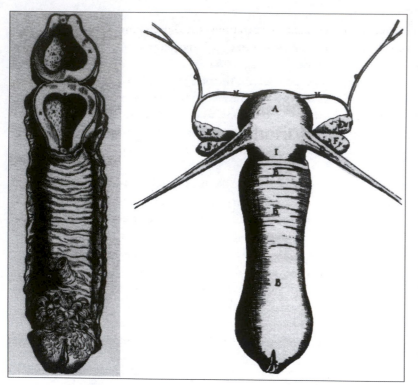

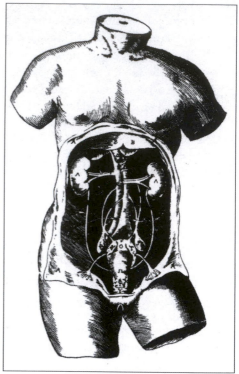

Figure 7.2 (left): Anatomical sketch from Vidus Vidius (detail)

Figure 7.3 (right): Anatomical sketch from Vidus Vidius

it meant "household," a married couple, their children, together with household servants and anyone else living with them; a father and husband ruled them all. In 1590, William Perkins (1558–1602) defined a husband as "he which hath authority over the wife."[2] So deep ran these attitudes that they could bring even an English aristocrat to execution. English nobles rarely suffered such punishment for anything but treason, but Mervyn Touchet (ca. 1592–1631), the earl of Castlehaven, had, it was said, compelled his wife to have intercourse with another man. The earl's offense was not so much violating her as violating his own authority as the head of the household. An example had to be made of him.

The rule of husbands over wives was natural, for nature made women to be ruled by men. The biology of the time explained how. In a theory that goes back to the ancient Greeks, women were held to be incompletely developed men (or, conversely, men were more fully developed women). Doctors still learned this theory in their textbooks. Consider Figure 7.2, taken from Vidus Vidius's work on human anatomy, *De Anatome Corporis Humani* of 1611. The sketch may appear to be that of man's penis and testes. It was, in fact, a sketch of a vagina and ovaries (see Figure 7.3). In a mature human being, these organs grew fully and so emerged from the body. Women, being less mature human beings, never got to see their reproductive organs. Indeed, this evidence brings home how

---

2 William Perkins, *Christian Oeconomie Or a Short Treatise On the Manner of Erecting and Ordering a Familie According to the Scriptures*, trans. T. Pickering (London: Felix Kyngston, 1609), 123.

powerful a thing a world view can be. Like modern medical illustrations, these drawings were made from cadavers. The men who made them were trying to draw what they saw. Instead, they drew what they knew.

So women, on this view, were immature human beings. As such, women did not fully develop the higher human faculties, mind and spirit. Lacking masculine minds, they were more driven than men by their physical needs, such as those for food and sex. Similarly, their passions more easily got the best of their reason, another higher human function. Thus, women were the hysterical, earthy sex. They needed to be ruled by the more rational, spiritual one.

This tendency to think in terms of nested hierarchies encouraged people to take analogies very seriously. Analogies did not simply suggest or illustrate relationships; they helped prove relationships, relationships expected to hold throughout nature. Not until 1742 did students of bees give up on finding the king bee that they knew must rule every hive (why they gave up in the eighteenth century will be considered later). Similarly, kings ruled over their kingdoms just as fathers ruled over their households.

Much of this world view—the tendency to take analogy seriously, the expectations of harmony, organic unity, and hierarchy—is evident in the metaphor of the kingdom as a "body politic." Society, it was said, was a "body politic" (a term sometimes used today to mean "society"), so it was structured like a human body. The king was its head and, like the head, directed the body. Other parts of society performed other functions—the peasants were the feet, supporting the body; nobles were the arms, protecting the body, and so on. The body politic was obviously hierarchical. It was also organic; each part had a function to perform, tied to the other parts and cooperating harmoniously with them like the organs of a human body. People had the rights appropriate to their place and function in the hierarchy. After all, for example, if the nobility's function was to fight, nobles needed the right to bear arms. And, because the body politic was part of the natural order set up by God, such rights were God-given, as well as justified by custom. This conception of society as a body had begun as a Christian idea, that of the community of Christians, the "body of Christ." But the Reformation had injured the notion of Christianity as the path to community (see 6.7). The more secular body politic was what remained.

It would be easy to conclude from this discussion that the king, being at the top of the divinely ordained hierarchy, was thought to have absolute power over the kingdom. The conclusion would be natural, but it would be wrong. Yes, the king was at the summit of the human hierarchy, but he was so tied to the rest of the body politic that he would suffer any harm he did its other parts. To destroy the peasants, for example, would be like the body's head cutting off its own feet. More fundamentally, if the king enjoyed his position by divine right or custom, so did the other parts of the body politic. As one of my own teachers put it clearly, the king had divine right, but so did everybody else. If the king had customary rights, so did everybody else. The ideal was harmonious cooperation in the exercise of these rights in an organic union. This expectation crops up in ways that may seem odd to modern eyes. In France, for example, the provincial estates sometimes referred to the taxes they granted the king as a *don gratuit*, a "free gift." Such grants were not merely government business; they were marks of friendship. These considerations applied to other kinds of rulers. The William Perkins who defined a husband as "he which hath authority over the wife" also noted a husband's duty "to love her as himself" and to take account of her as a "yoke-fellow," to use Perkins's term.[3] Husbands, it was thought, were to rule their wives, not abuse them.

Indeed, this talk of rights returns the discussion to the society of orders and corporations laid out in section 7.1. The groups of society with their various rights were thought of as the hierarchically arranged parts of the body politic, organically united. The tendency to think in terms of groups rather than equal individuals fit an organic notion of society. The limits on royal power posed by group rights made sense in a world in which kings topped the social hierarchy but lacked the authority substantially to change that hierarchy. Society and views of the universe were a good fit ca. 1600.

This world was not, however, that of the modern West. The seventeenth century set in motion two developments that ultimately help explain why the West of ca. 2000 is so different from that of ca. 1600. Absolutism assaulted the society of orders and corporations. The Scientific Revolution assaulted the assumptions that underlay it.

7.3 ABSOLUTISM I: MOTIVES, MEANS, AND IMPLICATIONS

In the seventeenth century, most Western countries saw attempts by monarchs to become absolute, that is, to gather more and more power in their hands, centralizing government and overriding that complex of rights (embodied, for example, in the English Parliament and French estates) that traditionally curbed them in. These attempts were, it should be noted, merely attempts. Although royal propaganda might trumpet the king's absolute authority, in no case did kings actually succeed in wholly defanging the political nation. Indeed, it is not always clear that kings consciously adopted absolutism as a goal even when, in practical terms, they moved in that direction. But in that direction most kings moved or tried to move. Some achieved relative success. Others failed, sometimes ignominiously. On the whole, central authorities were stronger ca. 1789 than they had been ca. 1600. To that extent, the society of orders weakened.

At the outset, however, a warning is necessary. In no case is the danger of making value judgments about the past greater than in a consideration of absolutism. Modern readers are likely to sympathize with absolutism's opponents. All-powerful government calls to mind Nazis or Communists, both nowadays usually seen as Bad Things. Yet, in attacking the society of orders and corporations and its different rights for different groups, absolute monarchs fostered greater equality, something most people in the modern West regard as a Good Thing. In the seventeenth century, however, absolutism and equality went together

---

3 Perkins, *Christian Oeconomie*, 125.

like bread and butter. Modern moral judgments that oppose equality (Good) and absolutism (Bad) can hamper historical understanding.

Why did the seventeenth century see the rise of absolutism? One explanation is momentum. The High Middle Ages had seen the emergence of centralized, bureaucratic government. Bureaucracies, one might suggest, naturally grow and kings naturally try to gather power. With the Reformation of the sixteenth century, kings had achieved further success in that regard, notably in gaining greater authority over the clergy in their kingdoms (see 6.6). But another development also helps explain the drive toward absolutism, a series of changes in warfare that have come to be called the "Military Revolution." These changes brought more expensive fortifications and a new stress on training and discipline that, in turn, rendered armies more expensive. These expenses made kings hungrier for revenue and pushed them to overcome the rights of orders, corporations, and provinces to limit the king's power to tax.

The Military Revolution was the culmination of important changes in warfare that had accumulated since the fifteenth century. The introduction of gunpowder and, with it, cannon meant that, starting in the fifteenth century, governments had to pay for new, costly equipment. Cannon also spurred the radical redesign of fortifications. Pioneered by Italian city states (and so called the *trace italienne*), expensive, thick, low walls replaced taller, thinner castle walls, making for yet more expense.

From Switzerland, a federation of independent towns largely lacking traditional knightly nobles, came a new kind of foot soldier, the pikeman. Holding his pike at an incline and backed by the weight of his fellows when packed together in a large block, this foot soldier was well positioned to hold off noble cavalry. Ca. 1500, pikemen displaced knights, the mounted, heavily armored warriors so characteristic of the High and Late Middle Ages. Gunpowder further encouraged reliance on pikemen. Most early modern muskets were inaccurate weapons, so there was little point to practicing at being a good shot. Musketeers did not, however, have to be very accurate shots anyway; aiming at a huge block of pikemen was rather like aiming at a barn. But musketeers needed pikemen. Muskets were cumbersome, slow-firing weapons; some required up to 98 commands to load, aim, and fire. And when musketeers had fired their shot and tried to reload, what then? They were defenseless, especially to (the now diminished) cavalry; they turned to the pikemen of their own side for protection.

Both pikemen and musketeers, however, reveal a way of warfare that put less store in training than did the kind of warfare to come in the course of the seventeenth century. Careful training of musketeers made little sense, given their lack of accuracy. Pikemen could do most of their work by holding their pikes at a correct angle, keeping up roughly with their neighbors in the block, and screwing up their courage when facing other pikemen, musketeers, or cavalry (although, of course, better-trained pikemen were better pikemen). This situation meant that war could be carried out by either professional mercenaries or even part-timers. When kings made war, they hired mercenaries or men who might otherwise have other occupations; when peace came, the men could find another war or go home. Wintertime was bad campaign weather, so many soldiers could be discharged and then hired back should they be needed in the spring. One advantage of this situation for kings was that it made war relatively cheap, and peace even cheaper. The fact that soldiers brought their own equipment—their own pikes or muskets—also saved money for their employers. So did the way armies ate, often by looting the neighborhoods through which they moved, especially if they were in enemy territory.

But rulers found that more experienced foot soldiers, including pikemen, fought better. One could hire mercenaries, an option followed especially by many Italian city states in the sixteenth and seventeenth centuries. The Swiss, who had invented the pikeman, became exporters of soldiers. (The colorful Swiss guards employed today by popes are a remnant of this development.) Mercenaries were professionals, but their lack of commitment to their employer made them suspect. Another option was to create standing armed forces that fought only for the ruler.

The problems of pikemen and musketeers started to bring about further tactical changes, ones that also fostered standing armies. These changes put a further premium on training and discipline and would further raise the cost of war. In the sixteenth century, musketeers began to protect themselves and more seriously harm the enemy by performing the *caracole*. That is, while one line of musketeers fired all their weapons, another line of musketeers waited behind them, loading; then, after the men in front had fired, the ones with newly loaded muskets moved up to take their place, firing in turn. Ten rows of musketeers working in this way could keep up enough fire to fend off cavalry, not to mention enemy pikemen. But performing this maneuver required better-trained musketeers who were able to keep their cool even in the heat of battle. In the seventeenth century, the *caracole* became more devastating when musketeers held their fire until all were ready. Then, on the order of their commander, they fired as one, producing a volley. The resulting front of fast-moving lead can be imagined. Again, however, the requirement that musketeers at the front of the line hold their fire while the enemy bore down on them required discipline, which in turn required training.

The *caracole* and then the volley had an even larger impact on pikemen. Pikemen ceased to be as necessary to defend musketeers, who could now fend for themselves. Musketeers began to replace pikemen. In the late seventeenth century, the invention of the bayonet made pikemen entirely obsolete. But to use musketeers more effectively, commanders began to arrange them not in barn-like blocks but in longer lines, spread out enough to maximize the width of the wall of lead shot flying toward the enemy. Arranging troops in long lines also made for better defense because the enemy had to spread its fire power when shooting at a longer line than when shooting at a more concentrated body of troops. Thinner lines also could mean faster-moving soldiers.

Sixteenth-century commanders had increasingly realized the theoretical advantages of long, thin lines. But they had trouble getting the troops to abandon more comforting, deep, square formations, in which less competent soldiers, in particular, could shelter from the demands of actual combat. Moreover, long, thin lines posed greater challenges to command and control. Men were farther apart from each other. More officers in the field were required to coordinate the many parts of the line. Even with more officers overseeing the troops, keeping soldiers together in a long, thin line was more difficult than keeping men together in a big (roughly) square block. And changing direction was harder. Turning a block of men was easier than getting a long line of soldiers to pivot and yet stay in a long line.

These military developments also meant that armies—increasingly professional, full-time armies—grew. The long sieges required by the *trace italienne* required more men to carry out. Long, thin lines meant larger battlefields. Spain was the superpower of the West in the sixteenth century with about 40,000 troops. By the end of the seventeenth century, the West's superpower was the France of Louis XIV, who numbered his troops in the hundreds of thousands.

Governments need to win wars. So governments bit the bullet. If cannon had to be purchased, later fifteenth-century governments bought them. If a few hundred or a few thousand soldiers had to be employed permanently, early sixteenth-century governments employed them, and built thicker fortifications too. If more officers were needed to coordinate the men, seventeenth-century governments paid them, and some began to employ troops in the many tens or even hundreds of thousands, dwarfing earlier standing forces. But all these developments required more money. (Having more officers also required more organization, hence the creation of a system of defined military ranks—general, colonel, major, captain.) And when it came to controlling the troops, officers were not enough. Ultimately, the long, thin lines of the seventeenth century required better-disciplined, prepared soldiers, men who could all fight rather than be carried by their better-prepared or braver colleagues, and men who knew how to follow more complex orders. The only way to get them in large numbers while avoiding the problems posed by mercenaries was to make them—in other words, to train them. The seventeenth century thus saw permanent armies of full-time soldiers more fully displace part-time temps. In wartime, of course, they went to war. In peacetime, however, they trained, as they now did in winter. Soldiers were drilled. These drills in camp kept the many troops in those long lines on the battlefield. Inspired by Roman military treatises—newly emphasized by Renaissance humanists—as well as by current needs, officers taught soldiers to march in step, still part of basic training. But permanent armies meant that armies had to be paid year round, and in peacetime too, even if wages were reduced at such times. Expenses rose.

Training also affected how soldiers were supplied. In 1599, the Dutch Prince Maurice of Nassau (1567–1625), a proponent of the *caracole*, ensured that all his musketeers would be supplied with muskets—the same muskets—by the government. Soldiers could more easily carry out the *caracole* if they had identical guns. Governments increasingly supplied guns rather than make do with whatever soldiers turned up with from home. The demand for discipline also encouraged governments to provide the men with food and clothing. By the end of the seventeenth century, commanders were prohibiting troops from despoiling even enemy civilians; soldiers engaged in pillage are not soldiers under control. And the clothing armies supplied was uniform; in 1600, soldiers had often worn whatever they brought with them. Uniforms were desirable not simply as a way to tell friend from foe; soldiers in uniform are more likely to think of themselves as soldiers and to feel the call of discipline. (Providing shoes for large numbers of men at one time produced an odd spin-off: shoes had previously been custom made, but now armies invented shoe sizes, three of them at first.) Monarchs had to find money for all these goods. They also found that soldiers living together under their commanders were more disciplined. The standing forces of ca. 1500 had not lived in barracks; but the much larger ones of the seventeenth century did. Kings also had to create and pay for the military bureaucracy needed to manage supply, training, and housing, the ancestors of institutions such as the Pentagon in the United States.

How does the Military Revolution help explain the rise of absolute monarchy? Kings, who traditionally led in time of war, had to raise more and more money to pay for war and, in peacetime, to prepare for it. But the privileges of society's orders, corporations, and provinces hindered the kings' ability to tax and manage resources freely in order to get the money. Those rights had to be curtailed—hence absolutism. Moreover, war's greater expense favored kings. In the Middle Ages, individual nobles, themselves knights, might recruit other knights to oppose the king in battle and had the resources to build castles from which to defy royal power. But such men lacked the deep pockets to pay for, say, cannon or the more expensive fortifications that cannon made necessary when even governments with access to national taxation had trouble doing so.

The Military Revolution had another consequence. It set in motion an arms race that, broadly defined, has run more or less into the twenty-first century. As one government improved its military—in terms of weaponry, organization, or size—neighboring governments had to keep up. In the course of the eighteenth century, the hothouse of competition was giving the West military superiority across the globe. By the end of the nineteenth century, Western governments would rule most of it. And in order to wage or prepare to wage war effectively, governments curbed the rights of their peoples. The "national security state" often linked to the Cold War of the twentieth century has a long lineage.

There may also have been a psychological connection between absolutism and the Military Revolution. Kings must have found it pleasant to see their orders carried down the ranks, ultimately moving distant privates on the field. By the early eighteenth century, some kings liked to think of themselves as heads of armies. Louis XIV of France (1643–1715), often regarded as the very model of an absolute monarch, had a medal stamped featuring the king reviewing his army, poking a cane at an imperfectly uniformed private in the rear: Louis, the commander in chief, drilling the troops. Absolutists such as King Frederick William I of Brandenburg-Prussia (1713–1740) and King Charles XII of Sweden (1697–1718) took military uniforms as their normal dress; the practice continued into the twentieth century. Perhaps such kings hoped that the sort of obedience gotten from the army could be had in politics too.

Desire alone, however, does not bring its fulfillment. Although no early-modern king became truly absolute, some succeeded in moving in that direction, overriding the rights of the political nation. How were they able to do so? Louis XIV's France provides some answers.

One means was raw force. In 1664, Louis XIV imposed the *gabelle* (a salt tax) on Béarn, overriding a traditional local right in absolutist fashion in order to raise revenue. When

Béarn resisted, Louis sent in the troops. The incident reveals how absolutism and the Military Revolution fed off each other. Kings overrode people's rights in order to pay for standing armies and fortifications. But standing armies, in lieu of largely non-existent police, gave kings the muscle with which to override people's rights. The cycle reinforced itself. But sometimes force could be applied more delicately. Louis XIV found that sending obstreperous members of the parlements and provincial estates into sometimes comfortable internal exile had the gratifying effect of being tough enough to intimidate the men who remained but not severe enough to provoke them to rebellion. Under Louis, the usual *don gratuit* (see 7.2) voted by the provincial estates increased by fifty percent. The Parlement of Paris came to accept all the laws issued by Louis, sometimes without even bothering to vote.

Another move was for kings simply to see what they could get away with. After 1614, French kings found that they could impose new taxes and make major decisions for the kingdom without bothering to summon that grand assembly representing the entire realm, the Estates General, much less getting its consent. The Estates General, already fading for much of the sixteenth century, would not meet again until 1789.

Persuasion was a more active approach. In the seventeenth century, effective propaganda could be rather intimate because the political nation was very small. Painting, sculpture, theater, and even buildings could serve, whereas today's politicians need television, radio, and the Internet to address a much larger audience. Kings commissioned works to exalt the monarchy. The most striking cases are to be found in the performing arts, for both king and nobles themselves took part. Masques—allegorical performances made alluring by elaborate costumes and spectacular special effects—proclaimed that the king was sovereign, his nobles his creatures. Louis XIV, fond of ballet, used it to show himself supreme. (In fact, ballet became systematized at his court, hence the French names of modern ballet steps.) Louis danced the role of the sun; leading nobles took the parts of the planets, which gave off a merely reflected light. The message, that nobles got their position from the king—not from the same God or custom that made the king—was an absolutist one, subverting the society of orders and the body politic alike. Presumably, such "active learning," to use modern jargon, was more powerful than passively absorbed propaganda.

Even the code of ritualized etiquette developed at the courts of absolutist kings served as a kind of participatory propaganda. Louis XIV's court at his new palace of Versailles is the classic example. Versailles was enormous; thousands of nobles and officials lived there, served by thousands of others. Louis made it the center of French, then Western, art and fashion. His nobles ached to live there, but when they did so, they found themselves in a world of elaborately polite ceremony. At Versailles, it was rude to knock at a door; one was supposed to scratch it. And scratch not with the right hand, but the left. And not with all the fingers of the left hand, but with the small finger. (People took care to grow that nail especially long for the purpose.) Ultimately, it was Louis who determined all these minute rules governing life at Versailles. Indeed, if anything, mastering elaborate etiquette drew the attention of leading members of the political nation from more traditional political affairs, leaving the latter to His Majesty. Moreover, the point of much of this ceremony was to reinforce the notion that it was the king who determined one's standing, an idea that quietly left both the force of tradition and God behind. This situation held until the end. Here Madame Jeanne-Louise-Henriette Campan (1752–1822), a former royal chambermaid, describes the ordeal of serving a glass of water to Marie Antoinette (1755–1793), queen of Louis XVI (1774–1792), France's last king before it all collapsed:

> the queen asked for a glass of water, the servant of the chamber handed to the first woman a silver gilt waiter, upon which were placed a covered goblet and a small decanter; but should the lady of honour [who was of higher rank] come in, the first woman was obliged to present the waiter to her, and if Madame or the Comtesse d'Artois [both ladies of even greater privilege] came in at the moment, the waiter went again from the lady of honour into the hands of the Princess before it reached the queen.[4]

The king endured similar treatment. In both cases, nobles found their standing determined by their relations with the monarch, who determined who took precedence over whom in performing such duties.

In making their case, absolutists were helped by the very hierarchical assumptions they attacked. Even ca. 1600, kings held an exalted place in society, perched at the top of God's and custom's hierarchy. Unsuccessful rebels against royal authority had long been subject to the severest penalties, such as public dismemberment. Absolutists could simply continue to stress this traditional message, discreetly leaving out the customary or divinely ordained rights of everyone else. The God-given right of kings was an important part of the theoretical arsenal of absolutists. Absolutists also liked to stress the authority of fathers. Absolute monarchs argued that they were indeed the fathers of their countries, neglecting to emphasize the political nation, the traditional authorities intermediate between king and household.

Yet, despite the effectiveness of the absolute monarch's toolkit, at the heart of absolute monarchies lay a profound limitation. Despite their propaganda, absolute monarchs were not absolute. In practice, "absolute" monarchs made critical compromises with the political nation. Consider Louis XIV himself. Although he overrode important rights of the political nation—neglecting to consult the Estates General, for example—he left other rights alone. He did not, for example, shut down the provincial estates or the parlements. He bullied them, yes. But even bullying was accompanied by negotiation; provincial estates petitioned for favors in return for those higher *dons gratuits*, and, to some extent, they got them. Dickering with such assemblies was easier than risking full-blown resistance by completely ignoring them. Moreover, the new standing armies offered opportunities to the nobility. Nobles continued their traditional warrior role by dominating the officer corps. Kings gratefully accepted their service, but, being dependent on their armies, they had to be wary of alienating too much of the nobility at any one time. Thus, the nobility, also

---

4   Mme Jeanne-Louise-Henriette Campan, *Memoirs of the Court of Marie Antoinette* (New York: Merill & Baker, 1900), 1: 154.

often employed in the government, received a share of the higher taxes collected by the state. Another example of the use of royal power on behalf of the nobility is the French king's use of the *lettre de cachet*, a royal order to imprison someone indefinitely without charge. Although the *lettre de cachet* symbolized a government that disregarded individual liberties, kings often used it at the request of noble families that wanted to bring wayward members to heel. (Some prisons were naturally more comfortable than others.) Finally, the rights kings left alone often had the effect of ensuring that most of the burden of absolutism fell not on the bulk of the political nation but elsewhere. In France, kings crucially left alone the exemptions from the *taille* and other taxes enjoyed by the first and second estates—the clergy and the nobility. Members of the bourgeoisie also largely obtained tax exemption one way or another. So the most burdensome of French taxes fell primarily on the peasantry. The French political nation might have to accept the king's raising of the *taille* to pay for the army, but at least the political nation did not have to pay for it. Such compromises made absolutism easier to live with—at least, for those who counted.

If absolute monarchs in practice compromised with the old order, there is one respect in which their success gave new life to an old phenomenon: the power of women exercised through the household. Absolutism meant that political decisions took place where the king was—in his household—rather than in public assemblies, such as the estates. Members of the royal household were thus positioned to exercise greater political power by influencing the one person who increasingly mattered, namely, the monarch. And this change, depending on the play of the personalities involved, boosted the political influence of women—royal wives and mistresses whose presence in the household gave them access to the king. Madame de Pompadour (1721–1764) is an example. The mistress of King Louis XV of France (1715–1774), she was interested in politics and, critically, Louis was interested in what she had to say. She advised Louis to embark on what historians have come to call the "diplomatic revolution" of 1756. For centuries, the kings of France had viewed the Habsburgs as enemies; a strong Germany, one unified under their rule, in particular threatened France. But that possibility had evaporated in the seventeenth century (see 7.4.1), and France faced new dangers. Now, at Madame de Pompadour's urging, Louis allied with the Habsburgs. One product of that alliance was a marriage between a Habsburg princess, Marie Antoinette, and the future King Louis XVI.

7.4 ABSOLUTISM II: SUCCESSES AND FAILURES

The previous section discussed the rise of absolutist states in general, drawing especially on French evidence. This section will try to flesh out the picture by surveying the drift toward absolutist governments in other parts of the West too. Most Western countries saw such moves. But they met with various degrees of success.

7.4.1 Germany

Like other countries, Germany in the seventeenth century saw attempts to create a stronger centralized state. But the Holy Roman Emperors, who by now were chosen from the Habsburg family, were at a disadvantage compared with some of their peers. By ca. 1600, the emperor's control over his dominion was weaker than that of most other monarchs over theirs (see 7.1). The Thirty Years' War (1618–1648), however, gave the Habsburgs a chance to change that. The war began as a religious war in which the emperor led the Catholic princes against the Protestant princes of the north. In 1629, Catholic success encouraged the Emperor Ferdinand II (1619–1637) to overreach. He issued the Edict of Restitution, returning to the Catholic Church lands confiscated from it years before by Protestants (even confiscations later validated by the courts) and outlawing Calvinism (Germany's second most common form of Protestantism) throughout the empire. Moreover, Ferdinand acted to put his relatives into re-Catholicized bishoprics, thereby increasing Habsburg influence. These measures appalled German Protestants. But they appalled German Catholics too— or, more precisely and importantly, German Catholic princes. For Ferdinand had issued the edict without consulting, much less obtaining the consent of, the imperial Diet (see 7.1). From the princes' perspective, whether Protestant or Catholic, the edict looked like a grab for power, an attempt to override princely liberties. Maximilian, the duke of Bavaria, the leading Catholic prince, and one of Ferdinand's erstwhile supporters, bolted. He refused to use his troops to enforce the edict, demanding that Ferdinand back down. When that failed, he helped persuade a meeting of the electors in 1630 not to elect Ferdinand's son as the emperor's successor. Ferdinand stuck to his guns. Events, however, were passing Ferdinand by. The Protestant princes regrouped and gained allies, most notably Sweden and France, the latter governed by Cardinal Richelieu (see 7.4.2). The Duke of Bavaria, too, allied with France; both wished to curb Habsburg power. And so the war ground on, Ferdinand giving way on the Edict of Restitution only when it was too late. It was the last significant attempt by the Habsburgs to strengthen their control over the empire. Their failure was written into the treaty that concluded the Thirty Years' War, the Peace of Westphalia of 1648. The treaty confirmed that the princes were subordinate to the emperor in name only. The Peace of Westphalia recognized their right to conduct even their own foreign policy without reference to any higher authority.

The Habsburgs' failure did not, however, spell the failure of absolutism in Germany. The emperor's control may have slipped, but what about the princes'? Over time, they worked to strengthen their own authority in their own territories. The dukes of Bavaria, for example, moved toward becoming absolute rulers of Bavaria.

The electors of Brandenburg, however, provide the most spectacular example of this development. In the early seventeenth century, the ruling family, the Hohenzollerns, faced an extreme version of the problem facing other rulers. There was, of course, the electorate of Brandenburg itself. To the east, the Hohenzollerns governed Prussia (after which their collection of lands would come to be named; see Map 7.1). The Peace of Westphalia added some new territories: eastern Pomerania and, to the west, Halberstadt and Magdeburg, which joined some smaller bits of western territory. This collection had been only recently assembled, and all its parts had their own rights, such as rights to their own assemblies, like French provincial estates, which imposed limits on the ruler. Indeed, before 1640, electors had rarely levied taxes and had almost no central bureaucracy to speak of. They lived the way most aristocrats lived, getting what revenue they needed from their own estates. In 1627, the elector had an army of only 900.

The Thirty Years' War, however, persuaded the elector that this was a situation he could not afford. His lands suffered terribly during the war, pinned between two of its leading contenders, the Habsburgs to the south and the Swedes to the north. Brandenburg lost more than half its population; its only substantial city, Berlin, declined from 14,000 to 6,000.

The Elector Frederick William (the "Great Elector," 1640–1688) sought a solution. He found it in the creation of a standing army that would leave his territories less vulnerable. In order to pay for it, however, he started to levy taxes on a regular basis, ignoring tradition and the rights of territorial assemblies. This move would create the most militarily oriented Western state of its time. (The reputation for militarism that Germans came to have in the nineteenth and twentieth centuries stems, in part, from the reputation of Prussia, which would come to dominate Germany.) The connection between the emergence of constant taxation and military needs was so tight that, until the mid-eighteenth century, all tax money collected by the Hohenzollerns was spent on the army. Indeed, taxes were not collected by some sort of civilian agency, such as the US Internal Revenue Service, but by a branch of the army, the "General War Commissary," set up in 1655. The very first bureaucracy to unify all the Hohenzollern lands was the army's. Moreover, the military, recruited from all the Hohenzollern territories, fostered a greater sense of unity among them, helping to overcome regional attachments. Training together can be a great integrator, as the experience of the modern US military suggests. The Hohenzollern lands were on their way to becoming what they were known as in the nineteenth century: "Prussia." Berlin, the capital of a centralizing state, grew. In the early eighteenth century, what had been a sleepy town now had 100,000 people, 20 percent of them soldiers. By that time, Prussia supported an army of 80,000. Prussian kings (as the various heads of the Hohenzollern family were known after 1701) came nearly always to appear in uniform.

How was the Great Elector able to consolidate power? Did not the nobility object? In the end, no, for Frederick William reached the same sort of compromise with his nobles that other absolute monarchs were reaching with theirs. In return for a free hand in taxation, he allowed noble landlords to deal with their peasant tenants however they liked. In fact, Brandenburg is an especially good example of this sort of arrangement because, there, the compromise was formalized explicitly in a document called the "Recess of Brandenburg" (1653), which was meant to last six years but became permanent. Usually such compromises simply evolved without being spelled out. The recess, however, states that Brandenburg's assembly will cease to meet and that the elector will not intervene in landlord-tenant disputes. This bargain had two results. First, it helped make Prussia into an absolute monarchy. Second, it fostered the enserfment of the peasants. And, of course, the elector was willing to use the army for more forceful measures. When in 1661 Prussia's Diet refused to accept his right to allow it to convene only as he wished, the elector occupied the city, where the Diet faced 2,000 troops.

Like the Hohenzollerns and other German princes, the Habsburgs also turned their efforts toward their own family lands, held by hereditary right, namely, Austria, Hungary, Bohemia, and others (see Map 7.1). Even at the end of the eighteenth century, these lands were not centralized, homogenous territories controlled from the Habsburg capital at Vienna. But the Habsburgs had at least a little success in moving in that direction, and they did so by making compromises of the sort seen elsewhere.

7.4.2 France

The king of France had greater success than the Holy Roman Emperor. The chief minister of King Louis XIII of France (1610–1643), Cardinal Richelieu (1585–1642), set out to strengthen his master's control over the kingdom. Central to this effort was gaining for his royal master something that most modern governments take for granted and that an absolutist government requires, namely, a monopoly on the legitimate use of force. A first step was to rob Huguenots of their right to garrison towns with troops under their own command (see 7.1). Richelieu chose his opponents well. The Catholic majority was not inclined to rescue a hated minority. Strikingly, however, as noted in section 6.7, Richelieu left the Huguenots' remaining rights alone. Although a Catholic and a cardinal to boot, his aim was to strengthen royal power, not to forward right religion.

Another move to eliminate force exercised other than by the king was to outlaw dueling. The point here was to curb the right of nobles to use force in resolving their own disputes (not to prohibit fun, the impression left by various "Three Musketeers" films). The French monarchy never entirely succeeded, but, in general, French nobles came to accept that they should use their arms only on the king's behalf. Their domination of the officer corps of the new army made that acceptance easier.

This expansion of royal power was not universally celebrated, but special conditions in France helped make it acceptable. France had been torn apart in the civil wars of religion of the sixteenth century (see 6.5). Some felt that, however unpleasant it might be, a strong hand at the helm was preferable to a return to chaos. But dissatisfaction spilled over in a major challenge to the crown when Richelieu's death, followed soon by Louis's, left behind the child King Louis XIV (1643–1715), on whose behalf his foreign mother and her Italian lover governed. The rebels of the Fronde, as the rebellion against the regent Anne of Austria was called, had various aims, and a defense of the political nation's power was among them. Doing away with monarchy, however, was not. Given the thinking of the time, even the rebels assumed that society must have a king, even if they preferred a weaker one. The Fronde failed in the end. That failure was also rooted in conflicts among the groups that made up the rebels and was perhaps helped by the fact that Louis XIV was a child, just as his being a child had helped make the Fronde possible. Louis, however, grew up to be an absolute monarch, a much-imitated one. By the middle of the eighteenth century, versions of his palace of Versailles (see 7.3) had appeared from Spain to Russia.

Both Richelieu and Louis XIV found that government solvency stood in tension with the rising cost of war. When Richelieu first took office, he aimed at reducing both government spending and taxes; he did not appear to be an advocate of what today would be called "big government." But war against the Huguenots and, especially, intervention against the Habsburgs in the Thirty Years' War proved expensive. He did manage to reduce the king's household expenses, but he nonetheless found himself raising the *taille* to more than double what it had been under Louis XIII's father.

The rising cost of war proved also to be Louis XIV's Achilles' heel. In the first ten years of his reign as an adult (1661–1671), Louis managed to run surpluses and even to double them. But these were years of relative peace. In 1672, Louis began a series of wars that changed everything. He expanded the standing army, recruiting even more troops in years of actual warfare, which became nearly constant. By the War of the Spanish Succession (1701–1714), his aggressive policies had united most of the major Western powers against him. France, the West's richest country, was able to hold them at bay, but only at enormous cost. At times, the king had to melt down his silver—along with that taken from others; the war's demands were so extensive that, today, French silver objects from before 1709 are scarce. When compromise brought the War of the Spanish Succession to an end, Louis's income met only 60 percent of his normal expenses. Indeed, the French monarchy would never free itself from enormous debt. No wonder Louis, dying, remarked, "I have loved war too much."[5]

7.4.3 Poland

At least France survived the eighteenth century. Poland's fate illustrated the dangers of not adopting the stronger central governments of one's neighbors. Ca. 1600, Poland was one of the great Western states, much larger than its modern successor (see Map 7.1). The Polish monarch, however, had little control over his ramshackle country. Polish kings were elected by the Polish nobility, a practice that, as in the Holy Roman Empire, discouraged a strong monarchy. The Polish Diet, a noble assembly, approved or rejected all major decisions of the king affecting the kingdom. Moreover, every member of the Diet had a particularly precious right, the *liberum veto*. Should any member wish to stop debate on an issue before the Diet and dissolve it, he could do so by simply announcing his veto of the proceedings. It was not a formula for effective government. That fact suited nobles used to handling their own affairs on their own estates. Polish kings never succeeded in curbing these rights. So they never succeeded in raising the expensive standing armies of their neighbors. In the eighteenth century, Poland's neighbors—Prussia, the Habsburgs, and Russia—repeatedly seized Polish territory, finally snuffing out the Polish state altogether by partition in 1795.

---

5   Quoted in Pierre Goubert, *Louis XIV and Twenty Million Frenchmen* (New York, 1970), 272.

7.4.4 Russia

The last of these countries, Russia, was new to the West in the seventeenth century. Russia had traditionally identified not with the Western half of the old Roman Empire but with the Eastern half, Byzantium. In the Middle Ages, its population had been converted by Byzantine (and so Greek Orthodox) missionaries sent from the Byzantine capital, Constantinople, also known as the "second Rome." After that capital fell to the Turks in 1453, Russians came to identify their chief city, Moscow, as the "third Rome." They called their ruler the *Tsar*, Russian for "Caesar."

Tsar Peter the Great (1682–1725) enormously complicated this situation. Fascinated by the Western artisans and merchants in Russia's few cities, he toured Western Europe for a year and returned determined to remake his country along the lines of what he had seen there. Some of his program was superficial. He insisted that his nobles go beardless in the (then) Western fashion, even shaving them personally; he similarly tried to impose Western dress. But even what might seem superficial could have larger repercussions. Russian noblewomen ceased to wear veils, but the move was part and parcel of Peter's insistence that noblewomen cease to hide behind closed doors. Peter also established a second capital for Russia. Saint Petersburg, on the Baltic, acted as a "window to the West." Greater communication opened Russia to further Western influence. By the middle of the eighteenth century, the Russian nobility spoke French. (Versailles, as the center of Western fashion, had ensured that French was the second language of most cultivated Westerners.)

Critically, this Westernization came at a time when absolutism was the rising fashion in the West. (It was also, of course, a form of government likely to gratify any ruler.) In developing a centralized state and bureaucracy, however, Peter had certain advantages. The absence of an extensive court system and its relative lack of economic development meant that Russia did not have the elaborate society of orders and corporations that had emerged in the West in the High and Late Middle Ages. Thus, Russia's dissimilarity to the West was an advantage to Peter. Moreover, Russian nobles had long tended to define their noble status in terms of their service to the tsar. Peter further encouraged this conception of nobility, issuing a Table of Ranks (1722) that more clearly defined status according to one's rank in the bureaucracy or in the new standing army (a move that some other absolute monarchs were attempting in the West). As in France, the tax structure cemented this alliance of ruler and nobility. Most taxes were paid by the peasantry. And, as in the West, taxes rose in order to pay for the new military and bureaucracy, staffed by the nobility. Outlying provinces, long autonomous, began to be brought to heel.

Even more than in the West, Peter and his successors made it state policy to encourage economic growth; Russia had to cover a lot of ground to catch up with the West. Here, however, the government ran into the fact that most peasants in Russia were serfs, most subject to absentee landlords; such serfs were not like the free laborers in the West, who might go from employer to employer as opportunity arose. The solution was not to free the serfs but to allow noble landlords to divert serfs to non-agricultural purposes, such as mining. Serfs left on the manor, pressed by rising taxes, replied by pooling their resources and responsibility even more than they had before. Doing so spread the risk that any one villager would be unable to pay the tax collector. But it also meant that decisions, including what to grow and how to grow it, had to be made cooperatively. Entrepreneurial innovation in Russian agriculture suffered. For serfs, however, the more immediate problem—whether dedicated to agriculture or not—was often the beatings their masters were entitled to give them.

These developments—the growth of centralizing, expensive government, the Westernization of segments of the country, the greater insecurity and suffering of the serfs—were explosive. The explosion came in the reign of the Tsarina Catherine the Great (1762–1796) in the form of Pugachev's Revolt (1773–1775).

Catherine herself is a good example of Russia's Westernization. Born in Germany, she married the heir to the Russian throne. After he became Tsar Peter III (1762), she had him killed and began ruling in her own right. She was a great patron of leading writers of her time—French writers, of course (see 8.4). In a move analogous to those of absolute rulers in the West, she also tried to bring the Cossacks, the horse people in the south of the country, under tighter central control.

But Catherine discovered that much of the country she ruled did not accept Western influence gladly. In 1773, a Cossack named Pugachev claimed to be the "lost" Tsar Peter III, calling on Russians to join him in taking back the throne. He recruited followers, Cossacks and serfs, in the hundreds of thousands. Landlords and government officials, and sometimes their families, died by the thousands, tortured, burned to death, beaten. The rebellion took two years to put down. Government and nobility responded ferociously; whole villages were leveled. In some places, rather than a normal hangman's noose, hooks were used to hang rebels by their ribs. Russia's rulers had been terrified.

Pugachev's promises are revealing. He promised to get rid of taxes—the higher taxes of the absolutist state. He promised to abolish serfdom, which, by now, bore down especially hard on the peasantry. He promised to restore Cossack independence. He promised to protect beards. And, revealingly, he said that he had been on pilgrimage to, among other places, Constantinople. In other words, he identified himself with traditional non-Western, Byzantine culture. One of the reasons for Russian serfs' increasing discontent in the eighteenth century was their sense that their landlords were becoming alien: dressing in non-Russian clothes, speaking French in front of the help, taking Western sugar rather than Russian honey in their tea. Pugachev promised to change all that, to get rid of this newfangled, foreign, Western government and aristocracy and make Russia Russian again, that is, Byzantine again. Indeed, Pugachev was not trying to get rid of the monarchy. Russia had to have a tsar, a Byzantine Caesar. Having a tsar/Caesar was part of the inheritance he was reclaiming.

Pugachev, however, failed. He did so in part because the Russian nobility stood solidly with the tsarina. Although Catherine may have been personally inclined to limit serfdom and took some tentative moves in that direction, she knew that, absolute ruler or not, she needed her nobles. In Russia, too, absolutism met its limits as the monarchy looked to the aristocracy for support.

7.4.5 England, Scotland, and Ireland

Catherine survived Pugachev's revolt. A seventeenth-century king of England, Scotland, and Ireland was not so lucky. In 1649, representatives of England's Parliament, which had fought a civil war against King Charles I (1625–1649), tried him for treason and beheaded him. For eleven years, a period in England known as the "Commonwealth" (1649–1660), the country was without a king. How had this "English Revolution" (1642–1660) come about?

It was a revolution nobody wanted. Two fears, inseparable, brought Charles down: fear of a plot to Catholicize England and fear of absolutism. Charles was the son of James I of England and VI of Scotland, who had brought the two countries under one ruler. He was, however, English rather than Scottish in outlook; Charles devoted his attention to his more populous and wealthy southern kingdom. There, however, his popularity suffered.

One of his problems was religion. Charles, head of the Protestant Church of England, married Henrietta Maria (1609–1669), a Catholic French princess, in order to ally with Catholic France. Worse, as head of the church, Charles appointed William Laud (1573–1645) archbishop of Canterbury, effectively the chief administrator of the church. The move appalled those members of the Church of England who did not think the church was purely Protestant enough, people sometimes called "Puritans." Puritans believed in predestination (that God had determined who would be saved or damned at the beginning of time). Like most Catholics, Laud did not. Moreover, Laud insisted on enforcing the observance of certain official church ceremonies, ceremonies that Puritans considered Catholic. Some local congregations had quietly modified them, but Laud insisted on enforcing rules. To Puritans, therefore, Laud, a committed Protestant, looked like a Catholic. That he overrode local autonomy made things worse. The conjunction of Laud and Henrietta Maria near the king produced a conspiracy theory; there was a plot to manipulate King Charles into Catholicizing the country. There was, in fact, no such plot. But the rumor ran just the same.

Charles had another public relations problem. He seemed to be aiming at an absolute monarchy. At the beginning of his reign, England had been at war with Spain. Warfare, of course, was getting more expensive in the seventeenth century, and Charles naturally turned to Parliament for more taxes. Parliament declined, even when expressing enthusiasm for the war. Charles responded by finding other ways to raise money, such as collecting "forced loans" from wealthy subjects. To members of the political nation, these moves were doubly troubling. Forced loans not only undermined the right to control one's own property but also seemed a way to get around Parliament's right to influence the king through control of the purse. In short, forced loans implied an absolutist program on the part of the king. It is not at all clear that Charles saw himself as aiming at a newfangled absolute monarchy. He always said he acted within law and tradition, and he may well have meant it. Relations between Charles and his Parliament got so bad, however, that, in 1629, Charles decided not to call Parliament again. Legally, he could take this decision as long as he needed no new taxes (but was satisfied just collecting the old ones) and no new laws, both of which required Parliament's approval. Charles governed for the next eleven years without calling Parliament, a period known as his "personal rule" (1629–1640). Making peace was eased by having no Parliament and therefore no venue for complaint about the peace. (English government, like most others, had long censored the press.) Yet, over time, Charles was naturally tempted to find ways to increase his income. He revived old fees due the king that had fallen out of use. He also found ways to stretch old taxes so they could bring in more money. "Ship money," for example, had been a tax paid since the Middle Ages by five seaports (the "Cinque Ports") to support the English navy. Charles, however, collected ship money from towns other than the traditional ones, even collecting it inland. From the king's point of view, he was simply extending an old tax, not creating a new one. Members of the political nation, however, were liable to see this as effectively a new tax, and one imposed in violation of parliamentary right.

Was Charles aiming at an absolute monarchy? Unfortunately, no surviving sources reveal his thinking in this regard. Perhaps the point of the personal rule was to get people used to not having Parliament, to raise a new generation accustomed to royal government without it. If this was Charles's plan, it might have worked had the personal rule lasted longer. When, during the English Revolution, Parliament and the king went to war, the king's supporters tended to be younger, Parliament's supporters older. This pattern also fit the trend of the time. Absolutism was the new fashion in the seventeenth century; more limited government in a society of orders and corporations was more old-fashioned. It is not surprising that the young would be more likely to support absolute monarchy. Older people felt more attached to tradition.

Although I have presented Charles's problems as of two different kinds, religious and political, that was not how his critics always thought about them. The Protestant nature of the Church of England was written into law, law made by Parliament. Hence, the fear of a Catholic conspiracy raised the fear that Parliament's rights—and so the political nation's rights—would be subverted. Yet, as dangerous as some feared the situation to be, dissatisfaction simmered but did not boil over. What brought the personal rule to an end?

Charles was king not only of England but also of Scotland, a land that zealously guarded its own rights, including its right to a firmly Protestant church. Indeed, so firmly Protestant was the Scottish church that many English Puritans preferred it over their own Church of England. In 1637, Charles chose to ignore Scottish rights, not to mention feelings, by announcing that, henceforth, a prayer book closely modeled on England's *Book of Common Prayer* would be used by the Scottish church too. It was, in a way, a classic absolutist move, an attempt to streamline his territories by overriding a right that made one different from another. And it was also a move the Scots hated. One hapless Scottish clergyman introduced the book in his cathedral in Edinburgh, only to have a market woman named Jenny Geddes (1600–1660) throw her stool at him, starting a riot. The Scots rebelled, raised an army, and seized control of the country. Stretching taxes such as ship money would not handle the emergency. Reluctantly, Charles called Parliament, which met for the first time in eleven years. England's political nation had eleven years' worth of resentment—about Catholic conspiracies and violations of English liberties—stored up. Now country gentlemen from all over the kingdom met together and found they had common fears and complaints. Not surprisingly, Charles found Parliament unmanageable. He dismissed it, apparently thinking the Scots could be talked down.

Then the Scottish army moved south, into the north of England. It was one thing for Charles to lose control of Scotland, but he had to defend his prize kingdom. So, later in 1640, Charles called another Parliament. This second Parliament, known as the "Long Parliament," was no better from Charles's point of view. Indeed, Parliament saw the Scots army not as a threat to the kingdom but as a guarantee that Charles could not act against Parliament. Members of Parliament used the opportunity to demand that the King choose as advisors only those approved by Parliament and that he remove William Laud, suppress the Catholic conspiracy, and renounce his activities during the personal rule. They did not, however, seek the abolition of the monarchy. They sought to restore tradition and the body politic, not to overthrow it.

At this point, critically, the English political nation divided. For, as Charles could point out, Parliament's demands on the king violated his customary and divinely ordained position in the body politic. Kings, not Parliament, chose royal advisors. Kings, not Parliament, made and unmade archbishops. Many peers and gentry agreed; many, on the other hand, felt that extreme measures were needed to defend the traditional constitution and right religion from attack.

The match that set off this powder keg was rebellion in Ireland in 1641. Most people on the island were Catholic, and most resented English, Protestant rule. Charles demanded funds to raise an army to put down the rebellion. To Charles's convinced critics, however, the Irish rebellion looked like part of the Catholic plot; the last thing they wanted to do was entrust Charles with command of an army to deal with it. Instead, in 1642, Parliament undertook to raise an army of its own to deal with the problem. Charles pointed out that commanding armies was a royal right and declared Parliament to be in rebellion. Some of the political nation responded to the king's call to arms, and some responded to Parliament's. With the peers and gentry divided, the civil war was on. Charles knew the situation was dangerous; he sent Henrietta Maria and their two sons to France. Parliament won, eventually making Charles himself its prisoner. The captive king was very small, very brave, and utterly untrustworthy. Efforts to get him genuinely to accept the reduction of his rights were futile, so he was executed. England was declared a "Commonwealth" rather than a kingdom.

Given these events, it may seem puzzling that, eleven years later, the English received Charles's son and heir as their new king, Charles II (1660–1685), as church bells rang in frantic celebration. The new king reasserted his rule in Scotland and Ireland too. Why was it that, after abolishing the monarchy, the kingdoms in 1660 happily saw its "Restoration," as this event is known?

In the first place, consider what civil war or, worse, the execution of a king meant to a society that saw itself as an organic body politic. The king and Parliament were supposed to cooperate harmoniously in a natural as well as customary hierarchy (see 7.2). For the king to be at war with Parliament was scarily perverse. This point was made very clearly by the author of the pamphlet whose cover sheet is reproduced in Figure 7.4. The date places it during the civil war. The cartoon shows how unnatural the situation was: a rat chases a cat; a man stands on his hands; the cart comes before the horse. Its author, T. J., announces himself a "well willer" to both sides, for neither side should triumph and eliminate the other. Seventeenth-century beliefs about the body politic made civil war more sickening than it usually is. To execute the king was like a body cutting off its own head. The Restoration seemed the restoration not just of monarchy but of the world as it ought to be.

The nature of the Commonwealth itself also helps explain delight at the Restoration. Parliament won the civil war because it had put together a trained army of the new type (see 7.3) more effectively than had Charles I and had raised the money to pay for it. That army's very name, "the New Model Army," suggests innovation. But with the king neutralized and then executed, Parliament lacked the standing to keep this new army's loyalties. Who, after all, had ever heard of a Parliament running a country? The soldiers turned to their brilliantly successful general, Oliver Cromwell (1599–1658), soon named England's "Lord Protector." Cromwell is sometimes described as becoming king in all but name. But, with a fully cowed Parliament and a standing army, he was more than king.

Figure 7.4: Cover Sheet, "The World Turned Upside Down"

Gentry who had fought against Charles to maintain an official Protestant Church of England and to defeat the king's absolutist tendencies drank disappointment under Cromwell. Cromwell, himself of Puritan inclinations, nonetheless believed in religious toleration (except for Catholics). Even Jews, expelled in the Middle Ages, were allowed back. England during the Commonwealth became a zoo of Protestant sects—Quakers rubbing shoulders with Anabaptists (see 6.4)—a development that appalled most English gentlemen, attached as they were to an official national church. As bad or worse, Parliament and then Cromwell overrode the local authority exercised by local gentlemen (see 7.1). The New Model Army stamped out resistance. Justices of the peace were no match for Cromwell's major generals, who were imposed as military governors on the country. (It did not help that the major generals were not socially top drawer.) In short, England experienced an absolutism that would have seemed familiar to the subjects of Louis XIV of France, and more effective too.

And so Cromwell's death in 1658 was quickly followed by the return of Charles II from exile in France. But the experience of civil war and revolution had left a permanent mark on Charles's kingdoms. The relationship among them was changed. For Cromwell's New Model Army had been unstoppable. It brought Scotland under English control and brought back rebellious Ireland too. Although the Scots would keep their own church and laws, the heart of Scottish political life had moved to London, where it would remain for centuries. Ireland, sullen, would also remain governed from London, not to gain its independence until the twentieth century. The three kingdoms were on their way to becoming "Great Britain."

The other long-term consequence is clearer from the next reign. Charles II ruled for twenty-five years, occasionally accommodating himself to Parliament, determined to remain king. He had the advantage of receiving substantial sums from the French king, Louis XIV, in return for help in Louis's military efforts. Raised in France by his Catholic mother (recall Henrietta Maria), Charles II converted on his deathbed to the Catholicism in which he had probably always believed. One of the greatest crises of his reign was the "exclusion crisis." Charles had no legitimate sons, so his younger brother James stood to inherit the throne on Charles's death. The problem was that James, more forthright than his brother, was a Catholic and let people know it. A movement gathered to exclude James from the succession; a Protestant Church of England could not have a Catholic king. The English political nation divided, with Charles working hard on his brother's behalf. Their supporters came to be called "Tories"; those who supported James's exclusion were known as "Whigs."

In the short run, the Tories won. Charles died, and, in 1685, James became King James II of England and VII of Scotland (1685–1688). He promised to leave the Church of England Protestant. But other measures led to a less lethal replay of the English Civil War of 1642–1649. The king declared that he favored religious toleration, issuing a "Declaration of Indulgence" to that effect. (James may have meant what he said. He sponsored a Quaker named William Penn [1644–1718] in his foundation of a colony in far-off North America, Pennsylvania, which, uniquely, offered full religious toleration.) Those afraid of a Catholic plot saw merely the thin edge of the wedge: first make Catholicism legal and then help Catholics take over the country. To the argument that the Test Act passed by Parliament required all members of Parliament and office holders to swear they were practicing members of the Church of England, James replied that he had a "dispensing power" to suspend parliamentary laws. As before, fears of Catholicism and fears of absolute monarchy fused. Worse, with a Tory-dominated Parliament at the start of his reign, James had been voted sufficient taxes for the standing army that was such an important part of the absolute monarch's equipment.

At least Mary, James's daughter and expected heir, was a Protestant, safely married to the Dutch (and Protestant) Prince William of Orange. But, in 1688, James's second wife gave birth to a son. The Whiggishly inclined were so outraged that they were ready to believe that some other baby had been smuggled in to give James an heir he could raise as a Catholic. Tories who had been willing to live with a Catholic king for the sake of the divinely ordained principle of hereditary monarchy had second thoughts. In 1688, leading elements of the English political nation, Whigs and Tories, invited William and Mary to bring an army to England to claim the throne; no one who counted wanted a return to the Commonwealth. The couple accepted the offer. When they landed, James fled the country without a shot being fired. The Glorious Revolution of 1688 is rightly also known as the Bloodless Revolution. Why had James lost his nerve? Perhaps he remembered his father's end.

At home, the political nation worked to make the world safe for the political nation. Parliament legislated to guarantee its place in English government. In 1689, it passed a "Bill of Rights" (not to be confused with the US Bill of Rights) that explicitly banned a royal "dispensing power." The king was also not to have a peacetime army except with Parliament's consent. In 1694, it passed its third Triennial Act. No longer would Parliament meet solely at the king's discretion; the king was legally required to summon it at least once every three years. In 1701, as it became clear that William and Mary (1689–1702) would die childless and that Mary's younger Protestant sister and heir Anne (1702–1714) would too, Parliament passed the Act of Settlement, laying down that, on Anne's death, the throne would go to a distant, but Protestant, relation, George, the duke of the minor German territory of Hanover. George I (1714–1727) was the first in the line of monarchs that reigns in Britain to this day. Parliament had asserted its power to bestow the throne. With monarchy safely contained, the political nation was even prepared to pass a Toleration Act for Protestant "dissenters"—that is, Protestants who were not members of the Church of England—so long as they did not seek to hold office.

Parliaments had been occasional events at the start of the seventeenth century, but they became central to British government by the century's end. The Triennial Act proved to be unnecessary; Parliament has met every year since 1689. Kings, and the occasional queen, found that running the government depended on having a majority of the members of the House of Commons willing to supply the taxes to support the expensive military establishment that Britain needed (a navy more than an army). This precept has held true since the start of a series of wars with the France of Louis XIV. Because the support of the House had become so significant, a monarch needed a member of Parliament who could organize and maintain that majority. This figure became known as the king's "prime minister." Robert Walpole (1676–1745) was the first, spending his days managing Parliament on behalf of King George II (1727–1760) and managing George on his own. Royal power was not dead in eighteenth-century Britain; kings, through their prime ministers, bought the support of many members of Parliament. In the very long run, however, prime ministers became more dependent on Parliament than on the king, choosing for their cabinets colleagues who could bring the votes of supporters in Parliament with them. Constant parliamentary manipulation was crucial in a way it had not been before. After all, kings could not do without parliaments. Moreover, kings could look back to two revolutions in the seventeenth century and wonder whether Parliament, if pushed, could do without kings, or at least without this or that particular king. Moreover, Whigs and Tories survived the exclusion crisis and the Glorious Revolution. They became early political parties, in which some members of the political nation competed against others for dominance in Parliament and, thus, for the position from which to decide who would be the king's prime minister. (The Tories still survive in Britain, as the Conservative Party.) Some of the essentials of the parliamentary government that has come to characterize most Western states, and some others too, were emerging by ca. 1789.

It is tempting to conclude that absolutism failed in Britain. In a way, it did. British subjects continued to enjoy, more or less, rights enshrined in the Common Law, such as the right of *habeas corpus* (the right to demand that the government charge people it arrests with a crime or let them go). Contrast this right with the lack of rights evinced by the *lettre de cachet* of the French monarchy (see 7.3). Yet Britain had to compete and survive in the eighteenth century. The demands of the Military Revolution did not slacken. An island state, Britain invested in sea power, building the most powerful navy in the world. Doing so required just the kind of centralized power and high taxes that absolute monarchs were imposing. Simple reliance on gentlemen amateurs in the shires would not do. But the gentry and peers were willing to allow greater central control because they, as members or voters or string pullers (remember pocket boroughs [see 7.1]), controlled Parliament, and Parliament could now count on weighing in on the conduct of government. Once kings were fully tamed, Parliament became as absolute as any absolute monarch (able, if necessary, to set aside rights like that of *habeas corpus*). It is not for nothing that modern British prime ministers have been described as elective dictators.

7.4.6 The United States

While Britain's political future was shaped in the clash of kings and parliaments, English settlers were building what they saw as another England on the other side of the Atlantic. Largely neglected by their home government, which had its own troubles in the seventeenth century, the northern colonies were thriving on trade by 1750. Influence was falling into the hands of merchants and small farmers. In the south, large plantations, relying more and more on slave labor imported from Africa, supported a class of southern gentlemen who saw themselves as the equivalent of the English gentry back home. Together, these merchants and landowners made up the American political nation. The colonial governments, dominated by property holders north and south, were largely self-governing. After all, English kings, and then English parliaments, were very far away. Britain imposed customs duties on goods going in and out of the colonies. But large-scale smuggling enabled the colonists to evade most of those taxes; even the British navy, the world's most powerful, could not fully enforce taxes on imports. In America, Britain did not collect "direct taxes," that is, taxes collected within the colonies themselves. The colonial political nation regarded this tax exemption and autonomy as customary rights, in the manner of the political nations of Europe. They had, they thought, the rights of Englishmen.

But their comfortable situation did not last. In the eighteenth century, Britain, like all major Western states, continually needed new revenues to finance its military. Moreover, the colonies only made things worse. In the French and Indian War (1754–1763), which overlapped with the war better known in Europe as the Seven Years' War (1756–1763), Britain had had to station troops in the colonies (which, in the end, brought Britain Canada). The war convinced both the British government and the colonists that British troops had to be kept in the colonies permanently in order to protect them from attack.

But how could the additional expense be supported? With new taxes, of course. The British Parliament first tried a new tax within Britain, on cider. British cider, it should be noted, is like beer, an alcoholic and popular drink. A tax on cider was thus not very tactful. Protests led Parliament to repeal it. Then Parliament made what seemed the logical move: as it had to pay for an army to protect the colonies, why not tax the colonies to support it? Raising indirect taxes on trade would not, however, do the trick; widespread smuggling made such taxes unproductive. So Britain imposed direct taxation. First, with the Stamp Act (1765), it tried a stamp tax on official documents; similar taxes were already in effect in Britain itself. This stamp tax not only violated the traditional exemption from taxes enjoyed within the colonies but also hit the literate and those who used official documents—in other words, the colonial political nation. In imposing the stamp tax, Britain followed the path absolutist monarchs had taken since the seventeenth century. Here was a central government that, in order to meet the rising cost of war, overrode traditional local rights and risked offending the political nation in the process. And offended it was. Protests and rioting met the stamp tax, as colonists insisted on their liberties. Britain repealed the Stamp Act in 1766 but replaced the tax with a succession of other direct taxes, hoping to find one the colonists would accept. Violent reaction accelerated in the colonies, provoking British countermeasures that only made relations worse. In 1773, Parliament granted the East India Company the sole right to sell tea to American dealers. One result was a sneak attack on tea-laden ships in Boston Harbor; their contents were dumped overboard in the Boston Tea Party (1773). Britain responded to such events by tightening control, or trying to. For example, Britain closed the port of Boston to business. These moves—which recall the use by absolute monarchs of their newly enlarged militaries to enforce their policies (see 7.3)—encouraged further resentment. Leading elements of the political nation responded to the closing of Boston harbor by convening the first Continental Congress in 1774 to work together in the face of British tactics. In 1776, the Congress declared the colonists' independence from Britain. In 1783 they achieved it.

Having thrown off one central government, the colonists feared setting up another. For this reason, the United States of America's new government, erected under the "Articles of Confederation" (in operation from 1781) could raise money only by asking the states (formerly the colonies) for voluntary donations. Elements of the American political nation soon concluded, however, that a stronger central government, one with the power to tax, was necessary if the United States was to have the expensive, standing military that most Western states had needed since the Military Revolution. The result was the adoption of the current United States Constitution in 1789. Yet the framers of the Constitution faced a political hot potato. On the one hand, the founding document of the new country, the Declaration of Independence penned by Thomas Jefferson, asserted that "all men are created equal, that they are endowed by their Creator with certain unalienable rights, [and] that among these are Life, Liberty, and the pursuit of Happiness."[6] Indeed, some

---

6   Henry Steele Commager and Milton Cantor, eds., *Documents of American History*, 10th ed. (Englewood Cliffs, NJ: Prentice Hall, 1988), 1: 100.

of the framers actually believed this assertion. On the other hand, in the southern states, Africans and their descendants lived as slaves, largely owned by the southern gentry. The contradiction provoked proposals to abolish slavery, sparking debate that threatened to wreck the attempt at a stronger central government. Southern slave owners ran a potential risk if they allowed a stronger central government that also might be hostile to slavery. The debate produced a compromise: proponents of the new federal government would get their stronger central authority, but slavery would also be protected in the South. It was a compromise that might have been familiar, in one way or another, to peasants from France to Russia.

Yet, if the American Revolution and its aftermath looks like earlier Western political conflicts discussed in this chapter, it also looks odd when set next to them. For one thing, it produced a republic. Since 1500, the West had seen only one other republic successfully declared—the Dutch Republic in the sixteenth century—and it had required the religious heat of the Reformation to forge it. The English had tried one in the 1650s, the Commonwealth, only gratefully to welcome back their king (see 7.4.5). Something had happened between the mid-seventeenth century and the later eighteenth. What?

A clue is provided by the Americans' founding document. Jefferson's declaration was a stunning assertion when compared with the assumptions common in the West ca. 1600 (see 7.2), namely, that there was a natural hierarchy and that rights were little different from property rights and so inheritable and alienable. Jefferson's use of the word "liberty," which to him meant natural human freedom, signals a departure from these older expectations. People who thought in Jefferson's terms could live without monarchy.

There were other signs of change. Americans, wary of their new federal government, tried to hobble it. Its three clearly defined branches—executive, legislative, and judicial—were set up as a system of "checks and balances." It was a system designed to promote conflict, which, ideally, would allow the central government to act only when the need was certain and pressing. Yet ca. 1600, conflict had been seen as unnatural. The point of the body politic had been not only hierarchy but also harmony. Checks and balances would have been abhorrent to early-seventeenth-century people. One of the parliaments with which Charles I of England had quarreled early in his reign (see 7.4.5) had been known as "the Useless Parliament" (1625), while one that similarly had failed to come to agreement with Charles's father James I became known as "the Addled Parliament" (1614). Now, however, political conflict was seen not only as acceptable but even as useful.

This acceptance of political conflict was not peculiarly American. Consider political parties. Such groups, permanently and deliberately organized for political combat, had been rare in the West ca. 1600. They were unlikely to appeal to people who thought harmony was mandated by nature. (This attitude died hard; the framers of the American Constitution themselves hoped to avoid party politics.) In Britain, however, Whigs and Tories became central to British political life (see 7.4.5). When they first emerged in Britain, they had been seen as disreputable. "Whig" and "Tory" had, in fact, started out as insults: "You are a Whig" or "You are a Tory," but never "I am a Whig" or "I am a Tory." But attitudes were changing in the eighteenth century. Whigs and Tories came to accept their own party labels. Some began to mouth a modern commonplace, that competition between two political parties is productive. One English observer noted in 1723 that "the Party who are OUT are always a Curb, and a Bridle to those which are IN, and the Parties which are In are always a Terror and a Stirrer up to Vigilance in those which are Out. In a Word, they are mighty useful...."[7]

How can one explain these new political assumptions, this embrace of conflict and a willingness even to dispense with monarchy?

7.5 THE SCIENTIFIC REVOLUTION I: NATURE

Ca. 1600, the common assumption was that the universe was ordered organically and harmoniously in a vast hierarchy and that this universe was best understood by examining the qualities of things, which explained their place in that hierarchy (see 7.2). The Scientific Revolution of the seventeenth century, however, produced a new framework of ideas. A standardizing view of the world undermined the notion of hierarchy by stressing the sameness of things. Standardization also, by reducing the variety of the universe, put less stress on the harmonious cooperation of different things. This standardizing approach also reduced the old interest in the qualities that made one thing fundamentally different from another: students of nature became more concerned with the quantifiable aspects of things. (Recall the example of the rising air bubble from 7.2. The modern, quantifiable explanation of its rise compares a measurable aspect of the air and water: their density, or mass per unit of volume.) Ca. 1700, these new assumptions were held by only a small fraction of the population—a few natural scientists, philosophers, and other interested parties. In the course of the eighteenth century, however, they became the common understanding of those with advanced educations. And, in the very long run, these changing ideas would arguably be the most important development of the seventeenth century.

The Scientific Revolution of the seventeenth century would have a wide impact only in the eighteenth century. But I will begin its story with the astronomical work of Nicolaus Copernicus (1473–1543) in the sixteenth. Copernicus proposed replacing the geocentric model of the Ptolemaic system with a sun-centered, or heliocentric, model. If one assumed that Earth and other planets revolved around the sun in perfect circles, Copernicus pointed out, one was left with a considerably simpler model than the Ptolemaic system, which required certain complications in the motions of the planets in order to make the model conform to observations. Copernicus approved publication of his work only as death approached. The preface, inserted after Copernicus's death by the theologian Andreas Osiander (1498–1552), was careful to point out that Copernicus's new model was a model only, designed merely as a convenience to make calculating (and so predicting) the motions

---

7 J.A.W. Gunn, ed., *Factions No More: Attitudes to Party in Government and Opposition in Eighteenth-Century England, Extracts from Contemporary Sources* (London: F. Cass, 1972), 86.

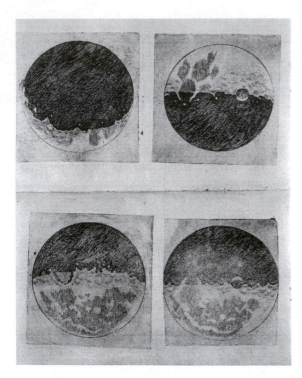

Figure 7.5:
Galileo's sketches of the moon seen through a telescope

of the heavenly bodies easier. Copernicus's system was not, Osiander said, intended as an actual description of what circled what. After all, more rode on the correctness of the Ptolemaic system than simply astronomy; in it was rooted a whole series of basic beliefs about the universe (see 7.2). Moreover, one could not actually observe sun, Earth, and the planets from a distance to see what was at the center. The sole evidence available for astronomical models was the observation of the heavens from Earth.

The Copernican system did not take the West by storm. More than fifty years later, its supporters were still in the minority, even among astronomers. Galileo Galilei (1564–1642) was one of the exceptions. Simplicity had long attracted Western intellectuals; the simplicity of Copernicus's model drew Galileo to conclude that it must indeed be a true description of reality, despite its implications for the rest of nature. Galileo sought further confirmation to persuade skeptics. Training the newly invented telescope on the heavens, he was the first person to observe satellites revolving around the planet Jupiter. The moons of Jupiter reassured those bothered by Copernicus's assertion that Earth was anomalous in having a moon. At the same time, Jupiter's moons reinforced the suggestion that heavenly bodies might not be so different from Earth, with its moon. Perhaps the planets were not ordered hierarchically, so perhaps Earth did not have to lie at the center of their orbits. Moreover, Galileo's observation of the moon (see Figure 7.5), published in his *The Starry Messenger* (1610), clearly revealed it to be far from the perfect quintessence that Ptolemaic theory asserted must lie in the heavens above a corrupt Earth. Such observations could be exciting. When he argued that people could live on the moon, John Wilkins noted of the heavenly bodies that "by the help of Galileus's glass, we are advanced nearer unto them, and the heavens are made more present to us than they were before."[8]

The Ptolemaic system, however, had many defenders. Simple conservatism explains some of their attachment to the old system. So does the fact that the Old Testament was more consistent with Ptolemaic views than Copernican (a point that eventually led to Galileo's trial and permanent house arrest by papal authorities in Italy). The way in which the Ptolemaic system was embedded in larger conceptions about nature and society also brought it support, as John Wilkins noted (see 7.2). But Ptolemy's defenders also had some good observational objections to a heliocentric model. For one thing, a moving Earth meant that one should be able to observe parallax, that is, the apparent motion of the stars relative to each other. Consider, for example, Figure 7.6. As Earth moves from A to B,

8   Wilkins, *Mathematical and Philosophical Works*, 26.

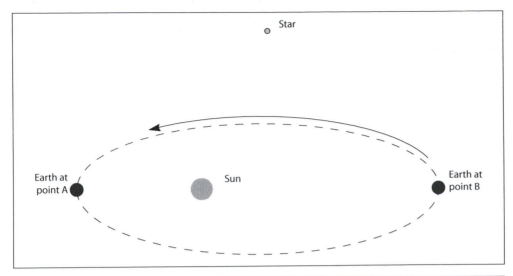

Figure 7.6: Parallax

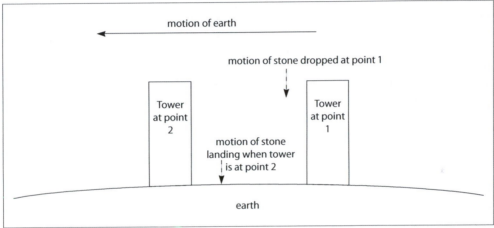

Figure 7.7: Stone falling from tower, with Earth moving, assuming Aristotelian principles of motion (stone is dropped when tower is at point 1 and lands when tower is at point 2.)

a fixed star ought to seem to move (think of the countryside appearing to move beside a speeding train). Yet parallax could not be observed; therefore Earth was at rest. (Parallax turned out to be undetectable until the nineteenth century. Only then were instruments sensitive enough to capture an effect so tiny because of the enormous distance of the stars from Earth compared with the piddling size of Earth's orbit around the sun. By that time, the heliocentric view had triumphed, partly because it fit so well with developments discussed later in this section.)

Galileo could do little about parallax. But he could reply to another objection. One obvious problem of the Copernican model was that it meant Earth is in motion. Yet Earth seems to be still. Supporters of Ptolemy put the point more precisely. Suppose one climbs to a high tower, leans over the edge, and drops a stone. The stone always lands at the foot of the tower. But consider Figure 7.7. If Earth were moving, the stone would not land at the foot of the tower but somewhere "behind" it, for, as the stone fell to Earth, Earth and so the tower would be moving away.

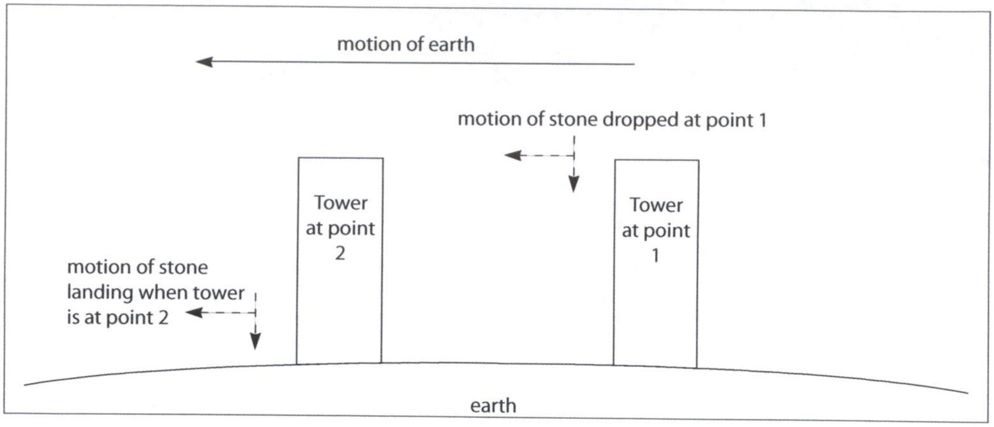

Figure 7.8: Stone falling from tower, with Earth moving, assuming inertia (stone is dropped when tower is at point 1 and lands when tower is at point 2.)

In order to counter this argument, Galileo found himself rethinking Aristotle's notion of motion (see 7.2). Aristotle had said that objects move either because of their inherent qualities or because they are pushed (or pulled). Galileo tackled this second explanation by proposing instead the principle of inertia: that an object, once in motion, will continue to move at the same speed and direction until or unless another force is applied. In other words, a moving object does not require further application of force to continue moving. Inertia explains why a stone dropped from a tower will land at its base even if Earth and the tower are moving. For the stone is moving in the same direction as the tower and Earth, and so continues to move with Earth as it falls toward it (see Figure 7.8).

Galileo's development of the concept of inertia illustrates something about the world view of a culture, namely, that it tends to be coherent, each element reinforcing the others. For this reason, challenges to one element (such as Ptolemy's astronomical model) encouraged challenges to others (such as Aristotle's ideas about motion). Galileo's Copernican views of astronomy led him to rethink principles of physics. The world view of ca. 1600, rooted in antiquity, was unraveling.

Further support for Copernicus, and with it further departure from the old science, came from the astronomer Johannes Kepler (1571–1630). Kepler's study of the planets' movements led him to formulate three laws of planetary motion. The first of these did away with the perfectly circular orbits that had been appropriate for quintessence spheres; Copernicus had kept these perfect circles for the orbits and spheres of his heliocentric model. Kepler's first law of planetary motion asserted that the orbit of each planet around the sun is an ellipse, with the sun as one of the ellipse's two focuses (see Figure 7.9). But why accept elliptical orbits, since no one could directly examine the orbit of a planet? In part, the answer is found in Kepler's second law, the law of equal areas: in any given amount of time, the area swept out by a planet in its elliptical orbit around the sun will be equal to the area swept out in the same amount of time elsewhere in the planet's orbit. Consider, for example, Figure 7.10. A planet orbits the sun in an ellipse, with the sun at A. Imagine that, in one month, the planet moves from B on its orbit to C on its orbit. The result is a sort of triangle with a round side, ABC. Now imagine that the planet continues along its orbit, and, at point D, one begins to time its motion, and, in one month, it moves

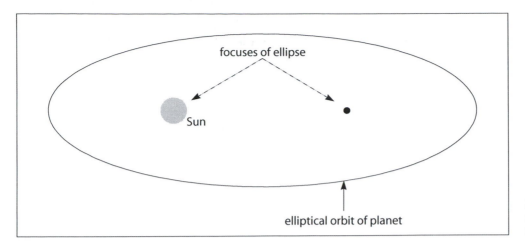

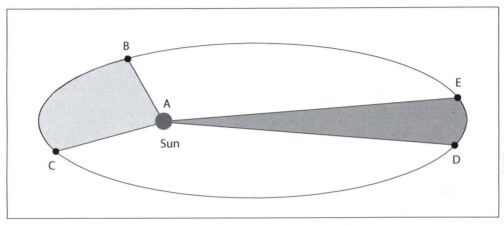

from D to E. That motion produces another soft-sided triangle, ADE. Copernicus's law of equal areas asserts that the area of ABC will be equal to that of ADE.

Kepler's third law is more difficult, and need not detain the reader.[9]

Aristotelian physics came under attack from another direction. While Copernicus's theory of inertia challenged Aristotelian ideas about how a force moves an object, a group of thinkers called the mechanists challenged Aristotle's idea that the motion of objects can be explained by their inherent qualities. The most influential of the mechanists, René Descartes (see 6.7), concluded that matter moves for one reason only, because an external force is applied. Also, continuous application of force is required for motion to continue. In other words, Descartes accepted Aristotle's notion of how an external force moves an object (which Galileo rejected), but rejected absolutely Aristotle's idea that objects move because of their qualities. Descartes held further that the universe is a *plenum*—that is, is full of matter, with no empty space—in which objects push other objects, which push

---

9 For the curious, it asserts that the time of a planet's complete orbit around the sun squared is in constant proportion to the cube of its average distance from the sun.

other objects, and so on. Thus, the universe was like a whirlpool in which one particle pushes the next, or it was like a large mechanical clock in which one cog moves because it is pushed by the next, which is pushed by the next, and so on (hence "mechanist"). Only some of those objects, however, are evident to the human senses. Thus, a ball flying through the air is pushed continuously by other objects, which are themselves pushed, but the elements pushing the ball appear to human beings as empty air because human nerves fail to register them. Indeed, argued Descartes, the various qualities people perceive in objects are not really there. The only variations in matter are volume, shape, and motion. According to this view, a red apple is neither red nor sweet. Rather, an apple is an object with a certain volume, shape, and motion that stimulates the nerves so as to make the observer experience red and sweet, illusions in the mind. The real world—colorless, odorless, tasteless—is without such qualities. The matter that makes up an apple is, in itself, no different from that which makes up a chair. Because qualities do not exist, they certainly cannot explain motion. The mechanists diverted attention from the qualities of matter to its quantifiable aspects, such as volume and mass. Indeed, Descartes furthered attempts to discuss shapes in quantifiable ways, helping to invent analytic geometry, that bane of high-school students.[10] The mechanists proposed a grand homogenization, and so standardization, of matter.

The work of Sir Isaac Newton (1642–1727) capped these developments, bringing them together into a powerful new description of nature. Newton combined Galileo's theory of inertia and the mechanists' rejection of the qualities of objects as an explanation of motion. For Newton, an object moves for one reason only: because a force is applied to it. But once in motion, an object will continue to move at the same speed and in the same direction until or unless another force is applied. Moreover, Newton proposed a theory of gravity that discussed gravity in quantitative terms rather than asserting that the qualities of objects led them to move closer to or farther from the center of the universe. The universe, Newton argues, is made up of particles of matter (some very big, like Earth, some very small, like a dust mote). Each particle of matter exerts on each other particle of matter a force of attraction; this force is gravity. The force of attraction between any two particles is directly proportional to the products of their masses, so the larger the masses involved, the larger the force. That force is also, however, inversely proportional to the square of the distance between the centers of the particles, so the farther apart two particles are, the weaker the force. Thus, the reason a dust mote falls from a bookshelf to Earth is that 1) the mass of Earth is very large, so, even though the dust mote is very small, the gravitational force between Earth and the dust mote is strong and 2) the dust mote is not very far from Earth, so the gravitational pull between them is strong. Rockets sent from Earth are able to get far enough from it that Earth's gravity is no longer strong enough to pull them back. And the sun's gravitational pull can affect a planet's motion, explaining

---

10 It is that branch of mathematics that expresses shapes as equations on an x/y axis (including, of course, the ellipses of Kepler's planetary orbits. Hence the term "Cartesian"—for De*scartes*—when referring to the coordinate system for such an x/y grid.

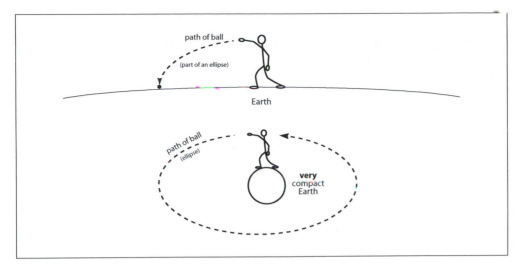

Figure 7.11: Path of a ball thrown horizontally on Earth: two possibilities

why, contrary to the mechanists' expectation, the sun could keep the planets in Kepler's elliptical orbits without touching them.

Newton's laws of gravity do away with qualities of matter as a fundamental point of analysis. Indeed, it is worth noting that, for Newton, gravity is a force exerted by every particle of matter on the rest. The dust mote pulls Earth to it just as much as Earth pulls the dust mote. As far as gravity is concerned, all matter is the same, except in terms of mass. Indeed, inertia and the laws of gravity put Newton in a position to reconsider Kepler's elliptical orbits. Consider a ball thrown horizontally on Earth (Figure 7.11). The force applied by the thrower sets it in a horizontal motion. Because of inertia it continues to move in the same direction with the same speed even though the throwing hand no longer supplies a force. There is also, however, a force of gravity between Earth and the ball, which is why the ball moves downward at the same time it moves horizontally. The result of moving in the two directions at the same time is that the ball moves in a curve (until, of course, it hits Earth, at which point Earth acts as a force to change the ball's motion, namely, stopping it). That curve, Newton calculated, is in fact a portion of an ellipse, a shape expressible in the analytic geometry of Descartes. Had Earth less mass, so its force of attraction on the ball were smaller, or were Earth compact enough that the ball could continue in its elliptical path without running into Earth, the ball could continue on its elliptical path around Earth. In other words, it would go into orbit. Kepler's laws of planetary motion, Newton concludes, govern motion in general. All matter is basically the same, whether on Earth or in the heavens. It was a stunning confirmation of what Galileo had seen through his telescope. Indeed, Newton's laws of gravity accounted for Kepler's law of equal areas. For Kepler's law required that planets move more slowly when they are farther from the sun and faster when they are closer to it. Reconsider Figure 7.10: The arc BC, when the planet is closer to the sun, is longer than DE, when the planet is further away. The planet is moving faster when closer to the sun. Gravity explained why. The force of attraction between the sun and the planet increases when the two are closer, speeding the planet's motion. Moreover, by developing a new kind of mathematics called the calculus (also developed by Gottfried Wilhelm Leibniz [1646–1716] roughly at the same time), Newton found ways to analyze changes in the speed of moving bodies, which, in turn, further encouraged analysis of nature in terms of quantity rather than quality. The modern scientific preoccupation with measurement was underway. This preoccupation now molds daily life. Imagine a weather forecast without an expression of the percentage chance of rain or speed limits on the roads without quantifiable terms.

7.6 EMPIRICISM

By the end of the seventeenth century, practitioners of the new science looked back on the science of ca. 1600 as mired in ignorance. Part of their criticism relied on the notion that those earlier students of nature had blindly followed ancient authorities rather than basing their conclusions on the direct observation of nature. Empiricism—the belief that true knowledge is empirical, that is, gained through the senses—became a critical part of the self-image of the new science. An important figure in this development was Sir Francis Bacon (1561–1626), who argued that people had been badly misled by old books and that nature should be studied only through careful observation. John Locke, whose writings on society and politics mirrored the new science's understanding of nature, went so far as to argue that all knowledge originates through the senses. The mind of a baby is, Locke asserted, a *tabula rasa*—a blank slate—on which nature writes perceptions through the senses, perceptions that give human intelligence the matter about which it reasons.

This self-image did not do justice to earlier thinkers. Students of nature ca. 1600 had, in fact, relied on observation as well as on Graeco-Roman authorities. Recall that one of the chief objections to Copernicus's views was that the Earth does not appear to move (see 7.5). In one respect, however, this self-image of empirical investigation did make an important difference in the new science. Newton and others deliberately created artificial observational events. Rather than simply observe nature as it is, they manipulated the conditions under which observations took place, changing them in order to find out what was an important factor in determining an outcome and what was not. In other words, they carried out experiments with controlled variables in order to test hypotheses. A day in the laboratory is different from a walk through the forest. This "scientific method" has wrought more radical changes in the understanding of nature over the last three hundred years than over the previous two thousand.

Along with this self-conscious empiricism went a new attitude toward probable knowledge. Traditionally, Western thinkers had had such a strong preference for absolutely certain knowledge that they tended to downgrade the reliability of what could be known with only probable certainty. (Of course, although they may have believed what they knew was certain, modern commentators generally disagree.) This distrust of what could only probably be known was not absolute—Aristotle was more willing to tolerate uncertainty than Plato—but it was influential nonetheless. Moreover, it tainted knowledge acquired through the senses, which had, since the ancient Greeks, been seen as deceitful. Indeed, this distrust of probable knowledge had fueled the crisis of authority of ca. 1600, leading Descartes systematically to doubt all that he had believed in an effort to find some conclusion so absolutely certain that he could not doubt it: "I think, therefore I am" (see 6.7). By the early eighteenth century, however, the successes of the Scientific Revolution were producing a new confidence in probable knowledge and, thereby, in knowledge gained through the senses. Although Locke admitted that sense perception is fallible, he also argued that it gives people the only knowledge of the world that is possible; one has no choice but to distinguish between ideas that are more and less probable. To say that something is very probably true, though not absolutely certain, is good enough. Not surprisingly, the new quantitative mindset turned to the study of probability itself. In France, Blaise Pascal (1623–1662) worked out the mathematics of probability. (The problem studied by generations of schoolchildren—"What is the chance that a coin tossed four times will come up heads once and tails three times?"—is one application of Pascal's mathematics.) Pascal was comfortable enough with uncertainty to propose an argument for belief in God in the form of a wager. If God does not exist, Pascal argued, one does not lose salvation by believing in him. But if God does exist, one will be damned if one does not believe in him, and saved if one does. The odds, Pascal calculated, favor belief. The corresponding new confidence in observation and the study of nature is summed up by an epitaph composed by the poet Alexander Pope (1688–1744): "Nature and Nature's Laws Lay hid in Night / God said, *Let Newton be!* and all was Light."[11] The crisis of authority of ca. 1600 (see 6.7) found its resolution in the acceptance of probable knowledge.

In turning to the rigorous assessment of probable knowledge, Western science came to rely on a body of ideas worked out in earlier centuries by lawyers. Law came to the rescue of science. The High and Late Middle Ages had seen the rise of courts staffed by professionals following legal rules. Such courts faced a problem: how to establish the facts of a case so as to apply the law correctly to it? For example, the law may define what a murderer is (i.e., someone who kills another person intentionally but not as an agent of the government and not in self-defense). But how can it be determined whether a particular defendant fits the definition of a murderer? One option was to ask God to decide, but the ordeal, a procedure by which God was asked to tell whether the accused was guilty, had disappeared in the High Middle Ages. The preferred method came to be the examination of witnesses (as it often continues to be). Of course, witnesses are often uninformed or even misleading. Over time, the authorities found themselves developing rules for how to weigh such imperfect evidence. For example, one should consider that a witness with an interest in the outcome of the case is less reliable than a witness with no such interest. In other words, courts learned, as best they could, to come to probable conclusions based on evidence. After all, with a job to do, they had no choice. Indeed, Sir Francis Bacon, that advocate of empiricism in the study of nature, was himself a lawyer.

---

11 Alexander Pope, *The Works of Alexander Pope*, ed. Joseph Warton (London: J.F. Dove and Richard Priestly, 1822), 379.

In the seventeenth century, the legal habits of self-consciously assessing evidence to arrive at probable conclusions spread to other fields. The practice of history was one of the first of these. Although the writing of history had long been thought of as a branch of literature, with the historian having license to depart from strict accuracy in order to make a point (usually a moral one), history writers had also occasionally tried to prove that their accounts were true. But, in the seventeenth century, the balance began to tip in favor of accuracy backed up by evidence over moral points and literary skill. Historians, in the manner of lawyers, began more frequently to cite their evidence, clogging the bottoms of their pages with footnotes.[12] They also subjected primary sources to more careful scrutiny. In France, Jean Mabillon (1632–1707) established various tests to determine the authenticity of medieval charters (a field called "diplomatic" because some charters were called diplomas). The ancient convention of making up speeches to put in the mouths of people in the past fell out of favor. It is worth noting that Bacon, lawyer and scientific empiricist, was also an historian.

By the early eighteenth century, these habits of weighing evidence, as well as the new ideas about nature, affected literature. The universe of nested hierarchies of ca. 1600 had fostered the use of metaphor. In his play *Richard II*, William Shakespeare (1564–1616) refers to King Richard as the sun, an eagle, a rose, and a lion. Audiences would have known that the sun was the chief planet, the eagle at the top of the hierarchy of birds, the rose at the top of the hierarchy of flowers. The lion, of course, is still sometimes called "the king of beasts." Such metaphors gained their meaning from a culture that conceived of the universe as a series of hierarchies, so that analogies could easily be drawn between one hierarchical element (a dog) and another (a peasant). This same mental habit allowed the authority of fathers to be viewed in the same terms as the authority of kings and demanded that a hive have a king bee. This habit means that modern readers often need the help of explanatory notes when reading literature written before the eighteenth century. But that world was dismantled by the Scientific Revolution. By the middle of the eighteenth century, the idea of a king bee was no longer compelling, as the series of nested hierarchies had come apart. An English poet, John Donne (1572–1631), saw the danger:

> And new philosophy calls all in doubt . . .
> 'Tis all in pieces, all coherence gone;
> All just supply [i.e., mutual support], and all relation:
> Prince, subject, father, son, are things forgot,
> For every man alone thinks he hath got
> To be a phoenix, and that then can be
> None of that kind, of which he is, but he.[13]

---

12 This book is an exception. Being a synthesis of largely conventional views, it follows the tradition of textbooks, citing only quotations.

13 John Donne, "An Anatomy of the World," in *John Donne: The Complete English Poems*, ed. A.J. Smith, 2nd ed. (Harmondsworth: Penguin, 1986), 276.

By ca. 1700, a simpler written style, sometimes referred to as the "classical" (not to be confused with "classical" as referring to ancient Greece and Rome) was gaining ground. Classicism valued straightforward reporting over metaphor. The new scientists and historians favored it, thinking it laid bare the evidence on which conclusions were based. But it also infiltrated literature. Even works of fiction reflected the new interest in weighing evidence. Novels were written in classical prose style, many in the eighteenth century as "epistolary novels." In these, the novelist composes a series of fictional letters so that the reader follows a story as an historian might who is trying to draw conclusions from a series of documents. Another tack was to write fiction in the same style as a newspaper account. Daniel Defoe (1660–1731), who wrote *Robinson Crusoe*, a novel about a traveler's fantastic adventures, was attacked by one critic for telling awful lies! Defoe's attacker had apparently not tumbled to the new literary style. Again, the law provided some precedence, for legal writers had long insisted that lawyers should avoid fancy rhetoric, so fact and argument could be weighed more clearly.

This new, self-conscious empiricism became characteristic of Western science in general and influenced other fields of study too. But empiricism became particularly pronounced in England, so much so that some now speak of an English or Anglo-American empirical tradition. It is worth noting that many of the figures mentioned in this section were English. This tradition contrasts with that of Descartes and his followers. Recall that, for Descartes, true knowledge should be certain, so it was to be found not through the senses but by reasoning from ideas entirely within the mind. "I think, therefore I am" requires no reliance on the senses. (Of course, not all English speakers were and would be empiricists, and not all non-English speakers, even outside the sciences, rejected empiricism.) What explains this English attachment to empiricism? The best explanation available is the role of the jury in English law. Other legal systems had juries in the Middle Ages, but, by ca. 1500, only English Common Law courts had held onto them. Originally, they had been made up of people from the neighborhood who would know what had happened. In other words, the jury was itself the witness. But, by the end of the sixteenth century, for reasons that are obscure, the jury's function had changed. Juries had gained their modern role of listening to witnesses, weighing their testimony, and concluding what had happened; in other countries, that job fell to judges. The English may have been drawn to empiricism because, although other Western legal systems required courts to weigh evidence, English experience in the formal weighing of evidence went beyond that of a small number of professional judges and lawyers. If so, the Anglo-American empirical tradition was a kind of historical accident. An accident, too, was the rescue from the crisis of authority of ca. 1600 (on which, see 6.7) carried out by products of a medieval legal tradition formed with very different problems in mind.

7.7 THE SCIENTIFIC REVOLUTION II: SOCIETY

The standardizing and leveling tendencies of the new views of nature also influenced discussions of society. After all, the hierarchical body politic of orders and corporations had been the social expression of principles that governed nature too. The rejection of hierarchy and organic harmony in nature fostered a similar rejection of these things when it came to society. This development is evident in the thought of Thomas Hobbes (1588–1679). Hobbes, an admirer and critic of Descartes, wrote his major philosophical work, the *Leviathan*, during the English Civil War and Commonwealth. Like many others, he thought his society was coming unglued (see 7.4.5); this perception inspired the starting point of the *Leviathan*'s political theory. Hobbes begins by imagining human beings in a state of nature, that is, as they are before the creation of an organized society and government. Such a life is, in Hobbes's words, "solitary, poor, nasty, brutish, and short."[14] Solitary because everyone would be on his or her own; poor, because such isolation made impossible the cooperation that economic development requires; nasty, because everyone being out for himself or herself means constant conflict; brutish, because such a life is fit for animals; short, because human beings seeking only their own interests and lacking any means of resolving their disputes will kill each other. Such a state, Hobbes says, is in fact a state of war of "every man against every man."[15] Humanity did, however, work out a solution. At some point, Hobbes argues, some people become so weary of a state of war of all against all that they band together, making an agreement among themselves to surrender up all their rights by promising complete obedience to a supreme authority, the governor. This contract thus sets up a governor that will be able to resolve disputes and keep order, allowing human beings to enter what Hobbes calls "civil society." True, some trouble-makers will resist the governor's decisions, but because everyone is contractually bound to obey the governor, the governor will be able to deploy enough force to deal with them. This governor—which will probably be a monarch but which, according to Hobbes, can be an assembly—has no limits on its authority. Such limits would, Hobbes argues, make it unable to carry out its proper function. Critical to this lack of limits is the fact that the governor itself is not party to the contract that creates it. If it were, the governor would have to judge disputes between itself and the people it governs—an impossibility. The only right against the government Hobbes leaves to human beings living in society is the right to self-defense.

How does all this relate to the Scientific Revolution? Hobbes's theory has no place for a society of orders and corporations, each with its own rights held independent of the ruler. To the extent Hobbes envisions hierarchy, it is a very simple one; the state is set over the people it rules. Indeed, Hobbes remarks that human beings are basically the same by nature: "though there be found one man manifestly stronger in body or of quicker mind

---

14 Thomas Hobbes, *Leviathan*, in *Hobbes: Selections*, ed. F.J.E. Woodbridge (New York: Charles Scribner's Sons, 1930), 253.

15 Hobbes, *Leviathan*, 252.

than another, yet when all is reckoned together, the difference between man and man is not so considerable...."[16] Instead of an organic body politic, Hobbes proposes a kind of artificial society, one created by human beings making a contract. Neither God (about whom Hobbes, to the scandal of his time, had doubts), nor nature, nor custom has a role in his scheme. Moreover, Hobbes's view of a society of equals brought together artificially is an atomized one; human beings, instead of being organically united according to their group and function, are like the free atoms of gas in a chamber, independent of each other and equal. His view of humanity was standardizing in a way analogous to the mechanists' view of matter.

In advocating an all-powerful government, Hobbes was laying out a theoretical justification for the up-and-coming government of his time, the absolutist state. Indeed, Hobbes's thought serves as a reminder that the new views of society and nature were quite compatible with absolutism. After all, absolutism implies equality; if no one has any rights, people are equal. In a sense, absolute monarchs and the new scientists of the seventeenth century had a common opponent: the assumption that the universe is an organically connected hierarchy.

The new standardizing vision could, however, lead to different political conclusions. This is evident in the Declaration of Independence, penned by Thomas Jefferson as a justification for the American Revolution against British rule. That revolution had begun as a defense of traditional liberties, and it was led by America's traditional political nation (see 7.4.6). In the Declaration, however, Jefferson argues for Americans' right to rebel in very different terms. He states, as already noted (7.4.6), that human beings are "created equal, that they are endowed by their Creator with certain unalienable rights, [and] that among these are Life, Liberty, and the pursuit of Happiness." He argues that, in order to secure these rights, human beings contract with each other to set up a government. That government is itself a party to the contract, and, should it fail in its contractual duty to protect the rights of the governed—especially if it violates them itself—the governed have a right to dissolve the government and set up a new one. Britain had violated the rights of Americans, and the Revolution was on.

Jefferson advocated limited government; Hobbes advocated absolute government. It is easy to see them as polar opposites. Yet, in fundamental ways, they agreed, an agreement that suggests the hold an atomized vision of society was coming to have. They both assume that human beings are free and equal—although, for Hobbes, that freedom was almost nonexistent in relation to government. They both avoid arguing for rights on the basis of tradition. For them, whatever rights people have are what today would be called human rights. Moreover, Hobbes and Jefferson both see government as something artificial, made by human beings. They both left assumptions commonplace in the sixteenth century behind. They embraced instead assumptions commonplace in the early twenty-first century.

---

16 Hobbes, *Leviathan*, 249, punctuation modernized.

Jefferson was not the first to turn these assumptions toward an argument for limited rather than absolute government—indeed, he was heavily influenced by earlier figures such as John Locke, who had previously argued for religious toleration (see 6.7) and by empiricism. Moreover, since ancient times, others in the West had tried to derive the nature of government by imagining human beings without it, in what Hobbes called the state of nature. The tradition that stems from the seventeenth century, however, came to be significant beyond a small band of intellectuals, for it now harmonized with larger assumptions about the universe. The Declaration of Independence is a sign that the atomizing vision of Hobbes, Locke, and others was coming to influence practical politics. That influence would grow.

7.8 LABOR

For most of Western history, those without full legal freedom did most of the heavy labor. Ancient Greece and Rome had been slave societies. The Middle Ages had seen serfs, peasants tied to the land, largely displace slaves as agricultural laborers. Serfdom in turn declined in the High Middle Ages, and largely disappeared in the Late Middle Ages. And outright slavery had become rare enough that the slaves from sub-Saharan Africa who occasionally appear in Spanish and Italian sources or the female slaves imported from eastern Europe (and often from further east) into Venice appear exotic to most historians of the Late Middle Ages. The tendency to use such slaves for household work rather than agriculture limited their numbers in a largely agrarian society.

The sixteenth and seventeenth centuries, however, saw the revival of slavery in the West on a large scale. Although some African slaves accumulated in Portugal, the critical development here was European conquest of the Americas. Enormous, fertile estates were available for the taking. The problem, from the point of view of their new owners, was a scarcity of labor to make them productive. Worse, the greatest profits were in cash crops that did not lend themselves to the arrangement common through much of the West, that of peasants cultivating small holdings in return for rent. Sugar, in particular, was best grown in tropical climates (such as that of the Caribbean islands—see Map 6.2) and on a large scale by laborers who had no choice but to do grueling work. And large sugar plantations would be followed by those producing cotton, tobacco, coffee, and rice. Slavery became a standard feature of the West's New World branch.

So large plantations became typical of New World agriculture in parts of Latin America, the Caribbean islands, and what became the southern United States. At first, their owners tried to compel indigenous Americans to work the land. But native populations plummeted as a result of contact with the new diseases brought from the Old World (see 6.2). Indentured servants—Westerners who contracted to work without wages for a certain number of years in return for payment for their voyage to America—also ultimately failed to fulfill the demand for labor. Slaves purchased from the coast of West Africa fit the bill.

Like Westerners, they enjoyed some degree of immunity from Old World diseases. Unlike Westerners, they had some immunity to tropical diseases and also were offered for sale. True, transporting them across the Atlantic drove up their price; with slaves crammed into the ships, death rates crossing the Atlantic were high, especially in the seventeenth century (about 25 percent). But planters' profits made slaves worth the price. By 1800, about nine million had been imported to the Americas. Indeed, sugar from the Caribbean islands was initially so profitable that it paid to work slaves on sugar plantations to death and buy replacements. Although most Africans perished before they could reproduce, others had children, establishing what would be a permanent population of African descent there and in the Americas generally.

Permanent, too, would be fluctuating hostility between black and white people in the Americas, both under slavery and after slavery's abolition. Slavery in the New World became identified as a black condition, freedom as a white one. Although the nineteenth century would see slavery ended in the West, conflict—sometimes violent—between black and white was not. Relations between social groups are often tense, such as those between ancient Greeks and barbarians or medieval Spanish Christians and Muslims. Those between blacks and whites have often remained so, no doubt in part because of skin color, visible and inheritable.

Work was also changing at home, in Europe. Between about 1500 and 1800, many European wage earners began to work longer hours, particularly in Western Europe. Many were peasants who mostly worked the land but who also took occasional employment in what is known to economic historians as the "putting out system." The method was a means of evading the gild regulations in force in many Western towns. An entrepreneur in, say, the cloth trade, might purchase raw wool and, instead of having it made into cloth in some urban workshop, would "put out" the work, hiring somebody outside of town to spin the wool into yarn. A peasant who happened to have the right equipment and skill and who wanted to devote spare time to earning some cash would contract to spin at home. The entrepreneur would then do the same with other steps of production, such as weaving the yarn into cloth, dying the cloth, and so on. Over time, some peasants, especially those with little or no land of their own, took on more and more work of this sort, becoming wage laborers and leaving the business of farming. By 1700, the putting out system was moving much of the production of goods for market from town to country-side, from urban workshop to rural household. The Dutch city of Haarlem is an example. In 1600, Haarlem was a center of linen production, although, by then, weavers in town were using yarn spun by peasants in the countryside. By ca. 1650, those weavers were out of business, the work taken over by cheaper peasant labor out of town. Soon after 1700, peasants were bleaching linen too. Haarlem's linen production was dead.

The movement of peasants to wage labor was a larger development than it might seem nowadays, in a world where most people work for wages. But ca. 1500, most peasants—and so the vast majority of the population—were largely economically self-sufficient. Not only did peasant families grow their own food but they often made their own cloth and their own clothes, their own shoes, and so forth. Only occasionally—as little, it seems, as possible—did they purchase goods on the market, such as metal tools from a smith. Even then, many such exchanges took place within villages and so did not stimulate broader trade. Agricultural life allowed peasants time to produce homespun goods; farming is a hard, but seasonal, occupation. As peasants moved from self-sufficient farming to wage labor, however, they not only produced goods that wound up being sold in the marketplace, but they also spent their wages on goods in the marketplace, in turn, increasing demand for such goods. In this way, the market for consumer goods grew enormously, serving most of the population rather than a small portion of it. The cash crops of the New World reinforced this trend. Tobacco and sugar could not be produced by Europeans at home but could be had only for cash, so, for most people in the West, purchasing these products required wage labor. Moreover, plantations single-mindedly geared to producing one crop for market added to the demand for inexpensive purchasable goods. Slaves on sugar plantations, for example, wore clothes made elsewhere.

Why were Western workers turning their labor from homespun to the marketplace? Many were trying to earn the cash needed to pay the higher taxes demanded by centralizing governments. Many were also following a new taste for ready-made goods. Following a fashion familiar today, wage laborers bought cheap versions of the luxuries of the rich. French inventories of recently deceased workers in the eighteenth century include items that most Westerners nowadays take for granted, such as fans and umbrellas. Workers and peasants of earlier centuries, however, had lived without such things.

This trend toward wage labor was especially pronounced in England, where agriculture underwent a vast reorganization ca. 1500–ca. 1800. As in most of the West, English peasants at the beginning of the sixteenth century often lived in communities with open fields. In other words, the land cultivated by a peasant household was not a compact plot but was scattered in strips in different fields around the village. Peasant households coordinated the farming of these fields, a cooperation that harmonized well with assumptions about the universe at large (see 7.2). They also pastured animals on common fields and let their pigs run in common woodland. These arrangements spread risk; if the harvest went bad in one field, at least one had strips in the others. If they limited risk, they also, however, limited agricultural innovation. A new crop or farming technique required the agreement of one's neighbors, so agricultural change proceeded at the rate the most conservative villagers were prepared to accept.

But the sixteenth century on saw a growing tendency to enclose open fields, creating individual plots of land farmed by individual households. In England in particular this movement accelerated after 1660. It should not be surprising that the act of Parliament enclosing this or that community's fields was the chief means of enclosure in these years; Parliament had long represented the interests of country gentlemen, and, from the later seventeenth century, it was less subject to royal control (see 7.4.5). (Indeed, France's absolute monarchy, by contrast, seeing peasants as generators of tax revenue [see 7.3], worked to keep them on the land, protecting them from non-tax-paying nobles and retarding enclosure in that country.) Peasants displaced from their land either became wage-earning agricultural laborers or wage-earning producers of goods for market via the putting out system. Enclosed fields, on the other hand, were subject to agricultural experiment, ultimately producing higher yields of food for the marketplace. Rising food production per person meant more people were available to work for wages in non-agricultural production.

FURTHER READING

Baumer, Franklin L. *Modern European Thought: Continuity and Change in Ideas, 1600–1950*. New York: Macmillan, 1977.

Birn, Raymond. *Crisis, Absolutism, Revolution: Europe and the World, 1648–1789*. 3rd ed. Peterborough, ON: Broadview Press, 2005. [Introductory text.]

Black, Jeremy. *Kings, Nobles, and Commoners: States and Societies in Early Modern Europe, a Revisionist History*. London: I.B. Tauris, 2004.

Brewer, John, and Roy Porter, eds. *Consumption and the World of Goods*. London: Routledge, 1993.

Curtin, Philip D. *The Rise and Fall of the Plantation Complex: Essays in Atlantic History*. Cambridge: Cambridge University Press, 1990.

Darnton, Robert. *The Great Cat Massacre and Other Episodes in French Cultural History*. New York: Vintage Books, 1985. [Particularly readable.]

Davis, Natalie Zemon. *Women on the Margins: Three Seventeenth-Century Lives*. Cambridge, MA: Harvard University Press, 1995.

De Vries, Jan. *The Economy of Europe in an Age of Crisis, 1600–1750*. Cambridge: Cambridge University Press, 1976.

Dixon, Simon. *The Modernisation of Russia, 1676–1825*. Cambridge: Cambridge University Press, 1999.

Elliot, J.H. *Imperial Spain: 1469–1716*. 2nd ed. New York: Penguin, 2002.

Gay, Peter. *The Enlightenment: An Interpretation*. 2 vols. New York: Knopf. 1966–69.

Goubert, Pierre. *Louis XIV and Twenty Million Frenchmen*. New York: Pantheon Books, 1970.

Hughes, Michael. *Early Modern Germany, 1477–1806*. Philadelphia: University of Pennsylvania Press, 1992.

Keen, Benjamin, and Keith Haynes. *A History of Latin America*. 7th ed. Boston: Houghton Mifflin, 2004. [Introductory text.]

Kramnick, Isaac, ed. *The Portable Enlightenment Reader*. New York: Penguin Books, 1995. [Primary sources.]

Levack, Brian P. *The Witch-Hunt in Early Modern Europe*. 3rd ed. New York: Pearson Longman, 2006.

Madariaga, Isabel de. *Catherine the Great: A Short History*. New Haven, CT: Yale University Press, 1993.

Outram, Dorinda. *The Enlightenment*. 2nd ed. Cambridge: Cambridge University Press, 2005.

Parker, Geoffrey. *The Military Revolution: Military Innovation and the Rise of the West, 1500–1800*. 2nd ed. Cambridge: Cambridge University Press, 1996.

Pomeranz, Kenneth. *The Great Divergence: China, Europe, and the Making of the Modern World Economy*. Princeton, NJ: Princeton University Press, 2000.

Rabb, Theodore K. *The Struggle for Stability in Early Modern Europe*. Oxford: Oxford University Press, 1975.

Rogers, C.R., ed. *The Military Revolution Debate: Readings on the Military Transformation of Early Modern Europe*. Boulder, CO: Westview Press, 1995.

Shapiro, Barbara J. *A Culture of Fact: England, 1550–1720*. Ithaca, NY: Cornell University Press, 2000.

Westfall, Richard S. *The Construction of Modern Science: Mechanisms and Mechanics*. Cambridge: Cambridge University Press, 1977.

Wiesner, Merry E. *Women and Gender in Early Modern Europe*. 2nd ed. Cambridge: Cambridge University Press, 2000.

THE EARLY MODERN WEST III

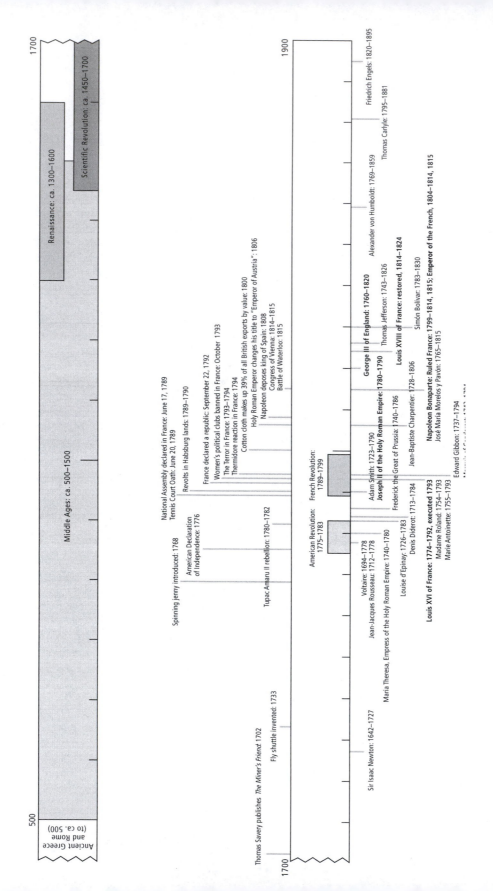

Ancient Greece and Rome (to ca. 500)

Middle Ages: ca. 500–1500

Renaissance: ca. 1300–1600

Scientific Revolution: ca. 1450–1700

1700

500

1700

1900

Thomas Savery publishes *The Miner's Friend*: 1702

Fly shuttle invented: 1733

Spinning jenny introduced: 1768

American Declaration of Independence: 1776

Tupac Amaru II rebellion: 1780–1782

National Assembly declared in France: June 17, 1789
Tennis Court Oath: June 20, 1789

Revolts in Habsburg lands: 1789–1790

France declared a republic: September 22, 1792
Women's political clubs banned in France: October 1793
The Terror in France: 1793–1794
Thermidore reaction in France: 1794
Cotton cloth makes up 39% of all British exports by value: 1800
Holy Roman Emperor changes his title to "Emperor of Austria": 1806
Napoleon deposes king of Spain: 1808
Congress of Vienna: 1814–1815
Battle of Waterloo: 1815

Sir Isaac Newton: 1642–1727

Voltaire: 1694–1778
Jean-Jacques Rousseau: 1712–1778
Maria Theresa, Empress of the Holy Roman Empire: 1740–1780
Louise d'Epinay: 1726–1783
Denis Diderot: 1713–1784

American Revolution: 1775–1783

French Revolution: 1789–1799

Adam Smith: 1723–1790
Joseph II of the Holy Roman Empire: 1780–1790
Frederick the Great of Prussia: 1740–1786
Jean-Baptiste Charpentier: 1728–1806

Louis XVI of France: 1774–1792, executed 1793
Madame Roland: 1754–1793
Marie Antoinette: 1755–1793

Edward Gibbon: 1737–1794

George III of England: 1760–1820

Thomas Jefferson: 1743–1826

Louis XVIII of France: restored, 1814–1824

Simón Bolívar: 1783–1830

Napoleon Bonaparte: Ruled France: 1799–1814, 1815; Emperor of the French, 1804–1814, 1815
José Maria Morelos y Pavón: 1765–1815

Alexander von Humboldt: 1769–1859

Thomas Carlyle: 1795–1881

Friedrich Engels: 1820–1895

EIGHT

THE EARLY MODERN WEST III: ENLIGHTENMENT, INDUSTRIALIZATION, AND AN UNRAVELED COMPROMISE

8.1 FUNDAMENTALS

Absolutism and the Scientific Revolution fundamentally challenged the society of orders, estates, and corporations that characterized the West as it entered the modern age. But that society had not disappeared ca. 1700, in part because of the compromises absolute monarchs had made with it (see 7.3). The result was what would, after the French Revolution of 1789, be called the "ancien regime" (from the French *ancien régime*, for "old [former] regime"): a juxtaposition of, on the one hand, the messy, complicated society of orders, estates, and corporations and, on the other, so-called absolute monarchy, theoretically contradictory elements of society that had learned to live with each other.

Eighteenth-century developments would, however, undo such settled conditions. The Enlightenment—an aggressive attempt to apply what appeared to be the lessons of the Scientific Revolution to society—leveled a continuing attack, at least in terms of ideas, on the ancien regime and so fostered a continuing tendency to atomize society. Toward the end of the century, the collapse of the compromises that had underwritten the ancien regime produced a crisis, one that the Enlightenment would influence fundamentally. And late in the eighteenth century, with gathering force in the nineteenth, the Industrial Revolution magnified those atomizing tendencies. The results shape the West to this day.

8.2 THE ENLIGHTENMENT I: ATTITUDES

In the eighteenth century, the Scientific Revolution and developments that flowed from it produced what has come to be known as "the Enlightenment." In a nutshell, the Enlightenment was an attempt to apply the lessons of the Scientific Revolution to all areas of human knowledge. The obvious success of Newtonian physics, so celebrated in Alexander Pope's line "God said, *Let Newton be!* and all was Light" (see 7.6), led to the conclusion that *all* ideas and institutions should be tested against the twin standards of observation and reason. Custom and tradition, which up to ca. 1600 had carried such great authority, were now held in contempt by the philosophes, as the Enlightenment's proponents were called. One of their leaders, Denis Diderot (1713–1784), wrote in his great work, the *Encyclopedia*, "All things must be examined, debated, investigated without exception and without regard for anyone's feelings.... We must run roughshod over all these ancient puerilities, overturn the barriers that reason never erected...."[1]

This attempt to root out the irrational did not exempt religion. Most of the philosophes concluded that reason and observation justified belief in God's existence because reason and observation revealed the universe to operate according to scientific principles, such as Newton's laws of gravity and motion. Such a universe was, they held, obviously planned, and therefore it must have a planner.[2] Indeed, Newton himself had described God as a clockmaker. Once that clockmaker God had made the universe with certain natural laws to guide its operation, he had left it to run on its own; no further divine action was necessary. The philosophes took up this view with a vengeance, generally becoming deists, that is, people who believe in the existence of the divine but not in the particular god of any organized religion. To most philosophes, belief in the god of Judaism, Christianity, Islam, or any other organized religion was, at best, mere superstition. Certainly religion might be tolerated, but it belonged in the heart, not in the halls of power. It was a view that accorded with the more fully personalized, internalized view of religion produced by the Reformation (see 6.7). Naturally, Christianity, as the West's dominant religion, came in for the most frequent criticism. Voltaire (1694–1778) called Christianity an "infamy" but pursued it with wit: "those who are called Papists eat God without bread, the Lutherans eat bread and God, while the Calvinists, who came soon after them, eat bread without eating God."[3] Disagreement over the communion, worth mayhem in the sixteenth century (see 6.1 and 6.4), was now a joke.[4] Edward Gibbon (1737–1794), another product of the

---

1   Denis Diderot, *The Portable Enlightenment Reader*, ed. Isaac Kramnick (New York: Penguin Books, 1995), 18.

2   The philosophes had, perhaps unwittingly, repeated arguments made earlier by, among others, medieval scholastics.

3   Voltaire, *Essai sur les Moeurs*, 2: 219, quoted and translated in *The Enlightenment*, vol. 1, *The Rise of Modern Paganism*, ed. Peter Gay (New York: Knopf, 1966), 154–55.

4   Along the same lines, Diderot's *Encyclopedia* referred the reader looking up "eucharist" to the article on "cannibalism."

Enlightenment, argued in his *Decline and Fall of the Roman Empire* that Christianity, an irrational ideology, had destroyed the character of classical civilization, leaving the empire vulnerable to invasion by barbarian tribes. The Middle Ages was characterized as an age of (Christian) faith, and so superstitious to its core. (Gothic architecture, a product of the High Middle Ages, got its name in the age of the Enlightenment; the style was named for the barbarian invaders of the Roman Empire, the Goths.) Although most people in the eighteenth-century West remained religiously committed and many accepted other Enlightenment ideas while remaining so, the Enlightenment represents the first significant attack on Christianity in the West since ancient Rome.

The atomized vision of a society of free and equal individuals that was encouraged by the Scientific Revolution became central to Enlightenment thought. Ca. 1600, a society of orders seemed both natural—because God had made the universe as an organic hierarchy—and justified by custom. Custom and nature were thus not necessarily opposed. To the philosophes of the eighteenth century, however, the society of orders, much of it left untouched by so-called absolute monarchs, no longer seemed natural, and custom alone justified nothing. Instead, the Enlightenment was a back-to-nature movement, one driven by a desire to strip away artificial custom to reveal nature as God had created it. The philosophes upheld natural human equality over irrational, customary rights. It should be evident that Thomas Jefferson, writing in 1776 (see 7.7), was part of this movement. So was Voltaire, a bitter critic of his society. A commoner, he had been beaten for insulting a noble, the chevalier de Rohan. De Rohan's family had also had Voltaire imprisoned for a fortnight in the Bastille for good measure in order to prevent the duel Voltaire wanted. Later, from the heights of international celebrity, Voltaire doused an irrational, unnatural society in scorn. He was not alone. No one, the philosophes argued, should have to bow low to an aristocrat. The celebration of natural equality had enormous theoretical consequences. It implied not only an end to noble privileges in the Old World but also an end to slavery in the New. And, although many philosophes came to identify powerful women with the elaborate artifice of the absolutist courts, some argued that women, sharing a common human nature with men, should enjoy the same rights as men, including the same political rights (see 8.4). Some of these aspects of Enlightenment thought would not have much practical impact before 1789, but all, in the long run, would have a vital influence on the West. In the short run, however, the desire to return to nature became fashionable, manifesting itself in some unexpected ways. Queen Marie Antoinette of France herself sought escape to the simple life from the now stodgy ritual life of Versailles created by Louis XIV (see 7.3). She embraced nature, having an imitation peasant's cottage built on the palace grounds where she and her ladies could dress up like shepherdesses. (The sheep wore pink ribbons.)

This assumption that society is naturally made up of free and equal people is evident in the work of Adam Smith (1723–1790), whose thought would prove the foundation of modern economic theory. Smith's *An Inquiry into the Nature and Causes of the Wealth of Nations* (1776) laid out what has come to be called the law of supply and demand: rising demand for an item in society will increase its price, while decreasing demand will lower its price; increasing supply of an item in society lowers its price, while decreasing its supply will raise its price. In order for these laws to work properly, buyers and sellers in the market should be roughly equal in their capacity to produce or consume. To illustrate with an extreme case: if many producers sell an item but most of those items are bought by only one consumer, that consumer can depress the price to an unnaturally low point; the laws of supply and demand will not operate. Buyers and sellers also need to act freely, in other words, independently of each other. If, for example, most of the producers of an item coordinate with each other—that is, if they act as a cartel—they can push the price of that item unnaturally high. The laws of supply and demand thus require an atomized marketplace of free and (roughly) equal producers and consumers; prices will then be set by what Smith called "the invisible hand." The best government policy to ensure such an operation, Smith's followers would conclude, is one of "*laissez faire*" (French for, loosely, "leave alone"), as government economic intervention tends to limit the free operation of producers and consumers.

Finally, the Enlightenment embraced the idea of progress. To many philosophes, it seemed obvious that the past several centuries had brought enormous improvement in human beings' understanding of the world. The Scientific Revolution had seen humanity, at least in the West, shake off the dead hand of tradition and superstition. Better yet, the eighteenth century had seen further progress, at least so far as the philosophes were concerned. After all, even Newton and Locke, heroes to the philosophes, had been firm Christians, despite Newton's talk of God the clockmaker. Locke had written that Christianity could be justified as good sense. That baggage had now been left behind. Only certain elements of Christian ethics could be preserved, as obviously consistent with reason. Jefferson took scissors to the New Testament, producing a pastebook of what a rational person could embrace regarding Jesus's life; the sayings of Jesus were all that remained. Indeed, while the philosophes celebrated pre-Christian, Graeco-Roman civilization as a distant golden age (see Gibbon's comments on the second century), they believed that those glories were now being recovered. In America, the framers of the Constitution adopted in 1789 sought a government with a democratic element, to be represented by the House of Representatives, but they sought to limit such democracy. Inspired by Rome, they established a legislature with an upper house. The American Senate, like the Roman body for which it was named, was to be made up of seasoned men (senators had to meet a higher minimum age than did members of the lower house) who would be less subject to popular passions (senators had six-year rather than two-year terms and, originally, were elected by state legislatures rather than directly by the voters). Indeed, Americans' very willingness to set up a republic was inspired by Rome's.

But perhaps progress could go farther than simply the recovery of ancient virtues. After all, ancient science had been surpassed. Some philosophes suggested that progress could become a permanent feature of human history. Indeed, humanity might be perfectible.

8.3 THE ENLIGHTENMENT II: CONTINUITY WITH THE PAST?

The philosophes were clearing the path to human progress, a path they expected to continue, even to a perfect future—or so they generally thought. To them, the Scientific Revolution of the seventeenth century had triumphed over an irrational attitude toward nature inherited from the Middle Ages. True, that victory had been accomplished by believing Christians. But what might have been an inconvenient truth pointed to further progress yet. The philosophes of the eighteenth century may have stood on the shoulders of seventeenth-century giants, but they could nonetheless see farther than their predecessors for having left off the blinkers of organized religion. Thus, the eighteenth century marked progress over the seventeenth. With humanity at last recovering from barbarism and superstition, the future was bright. That was why Diderot insisted on challenging all received opinion (see 8.2); the wreckage of custom, of the past, had to be cleared away for a better tomorrow.

But the past is not easily escaped. In the first place, of course, much of the past was still around for the philosophes to attack. For example, most people in the West continued to be Christians, even if Enlightenment deism was fashionable. Moreover, it is one thing to attempt systematically to challenge all one has known or believed; it is quite another to succeed in doing so. Indeed, the philosophes, despite themselves, wound up building into their view of the world much of what they had drunk in with the Christian education that was unavoidable in a society where nearly all educational institutions had a religious affiliation.

Consider the philosophes' view of history. For them, the world of classical civilization was a kind of golden age. Edward Gibbon thought that the second century AD, the high point of the Roman Empire, was the happiest period in human history, an age brought low only by the infection of a superstitious Christianity that turned peoples' attention from this world to the next, and from reason to faith, allowing barbarians to attack. A thousand years and more of barbarism followed, as the Christian Middle Ages succeeded Graeco-Roman civilization. The Scientific Revolution marked the recovery, and an even more enlightened future beckoned.

In broad outline, however, this vision of history resembled the Christianity the philosophes so vehemently attacked. Christians, too, looked to a golden age in the distant past, to the Garden of Eden in which there was no sin and no death.[5] Moreover, whereas Christians assigned the Fall from Eden to the sin of the first human beings, Adam and Eve, the philosophes saw Christianity as responsible for the fall from a blessed state of civilization. While Christians had the high drama of the birth and death of Jesus to bring in a new and better age, the philosophes had the more gradual enlightenment brought by the Scientific Revolution. And whereas Christians looked with certainty to the second coming of Christ and the reign of heaven, the philosophes at least hoped for a perfect society here on earth in the future. The philosophes' vision of the larger contours of history replicated,

---

5 This idea of a golden age in the past had, in fact, been a commonplace of ancient Western society even before Christianity.

in a secular guise, the vision Christians had accepted for centuries: a long-ago golden age, followed by a fall, which led eventually to a partial triumph in this world, with a future as golden—or perhaps even more so—than what had been lost.

It is that perfect future state that helps explain why the philosophes reshaped a Christian vision of history. For that vision gave history a happy ending. That happy ending, in turn, gave history meaning. Indeed, it gave meaning to suffering in one's own time. While Christians could hope for a future divine judgment and reward, the philosophes could hope that the more enlightened future generations to be delivered by the force of progress would judge them—and judge in their favor. Such judgment would provide the comfort of a good reputation in the future, if not eternal life. Madame (Marie-Jeanne Phlipon) Roland (1754–1793), languishing in prison on dubious charges, was consoled by the good opinion that posterity, at least, would hold of her. Diderot remarked that posterity took the place of heaven for the philosophes. A generation raised on a Christian view of history could not so easily give up on the attractions of a history with meaning.

Indeed, the philosophes thought they needed this kind of future judgment. In order to understand why, consider Christianity again. The simplest version stresses that people should be good and not be bad for two reasons. Good people are rewarded; they go to heaven. Bad people are punished; they go to hell. To put it crudely, people, like horses, respond to carrots and sticks. Of course, this approach to morality was even older than Christianity. The god of the Hebrews also punished the wicked and rewarded the just (at least he usually did), but he did so in this world rather than after death.

But the philosophes had a problem. If you believe in a God the clockmaker, then why be good? Who is going to punish the wicked or reward the just? One possible answer is that one should be good because it is simply right to be so: punishments and rewards are irrelevant. That answer (among others) was offered by the Greek philosopher Plato in the fifth century BC. But the philosophes had all been raised in the Christian tradition. It was hard for them to conceive of a way to ensure good behavior without carrots and sticks. Heaven and hell were out of the question because of God the clockmaker. The judgment of posterity—having a good reputation in the future—was the next best thing. As Diderot noted, posterity really was the heaven of the philosophe.

The philosophes rejected all organized religion, including Christianity. That is certainly what they said they were doing, and, in some important ways, they were true to their word. But the philosophes kept more Christian ideas than they realized. In this way, certain elements of Christianity, including its morality, became secularized—that is, they were given a nonreligious form. And so, in the future, even when many Western intellectuals had given up on religion, they still dealt in Christian assumptions about the world that had been preserved in a secular guise by the philosophes.

8.4 THE ENLIGHTENMENT III: EQUALITY AND GENDER

The ancient god Janus had two faces; one looked toward the past, the other toward the future. That image fits Enlightenment thinking about the sexes well. For the Enlightenment produced not one but two views of the sexes, in other words, two accounts of gender. Moreover, these views were not only different, but contradictory.

On the one hand, some philosophes developed a now familiar position, familiar because of the Enlightenment's own influence. They argued that all rights are—or at least should be—natural human rights. Because people are naturally equal, people naturally should have the same rights. And, because they share a common human nature from which rights spring, women and men should have the same rights. Louise d'Épinay (1726–1783) made a classic Enlightenment argument that "men and women have the same nature and the same constitution. The proof lies in that female savages are as robust as male savages: thus the weakness of our constitutions and of our organs belongs definitely to our education, and is a consequence of the condition to which we have been assigned in society"—in other words, is a product of custom.[6] Such an argument would be the basis of feminism from the eighteenth century through much of the twentieth. In this way, feminism is an Enlightenment creation.

And yet.... Some philosophes reached a very different conclusion: that women are less rational, less serious, and so less suited to public life than men. Being less rational, women were, in the minds of these philosophes, opposed to nature, which philosophes assumed to be rational and to which the Enlightenment turned for guidance. Women could thus appear, odd as it might sound, naturally unnatural. Being less serious, women were more given to fashion, in other words, up-to-date convention, itself a sign of their opposition to nature. Being less suited to public life, women were best confined to the home.

Such attitudes are evident in Diderot's discussion of how a man must talk to a woman. "We [men] are afraid," he wrote, "of tiring them or boring them [women]. Hence we develop a particular method of explaining ourselves easily that passes from [simple, natural] conversation into style."[7] Such refinement contrasted with natural simplicity. The philosophe Jean-Jacques Rousseau (1712–1778) made it clear in his *Second Discourse* that fashion and luxury and pleasure were for women—and feminized men. He describes his native Geneva as an ideal society: "Let dissolute youth go to seek easy pleasures and long lasting repentance elsewhere; let the supposed men of taste admire in other places the grandeur of Palaces, the beauty of carriages, the superb furnishings, the pomp of

---

6   Dena Goodman and Kathleen Wellman, eds., *The Enlightenment* (New York: Houghton Mifflin Co., 2004), 167.

7   Denis Diderot, *Dialogues by Denis Diderot*, trans. Francis Birrell (Port Washington, NY: Kennikat Press, reprint 1970), 196.

spectacles, and all the refinements of softness and luxury. In Geneva one will find only men...."[8]

Many readers will find here a familiar, modern stereotype. Women are attracted to luxury, style, and fashion. Men, simple, down-to-earth, straightforward (natural) creatures, wear whatever is comfortable and go camping, close to nature. For Rousseau and others, the conclusion seemed obvious: flighty women could not be trusted with a role in government but belonged at home. This stereotype, against which modern feminism rebelled, shows the long-term influence of the Enlightenment, or at least that of one of its faces.

A look at eighteenth-century, and modern, attitudes toward eighteenth-century art and design reveals that influence too. Consider, for example, a picture of the Duke of Penthièvre's noble family drinking chocolate (Figure 8.1), painted by Jean-Baptiste Charpentier (1728–1806). It is an example of the dominant artistic and decorative style of the time, known as the rococo. The décor is delicate, elaborate, and not especially sober. Today, most viewers will, I think, also see it as rather feminine, something that belongs more on the wall of a woman's living room than a man's. But, in the eighteenth century, the attitudes that would characterize this painting as feminine were only just being created by the philosophes. The men and women who first viewed this painting would not have seen it as a particularly feminine work. Similarly, both women's and men's fashions were, by modern standards, elaborate and colorful, as in Charpentier's painting (Figure 8.1).

Despite all this, the assertion of natural male and female equality flows easily from Enlightenment assumptions about natural rights. So how did a movement that attacked traditional inequalities in the name of human nature come to assert that the sexes are inherently different and unequal?

The story is rather complicated. It requires a look at the place of women, especially aristocratic women, under the ancien regime.[9] Women, including noblewomen, were generally subordinate to men (in particular, to their husbands). But there were certain exceptions, for example, the royal wives and mistresses at the courts of absolute monarchs (7.3). Such women sometimes exercised influence over the king, and, by doing so, became power brokers through whom men of the political nation sought influence. These women, moreover, operated in a royal household marked by elaborate manners and social distinctions (7.3), characteristics that the philosophes had come to attack as artificial convention. In their minds, women exercising power behind the scenes came to be associated with an unnatural addiction to court life, to its luxuries and manners and, most frivolous of all, gambling. The philosophe Montesquieu remarks of gambling that "women are especially devoted to it.... Clothes and carriages begin the disruption ... and gambling completes it."[10] Moreover, their frivolous shallowness made women naturally two-faced—indeed,

---

8 Jean-Jacques Rousseau, "Discourse on the Origins of Inequality," in *The Collected Writings of Rousseau*, eds. Roger D. Masters and Christopher Kelly (Hanover: University Press of New England, 1992), 3: 11.

9 For a definition of ancien regime, see 8.1

10 Montesquieu, *The Persian Letters*, trans. C.J. Betts (London: Penguin Books, 1993), 120.

natural conspirators. Diderot, perhaps thinking of powerful women at court arranging decisions behind the scenes, remarks that women "seem linked in a loose plot for domination."[11] Indeed, such domination means their lack of seriousness infects the nation generally. Montesquieu remarks that women's addiction to banter—another sign of their frivolity—"which is so natural round a woman's dressing table, seems to have spread so far [in France] that it has influenced the character of the nation at large."[12]

The salon offered another exception to women's subordination to men. A salon was a room in a great house; the term also came to be applied to periodic social gatherings that some wealthy people had in that room. Such gatherings were often geared toward discussion of intellectual and artistic matters: literature, politics, painting, science, and so on. The dominant figure of the salon was the lady of the house, the *salonnière*. She determined who was invited and who might come back. This control had greater repercussions than one might think. In this case, it's worth noting that many writers—including most philosophes—did not make a living from sales of their work. Best-selling writers did; Voltaire was an example. Some near the bottom eked out a living by writing fast and cheap, often,

Figure 8.1: Jean-Baptiste Charpentier, *Duke of Penthièvre's Family Drinking Chocolate* (ca. 1767)

---

11 Diderot, *Dialogues*, 187.

12 Montesquieu, *The Persian Letters*, 130.

in fact, by writing pornography. (Diderot himself sometimes made ends meet by writing some milder stuff.) Otherwise, however, a successful writer needed a wealthy, usually aristocratic, person to take an interest in his work, to serve as a patron. With a patron to provide for at least some expenses, the writer could write. Diderot, for example, fared especially well in this regard, receiving support from Catherine the Great of Russia and Frederick the Great of Prussia (1740–1786), among others. (For these monarchs, see 7.4.4 and 8.5.2.)

But how to find a patron? That was where the salon came in. It was a place where a writer on the make could rub shoulders with well-to-do readers. In other words, it was a place to hook a potential patron. But the lady of the house was the gatekeeper. In this way, a *salonnière* could be critical to the careers of (male) artists and writers, men like the philosophes. Yet to flourish in a salon, one had to be fashionable: not only talk the right talk, but wear the right clothes and display the right manners. Despite the philosophes in them, salons were centers of those very elements that philosophes associated with artificial convention; the fact that some were only that, and not geared to intellectual matters, only heightened their association with fashion and style. And the salons were dominated by women.

So why did male philosophes latch on to powerful women as the root of the trouble? These men had grown up in a world in which women *were* expected to be subordinate to men, in general at least. And so they were especially liable to resent finding themselves at the whim of some aristocratic female power broker, a royal mistress or a *salonnière*. Montesquieu wrote that the women at the court of the king of France "were like another state within the state, and a man who watches the actions of ministers, officials, or prelates at court, in Paris, or in the country, without knowing the women who rule them, is like a man who can see a machine in action but does not know what makes it work."[13] The result was a tendency to focus on powerful women as the very source of aspects of the ancien regime of which the philosophes disapproved. Hence the creation of what might be called the antifeminist Enlightenment that ran counter to the feminist Enlightenment.

8.5 THE CRISIS OF THE ANCIEN REGIME: REBELLION AND REVOLUTION

Early modern "absolute" monarchs were not absolute (see 7.3). Although they overrode some of the rights of the political nation, governments often compromised in practice, leaving some of those rights alone. Yet the forces that drove absolutism did not abate in the eighteenth century. In particular, the expense of war continued to rise, and governments continued to look for revenue, a search that was hamstrung by the compromises governments had made. Moreover, the Enlightenment encouraged governments to attack the traditional privileges that held them back. Thus, governments renewed their attack on

---

13 Montesquieu, *Persian Letters*, 197.

orders and local authority. The result, starting in about the third quarter of the eighteenth century, was the "crisis of the ancien regime." Newly challenged by central authority, the political nation revolted. In some countries, governments compromised before they were overthrown, and survived—a kind of replay of the creation of absolute monarchy in the seventeenth century. Sometimes, however, governments lost control of territories in rebellion or were overthrown altogether. Moreover, the later eighteenth century was a different world from the seventeenth: it was the age of the Enlightenment, which deeply influenced the impact of the crisis. Rebellions that began in the name of a defense of traditional rights in a hierarchically ordered society sometimes ended as rebellions in the name equality, freedom, and nature.

8.5.1 The American Revolution

I have already told the story of the rebellion of North American colonists against British rule—the American Revolution, which culminated with British recognition of the new United States of America in 1783 (see 7.4.6). That story was, in fact, part of a larger eighteenth-century story: the crisis of the ancien regime. In the first place, when Britain imposed those unheard of direct taxes on the colonists, it was undoing a quiet, little-considered compromise it had earlier made with the American political nation. And it undid that compromise in order to cope with rising military expenses.

For their part, the colonists began to resist in the name of their traditional liberties—tax exemption. The colonists were, in that way, reacting conservatively and not in order to found something new. One indication of their frame of mind was the proposal that the colonies remain under the rule of King George III (1760–1820) and independent from all parliamentary jurisdiction. The idea was a no go, but the proposal indicates a conservative attitude.

The Declaration of Independence of 1776, however, signaled a shift in the Revolution. The movement had begun in defense of tradition. But the Declaration justifies the break from Britain in very different terms: as a demand for "Life, Liberty, and the pursuit of Happiness." Indeed, the Declaration asserts human equality and natural human rights (see 7.7). The Revolution had embraced the Enlightenment, a movement hostile to tradition. This pattern—a rebellion begun to defend traditional rights transmuted into a rebellion in the name of Enlightenment values—would be repeated in the crisis of the ancien regime.

8.5.2 The Habsburg lands

Maria Theresa (1740–1780), head of the Habsburg family, had a problem. Her family had collected territories over generations, all bound together by nothing but the coincidence of being ruled by the house of Habsburg: Austria, Hungary, the "Austrian Netherlands" (roughly, modern Belgium), Moravia, Transylvania—a partial listing (Map 8.1). The

Habsburgs had also traditionally held the title Holy Roman Emperor, a nearly empty title (see 7.4.1).[14] Moreover, the Habsburg lands were hard to rule. They were riddled by the same kinds of tradition-minded assemblies, dominated by the nobility, that hampered Western rulers elsewhere. The continuing existence of serfdom in some of their territories also limited the Habsburgs. Being tied to the land, wholly subject to their landlords, serfs were not available to the army. Moreover, rendering in-kind payments to their landlords rather than selling the produce of their fields, serfs did not have cash available for the Habsburgs' tax collectors. These weaknesses were underlined in 1740, when Frederick the Great of Prussia mobilized the kind of army that an absolute monarchy could support and that Maria Theresa could not afford. Frederick seized one of the Habsburg provinces, Silesia (Map 8.1). Maria Theresa drew the obvious conclusion regarding her lands: centralize them or face their dismemberment.

She chose to centralize, cautiously. A vital element was a property tax to support the army, to be paid throughout her dominions. Unlike earlier taxes, this tax was not voluntarily surrendered up by the estates of her various territories. But she compromised too, not pushing the political nation too far. Yes, there was an annoying new tax, but at least the estates were able to exercise the right to assess it. And Hungarian nobles gained a large measure of exemption. Maria Theresa was able to get what she needed; the size of the army more than doubled from what it had been under her father. This increase was not enough to regain Silesia, but it sufficed to protect what was left. She reduced labor services owed by serfs if opportunity allowed, for example, in Bohemia in 1775 after a rebellion by serfs provoked by famine.

Maria Theresa died in 1780. Where she had been cautious, her son Joseph II (1780–1790) was bold. Joseph sought to abolish serfdom throughout his lands outright. In Hungary, where the nobility was tax exempt, Joseph prepared a new property tax that would not exempt them, bypassing the noble-dominated assemblies. In the Austrian Netherlands, Joseph, ignoring the wishes of the local estates, brought the Catholic Church under tighter state control; in some places, he declared the estates' rights at an end.

So Joseph applied greater pressure to the political nation than had his predecessors. Not only was this a practical matter but it fit the rejection of tradition's authority that characterized the Enlightenment. Indeed, in a sign of changing times, Joseph put his case less in terms of his own divine right than in terms of the conclusions he drew from a social contract that, according to some of the philosophes, created government in the first place (see 7.7). The fate of Count Podstacky illustrates Joseph's dedication to legal equality. The count, a young wastrel, was convicted of forgery. When such a culprit was a nobleman, imprisonment, perhaps comfortable imprisonment, was the usual result; public humiliation was off limits for nobles except in cases of treason. Joseph, however, made certain that the count was treated like other criminals: his hair cut off, he was dressed in a rough uniform, put in a chain gang, and made to clean the streets of Vienna.

---

14 Being a woman, Maria Theresa was not eligible to hold the title Holy Roman Emperor; her husband was, and eventually was elected Emperor.

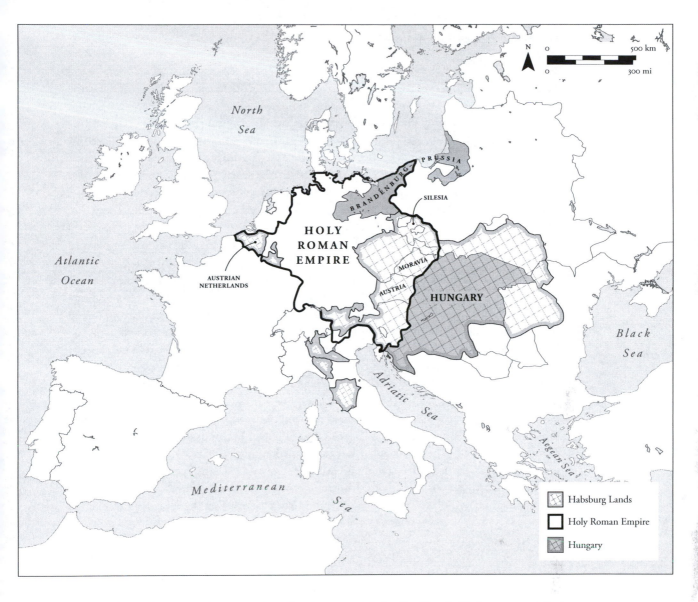

Map 8.1 : Germany and Habsburg family lands in the eighteenth century.

Joseph's policies produced crisis. The Austrian Netherlands rebelled in 1789. The Hungarian nobility considered rebellion and asked for support from Prussia, the Habsburgs' chief rival since the seizure of Silesia. Reports of noble unrest poured in from the other Habsburg lands. Joseph, dying, despaired; he revoked most of his reforms. But these concessions, sealed by Joseph's death, resolved the crisis in the Habsburg lands. Outright rebellion did not materialize beyond the Austrian Netherlands. Nor did resistance to the government come to be dominated by the language of the Enlightenment, as it had in America or would be in France and Latin America. Moreover, the Habsburgs kept their collection of thrones. In France, however, events were proceeding differently.

8.5.3 The French Revolution

Just as the France of Louis XIV provided the model case of absolutism (see 7.3), so the French Revolution serves as the model case of the crisis of the ancien regime. That crisis was rooted in finance. Facing debts going back to the wars of Louis XIV (see 7.4.2), King Louis XVI could not pay his own military expenses. The tipping point was Louis's intervention in the American Revolution on the side of the colonists, a move calculated to weaken France's old enemy, Britain. The British lost the heart of their North American empire, but the French king had to borrow every sous to pay for his part in that victory. By 1788, about half the government's revenue went to service debt. Louis decided against bankruptcy, even though his predecessors occasionally had simply repudiated some of their debts. The alternative was to raise taxes. The problem here was France's tax structure. Most taxpayers were peasants, already taxed so heavily that taxing them more would not produce much additional revenue. The wealthiest members of society were largely tax exempt: these were the first estate (the clergy) and the second estate (the nobility). Their willingness to accept an absolute monarchy had, in part, been built on the king's willingness not to touch this traditional right of tax exemption (see 7.3). Now Louis announced plans to levy significant taxes on all his subjects, including those of the first two estates. The grand compromise that underwrote absolute monarchy in France was unraveling.

Resistance set the stage for revolution. The Parlement of Paris, the kingdom's chief court, staffed by noble judges, declared this tax reform (as Louis considered it) illegal; it had not been approved by the Estates General, the body that legally and traditionally approved taxes to be collected throughout the kingdom (see 7.1). Of course, earlier absolute monarchs had imposed taxes in just this way, without bothering to convene the Estates General; they had simply taken care not to tax the political nation—i.e., the first two estates. Indeed, the Estates General had not met since 1614. Louis's predecessors had also dealt with obstreperous assemblies, like the parlements, by calling in the troops. But the officer corps was dominated by the nobility, and Louis feared that the army was unreliable. Reluctantly, Louis summoned the Estates General to meet in May of 1789.

The meeting was not a success. No one living had ever seen a meeting of the Estates General. Some had imagined some sort of representative assembly along the lines of England's Parliament or perhaps the American Congress, which were both, in practice, assemblies of property holders. It is the case that the Estates General was dominated by men of property. True, the representatives of the third estate sat for all those who were not clergy or nobles and so everyone from peasants to merchants. But those representatives themselves were largely property holders; no peasants sat in the Estates General. But the first two estates insisted that voting in the Estates General take place in the way it had in 1614: by estate rather than by head. Each estate had one vote. The first two estates could, thereby, always together outvote the third, even though the representatives of the third estate were about equal in number to those of the first two estates put together, and represented the vast majority of the population besides. A fierce debate gripped the country just before the opening of the Estates General: should voting be by estate or by head?

Jacques Mallet du Pan (1749–1800), a Swiss journalist in Paris, observed that "The public debate has changed. Now the King, despotism, the constitution [i.e., the issue of absolute monarchy] are merely secondary; it is a war between the Third Estate and the other two orders."[15] In defending voting by estate, the clergy and nobility defended a traditional, organic society, a society of corporations and estates; a person's rights were determined by membership in those corporations and estates. Yet the West had changed since 1614. The philosophes had argued that rights were rooted not in tradition or in membership in some artificial legal group but in a common humanity as decreed by nature. It was that conception for which representatives of the third estate argued. Indeed, the Enlightenment ran deep; many nobles and clergy themselves agreed with their colleagues in the third estate. What had started as another attempt by an absolutist government to override traditional rights had become a conflict over Enlightenment principles.

After weeks of stalemate, on June 17, 1789, representatives of the third estate had had enough. They went ahead and simply declared themselves "The National Assembly." They invited the representatives of the other two estates to join them, but made it clear that voting would be by head, not by estate. Some members of the nobility and clergy accepted the invitation. One could argue that the formation of the National Assembly was the formal beginning of the French Revolution. After all, the representatives had had no legal authority to declare themselves a national assembly. The pressure on Louis to summon the Estates General had been, by contrast, a call on Louis to follow the law.

One might have expected Louis to side with the National Assembly. Not only did its existence undermine distinctions between the estates and therefore noble and church privileges—an old aim of absolute monarchs—but it was a step toward solving the king's immediate problem of raising taxes. It might have been the wildest dream of that old absolutist, Louis XIV. The problem was that Louis XVI had not decided to form the National Assembly; representatives of the third estate had. Louis, losing control of the situation, had the third estate's meeting hall locked up on the night of June 19. The next day, members of the National Assembly found a nearby tennis court and swore "the Tennis Court Oath" to continue to meet—and to give the country a written constitution. Louis, without troops in place to quash dissent, lost his nerve, accepted the situation, and ordered the representatives of the other two estates to take their seats in the National Assembly.

And so—to make a long story short—France came to be ruled by the National Assembly, eventually called the National Constituent Assembly. The Assembly and its successors proceeded to restructure France along the lines a philosophe would admire. It abolished the tax privileges of the first and second estates, as expected. With strokes of the pen, the Assembly erased France's millennium-old provinces and their traditional assemblies, the estates and the parlements, that had acted to limit royal power. The provinces were replaced by 83 "departments," all roughly the same size, all with identical institutions. Eventually, all would respond to direction from Paris. Limits on central authority

---

15 Quoted in T.C.W. Blanning, *The French Revolution: Class War or Culture Clash?* 2nd ed. (Basingstoke: Macmillan Press, 1999), 48.

that had troubled even "absolute" monarchs were thus disappearing. Enlightened reform, and so standardization as regional differences were erased, became the order of the day. In 1793, as the Revolution entered its most radical phase (more on this to follow), the government scrapped the various traditional systems of weights and measures from the different provinces in favor of a single, symmetrical system—the metric system, which now got its start. (The American system of 12 inches to a foot and 3 feet to a yard is a holdover from the kind of measures in use under the ancien regime.) The old calendar was eliminated, replaced by one with new names for the months, each to be made of three ten-day weeks. The year 1792 became Year I, suggesting that a new age had begun. Paris's great cathedral of Notre Dame became the Temple of Reason. The government went on to sponsor the worship of a generic, and so non-Christian, Supreme Being.

Outside the government, fashion changed in a way that reflected the new emphases on nature and classical virtue. The Enlightenment had long held up classical civilization as a model, its supposed simplicity and solidity a contrast with rococo complexity and frivolity (see 8.4). Now the Revolution marked, or at least seemed to mark, a clean break with the immediate past and a return to natural simplicity and classical values. Compare the painting by Jacques Louis David (1748–1825) of Brutus receiving the bodies of his sons, whom he had sentenced to death to preserve the Roman Republic (Figure 8.2) with the rococo work of Charpentier (Figure 8.1). The style is simple and somber compared with that of Charpentier; the subject is self-sacrifice for the common good, a traditional Roman value.

The National Constituent Assembly proceeded to write a constitution for France. There was much debate. For example, should France continue to have a king? In 1791, the decision was to retain the monarchy but not an absolute one. The king would control foreign policy and the army; otherwise, he could only delay legislation not stop it. Moreover, the legislature, called the National Legislative Assembly, had the power to declare war and peace. The new political system was not democratic. The Assembly was made up of propertied men. Its composition should come as no surprise. Even Locke had held that, although all men may be born equal, only property holders could be expected to protect the right that all people have to keep their property if they have it; this idea was commonly accepted by Enlightenment thinkers. Moreover, the representatives in the National Assembly, noble and non-noble, had been property holders themselves, as were the representatives of the National Constituent Assembly. France's new constitution also required a minimum amount of property of those who were eligible to vote for the representatives, even wealthier than themselves, who would, in turn, choose the members of the National Legislative Assembly. These members were themselves eligible to serve based on the taxes they paid, so all would also be men of property.

But how was the government able to enforce its will? Absolute monarchies had relied on the army (see 7.3), but Louis's army was unreliable in the early days of the Revolution. Here it is necessary to consider a new player in French, indeed, Western, politics: the *sans culottes*. The term refers to those men "without breeches," who wore trousers instead. Among men, trousers were a marker of lower class status, whereas breeches, with stockings

below the knee, were a sign of membership in the upper ranks of society, the political nation. (For men in breeches, see the painting by Charpentier, Figure 8.1). It was the *sans culottes*, both men and women of the same class, who provided the muscle on which the National Assembly and its early successors relied. The common people flexed that muscle on July 14, 1789. Louis had been summoning troops toward Paris, presumably in order to use them to close down the National Assembly. Crowds responded by showing up in front of the military prison in Paris, demanding the arms stored there be turned over to them in order that they might defend the Assembly. The commander refused. The Bastille was stormed; it turned out to have few weapons. But this was the first large-scale use of force of the Revolution, and it was exercised by the *sans culottes*, traditionally excluded from the political nation.

The result was an uncomfortable alliance between the common people of Paris and the representatives of the traditional political nation—including leading members of the

Figure 8.2: Jacques Louis David, *The Lictors Bring to Brutus the Bodies of His Sons* (1789)

third estate—who made up the revolutionary government. The new constitution was designed to give political power to property holders, not the *sans culottes*. But proponents of that constitution also needed the *sans culottes*. It was they, for example, who in October marched to Versailles and forced the king and queen to move to Paris, where the government could keep an eye on them.

The suspicions that surrounded the king were justified. Despite public statements of support for the Revolution, Louis worked behind the scenes to reverse it, thereby making the position of those in the political nation who wanted to keep a (limited) monarchy awkward. Moreover, a divide opened among the revolutionary-minded segment of the political nation itself in 1791. There were the moderates, who favored keeping political decisions in the hands of the propertied classes and who generally favored a clipped monarchy to a republic. And there were the Jacobins, named after their club's meeting place in an old Jacobin monastery, who favored some sort of democracy. They also favored a republic, that is, no king at all. In June of 1791, Louis, Marie Antoinette, and their son attempted to flee the country in disguise; they were caught at the French town of Varennes and returned to Paris. This "flight to Varennes" strengthened the hand of the Jacobins.

The Jacobins and the *sans culottes* were natural allies. Events outside France strengthened that alliance. In August 1791, the Prussian and Austrian monarchs, concerned that revolution might spread to their countries, issued the Declaration of Pillnitz, expressing concern for the safety of the king and queen of France and a willingness to intervene in France to restore order. The move only made Louis look like a tool of hostile foreign governments and made things harder for French defenders of monarchy. By this time, aristocrats known as *émigrés* had been leaving France in large numbers, either resentful of the changes that had taken place or fearing worse. Some *émigrés* welcomed the declaration. The Jacobins could thus claim that aristocrats were plotting to undo the Revolution. In April 1792, France declared war on Austria. Now opposition to the Revolution looked like betrayal of France itself. In August, the *sans culottes* stormed the royal palace in Paris, slaying the royal guards. The government, both dependent on the *sans culottes* of Paris and afraid of them, soon imprisoned the royal family, declared France a republic on September 22, 1792 (which would become the first day of Year 1 in the new calendar), and called for the vote to be extended to all adult men.

The stage was set for what has become known as "the Terror" (1793–1794), the Revolution's most radical phase. With the war going badly, fear that nobles, clergy, and the former king were conspiring against the country was hard to resist. The government went onto an emergency basis, with leadership falling upon the Committee of Public Safety in Paris. This committee was dominated by Maximilien Robespierre (1758–1794), who sought to institute a "Republic of Virtue." He and his colleagues, certain of the need to complete the reform of France and purge it of enemies, led a campaign to eliminate anyone who threatened the country, anyone, in fact, who could be classified as "an enemy of liberty," as the government put it. A kind of *lettre de cachet* (see 7.3) was reinstituted. Aristocrats, clergy, and those accused of sympathizing with them were executed in the tens of thousands—the greatest bloodletting off the field of battle that France had seen since at least the religious conflicts of the sixteenth century. Louis XVI was tried and executed. The Terror's speed was fostered by simply shooting rather than hanging the accused and by using a new tool for execution, the guillotine, which cut off its victims' heads with little fuss. Opposition to the government was equated with treason to France and the Revolution. Even revolutionaries themselves were liable to a quick trial and beheading.

Indeed, the Terror was not aimed only at members of what had been the political nation. More than half its victims were themselves *sans culottes*. That even non-aristocrats were vulnerable suggests that the Terror was a symptom of the collapse of organic notions of society that had been weakening since the seventeenth century (see 7.5 and 8.2). The Terror was not simply an expression of hostility to noble privilege. The French could now consider themselves free and equal. But freedom and equality did not offer a feeling of community, a feeling of connection with others. Although the motto of the Revolution was "Liberté, Égalité, Fraternité"—"Liberty, Equality, Brotherhood"—the first two overshadowed the third. At the same time, perhaps the Terror itself also fostered a sense of unity, indeed, of brotherhood in the face of a common threat, both internal and external, even though anyone might at any time be defined as being a part of that threat.

The Terror also saw a decision on an issue that had been ambiguous during the Enlightenment: the correct role for women (see 8.4). If France was to be restructured according to reason and nature, which Enlightenment view of women would prevail? Did women share human equality with men, or did reason and nature decree that women should be confined to private life? At first the question appeared open. The Marquis of Condorcet (1743–1794), a philosophe and noble revolutionary, argued for women's political equality on the floor of the National Constituent Assembly. Women were well represented among the crowds of *sans culottes* who provided the Revolution's force in the early days. Members of the Society of Revolutionary Republican Women, one of a number of women's political organizations that sprang up, patrolled the streets, armed and wearing trousers, ready to defend the Revolution from its enemies. The government passed laws giving women greater rights over property and in divorce. But, late in 1793, the other side won the day. In October, the former queen, Marie Antoinette, charged with, among other crimes, wickedly influencing her husband in political matters—that very mingling of public and private life that the Enlightenment had criticized—was executed. In the same month, all women's political associations and clubs were banned. Women were excluded from attending France's legislature unless accompanied by a man. Madame Roland (see 8.3), whose salon had included such revolutionary figures as Robespierre and who had written some of the official papers of her husband, a minister in the new government, was executed in November. The new laws regarding women's rights over property and in divorce were revoked. The age of the *salonnière*, and of the royal wife and mistress, was over. Women in the new society would be more systematically subordinate to men than before, and the line between private life and public power would be sharper.

While these issues pertaining to Enlightenment thought were being worked out, large military changes led to a new atmosphere. The army was being radically reorganized—and enlarged. In a move that earlier absolutists might have envied, the government instituted mass conscription. French victories followed in 1794. Another result was a military force in the hands of the government, one that made it less reliant on *sans culottes* in the streets. This change set the stage for the end of the Terror and a swing back to calmer times.

8.5.4 Latin America

Latin America was far larger and arguably more complex than the other societies that experienced the crisis of the ancien regime. Most of the region was governed by Spain; Brazil was under Portuguese rule. Its crisis fit less well into the pattern set by Europe and England's thirteen colonies. International events played a larger role. Eighteenth-century Spanish America was also marked by various tensions. One such tension was among racial groups. White Creoles, descended from Spaniards but born in the Americas, made up the native ruling class; some were quite wealthy and aristocratic. Native Americans, whose ancestors had been conquered by Spain, still made up the majority of the population. Their discontent, especially with Spanish taxation, became evident in Peru in 1780, when many rebelled and followed the standard of a man who claimed to be Tupac Amaru II, the last of the Inca royal family. At first Creoles supported the rebellion, but that stopped when the rebels began to massacre them. "Tupac Amaru" failed to unite even native Americans, and the rebellion was put down in 1782. Black slaves had been imported in large numbers from Africa. They constituted a class of disaffected laborers whose resistance the Creoles feared. More threatening to the Creoles even than slaves were the *pardos* (the "browns"), free persons of partial African ancestry. Colonial legislatures, controlled by Creoles, prohibited *pardos* from attending universities and marrying whites, although these laws were sometimes evaded. Creoles, in turn, faced competition from the peninsulars—that is, Spaniards from Spain, some poor immigrants looking to make their way and some sent to govern the colonies. Worse for the Creoles, Spanish policy favored peninsulars—who were arriving in increasing numbers—giving them a monopoly on higher office. Indeed, Creoles were ceasing to identify with Spain. The Prussian visitor Alexander von Humboldt (1769–1859) noted both Creole hostility to the monopoly on government offices enjoyed by peninsulars and Creole disaffection from Spain, often hearing Creoles say, "I am not a *Spaniard*, I am an *American*."[16] It did not help that Spanish authorities were overriding Creole privilege by selling *pardos* the right to equal legal status with whites. Moreover, Spain was increasing taxation in the colonies; the province of Mexico furnished nearly quintuple the taxes at the end of the eighteenth century than it had at the beginning. In some cases, Spain simply twisted the arms of wealthy Creoles, forcing them to donate money for Spain's military expenses. Albeit less aggressively than in France, British America, or the

---

16 Helen Delpar, ed., *The Borzoi Reader in Latin American History* (New York: Knopf, 1972), 1:164.

Habsburg lands, the central authority in the colonies was overriding the traditional privileges of the political nation.

International events also fostered growing distance between the Creole elite and Spain. The American Revolution showed that American colonies could break away from the mother country. The French Revolution showed that monarchies, such as Spain's, were vulnerable. Indeed, Humboldt wrote that Creoles began to claim to be Americans rather than Spaniards after the conclusion of the American Revolution and especially after 1789.[17] Such attitudes were also fostered by the nationalism that became fashionable in the early nineteenth century (see 9.3).

Creoles could at least hope that Spain would maintain order and so keep the lower orders in their places. But international events intervened. In 1808, France under Napoleon (more on him in 8.6) occupied Spain, deposed the king, and installed a puppet monarchy. With the colonial administrations rudderless, Creoles seized control of various provinces of Latin America, forming ad hoc *juntas*, or administrations, ironically acting in the king's name. The Creoles could thus achieve practical independence—a captive king was in no position to give orders—and protect, even bolster, Creole privilege. It would be fair to describe these developments as, in some sense, conservative.

But Spain's king was restored with Napoleon's defeat in 1814 (see 8.6). When the monarchy attempted to reassert control in the colonies, it was resisted. The resulting liberation movements played out in different ways in different parts of this huge and diverse region. The various fissures within colonial Spanish society added to the complexity. In Peru, for example, Creoles remembered the Tupac Amaru rebellion of 1780–1782, which made them cautious about embracing rebellion of any kind. Other Creole leaders feared that disorder would favor a black or native takeover. At the same time, in over a decade of war, each side needed black, native American, and *pardo* support.[18] And here supporters of independence could draw on Enlightenment thought. Simón Bolívar (1783–1830), a freethinker in religious matters, advocated legal equality for Latin America's various racial groups, in line with the philosophes' stress on equality. (Although, like many Enlightenment-minded men in the new United States, he also feared influence exercised by non-whites.) Even a revolutionary of a conservative stamp such as José María Morelos y Pavón (1765–1815), who proclaimed that independent Mexico should tolerate only Catholicism, declared that "slavery is proscribed forever, as well as distinctions of caste, so that all shall be equal."[19]

---

17 He must, however, have been relying on earlier reports, for he arrived in Latin America only in 1799.

18 Britain had attempted a similar move during the American War of Independence, offering slaves their freedom in return for fighting for Britain, but this sort of competition for the allegiance of slaves did not go very far there.

19 Gilbert M. Jones and Timothy J. Henderson, eds., *The Mexico Reader: History, Culture, Politics* (Durham: University of North Carolina Press, 2002), 190.

Venezuela's constitution, the first adopted in Spanish America, laid down legal equality among all persons regardless of race, and later constitutions followed suit. Revolution in Latin America could thus also be described as starting as a defense of traditional order only to mutate into an Enlightenment program of attacking it. In this way, Latin American developments were similar to those occurring during the crisis of the ancien regime in the British colonies and in France. By the end of the 1820s, the series of Latin American wars had ended in independent governments throughout most of the region.

8.6 COUNTERREVOLUTIONS: THERMIDOR, NAPOLEON, AND THE CONGRESS OF VIENNA

Historians have observed that revolutions often enter a radical phase only to enter a subsequent phase that undoes some, although not all, of that radicalism. The French Revolution is a textbook case. The Terror was radical, a case of widespread violence carried out in order to create and defend a democracy that would have appalled most people before 1789 (see 8.5.3). By the middle of 1794, however, the military emergency that seemed to justify the Terror had abated. A powerful central government had instituted the draft and rebuilt a massive French army from the ground up, and that army was gaining France victories, even conquests. On July 27, Robespierre's colleagues, afraid that he was turning on them too, had him arrested; he was executed the next day, an illustration of the Terror's measured justice. In France's new calendar, the month was Thermidor ("the month of heat"). Ironically, Thermidor came to give its name to any conservative turn, any cooling of a revolution after a heated, extreme phase.

France now received a new constitution, known as "the Directory," in November 1794. Five men, called "directors," formed a board with executive power. Once again, indirect voting protected the political dominance of property holders. Moreover, the stabilized military situation meant that elements of the army were available to keep order in the streets. The government thus no longer had to depend on and be dependent on crowds of *sans culottes*. This independence became clear in October 1795, when supporters of the old monarchy rebelled in the streets of Paris. The government called on a young officer, Napoleon Bonaparte (1769–1821), to order his troops to act. The rebellion collapsed.

The Directory, however, was powered primarily by exhaustion. Few passionately supported it, but most accepted it as better than some other form of government that others wanted—perhaps a restoration of democratic Terror, perhaps a restoration of monarchy. Bonaparte's "whiff of grapeshot," as it was later called, was only a sign of things to come, as the Directory resorted to military force to stay in power. When royalists aiming to restore the monarchy were elected to the legislature, the directors deployed the army, again including Bonaparte, to override the results. Bonaparte was, in turn, realizing that the government's dependence on the army made it vulnerable to the army, just as the earlier revolutionary government's dependence on the *sans culottes* had made it vulnerable to them. The fact that Bonaparte had achieved a string of triumphs—he had brought most of Italy under French control—gave him that special aura of competence that only success in the field confers. The fact that he was only 30 years old added to his allure. In 1799, Bonaparte seized power. He created an elected legislature that made the laws he desired, keeping real power in his own hands. He erased local control of the departments, appointing prefects without local ties and so completing the centralization of power begun by the absolute monarchy. He also made a place in his government for all who would serve it—whether old aristocrats or old proponents of the Terror. *Émigrés* began to return to France. In 1802 he had himself "voted" in as the country's executive for life. In 1804, he had himself declared, by another partially stacked vote, Napoleon, "Emperor of the French." This reliance on popular votes, however manipulated, and on military rigor has led some historians to conclude that Napoleon marks not a final height of monarchy but the prototype of the modern dictatorship. I do not see why Napoleon could not have been both.

Monarchy, of a kind, was thus restored to France. It is tempting to say that the Revolution had been undone. But that would not be entirely true. Napoleon maintained France's departments. His Napoleonic Code asserted the legal equality of all adult, male citizens, not to mention legal homogeneity across the country. It also maintained the systematic confinement of women to private life. Even when Napoleon began to hand out noble titles, these did not confer special legal rights as in the ancien regime, although he did ensure that recipients had the wealth necessary to support their new standing. So Napoleon could certainly be said to have preserved the Revolution. On the other hand, Napoleon offered, if not something for everyone, then something for most people, including those who distrusted the Revolution. To those who looked back to absolute monarchy as France's last stable government, he gave monarchy—monarchy even more effective than the one overthrown in 1792. At the same time, he reconciled many republicans to monarchy by being an "emperor" rather than a "king" and by not being one of the Bourbons, France's former royal family. He also offered such people the preservation of legal equality, not to mention a promise not to recover the church property redistributed during the Revolution. In 1799, he proclaimed, "Citizens, the Revolution has been made fast to the principles that started it. The Revolution is ended."[20] To the old nobility, he offered government position and the rewards that went with it, so long as he received faithful and competent service; at the same time, he opened such paths to anyone else with the right skills. This policy of "careers open to talent" is evident from the backgrounds of Napoleon's marshals, the highest rank in his army. Of the eighteen men appointed in 1804, five had noble backgrounds dating to before the Revolution; five were—or had been—*sans culottes*; the rest were bourgeois. Indeed, Napoleon said that every private's bag carried a marshal's baton.

---

20 Napoleon, quoted in *The Mind of Napoleon: A Selection from his Written and Spoken Words*, ed. and trans. J. Christopher Herold (New York: Columbia University Press, 1955), 72.

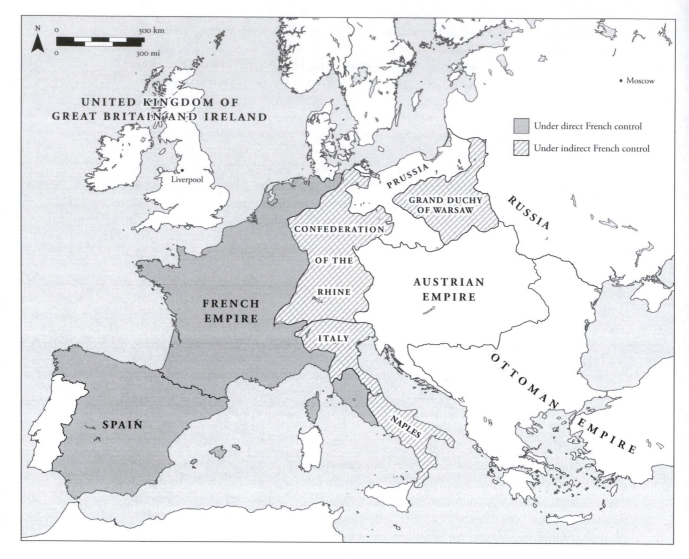

Map 8.2: Napoleon's conquests

Napoleon also exported aspects of the Revolution to much of the rest of the West. He was a great conqueror, bringing under French direct or indirect rule Italy, Spain, most of Germany, and more (see Map 8.2). Kings and princes in these lands were often replaced by Napoleon's relatives (for the consequences for Spanish America, see 8.6). He or his agents imposed the Napoleonic Code in the conquered lands, as well as in the French colony of Louisiana in North America. The revolutionary drive to simplify complex traditional arrangements was felt, in limited form, in Germany. The Holy Roman Empire had consisted of more than 300 states before Napoleon. The Emperor of the French consolidated them, reducing their number to 39—not the sweeping change of replacing France's traditional provinces with the departments but still a change that moved in a similar direction. The Holy Roman Empire was clearly at death's door in 1806; the head of the house of Habsburg discreetly renounced his title of "Holy Roman Emperor" for that of "Emperor of Austria."

Like other great conquerors, however, Napoleon reached too far. The major powers of Europe—in particular Britain, Austria, Prussia, and Russia—did not trust him to limit his ambitions and formed various alliances against him. Finally, in 1812, he invaded Russia with his "Grand Army" of some 600,000. Victory on the field led to disaster. His army penetrated all the way to Moscow, only to find the city stripped of supplies and an enemy simply retreating into Russia's huge interior. The troops starved. The long retreat of unprepared and underfed men through the fierce Russian winter was fatal. Only about 50,000 troops returned home. Napoleon raised another army in France, but it met defeat at the battle of Leipzig (1813), and Napoleon met exile at the hands of the coalition against him. The victorious allies restored Louis XVIII (1814–1824) as the king of France.[21]

Yet the Revolution was not erased. Although one prominent French politician said Louis and his supporters had learned nothing from the Revolution, Louis had, in fact, learned a great deal. True, the king in principle rejected the notion that he governed by his country's consent, which even Napoleon had accepted, even if he had to manipulate votes to achieve that consent. Louis certainly rejected the principle of one man, one vote—but so had most French regimes since 1789. In practice, however, Louis accepted much of what the Revolution had accomplished. Legal distinctions between nobles and non-nobles were not restored. The provinces were revered as part of French culture, but the legal divisions of France remained the departments, fully subject to Paris. Even the nobles created by Napoleon kept their titles.

A similar phenomenon—a theoretical setting of the clock back to before 1789 accompanied by practical acceptance of much that had changed—characterized international affairs. Representatives of the various European states gathered at the Congress of Vienna in 1814–1815. The goal was to make peace, a workable peace that would bring Europe stability after decades of war. The principle that the congress ultimately accepted, in theory at least, was "legitimacy": that stability could be had through a return to arrangements that people could accept because they had the stamp of tradition rather than of being imposed by a French army. Perhaps not surprisingly, this principle of legitimacy was pressed by Louis XVIII's representative to the congress; the same argument had been used to urge the Bourbon restoration. The papal states in Italy were resurrected, having vanished in the wake of French armies. But, in practice, the interests of the great powers and an interest in stability prevailed. France, not surprisingly, was reduced to earlier boundaries, ultimately to those of 1789; all conquests since then were lost. Austria—as the Habsburg state was now known—added Venice to its holdings in Italy. Prussia gained German territory along the Rhine, the better to contain France. And, perhaps most stunning of all for traditionalists, the Holy Roman Empire remained on the scrapheap. So did hundreds of its statelets

---

21 Louis XVIII was Louis XVI's brother. He was counted the eighteenth of this name because Louis XVI's young son, who died in captivity after his father's execution, was regarded as Louis XVII by supporters of the monarchy.

eliminated by Napoleon, although their rulers appealed for their restoration. The German states remained 39 in number, organized in the "Germanic Confederation." (The greatest thrill of the Congress of Vienna may have been Napoleon's escape from exile back to France, where he quickly gained the support of the army and drove out Louis XVIII. But the victorious great powers moved promptly and ended Bonaparte's "100 days," defeating him at the battle of Waterloo in 1815 and sending him to a safer, more remote, exile. Louis XVIII and peace were speedily restored.)

The restoration of Louis XVIII and the work of the Congress of Vienna may appear to have been the ultimate "Thermidor." The creation of a new, stronger central government for the United States in 1789 (see 7.4.6) was also a kind of Thermidor. But, although the pendulum had swung back from the extremes of the Revolution, it had not swung all the way back.

In independent Latin America, power tended to fall into the hands of *caudillos*—strong men—for much of the nineteenth century. These men ignored constitutional constraints and looked to support from similar *caudillos*. Many Creole heirs of the Enlightenment came to see such men as bulwarks against a tradition-minded and Catholic society, not to mention against a takeover by racial minorities. At least they could enjoy a facade of elective government, as in Napoleon's France.

Indeed, many still looked back to the Revolution and the Enlightenment with admiration. Such people would come to be known as "liberals" in the nineteenth century: persons who favored the largely unfettered freedom of the individual over tradition and government regulation. Nineteenth-century liberals favored market forces over government regulation of the economy, i.e., laissez-faire economics (see 8.2). They favored legal equality over distinctions between noble and non-noble. They favored republics or limited monarchy over absolutism. Liberalism was in retreat in Europe in 1815 but not in English America. And liberals, although largely defeated, did not disappear from the scene elsewhere. Instead, the Revolution bequeathed a long-standing division in Western politics between "right" (associated at the start of the new century with conservatism) and "left" (associated with liberalism). Even the use of "left" and "right" as political labels had originated during the Revolution; it referred to where radical and conservative members sat in France's National Constituent Assembly (see 8.5.3). What exactly people on the right and left believed would evolve over time. But constant opposition between political ideologies at different ends of a political spectrum would not. The crisis of the ancien regime had permanently marked the West.

8.7 THE INDUSTRIAL REVOLUTION

The rise of absolutist governments and the Enlightenment—itself an outgrowth of the Scientific Revolution—worked in the eighteenth century to atomize what had been an organic society. But economic developments were also pushing the West in the same direction. I have already explained how many peasants who had lived in tight-knit communities and labored together on the land were becoming, in the seventeenth century, wage laborers who simply worked for an employer (see 7.8). Although some scholars have minimized their importance, technological changes of the later eighteenth century had a leading role in transforming that seventeenth-century landscape. Historians have labeled this fundamental economic change the "Industrial Revolution," which can be defined, at bottom, as the application of the nonhuman, nonanimal power of machines to the mass production of goods. Britain, in the later eighteenth century, was the first to experience the Industrial Revolution, but, in the course of the nineteenth and twentieth centuries, most of the West and beyond would undergo it too. And industrialization, in turn, had a further atomizing impact. It strained human connections in the workplace. It threw people without neighborly ties together in new towns. It even threatened to tear asunder the family.

The Industrial Revolution may have been technological, but a consideration of its origins in Britain shows other factors at work: British colonies, social conditions, and geographic accident. Textile production was the first to industrialize. The invention of the fly shuttle (1733) halved the labor needed for a loom, increasing demand for yarn; urban gilds were powerless to limit this development in the countryside. Attempts to meet that demand fostered the development of the spinning jenny (ca. 1764), which allowed one worker to operate as many as 100 spindles. Soon, these machines were adapted so as to use waterpower. But, in the longer run, the greatest impact would be from the steam engine, which increasingly made its mark from the 1780s. Steam engines had first interested the English as a way of powering pumps to get water out of coal mines. (One of the earliest manuals on their construction was Thomas Savery's *The Miner's Friend: Or, an Engine to Raise Water by Fire* [1702].) The English mined coal—which happened to be plentiful in England—because, by the eighteenth century, they had cut down most of their forests and needed fuel for heating and cooking. Because they were used in coal mining, steam engines were generally powered by burning coal. The application of such coal-powered steam engines to spinning jennies and looms released enormous productive energy. In the early nineteenth century, coal yielded more energy than all of Britain's agricultural land could have done had this land been devoted solely to producing wood for fuel. Indeed, England's coal-driven capacity to turn wool into cloth threatened to outstrip Europe's ability to produce wool.

Here New World plantations became critical. Another technological development, the invention of the cotton gin in 1793, meant that cottonseeds could be removed quickly from cotton fibers, opening the way to the use of cotton in large quantities. The new machines worked best with cotton fibers anyway; wool tended to gum up the works. And American cotton plantations worked by slaves on seemingly endless supplies of land could supply what European shepherds could not. Moreover, cotton cloth was more suitable to warm weather markets—such as the New World's plantations—than wool. In 1700, British cotton cloth exports had been practically nonexistent. By 1800, cotton cloth made up 39 percent of all British exports by value—this from a country where cotton would not grow. Moreover, steam-powered machines made cloth so cheaply that it easily became the fabric of choice for the burgeoning population of wage laborers at home, and one that could be worn by slaves in the Americas. In the nineteenth century, traditional producers of cotton cloth could not compete with British industry. India had long exported cotton cloth. There, however, hand spinners had to labor 50,000 hours to produce 100 lbs. of cotton yarn. By ca. 1825, one of the new machines in Britain could achieve the same task in 135 hours.

The new machines also changed the workplace. Before, workers had used simple, human-powered machines such as looms or spinning jennies at home as tools to make cloth; now, workers left home to work with heavy, more expensive machinery powered by water mills and, increasingly, coal-burning steam engines. The factory was born. Children had always worked, but now they worked outside the home and away from the influence of parents who might soften the demands put on them. Children, like their parents, worked in dangerous conditions for half a day and more. Work also in this way became standardized. Everyone had to work according to regulated shifts, responding in the same way when the bell rang or the whistle blew. In fact, people had to become, in a sense, part of the machines that they tended, a development that seemed to undermine workers' humanity and so human ties. James Kay-Shuttleworth (1804–1877) observed in 1832 that "Whilst the engine runs, the people must work—men, women, and children are yoked together with iron and steam. The animal machine . . . is chained fast to the iron machine, which knows no suffering and no weariness."[22]

These factories also created new cities. Sparsely populated northern England, in particular Lancashire, drew workers to new factory towns situated near coal mines. Liverpool, a mere village ca. 1650, grew to 78,000 people by 1800; it was on the coast and so well placed to receive cotton imports—and it was also near coal deposits. People who moved to find factory work found themselves living in cities seemingly built overnight, cities much larger than their old villages and without the traditional ties among neighbors characteristic of older communities. Friedrich Engels (1820–1895) wrote in 1845 of the inhabitants of such cities that "they crowd by one another as though they had nothing in common, nothing to do with one another, and their only agreement is a tacit one, that each keep to his own side of the pavement"; it was, he said, a "world of atoms."[23] Contemporaries observed that crime was rampant in the new towns. In these ways, workers in England were experiencing their own version of the atomized society promulgated by the philosophes.

These developments were not without their critics. Why purchase a lovingly made pair of shoes when a less expensive, mass-produced pair would do as well? Skilled artisans faced unemployment as cheap factory goods soaked up demand for their own, painstakingly produced, products. Some saw in industrialization a reduction of all relationships

---

22 Quoted in John F.C. Harrison, *The Birth and Growth of Industrial England, 1714–1867* (New York: Harcourt, Brace, Jovanovich, 1973), 90.

23 Friedrich Engels, *The Condition of the Working Class in England*, ed. Victor Kiernan (London: Penguin Books, 1987), 69.

to economic ones, an atomizing tendency that tore the community asunder. Writing in 1839, Thomas Carlyle (1795–1881) complained that cash payment was now "the universal sole nexus of man to man."[24]

Labor conditions became another point of controversy. The dangers of working with heavy machinery and for long hours led to calls for government action. Such demands stood in tension with the vision of factory owners and factory workers as atomized free and independent actors in the market place, a laissez-faire vision rooted in the Enlightenment (see 8.2). Nonetheless, 1802 saw the first factory regulations bill passed in Britain. It would be followed by others, but factory conditions remained an object of complaint and reform throughout the nineteenth century and into the twentieth.

FURTHER READING

Baumer, Franklin L. *Modern European Thought: Continuity and Change in Ideas, 1600–1950*. New York: Macmillan, 1977.

Becker, Carl. *The Heavenly City of the Eighteenth-Century Philosophers*. New Haven, CT: Yale University Press, 1932. [A classic, not always now in favor.]

Birn, Raymond. *Crisis, Absolutism, Revolution: Europe and the World, 1648–1789*. 3rd ed. Peterborough, ON: Broadview Press, 2005. [Introductory text.]

Black, Jeremy. *Kings, Nobles, and Commoners: States and Societies in Early Modern Europe, a Revisionist History*. London: I.B. Tauris, 2004.

Blanning, T.C.W. *Joseph II*. London: Longman, 1994.

Bushnell, David. *Simón Bolívar: Liberation and Disappointment*. New York: Pearson Longman, 2004.

Curtin, Philip D. *The Rise and Fall of the Plantation Complex: Essays in Atlantic History*. Cambridge: Cambridge University Press, 1990.

Darnton, Robert. *The Great Cat Massacre and Other Episodes in French Cultural History*. New York: Vintage Books, 1985. [Particularly readable.]

Doyle, William. *Origins of the French Revolution*. 3rd ed. Oxford: Oxford University Press, 1999.

Ellis, Geoffrey. *The Napoleonic Empire*. 2nd ed. New York: Palgrave Macmillan, 2003.

Gay, Peter. *The Enlightenment: An Interpretation*. 2 vols. New York: Knopf. 1966–69.

Goodman, Dena, and Kathleen Wellman, eds. *The Enlightenment*. New York: Houghton Mifflin Co., 2004. [Primary sources.]

Hardman, John, ed. *The French Revolution Sourcebook*. 2nd ed. London: Arnold, 1999.

Hughes, Michael. *Early Modern Germany, 1477–1806*. Philadelphia: University of Pennsylvania Press, 1992.

Hunt, Lynn. *The Family Romance of the French Revolution*. Berkeley, Los Angeles: University of California Press, 1992.

---

24 Thomas Carlyle, *Selected Writings*, ed. Alan Shelston (London: Penguin Books, 1971), 193.

Keen, Benjamin, and Keith Haynes. *A History of Latin America*. 7th ed. Boston: Houghton Mifflin, 2004. [Introductory text.]

Kramnick, Isaac, ed. *The Portable Enlightenment Reader*. New York: Penguin Books, 1995. [Primary sources.]

Morgan, Kenneth. *The Birth of Industrial Britain, 1750–1850*. 2nd ed. London: Longman, 2011.

Outram, Dorinda. *The Enlightenment*. 2nd ed. Cambridge: Cambridge University Press, 2005.

Palmer, R.R. *The Age of Democratic Revolution: A Political History of Europe and America, 1760–1800*. 2 vols. Princeton, NJ: Princeton University Press. 1959–64.

Pomeranz, Kenneth. *The Great Divergence: China, Europe, and the Making of the Modern World Economy*. Princeton, NJ: Princeton University Press, 2000.

Sutherland, Donald. *The French Revolution and Empire: The Quest for a Civil Order*. Malden, MA: Blackwell, 2003. http://dx.doi.org/10.1002/9780470758410.

Valenze, Deborah. *The First Industrial Woman*. Oxford: Oxford University Press, 1995.

Wiesner, Merry E. *Women and Gender in Early Modern Europe*. 2nd ed. Cambridge: Cambridge University Press, 2000.

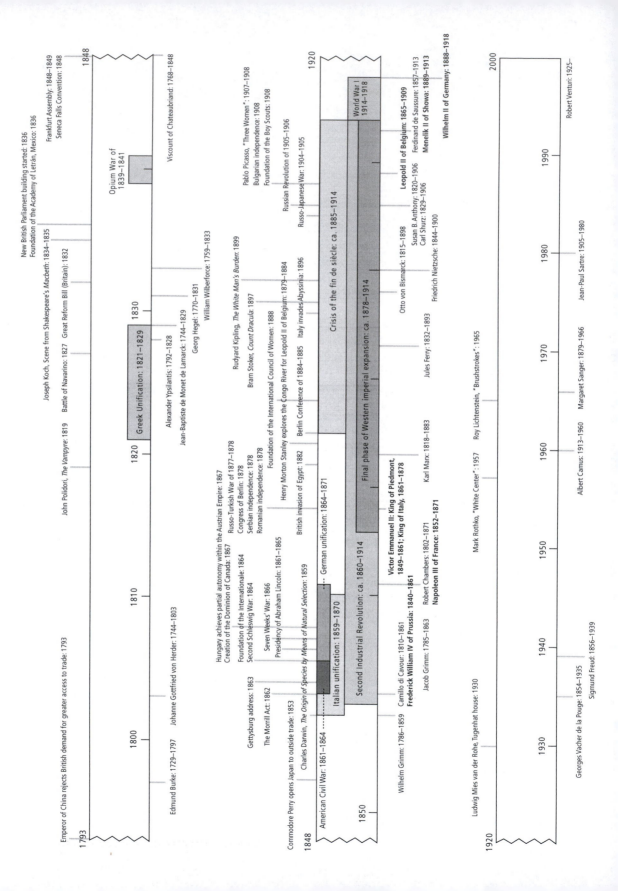

THE WEST, 1815–1914

1793

Emperor of China rejects British demand for greater access to trade: 1793

Edmund Burke: 1729–1797

Johanne Gottfried von Herder: 1744–1803

John Polidori, *The Vampyre*: 1819

New British Parliament building started: 1836
Foundation of the Academy of Letrán, Mexico: 1836

Joseph Koch, Scene from Shakespeare's *Macbeth*: 1834–1835

Battle of Navarino: 1827   Great Reform Bill (Britain): 1832

Frankfurt Assembly: 1848–1849
Seneca Falls Convention: 1848

1848

Viscount of Chateaubriand: 1768–1848

Opium War of 1839–1841

Greek Unification: 1821–1829

Alexander Ypsilantis: 1792–1828

Jean-Baptiste de Monet de Lamarck: 1744–1829

Georg Hegel: 1770–1831

William Wilberforce: 1759–1833

Rudyard Kipling, *The White Man's Burden*: 1899

Bram Stoker, *Count Dracula*: 1897

Hungary achieves partial autonomy within the Austrian Empire: 1867
Creation of the Dominion of Canada: 1867

Foundation of the Internationale: 1864

Second Schleswig War: 1864

Seven Weeks' War: 1866

Presidency of Abraham Lincoln: 1861–1865

Russo-Turkish War of 1877–1878

Congress of Berlin: 1878

Serbian independence: 1878

Romanian independence: 1878

Foundation of the International Council of Women: 1888

Henry Morton Stanley explores the Congo River for Leopold II of Belgium: 1879–1884

Berlin Conference of 1884–1885   Italy invades Abyssinia: 1896

British invasion of Egypt: 1882

German unification: 1864–1871

Pablo Picasso, "Three Women": 1907–1908

Bulgarian independence: 1908

Foundation of the Boy Scouts: 1908

Russian Revolution of 1905–1906

Russo-Japanese War: 1904–1905

1920

World War I
1914–1918

Leopold II of Belgium: 1865–1909

Ferdinand de Saussure: 1857–1913

Menelik II of Showa: 1889–1913

Wilhelm II of Germany: 1888–1918

Crisis of the fin de siècle: ca. 1885–1914

Final phase of Western imperial expansion: ca. 1878–1914

Otto von Bismarck: 1815–1898

Susan B. Anthony: 1820–1906

Carl Shurz: 1829–1906

Jules Ferry: 1832–1893

Friedrich Nietzsche: 1844–1900

Karl Marx: 1818–1883

Gettysburg address: 1863

The Morrill Act: 1862

Charles Darwin, *The Origin of Species by Means of Natural Selection*: 1859

Italian unification: 1859–1870

Commodore Perry opens Japan to outside trade: 1853

1848

American Civil War: 1861–1864

Second Industrial Revolution: ca. 1860–1914

Victor Emmanuel II: King of Piedmont,
1849–1861; King of Italy, 1861–1878

Camillo di Cavour: 1810–1861
Frederick William IV of Prussia: 1840–1861

Robert Chambers: 1802–1871
Napoleon III of France: 1852–1871

Jacob Grimm: 1785–1863

Wilhelm Grimm: 1786–1859

1800   1810   1820   1830

2000

Robert Venturi: 1925–

1990

Jean-Paul Sartre: 1905–1980

Margaret Sanger: 1879–1966

Roy Lichtenstein, "Brushstrokes": 1965

Mark Rothko, "White Center": 1957

Albert Camus: 1913–1960

Ludwig Mies van der Rohe, Tugenhat house: 1930

Georges Vacher de la Pouge: 1854–1935

Sigmund Freud: 1856–1939

1920   1930   1940   1950   1960   1970   1980

NINE

THE WEST, 1815–1914: THE SEARCH FOR COMMUNITY, AND RESPONSES TO THE ENLIGHTENMENT AND REVOLUTION

9.1 FUNDAMENTALS: THE SEARCH FOR COMMUNITY

What does "modern" mean? Sometimes it means "right now," the early twenty-first century—which is what most people mean by it. But historians sometimes call "modern (Western) history" everything following the Middle Ages, i.e., everything from ca. 1500 on.[1] For other historians, "modern" refers to the West from the time of the Enlightenment, the French Revolution, and the Industrial Revolution on. That use presumes that these developments set the West on its path to the present. As seen in the last chapter, there is much to be said for this view. Certain aspects of Enlightenment thought are now commonplace; the standardized, republican world of mass production ushered in by the revolutions of the late eighteenth century are more familiar to people today than the ancien regime. But the influence of these eighteenth-century changes runs deeper than that. Reactions against the Enlightenment, the French Revolution, and industrialization were also profound. The story of much of the nineteenth century is about the continuing influence of the eighteenth *and* of reactions against it. (The same would also be true of the twentieth century, to be considered in the next chapter.)

---

1 Or perhaps earlier.

A word on what is meant by "nineteenth century" is also in order. Historians often see World War I (1914–1918) as the great turning point in the West between the nineteenth and twentieth centuries. So, as odd as it might sound, for purposes of historical analysis, historians often consider the nineteenth century to have continued until the eve of World War I. In the discussion below, "nineteenth century" will include the years to 1914.

The direction of the eighteenth century had been toward an atomized society (see 8.2 and 8.7). Continued industrialization only fed that atomization in the nineteenth century as factories and industrial cities spread to other parts of the West. In the course of 50 years, the populations of major capitals, such as Paris and Berlin, doubled or tripled, swollen with factory or government workers.

An atomized society leaves people without a sense of community, that feeling of connection with others and the larger society. Such connections had been clearer in the earlier, organic society represented by the body politic (see 7.1). Yet most people want a sense of community, a sense of belonging. Critical nineteenth-century developments stemmed from this desire to recreate a sense of connection with others. In particular, the great rival forces of the nineteenth century—nationalism and Marxism—both drew much of their appeal from their promise of community. These forces would also dominate much of the twentieth century. But before exploring these developments, it will be necessary to discuss the reaction against the Enlightenment from which both nationalism and Marxism flowed.

9.2 CHANGE AND *GEIST* I: ROMANTICISM

As the eighteenth century drew to a close and the nineteenth began, many Western intellectuals rebelled against the Enlightenment. This movement is known as "Romanticism" and its proponents as "Romantics." But these terms should not mislead. Romanticism was more a family of ideas and tendencies than a coherent system of thought designed to displace the Enlightenment.

Romantics often rejected the authority of reason. They celebrated the unconscious mind as a source of artistic creation freed from the constraints of reason. Consider the tales of the supernatural that became fashionable in the nineteenth century. *The Vampyre*, by John Polidori (1795–1821), achieved great popularity in the 1820s; the story's vampire, the aristocratic Lord Ruthven, was a predecessor of *Dracula*, penned by Bram Stoker (1847–1912) in 1897. This was not the sort of literature likely to have been approved of by the philosophes.

True, there were lines of continuity between the Romantics and their Enlightenment predecessors. Both revered nature. Yet that common interest belied rather different approaches to the natural world. For the philosophes, nature was something to be understood, to be studied in order to perceive the natural laws that govern it. Earth's movement around the sun demonstrated Newton's laws of motion at work, laws regulating all the

planets. If the movement of Earth around its axis causes sunsets, then sunsets too are to be understood as products of scientifically understandable natural laws. But Romantics disdained this emphasis on reason in the understanding of nature. For them, nature was something to be experienced, not analyzed in order to identify natural laws. To experience a sunset in its majesty—its power and beauty—is a very different thing from producing a theory of sunsets. This contrast also points to another between Romantics and the philosophes: a concern with the particular (the Romantics) over the general (the philosophes). Better to appreciate the beauty of one sunset—to be ravished by its beauty—than to understand and predict sunsets, which is to understand individual instances as simply reflections of a general rule. Rapture might be said to be Romanticism's characteristic mood. This emphasis on experience over analysis and the particular over the general was also of a piece with Romanticism's de-emphasis on reason's authority. Indeed, Romantics were attracted to nature at its most wild, its most uncontrolled, not the sort of world one would expect from a rational "God the Clockmaker." The storminess of the scene of Shakespeare's *Macbeth* greeted by three witches, painted by Joseph Koch (1768–1839) in 1834–1835 (Figure 9.1) is an example—and has an appropriately supernatural subject.

Figure 9.1: *Macbeth and the Witches*, Painting by Joseph Koch of scene from Shakespeare's *Macbeth* (1834–1835)

A related contrast concerns attitudes toward change. The philosophes had been drawn to the constancies in the universe, such as the laws of nature. Objects might move on earth or around the sun, but the laws of gravity and motion governing them were fixed eternally. Romantics, however, were drawn to the idea that the world and the things in it are in flux (and so unique and not part of some eternal pattern). They saw everything as always changing—and not only changing, but developing. This was the century that saw history, the story of development over time, become well established as a university discipline.

Such change was pushed forward by spiritual forces embedded in developing things—a protest against the mechanistic views on which the Scientific Revolution had been built (see 7.5). The philosopher Johann Gottfried von Herder (1744–1803) wrote of nature that "the more we learn about matter, the more forces we discover in it, so that the empty conception of a dead extension [i.e., material world] completely disappears.... All that we call matter is more or less imbued with life."[2]

Germany was a leading center of Romantic thought, so it should not be surprising that the German term *Geist*—spirit—was often applied to such forces. Regarding history, Georg Hegel (1770–1831)—more on whom in section 9.5—wrote that "the principle of *development* . . . is based on an inner principle . . . [which] is essentially the spirit."[3] Not only might a thing's *Geist* direct its development, but it was to its *Geist* that it owed its particular character. Such a *Geist* could be compared to Herder's hidden forces. On this basis, God was no longer a clockmaker but the great *Geist* of the universe that drove it continuously forward. Herder identified the forces in matter with the divine.

Tradition came to be viewed more positively. It both expressed a people's *Geist* (more on this soon) and reflected an unconscious wisdom. The Irishman Edmund Burke (1729–1797) expressed these views early on. Burke was appalled by the violence of the French Revolution, which he came to see as rooted in attempts to overthrow tradition in the name of reason. Burke argued that human reason was only of limited use as a guide for society—at best, reason was what bright people happen to think in their own fleeting present. Custom, on the other hand, represented the slowly accumulated experience of many generations. Hence, although custom was not certainly always right, it was more likely to be right than reason, which, after all, represented the thought of only one generation, the present generation. Moreover, to follow custom meant to avoid extremes, whereas reason could dictate radical change; Burke allowed that one might depart from tradition, but the wise would do so only in small increments. Hence, where the philosophes attacked the authority of tradition, Burke defended it. Burke's attachment to tradition was a harbinger of the Romantics of the nineteenth century. Herder, perhaps not surprisingly, collected folk songs—handed down from one generation to the next, they manifested the *Geist* of the nation. Indeed, folklore of various sorts came to be celebrated in the nineteenth

---

2   Johann Gottfried von Herder, *God, Some Conversations*, trans. F.H. Burkhardt (Indianapolis: Bobbs-Merrill Company, 1940), 105, 172.

3   G.W.F. Hegel, *Reason in History: A General Introduction to the Philosophy of History*, trans. Robert S. Hartman (Indianapolis: Bobbs-Merrill, 1953), 68–69.

century. The efforts of the Brothers Grimm, Jacob (1785–1863) and Wilhelm (1786–1859), who preserved fairytales such as *Snow White*, were one result of this movement.

A new, more positive attitude toward the Middle Ages also points to Romantic influence. Whereas philosophes had criticized the Middle Ages as an age of faith (see 8.2), Romantics celebrated it for the same reason. In fact, although some Romantics were deists, many embraced organized religion, Christianity specifically. And where Locke had defended Christianity as rational, Françoise-René, vicomte de Chateaubriand (1768–1848), defended it by seeing virtue in its irrationality: "There is nothing beautiful, pleasing, or grand in life but that which is more or less mysterious."[4] The nineteenth century saw a "Gothic revival," as public buildings and private homes were built to look like medieval churches in a style that the Enlightenment had labeled "barbaric" (see 8.1). England's new parliament building, started in 1836 (see Figure 9.2), was resplendent in Gothic decoration even if it was built to up-to-date nineteenth-century engineering specifications.

Figure 9.2:
Parliament Building, Great Britain (commenced 1836)

---

4   Viscount de Chateaubriand, *The Genius of Christianity or the Spirit and Beauty of the Christian Religion*, trans. Charles I. White (Baltimore: J. Murphy, 1856), 51.

9.3 NATIONALISM: THINKING ABOUT THE NATION IN THE FIRST HALF OF THE NINETEENTH CENTURY

The nineteenth-century West was searching for a sense of community. How could people feel a connection with others? Answers were needed, and they were found. One was nationalism, the belief that people are essentially bound to their nation and should serve it. Of course, that answer raises a question: what is a "nation" anyway? The usual answer in the nineteenth century, especially in the earlier nineteenth century, was that a nation is a people who share a common language and common customs. Thus, living under the same government did not make people a nation. For example—an important example ca. 1800—Germans spoke a common language and shared common customs (a fondness for sausages for breakfast, for example), but they did not live under a single government. Rather, Germans lived under various governments, from tiny Hesse to large Prussia (Map 9.1); some Germans lived under rulers who also ruled many non-Germans, such as those in the Austrian province of the Habsburg lands (see 8.5.2).

Of course, this definition of "nation" was not really fully satisfactory even in the nineteenth century. Americans and Britons, for example, largely shared a language (English) and could also be said to have shared customs (by the end of the century, having Christmas trees, for example). But Americans and Britons did not commonly see themselves as a single nation, although some were tempted to do so. In the middle of the century, peoples of the provinces of what is now Canada did not agree as to whether they made up one nation or several. Perhaps the provinces were nations, not Canada. And what customs counted? Germans, after all, invented Christmas trees, but putting up Christmas trees did not make Britons or Americans German. Nations could also decide they were not nations. During the American Civil War (1860–1865), American southerners decided that, English-speaking or not, they were not the same nation as northerners. Perhaps it's best to conclude that a nation can be defined as "a group of people who consider themselves to be a nation." Even a "common language" could be something of a mirage: nineteenth-century Italians spoke dialects that were so various that, according to some estimates, as late as 1861, only 2.5 percent of the population spoke a language that could be clearly called "Italian." There is an arbitrary aspect to definitions of nationhood. Indeed, sometimes nations were thought of as being clumped into what one might call "supernations." The Slavic nations spoke related languages; a "Pan-Slavic" movement grew (especially in Russia), a movement that urged all Slavs—Czechs, Serbs, Poles, and Russians, for example—to stand together.

Arbitrary or not, nations were a matter of custom and language in nineteenth-century thinking. Another contrast with the Enlightenment of the eighteenth century is evident here. The philosophes of the Enlightenment had seen custom as the rust that obscured nature and reason. Custom was something to be overthrown or scrubbed off. Nineteenth-century nationalists saw custom much more positively, as that which made people part of a community. Language itself was a kind of custom; like custom, it evolved over time, handed down from one generation to the next. It was custom on the tongue.

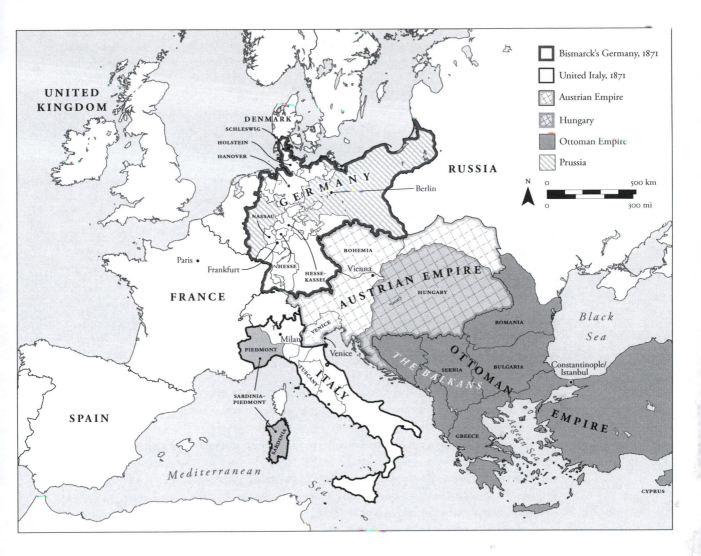

Map 9.1: Europe in the nineteenth century (with unification of Germany and Italy and changes in the Balkans)

Indisputably, new nations could be especially self-conscious in their nationalism. In 1836, the Academy of Letrán was founded in Mexico in order to "Mexicanize" the country's literature and make it distinct from that of all other countries. In the search for a long-standing Mexican tradition, some turned, without too much effort, to the world of Mexico before the Spanish conquest.

Did in-born traits account for the differences between nations? Some certainly spoke of nations as "races"—a tendency that would become more marked in the later nineteenth century (see 9.6). Enlightenment thinkers had sometimes categorized humanity into races, most often, however, attributing such distinctions to differences in climate. Sometimes, nationalists applied the same thinking to nations. By the early nineteenth century, however, some racial thinking had come to see racial and national distinctions as hereditary.

A great deal of nationalist thought in the early nineteenth century was German. Perhaps the most influential of these proponents of nationhood was Herder (see 9.2), whose influence would run long in the nineteenth century. Herder asserted that humanity was not one massive, homogenous whole. Rather, the world was made of individual nations. Each such nation—in Herder's German, *Volk*—was different from the next, distinguished by special characteristics, a sort of personality that made it unique. This special national character was its *Volksgeist*, or "national spirit." On this view, Germans, Italians, the French, and the Chinese were different from each other not because they lived under different governments but because of their individual and special *Volksgeist*. That *Volksgeist* was expressed through a nation's language. The exercise of language, Herder argued, was a community activity and so defined the community. Embedded in different languages were different ways of thinking about the world—again a reflection of one's *Volksgeist*.

In one sense, Herder did assert a kind of human equality in his discussion of nationhood. He held that each nation made a unique contribution to a common human store of characteristics and so was to be valued. And he denied that some nations are superior to others. Like other nationalists, Herder assumed a special bond between a nation and the land it occupies, which could serve as another environmental explanation for the differences among nations. Given such ties to their own lands, nations could be expected to live peaceably together, not coveting the land of others. But Herder's assertion of the uniqueness of each *Volk* also cut against the Enlightenment's standardizing tendency of thinking in terms of human nature. Nationalists like Herder significantly encouraged people to think not in terms of what humanity has in common but in terms of the differences among nations.

Indeed, nineteenth-century nationalism can be termed a species of Romanticism. Like other Romantics, nationalists were more interested in the specific (this nation or that) than the general (humanity). Nationalists thought in terms of a *Volksgeist*, which not only gave a nation its unique character but also drove the development of the nation over time, just as *Geist* drove the development of other things (see 9.2). Also, both Romantics and nationalists tended to revere tradition, with nationalists seeing custom, built up over time, as an expression of the *Volksgeist* that revealed the character of the nation. The Romantic Herder who collected folksongs was also the nationalist Herder.

Romantic interest in the Middle Ages played a role here too. The Middle Ages was seen, with some justice, as the seedbed of nations, at least in western and central Europe. The languages (and other customs) that defined many of those nations were medieval creations. Spanish, French, and Italian, for example, evolved from Latin in the course of the Middle Ages. The Gothic revival was a vehicle for celebrating nationhood. When the British built a new parliament building to house what was for them their characteristic national institution, they built in the Gothic style (Figure 9.2). When Hungarians achieved a measure of national independence from Habsburg rule in 1867 (see 9.4.3), they did the same thing (see Figure 9.3).

To feel the *Volksgeist* was to feel the connection with one's nation. In this way, nationalism was not just a response to the emergence of Romanticism or even a variant of it.

Nationalism was a response to that need for a sense of community produced in the West by developments since the seventeenth century. Nationalists, like the Romantics, sometimes criticized the atomizing thought of the Enlightenment. A nation held together by a common spirit is very different from a society formed by people who had decided to make a contract with each other to do so. An atomized society encouraged and reflected a rootless individualism. That critique of the Enlightenment, and the nationalist response, would be powerful.

Figure 9.3:
Parliament Building, Hungary

9.4 NATIONALISM AND POLITICS: MOVEMENTS OF NATIONAL UNIFICATION AND INDEPENDENCE

If the true community was the nation, then the appropriate government for the nation was the "nation-state": a government that governed only members of one nation—and all members of that nation. Or so nineteenth-century nationalists concluded. Ca. 1815, there were some nation states in the West: France, Britain, and Spain have all been described as more or less nation states by this point. Many peoples, however, clearly did not live under a nation state. Italy was fragmented into a number of different states (Map 9.1); parts of it were under Habsburg domination, ruled from German-speaking Vienna. The same can be said of Germany (Map 9.1). The eighteenth century had seen Poland partitioned among Prussia, Russia, and the Habsburgs (see 7.4.3). Indeed, many people were governed by large, multinational empires. The various nationalities of the Balkans—Serbs, Greeks, Croats, Romanians, Bulgarians, and others—lived under Turkish (Ottoman) or Habsburg rule, as did the Hungarians.

German and Italian nationalists sought to unify their nations into nation states. These nationalists thereby became opponents of their current governments. Because those governments had set themselves against the French Revolution and all that it stood for (see 8.6), early nineteenth-century nationalists also tended to see themselves as heirs of the French Revolution and, with it, of the Enlightenment. In this way, although Romantic nationalism in certain important ways ran contrary to the Enlightenment (see 9.2), the nationalists of the first half of the nineteenth century were usually liberals (on liberalism, see 8.6). The nation states they envisaged were not the authoritarian (and often multinational) states of their own day. Instead, they agitated for governments based on certain Enlightenment principles: equality before the law, with power exercised by an assembly that was either democratically elected or (more usually) elected by property owners. Such a state—in the form of a constitutional monarchy or even a republic—would, it was hoped, emerge through a grassroots (and fairly peaceful) movement of the *Volk*, led by its better educated, middle-class elements. Of course, liberalism stood in tension with nationalism. Liberalism emphasized individual freedom and equal human rights founded in a common human nature, while nationalism focused on national differences and the individual as part of a community. Liberalism's stress on the authority of reason over custom ran counter to nationalists' stress on the authority of tradition. But this tension went unnoticed by many, perhaps most, nationalists in the early nineteenth century. This situation was not, however, merely the result of two separate groups, nationalists and liberals, allying against a common opponent, authoritarian non-nation-states. Instead, the urge to overthrow such governments made nationalism and liberalism appear to go hand in hand. Most nationalists *were* liberals.

Nationalism was thus politically explosive among people who did not live in nation states. The pull of the nation fed the movements for national independence in Latin America, where the various provinces of Spain's empire were coming to be seen as nations distinct from Spain (see 8.5.4). In south, central, and eastern Europe, nationalist movements similarly sought to overthrow multinational empires in favor of nation states.

This stress on rebellion is correct, but it can mislead. Nationalism could also be a more or less artificial creation of governments. In 1867, the disparate provinces of British North America were brought together in a Dominion of Canada—the better to encourage economic development, to reduce their cost to the British Empire, and to provide for a coordinated defense against the United States, newly strengthened after the North's victory in the American Civil War (see 9.4.6). It was only following this confederation that many Canadians came to see themselves as members of a Canadian nation rather than as one of several North American provinces, willingly or unwillingly part of the British Empire.

9.4.1 Greece

The Greeks were the first in Europe to rise up and create a new (more or less) nation state in the nineteenth century, one that included most of what is today Greece. Ca. 1800, that region had been ruled for centuries from Constantinople (Istanbul) by the multinational Ottoman Empire, dominated by the Turks. Greek speakers also lived in many other parts of the empire, while many others had emigrated to other parts of the West. Greeks' sense of identity as Greeks was not strong. Greek speakers called themselves many things—some even referred to themselves as "Romans," harking back to the old Roman and Byzantine empires. By contrast, they rarely called themselves "Hellenes," the term on which Greek identity had centered in the ancient world. Many Greeks served the Ottoman government. The commander of the Ottoman fleet that would attempt to suppress the Greek rebellion to come was himself a Greek.

But the Ottoman Empire was weakening. The sultan's hold on outlying provinces had slackened, as had his authority over the central government. Bandit leaders on the Greek mainland, as well as the local Greek officials who opposed them, were largely untouched by nationalism; nonetheless, they all looked to tighten control over their own communities. Greeks on the Aegean Islands (see Map 9.1), however, influenced by their seafaring ties to the West, were developing nationalist ambitions; they would provide the naval power critical to any rebellion against Ottoman rule. Along with Greeks living abroad in Britain, France, the United States, and other countries, the Greeks of the Aegean formed nationalist societies that sought an independent Greece (at first conceived as encompassing all the territory of the former Byzantine Empire). The term "Hellene" saw a quick revival as Greek nationalists looked back to what they saw as a glorious past waiting to be revived.

It was one of these societies, the secret "Friendly Society," that succeeded in sparking rebellion in 1821. Alexander Ypsilantis (1792–1828), the society's first president and a Russian army officer, began hostilities by leading armed rebels in an invasion from Russian territory. Victory also depended, however, on the cooperation of mainland Greeks with their own agenda, and this was not easily achieved. Moreover, although the Ottoman Empire was weak, it was not toothless. Intervention by Britain, France, and Russia, in the form of the destruction of the Ottoman fleet at the battle of Navarino (1827), helped bring the beginning of the end, and Greek independence was achieved in 1829 (see Map 9.1). But liberal nationalists were not the predominant group in the new country. The grip of local strongmen on the mainland was powerful, and most parties looked to foreign support from the countries that had intervened at Navarino. The new Greece, when it was not engaged in civil war, would not be the liberal state for which some, mostly expatriates and islanders, had hoped.

9.4.2 Serbia and Bulgaria

Other Balkan peoples were moving toward independence from Ottoman rule, heeding the call of either the *Volksgeist* or Ottoman weakness and helped along by the larger Western powers and their conflicts. As Ottoman power declined, Russia viewed the Balkans as a natural field for expansion, with the ultimate goals of gaining control of Constantinople—which long had a role in Russian identity (see 7.4.4)—and free egress out of the Black Sea. Austria, itself drawn to Balkan expansion, saw Russia as both a rival and a threat. By midcentury, Britain, concerned that Russian influence would threaten British interests in India and Egypt, came to regard support of the Ottoman Empire as vital to its interests.

To the north of Greece (see Map 9.1), Serbs had begun to rebel even before the Greeks. Supported by Russia, they achieved autonomy but, as a concession to Austrian fears, autonomy within the Ottoman Empire. In 1858, Romania was carved out of Ottoman territory. Romania, too, was to be an autonomous territory under Ottoman rule, but it looked to Russia for support. War between Russia and the Ottoman Empire in 1877–1878 promised a Russian triumph. Their backs against the wall, the Turks agreed to complete independence for Serbia and Romania—both under Russian influence. The Turks also accepted autonomy for a new province, Bulgaria, also expected to look to Russia. Britain, however, worried about this expansion of Russian influence, threatened war. At the Congress of Berlin in 1878 (see 9.9), Russia agreed to some curtailment of Bulgarian autonomy. Austria was compensated for Russia's increased Balkan influence with the control of the province of Bosnia, which would nonetheless remain technically within the Ottoman Empire. Britain acquired the island of Cyprus from the Ottoman Empire. Other powers gained influence in various provinces of the Ottoman Empire. As Ottoman power continued to slip, Bulgaria became independent in 1908.

9.4.3 Hungary

Austria, another multinational empire, also felt nationalist tremors in the nineteenth century. For centuries, the Habsburgs had ruled a collection of peoples with little in common except for the house of Habsburg (see 8.5.2). One of the largest of these nations was Hungary, long ago an independent kingdom but now governed from German-speaking Vienna. By midcentury, the situation did not sit well with increasingly nationalist Hungarians.

Revolution broke out in France in 1848. The restored Bourbon monarchy (see 8.6) was overthrown in favor of a republic. The sight of a king deposed in the name of "the people" naturally inspired nationalists in other countries. The fact that nationalism was aligned with liberalism helped make the connection (on that alignment, see 9.3).

In Hungary, the response to revolution in France in 1848 was a move to create a Hungarian nation state. The Hungarian Diet—the traditional assembly dominated by the nobility—declared that Hungary would henceforth be governed by Hungarians, although the Habsburg emperor would still be recognized as its king. Hungarian was to be the official language. At the same time, the Habsburgs' Italian possessions fell under attack. Rebels in another Austrian territory, Bohemia (roughly the modern Czech Republic) declared its independence and called a meeting of all Slavs (on Pan-Slavism, see 9.3). Riots broke out in Vienna.

The rebellions against the Habsburgs were put down. Although the central Habsburg administration fell into crisis, its armed forces did not collapse. The Habsburgs turned back the invasion of their Italian possessions. They restored their control in Bohemia. And Hungary, on the brink of independence, dissolved into civil war. That war's causes are revealing. The kingdom of Hungary included large ethnic minorities: Germans, Serbs, Romanians, and others. They resented the Hungarians' attempt to impose their language. The interests of nations could conflict; a multinational alliance of nationalists was easier when they were far from achieving their aims.

The Habsburg emperor had, under duress, made various promises to the revolutionaries. Now that the government was gaining the upper hand, the emperor abdicated to be replaced by his heir, Franz Joseph (1848–1916), who could more easily renege on these concessions. Franz Joseph finally retook control of Hungary by asking for Russian help. The Russians, fearing revolution, obliged in 1849 with an invasion of Hungary.

But Hungarians would gain a delayed victory. As the largest minority after the empire's Germans, their demands were hard to ignore. In 1867, Franz Joseph, under pressure because of his defeat by Prussia (see 9.4.4), conceded a large measure of autonomy in internal affairs to a Hungarian government in Budapest. Representatives of the parliaments in Vienna and Budapest would meet periodically, and the two governments' militaries, foreign policies, and finances would be one. Thus a "Dual Monarchy"—an Austro-Hungarian Empire—was created. It satisfied all but the most extreme of Hungarian nationalists.

Other nations of the empire—Czechs, Serbs, Romanians, and others—found these developments less satisfactory. By the end of the nineteenth century, some of these groups would achieve their own nation states—almost. As has been seen, Serbia and Romania were carved out of Ottoman territory. In both cases, however, these nation states were incomplete: many Serbs and Romanians continued to live under Habsburg rule. So did virtually all Czechs, who did not even have a state of their own outside Habsburg territory to provide greater hope of national independence.

9.4.4 Germany

Germany also became a nation state, or largely so, in the course of the nineteenth century. Although the settlement of the Congress of Vienna confirmed Napoleon's consolidation of the "German Confederation" into a smaller number of states in 1815 (see 8.6), that nation was still far from being a nation state; thirty-nine states are many more than one. Of these states, the two best positioned for leadership were Prussia, which had the most German territory, and Austria, led by the Habsburgs, Germany's traditional leaders.

German nationalists, like other nationalists in the earlier nineteenth century, dreamed of a liberal German nation state created from below (see 9.3). For them, as for other nationalists, the overthrow of the French monarchy in 1848 was electric. Germans demanded liberal reforms, such as a free press and power exercised by representative assemblies. Indeed, their governments, observing events in France and the Habsburg Empire, suffered a collective failure of nerve; even the king of Prussia, Frederick William IV (1840–1861) abandoned his capital of Berlin, leaving it to protestors. Middle-class German liberals met in Frankfurt to lead their countrymen to the promised land of a united Germany. The resulting Frankfurt National Assembly set to work on a written constitution, which was to include a limited monarchy with real power in the hands of an elected assembly. Echoing the French Revolution's Declaration of the Rights of Man and Citizen, the assembly produced a Declaration of the Rights of the German People, a liberal, but as the title also indicates, nationalist, document.

The composition of the assembly proved its undoing. True, hope that all classes would join together in a wave of nationalist feeling was high. Carl Schurz (1829–1906), then a university student, remembered the Frankfurt National Assembly's early days as a time when an "enthusiastic spirit of self-sacrifice for the great cause . . . pervaded almost every class of society with rare unanimity."[5] Professionals and professors (whom Schurz also recalled as "squandering in brilliant, but more or less fruitless, debates much of the time which was needed for prompt and decisive action"[6]) could not easily ally with working-class agitators. The latter by now often had socialist inclinations and so did not see their interests aligned with those of the middle class (see 9.5); the alliance between the National Assembly and the *sans culottes* of the French Revolution (see 8.5.3) was not to be repeated. Holding popular violence at arm's length, the Frankfurt National Assembly found itself turning to the king of Prussia for the use of force ultimately necessary for any government. The Austrian Habsburgs were the traditional leaders of Germany, but they also ruled a multinational state in which Germans were a minority. Prussia was a more credible protector of a movement to create a German nation state. The assembly offered the king of Prussia the imperial crown of a united Germany.

The king was not, however, prepared to pick up a crown "from the gutter," as he put it, a crown that came to him from a revolutionary assembly rather than by divine right. His own supporters, not to mention the heads of the other German states, had much to fear. A united Germany would mean the end of their own states. A liberal Germany would mean an end to their own power. Meanwhile, the Frankfurt National Assembly, having debated and dithered about whether Austria could be included in a united Germany, was at a loss. The various German governments, especially Prussia, recovered their nerve. Most of the assembly's members went home in defeat; the Prussian army threw the extremist rump out of town in 1849. Schurz fled the country, with many other "forty-eighters," eventually winding up in America.

---

5   Carl Schurz, *The Reminiscences of Carl Schurz* (New York: The McClure Company, 1907), 1: 126.

6   Schurz, *Reminiscences*, 1: 134.

The Frankfurt National Assembly's defeat did not, however, put an end to German nationalism. That was the (correct) conclusion of an unsympathetic Prussian nobleman, Otto von Bismarck (1815–1898). On the one hand, Bismarck was a traditionalist, who saw his mission as serving not the German nation but the Hohenzollerns, Prussia's ruling dynasty. On the other hand, Bismarck saw that nationalist feeling in Germany was strong. A united German nation might be inevitable. Furthermore, even if the Prussian monarchy were preserved, a liberal Germany threatened the dominant role of the nobility under the monarchy. What to do, in this situation? Bismarck decided that, if he couldn't beat them, he would join them. In 1862, he became the Prussian king's first minister, the chief architect of his policy. From this position, he, heretofore an opponent of German nationalists, undertook to strengthen Prussian leadership in Germany by allying with the nationalists. It is hard to know how far ahead Bismarck planned his steps, but this course of action meant that, if Prussia gained an opportunity to unite Germany, it would be positioned to create a united Germany in which liberalism would be restrained: a Germany safe for the Hohenzollern monarchy and Prussian nobility. If that was Bismarck's long-term plan, it worked.

The provinces of Schleswig and Holstein provided an opportunity (Map 9.1). Ruled by Denmark, the duchy of Schleswig had a large German-speaking population, while Holstein was largely German; both situations were bound to grate on German nationalists. Both, however, were considered distinct from the rest of Denmark and were governed separately. When Denmark announced that Schleswig was to be amalgamated with the rest of the kingdom, German nationalists agitated for both provinces to be transferred to a German ruler, the duke of Augustenburg. Bismarck, however, had other plans. Prussia declared war on Denmark in 1864, in cooperation with Austria; the two leading German powers would thus defend the German nation from Danish tyranny. The Danes were defeated easily in this "Second Schleswig War"; Prussia occupied Schleswig, and Austria occupied Holstein.

In going to war with Denmark on behalf of Germans, Bismarck gained some credibility with German nationalists suspicious of his conservative, anti-liberal tendencies. But if Prussia were truly to lead the other German states, Austrian influence had to be extinguished. In 1866, Bismarck used tensions over the administration of Schleswig and Holstein to go to war with Austria. This "Seven Weeks' War" was another easy victory for Prussia. Better equipped and using the advantage of rail transport, Prussian forces routed the Austrian army. Prussia's victory meant that now there would be only one great German power. Moreover, some of the states that had made the mistake of siding with Austria (Hanover, Nassau, Hesse-Cassel, and Frankfurt) were simply added to Prussian territory, along with Schleswig and Holstein. In this way, Germany inched toward unification—by being swallowed by Prussia.

Prussia would have the entire meal—save for the German-speaking part of the Austrian Empire—as a result of another war, this one with France. France was the bogeyman of German nationalists, who remembered their country's subjection to Napoleon (see 8.6). In 1870, Bismarck was able to manipulate France into declaring war on Prussia. The fact that France was now ruled by another Bonaparte, Napoleon III (1852–1870), who had come to power after the revolution of 1848, only heightened the feelings of German nationalists. All the remaining independent German states (excepting Austria, which remained neutral) felt compelled to ally with Prussia. At least they chose a winner. Prussia easily defeated the French armies, even capturing Napoleon III. The flood of nationalist feeling saw the Prussian king declared German kaiser, or emperor, in 1871. Bismarck became Germany's chancellor, charged with the day-to-day management of the government. A German nation state had been born. Alsace-Lorraine, descended from the Lotharingia that divided Germany from France in the time of Charlemagne's grandsons, was transferred from France to the new German Empire.

It was not, however, the nation state envisioned by earlier nationalists. In the first place, it had been created by force and from above by a preexisting state, not by some peaceful, grassroots movement as the Frankfurt National Assembly had attempted in 1848. Second, it was an empire ruled by the kaiser and his chosen chancellor. Bismarck did create a representative assembly, the Reichstag. He even had representatives elected by universal male suffrage, making it one of the most democratic assemblies in the West. But the Reichstag had little power. It might reflect public opinion, but power was in the hands of the chancellor, in turn responsible only to the emperor; otherwise, the government was dominated by the aristocracy. The new Germany was not a liberal Germany.

9.4.5 Italy

In the early nineteenth century, Italy was described as a "geographical expression": a peninsula of various states, not a nation state. Much of the North—Milan, Venice, and Tuscany—was part of the Austrian Empire. But like Germans and others, Italians felt the pull of nationalism. Liberal rebellion broke out in January 1848, in Sicily in the south, spreading north. Then the overthrow of the French monarchy, a source of combustion in Germany and Hungary, added fuel to the Italian fire. A crowd of 10,000 in Milan demanded an elected assembly, freedom of the press, and a militia made up of Milanese citizens; the Austrian military commander, unprepared for such a revolt, took his troops out of the city. The Austrian commander in Venice, fearing that his Italian troops were unreliable, surrendered; Venice declared itself an independent republic. The pope was driven out of Rome and a "Roman Republic" was declared. The head of the only native Italian dynasty ruling an Italian state, the king of Sardinia-Piedmont (henceforth referred to in this book as Piedmont), quickly conceded a liberal constitution to his subjects. He then tried to ride the storm by declaring war on Austria in an attempt to seize Austrian territory in Italy. Italian nationalists north and south marched to take part in a crusade against the Habsburg foreigners. Italy was falling into the grip of a nationalist fever. But the government in Vienna, bolstered by Russian aid, regained confidence. It defeated the Piedmontese invasion. French troops marched to Rome to restore the papal states, and the other Italian republics were suppressed. Liberal nationalism had failed in Italy as it had failed everywhere else.

In Italy, as in Germany, national unification would be directed from above. The Italian analogue to Otto von Bismarck was Camillo Benso, conte di Cavour (1810–1861), the chief minister of the king of Piedmont. Unlike Bismarck, Cavour was a nationalist as well as a liberal; the constitution conceded by the king in 1848 continued in force with Cavour's support. But Cavour determined that liberal uprisings, even in conjunction with action by little Piedmont, would not be enough to unify Italy. Piedmont would have to direct unification, using strategic alliances with major powers outside the country. Cavour maneuvered Austria into declaring war on Piedmont in 1859, surprising the Austrians by bringing his ally Napoleon III into the war. Defeated, Austria turned Lombardy over to Piedmont. Revolutions broke out in the other Italian states north of Rome, and their inhabitants voted to join Piedmont. In 1860, the kingdom of the Two Sicilies tottered from rebellion; its people voted to become part of Piedmont, the kingdom that was coming to be seen as the cockpit of an Italian nation. The king of Piedmont, Victor Emmanuel II (1849–1861), was declared king of Italy (1861–1878). The next few years would see further additions, guided by Cavour's approach if not by Cavour himself, who died in 1861. In 1866, Piedmont supported Prussia in its war against Austria (see 9.4.4); its reward was Venice. Prussian victory against France in 1870 (see 9.4.4) meant French troops could not be kept in Rome to protect the pope, so the papal states were added to the Italian kingdom, and the capital was transferred to Rome. Although Piedmont had had a liberal constitution, one should not mistake the new Italian kingdom for a democracy. Although an elected assembly was central to its political life, only a small portion of even the male population had the vote.

9.4.6 The United States

Unlike Germany or Italy, the United States began the nineteenth century politically united. But was the United States a "nation"? The answer was unclear. Americans referred to the United States in the plural—"these United States do" not "the United States does." Individual states sometimes asserted the right to nullify laws made by the central government, or even to secede from the United States altogether. Strong sectional conflicts threatened to tear the union of states apart. By the middle of the century, these conflicts centered on the issue of slavery. Much of the South's economy depended on slave labor, and even poor white southerners who could not afford slaves enjoyed free status in contrast with enslaved persons of African descent. In the North, however, a movement to abolish slavery was growing.

The election of Abraham Lincoln (1809–1865) as president in 1860 prompted the South to secede from the Union. Lincoln disapproved of slavery, although he was not committed to its abolition. But he was committed to preventing slavery's expansion into territories being settled by Americans in the West. Southerners saw that extension as essential to preserving slavery where it was—hence secession, and the beginning of the American Civil War (1861–1865).

Much attention has been given to the question of exactly why southerners sought to leave the Union. Much less has centered on why northerners like Lincoln sought to preserve it. Of course, the Union was preserved, so its existence seems natural, needing no explanation. But the question is worth asking: why preserve the Union? One reason was that, by the middle of the nineteenth century, many Americans had come to define themselves as a nation, and nations, nineteenth-century nationalists believed, should have nation states. According to this view, the United States was not simply a collection of states that had agreed to enter a union in 1789, when the US Constitution was adopted. Instead, the Union was the political expression of an American nation.

Consider, for example, the opening words of Lincoln's Gettysburg address (1863):

> Four score and seven years ago our fathers brought forth on this continent, a new nation, conceived in Liberty, and dedicated to the proposition that all men are created equal.
> Now we are engaged in a great civil war, testing whether that nation or any nation so conceived and so dedicated, can long endure.[7]

For Lincoln, America is a nation. Moreover, he asserts that this nation has a kind of *Volksgeist*—a dedication to liberty and equality. In this way, Lincoln and other Americans cast a universalist Enlightenment program—freedom and equality belong to all human beings because of their shared human nature—as a specifically American characteristic. The North fought the war to preserve this nation, to maintain its political unity—and, for Lincoln, to maintain and fulfill its character. To Lincoln, slavery, important as it was, was a secondary issue. He said that if maintaining slavery were required to preserve the Union, he would maintain it. Indeed, Lincoln was criticized for having a rather mystical attachment to the Union, just as Bismarck had viewed German Romantics' attachment to the German *Volk* coldly. But Lincoln the American nationalist won. After the war, the United States was singular, not plural.

9.5 CHANGE AND *GEIST* II: MARXISM

The nineteenth-century preoccupation with change and development marked thinking about society. Philosophers worked to understand how society had changed over time, as is evident in the work of the German philosopher Georg Friedrich Hegel (1770–1831). Karl Marx (1818–1883), in turn, fundamentally reworked Hegel's view of history to produce an account of society that would, in the long term, influence the political left more than anyone else's.

---

7   Henry Steele Commager and Milton Cantor, eds., *Documents in American History* (Englewood Cliffs, NJ: Prentice-Hall, 1988), 1 : 428–29.

Hegel, a product of the Romanticism of his time, was preoccupied by historical change. He produced a theory that history is divisible into clearly defined periods. Each period, according to Hegel, was characterized by a dominant idea, a *Zeitgeist*, or "spirit of the age." His emphasis on *Geist* showed Hegel's Romantic inclinations (for Romanticism and *Geist*, see 9.2). This dominant idea was a period's "thesis" (a point reminiscent of how an essay is dominated by its thesis). How does one historical period succeed another? Every age, according to Hegel, eventually gives rise to an idea that counters the dominant one, an "antithesis." The thesis and antithesis struggle with each other, until, eventually, they fuse together to produce a new idea, called a "synthesis." The emergence of such a synthesis heralds the beginning of a new period, one in which the synthesis serves as the new thesis. That thesis would eventually give rise to its own antithesis, and the cycle would continue. Hence, for example, one might argue that the dominant idea of ancient Greece and Rome was a rational understanding of nature, grounded in Greek philosophy. That thesis was eventually countered by a faith-based Christianity, which rejected the Greek philosophical tradition. The eventual synthesis was the scholasticism characteristic of a new period, the High Middle Ages, in which Christian thinkers endeavored to use Greek philosophy to bolster their faith.[8] This process of thesis giving rise to antithesis, leading to a synthesis, was termed by Hegel the "dialectic," like a dialogue between two parties.

Marx argued that Hegel was right in some ways. History did evolve over time, and through dialectic. But, as Marx put it, Hegel also had to be turned on his head. Hegel had gone wrong in thinking in terms of a dialectic of *ideas*. What mattered, according to Marx, was the relationship of people to the means of production—to put it crudely, who owns what. Marx argued that society in his own time was defined by conflict between two classes: industrial workers, or the proletariat, and the owners of factories, the middle class, or bourgeoisie. What separated these classes was their relationship to the means of producing industrial goods. The bourgeoisie owned the factories and the raw materials. The proletariat owned only their own labor. What made a person a member of one class rather than another was a person's relation to the means of production.

History, according to Marx, is largely—but not entirely—characterized by conflict between classes, between a dominant class and a subordinate one. Consider the periods into which Marx divided human history. First, there was primitive society. All things were owned in common. Primitive society, then, was a "classless society." After all, if everyone had the same relations to the means of production, everyone was a member of the same class; another way of saying this is that there were no classes. And if there were no classes, there was no conflict between classes.

But this happy state did not last. The classless society gave way to a new period of human history, slave society. Here, there were two classes, defined as classes because of their different relations to the means of production: slave owners, who owned everything

---

8   This example is for illustrative purposes only. It is not one that Hegel used, nor is it meant as an accurate assessment of the move from the ancient to medieval West.

(land, seed, tools, and the labor of slaves) and slaves (who owned nothing, not even their own labor). Slaves and slave owners naturally had contrary interests, so conflict between them was inevitable. The class structure of this society was its dominant characteristic—its thesis, in Hegelian terms. Note the absence of *Geist* here. The means of production, not some sort of spirit, determine the nature of an age.

The conflict between slaves and the dominant class of slave owners was the working of the dialectic, which eventually produced a new class structure (a synthesis) and so a new period: that of feudal society in which lords (the dominant class) owned the land and seed but did not quite own serfs (the subordinate class), who were nonetheless tied to the land and bound to work it.[9] The dialectic ground on. Conflict between these classes eventually produced, as a result of the French Revolution of 1789, a new society—bourgeois society—in which heavy industry dominated production and the bourgeoisie dominated the proletariat through its control of the means of production other than labor. In this way, for Marx, rather than a dialectic of ideas or *Geist*, the engine of history was "dialectical materialism"—the struggle over who owned what.

Although Marx's interest in change over time betrays the influence of early nineteenth-century Romantics such as Hegel, his dialectical materialism points to the influence of the Enlightenment too. For Marx believed that dialectical materialism was scientific. He believed it was scientific because he thought it flowed from the application of reason and observation to the study of history and because it rejected Romantic rubbish about *Geist* for what was down to earth and knowable. The image of Marxism as scientific would be part of its attraction and is evidence, if evidence were needed, that the Enlightenment tradition, in modified form, did not die with the eighteenth century.

Where was the dialectic headed? Marx believed that the struggle between the proletariat and the bourgeoisie would inevitably result in a successful revolution of the proletariat. That revolution would bring an age in which all things would be owned in common, therefore a "communist" society. Because everyone would enjoy the same relationship to the means of production, this society would also be classless and so unmarred by class struggle. It was this revolution that many on the political left would hope for over the next century and a half.

Marx's larger scheme of history will be familiar given the discussion presented in section 8.3. Just as philosophes of the Enlightenment replicated a Christian history that began in the garden of Eden, recounted a fall of humanity, and looked forward to another golden age, so too did Marx. Humanity started in an Eden-like classless society. The seizure by some of the labor of others—slavery—ushered in millennia of class conflict, but we can all look forward to a new golden age: not only a classless society but a classless society more productive than the first one because marked by industrial production. Like Christian and Enlightenment accounts of history, this story of humanity's past, present, and future gave history meaning. There was a happy ending toward which humanity was moving that

---

9   I am here explaining Marx's view of the Middle Ages and not necessarily describing medieval society as historians now see it.

gave present suffering a point. Marx argued that humanity inevitably must pass through each phase of history he identified; there were no shortcuts to paradise. This end point of history was part of Marxism's allure. It held out heaven to those on the political left without religion. And it did so as science.

But what about all the other things that preoccupy historians? What about art, philosophy, religion? What about the most common subjects of historical writing in the nineteenth century, politics and government? Marx argued that these are side-shows to the main event, the material dialectic. A society's fundamental structure was its class structure, determined by relations to the means of production. The rest—a society's laws, government, religion, art, everything—was what he called "superstruc-ture." Furthermore, a society's superstructure was merely a tool used by the dominant class in order to maintain its position and so a product of the fundamental structure. Did Enlightenment thinkers like Locke assert that the right to keep one's property was a human right? They did so to support the aristocracy and then the bourgeoisie, all those who owned property. Did nineteenth-century governments write and enforce laws to protect property? They did so because they served the interests of the dominant class; all government has always existed to serve the dominant class. Marx's analysis of reli-gion worked the same way. Christianity preached that troubles in this world do not matter because all that is important is the next. Thus, Marx concluded, religion works like a drug to reconcile workers to the misery of the factories and to discourage them from rebellion against the bourgeoisie. Come the Revolution, government, along with the rest of superstructure, would become unnecessary because no class would need it to retain power. A happy ending indeed!

Marx's focus on the needs of the working class also held appeal, in two ways. In the first place, Marx explained—at least to the satisfaction of many—why working condi-tions in the factories of the Industrial Revolution were so poor (see 8.7) as well as what had to happen to fix the situation. Second, Marxism addressed that need for a sense of community that marked the increasingly atomized society of the nineteenth century. Marx and his colleague Friedrich Engels vigorously criticized capitalist society in terms drawn from Romantic nationalists as a soulless, atomizing one (for Engels, see 8.7). What solution did Marx offer? It helps to understand that, according to Marx, an oppressed class could not rise up against its oppressor until the members of that oppressed class came to think of themselves *as* a class. Individuals of the bourgeoisie were able to over-throw the aristocracy when they came to identify with the bourgeoisie; workers would not overthrow the bourgeoisie until they identified with the proletariat. Marx called this identification "class consciousness" and argued that no class revolution could happen without it. Thus, Marxists believed that their movement had to be international. Workers the world over had more in common with each other than with the bourgeoisie of their own nations. Class consciousness, once developed, would be a powerful and interna-tional source of unity. In this way, Marxism offered a sense of community, but one that served as a competitor to nationalism. For nationalists, the nation was the community; for Marxists, class was.

9.6 CHANGE AND *GEIST* III: DARWINISM

Darwinism's impact in the later nineteenth century was similar to that of Marx. Both appeared to put a scientific seal on the earlier century's fascination with change over time. The theory of evolution by means of natural selection formulated by Charles Darwin (1809–1882) became orthodox among scientists very quickly. Yet the book in which Darwin announced his theory, *The Origin of Species by Means of Natural Selection* (1859), also shocked his society. It called into question two beliefs held by both the philosophes and the Romantics: the benevolence of nature and an inherent force of progress in it. Darwin later said that publishing his work felt like admitting to murder.

In fact, interest in the idea that plant and animal species had changed over time—evolution—preceded Darwin; it was a characteristic concern of an age preoccupied by change. Jean-Baptiste Pierre Antoine de Monet de Lamarck (1744–1829) argued early in the nineteenth century that species evolve over time. These changes were driven by two forces, according to Lamarck. One was adaption to the environment. The ancestor of the modern giraffe might have had a short neck, but, because giraffes fed on leaves on high branches, they stretched their necks to reach those leaves. Such giraffes then reproduced and passed on their slightly longer necks to their offspring.[10] The repetition of this process over generations had resulted in giraffes with long necks. But such evolution was not simply a response to environment. True to his time, Lamarck also held that species were driven to evolve by a "life force"—what others of his age might have been tempted to call a *Geist*—which pushed them to grow in complexity (and superiority) and thus to adapt to their environments. In 1844, Robert Chambers (1802–1871), too, wrote in support of the evolution of plant and animal species, also arguing that they achieved greater superiority over time. Although he caused some scandal by claiming that no divine force was present in species as they evolved, he nonetheless asserted that they did so as part of a divinely laid-down plan, an attitude that harmonized with the century's expectation of progress.

Hence, in one respect, Darwin's book *Origins of Species* did not fall on an unprepared public when it was published in 1859. Many were familiar with the notion that species had changed over time. Chambers's book had even been a best seller. Darwin's picture of an evolving nature harmonized with the nineteenth century's general interest in change over time. Nature was already being "historicized," and Darwin was following the trend.

What was shocking about Darwin was the mechanism he laid out by which evolution takes place: natural selection. He observed that some variety always marks the offspring of any living thing. Consider dogs. Not even puppies born of the same parents are identical; they are characterized by small, random variations. The puppies that survive to reproduce can pass those variations on to their own offspring. The puppies that do not survive will not. Variations that contribute to a puppy's survival will thus be more likely

---

10 This theory of heredity is known as that of "acquired characteristics" and is rejected by modern biology.

to be transmitted to the next generation than those that do not. Over time—millions of years—the variations so transmitted will mean a species changes, as a particular variation becomes the dominant form. Chihuahuas and German Shepherds may be a single species, but, should the breeds continue to develop in different directions, that might not always be the case.

Gone here is the idea of progress according to some plan or *Geist* inherent in nature. Instead, evolution is a matter of chance variations, some of which are "selected" by nature for survival, but selected unconsciously. Moreover, although Darwin believed that evolution was a process that led to improvement—he accepted the phrase "survival of the fittest" as a description of what he was talking about—others were not so sure. After all, a plant or animal might survive to reproduce because of chance rather than because it possessed a characteristic making it better able to survive. Darwin himself pointed out that species often retained useless parts, such as the shriveled wings carried by beetles that only crawl. And the planlessness of nature seemed to be underlined by the conflict at work within it. Darwinism highlighted a world of death as well as life, a world in which plants and animals were ruthlessly weeded out by competitors in a struggle for existence. Moreover, random variation followed by struggle—and so evolution—would presumably take place as long as there are living things with natural variations in each generation. There was no final, perfect state toward which evolution was moving. In the end, Darwinism was disturbing because it, more than any other scientific theory, seemed to undermine that belief in progress toward perfection that had underlain the Enlightenment and Christianity before it. At the same time, it opened the door to a planless, random universe. For a Darwinian, even God the clockmaker appeared to be dead.

Darwin's thought did not, however, pertain to the study of nature alone. His theories were soon applied by others to society as well, producing what has come to be known as "social Darwinism." After all, some reasoned, if some varieties of a species are fitter than others and so will ultimately survive in a struggle for existence, would this not apply to humanity as well? Some social Darwinists saw this competition in biological terms: social classes, nations, groups of nations (e.g., the "Nordic" nations of Germany, Scandinavia, and Britain), or races are biologically distinct; some are superior to others; winners would naturally take all in a scientifically determined outcome. Earlier tendencies to categorize humanity into races and to see nations as races (see 9.3) received a significant boost in the later nineteenth century; Darwinian thought played a role in this shift. Some social Darwinists thought in cultural rather than biological terms: national cultures, in particular, are distinct, and some cultures will triumph over others because of their superiority.

Social Darwinism, in one sense, extended earlier developments of the century. Nationalists had already promoted the idea that nations are unique and thus deemphasized the Enlightenment's notion of a universal human nature shared by all. The distance between social Darwinist and Enlightenment thought in this respect can be seen in the work of the Frenchman Georges Vacher de Lapouge (1854–1936), who believed the motto of the French Revolution of 1789—"Liberty, Equality, Fraternity" (see 8.5.3)—should be exchanged for "Determinism, Inequality, Selection." Social Darwinists added to this supposition a clear biological basis for such differences. Where an earlier nationalist such as Herder had been willing to think in terms of nations being different but equal, social Darwinists stressed that some nations are superior to others. In this way, nationalism came to be seen as scientific, as did racism.

9.7 THE NEW TOUGHNESS OF MIND

There was much continuity between the first and second halves of the nineteenth century. For example, nationalism remained powerful to the end of the century (and beyond). In one respect, however, a change in tone distinguishes the latter from the first part of the century. This new tone can be described as a self-conscious tough mindedness, a desire to think in hard, even ruthless, terms.

Marx's criticism of Hegel can be seen in this light. While remaking Hegel's vision of history, Marx accused his predecessor of excessive idealism. Real history, Marx argued, is the story of dialectical materialism, of class conflict over the means of production, and not of airy ideas such as faith and reason. Evolutionary thought made a similar transition. The rosy views of Lamarck and Chambers (both published before 1850) fell before the harsher account of Charles Darwin (publishing in 1859); a mindlessly competitive world explained the evolution of species, not some inherent, God-given drive toward progress. One way to describe the contrast between Marx and Hegel, on the one hand, and Darwin and his predecessors, on the other, was that these later-nineteenth-century figures were concerned with change without *Geist*. The Romantic assumption that change was to be explained by some spirit or force (see 9.2) was fading.

The nationalism of the early nineteenth century underwent this kind of transformation too. This change is most obvious in the emergence of social Darwinism, which stressed the competition among nations to survive. But it is also evident in the actual political experience of nations. After all, with the exception of the Balkans, the earlier movements to create nation states had tended to stress grassroots, peaceful unification from below resulting in a liberal, moderately democratic government. That was not, however, the actual experience of Italy or Germany, which were unified through force exercised from above. Bismarck himself drew the contrast. Speaking of German unification in 1862, he told his listeners that "Not to Prussia's liberalism but to her power is Germany looking... not by speeches and majority votes are the great questions of the day to be decided—that was the great mistake of 1848 and 1849—but by blood and iron."[11] The United States, too, saw extreme measures taken to defend a united nation state: a bloody civil war, which, until World War II, had the distinction of killing more Americans than all other US wars put together (see 9.4.6). Such tough-mindedness in the realm of actual politics should

---

11 Jonathan F. Scott and Alexander Baltzly, eds., *Readings in European History since 1814* (New York: F.S. Crofts and Co., 1930), 242.

probably not be seen as a response to social Darwinism. But it reinforced social Darwinist thought, serving as a demonstration that, for nations, existence requires conflict and that eggs had to be broken to make omelets. It seemed a blood and iron world.

9.8 IMPERIALISM I: MEANS

Five of the great Western powers went to war in 1914: Britain, France, Germany, Russia, and Austria. In 1917, the United States joined them. The conflict has become known as World War I (1914–1918) because so much of the world beyond Europe or even the West was involved. The chief reason for the war's global reach was that several of its participants were world powers when the war started, governing among them most of Asia and Africa. In 1914, Western countries ruled, directly or indirectly, some 84 percent of the planet's land surface (Map 9.2). The British Empire alone, from its small homeland off the coast of mainland Europe, governed a quarter of the globe (Map 9.2). In addition, some historians argue that Britain and later the United States enjoyed an "informal empire" over much of Latin America, as they exercised a great deal of influence in the region in order to protect their commercial interests, especially after ca. 1860 and the "Second Industrial Revolution" (see 9.10). Given their world domination, when the major Western powers went to war, the world went to war. Western imperialism—by which Western powers came to dominate the rest of the world—was at its high-water mark.

The imperial activity that led to this situation came in three broad phases. First was the conquest of the Americas by Spain, Portugal, Britain, and France in the sixteenth and seventeenth centuries. In the second phase, Western trading powers took over smaller territories in the seventeenth and eighteenth centuries, usually in order to establish merchant outposts in Africa and Asia. The emphasis on trade is highlighted by the fact that such conquests were not generally carried out by Western governments but by Western trading companies, which found that political control of territory promoted and protected their commercial interests. The most significant move of this sort was the conquest of Bengal (in what is now India) by Britain's East India Company. It began the expansion of British territory on the Indian subcontinent. Such conquests were encouraged by political divisions among the company's potential opponents. India had been a united empire in the seventeenth century but, by the eighteenth century, was broken into many independent states. The East India Company became adept at allying with one Indian state against another. The third phase of imperialism came in the nineteenth century, particularly accelerating in the 1880s. This last phase witnessed Western powers coming to dominate nearly all of Africa and Asia, and it is this phase that is my focus here.

What made it possible? How was the West able to seize so much of the world?

In some cases, Western states made imperial control easier by resisting the temptation to assert direct authority over the peoples of defeated states, a technique that, in a broad sense, had a long imperial pedigree. This indirect control was a particular feature of the

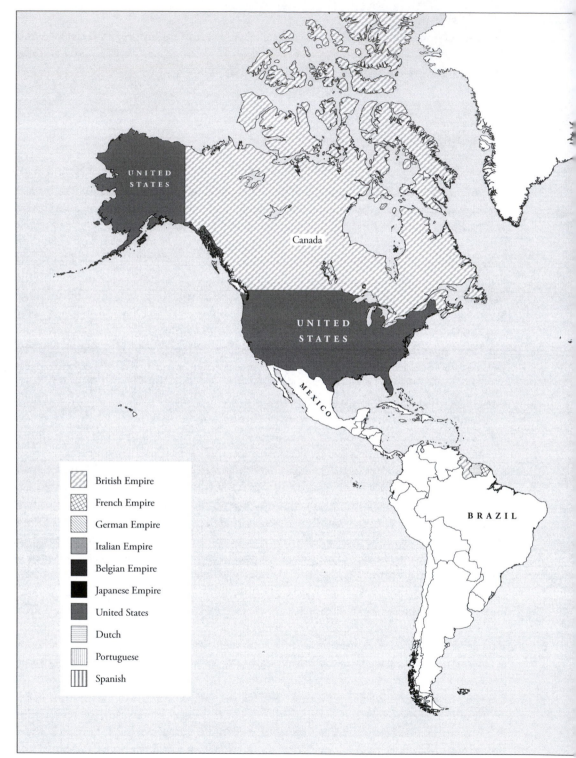

Map 9.2: Western world empires in 1914

British Empire
French Empire
German Empire
Italian Empire
Belgian Empire
Japanese Empire
United States
Dutch
Portuguese
Spanish

British Empire. In the eighteenth century, the East India Company had found it convenient to sign treaties with some of the states it defeated, leaving the rulers in those states on their thrones, some with greater autonomy, some with none. In the nineteenth century, the British government often followed the same practice. This form of administration was known as "indirect rule" and had several advantages. Indigenous people would more easily accept traditional authorities than foreign rule, and Britain could limit administrative costs. Kenya (British East Africa), for example, could be governed by one administrator for every 19,000 people. In some places, a colonial administrator might not see a colleague from home for months. In 1882, Britain invaded Egypt, technically, part of the Ottoman Empire but, in practice, an independent state ruled by its governor, the khedive; the khedive remained in place but was now subject to Britain. Two-thirds of British India was ruled indirectly. "Princes," rulers the British brought under their control rather than displace, governed small territories. Each was monitored by a British "advisor" prepared to call in British troops should his advice be rejected. Of course, where traditional authorities were weak, Britain could bolster them, making them more dependent on British rule. At the same time, of course, British power and influence meant that, even under indirect rule, non-Western societies were altered to suit Britain's requirements (see 10.9).

As technological change had fed the atomization of the West, so it also made possible Western imperialism. An example of this connection was the development of medical knowledge. Tropical diseases—to which natives of the region often had some immunity and Westerners had little—blocked Western penetration of much of the world at the beginning of the nineteenth century. The problem for Western powers is illustrated by the death rates of British soldiers sent to the coast of Africa in order to stop the slave trade. Two-thirds of those stationed in the Gold Coast in the years 1823–1827 perished as a result of disease. (One of the ways Britain managed to find sailors for this duty was by offering criminals the option of service there rather than punishment at home.) Various diseases struck down European visitors to Africa, an especially virulent form of malaria chief among them. In 1820, however, the drug quinine was first extracted from the bark of the cinchona tree, and, in 1830, large-scale commercial production began. Its use to ward off malaria through preventive doses spread in the 1850s.

The other technological component of imperialism's success was military. Starting with the Military Revolution of the early modern period (see 7.3), Western states had stewed in a pressure cooker of military competition with each other. By the middle of the nineteenth century, the constant search for military superiority had produced Western states armed with military technology far more devastating than that of the rest of the world. In the first half of the century, technical limits on the large-scale military use of rifles— more accurate and able to fire at longer range than the earlier musket—were resolved. By 1914, such rifles were, in terms of firepower, as superior to muskets as muskets had been to bows and arrows. The 1880s witnessed the widening use of reliable machine guns, such as the Maxim gun, an improvement on its predecessor, the Gatling gun. Such equipment gave an overwhelming advantage to even small numbers of Western troops facing opponents armed with muskets at best and swords and spears at worst. In Chad (Map 9.2) in 1899,

320 French troops defeated 12,000 men under the slave trader Rābih az-Zubayr, who also had 2,500 guns, but inferior guns. In the Sudan (Map 9.2), the British defeated a Dervish army at the battle of Omdurman (1898). The British lost 20 men, along with about 28 Egyptian troops. Their opponents lost 11,000 men. Such imbalances of firepower encouraged conquest by making it easy—so easy that even an insult to a minor official could lead to imperial conquest. One British naval commander, Commodore Lambert, was infuriated when a Burmese governor refused to meet with him to discuss British concerns over two British merchants who had been shaken down by Burmese. In 1852, Lambert attacked against orders, forcing his superiors in India to support him reluctantly in order to maintain British prestige. British victory swiftly followed. The result was, contrary to British policy, Burma's surrender of territory to British rule.

The critical nature of this technological advantage is also evident in Western imperialism's few failures. In the 1880s, Abyssinia (modern Ethiopia) was torn by civil conflict. Western arms manufacturers flooded the country with weapons. Eventually, Menelik II (ruler of Shewa, 1863–1889) managed to unify the country as emperor of Abyssinia (1889–1913), and he even proceeded to use his technological advantage to conquer neighboring territory. In 1896, however, Italy invaded Abyssinia. Italians expected an easy victory. They did not get it. Menelik's army, equipped with plenty of rifles and three machine guns, defeated the invaders in the battle of Adowa (1896); the country remained independent. Japan is an analogous case. Since the seventeenth century, Japan had largely shut itself off from Western contact, including Western trade. In 1853, the Japanese suddenly discovered their vulnerability to Western arms when the American Commodore Matthew Perry (1794–1858) sailed to the capital and, backed by gunboats, forced the government to open the country to American commerce. In 1868, in an effort to preserve Japan's independence from mounting foreign pressure, the Japanese began to Westernize their military and industry. By 1904, Japan's navy rivaled Western navies of a similar size. Japan's industrialization encouraged its designs on Manchuria and Korea, then ruled by a weak China (Map 9.2). Russia, however, also had ambitions there, resulting in the Russo-Japanese War of 1904–1905. The Russians discovered that Japan was not the usual, vulnerable Asian state. Russia sent its Baltic fleet to the Pacific, only to see it destroyed by the Japanese fleet. Defeated, the Russians accepted a brokered peace; Japan gained Korea and a position of influence in Manchuria. Abyssinia and Japan were exceptions that tested the rule. Western technology opened the door to Western imperialism.

9.9 IMPERIALISM II: MOTIVES AND ATTITUDES

But why did Western powers go through the door? Even at the time, people debated the motives of Western empire builders. In the end, it appears that different motives underlay different imperial adventures.

Sometimes economic benefits drew Western states to assert control over other parts of the globe. Foreign commercial practices, not understood by Westerners, occasionally interfered with Western trade. Western attempts to solve the problem were on Western terms, and brought Western political control. China is an example. By the early nineteenth century, British traders found themselves importing many goods from China, in particular, tea. The Chinese emperor, however, limited their activities to one city, Guangzhou (also known as Canton). That limitation flowed from the attitude of the emperor's government, which saw Chinese trade as a privilege that foreigners received in return for contact with the supreme ruler on earth, the emperor. Indeed, British merchants offered very little that interested the Chinese in return. As a result, huge sums of cash accumulated in Chinese coffers. For the British, trade was a means of generating wealth through exchange. Orthodox British liberals held that an unregulated market would do so most effectively; the limitation of trade to Guangzhou was not only inconvenient but contradicted Western practice and theory.

Then the British discovered that China was a potentially vast market for opium, which could be grown in British India. Opium exports to China came to balance British imports from China. The Chinese government, however, resisted the opium trade, fearing the effect of the drug on the population; one official began to confiscate British-owned opium and destroy it. To Britain, this move both threatened British commerce and violated property rights. The British government replied with force, sending in warships and troops and quickly defeating the Chinese in the First Opium War (1839–1842). China opened more than a dozen ports to Westerners, where they not only could trade but would also be subject to their own laws. Over the years, the emperors would—under pressure—open up further territory on similar terms to Britain and other Western countries, eventually also turning its collection of taxes on trade over to Western governments. China was becoming a de facto Western colony.

Belgium's African colony of the Congo is another case of imperialism driven by economic interests. The territory was not controlled by the Belgian government but was the personal holding of the Belgian king, Leopold II (1865–1909), a constitutional monarch. Leopold, in search of a good investment, sponsored the travels of the journalist Henry Morton Stanley (1841–1904) along Africa's Congo River in 1879–1884. Leopold's goal was to lay claim to the country and assess its commercial value. The Congo did indeed yield Leopold a profit, by the export of rubber in particular. Leopold's agents, however, lowered labor costs by virtually enslaving the population. The Congo became a byword for the abuses of Western imperialism. Reports of atrocities found their way out; the outcry in Belgium itself became so strong that, in 1908, the Belgian government seized control from Leopold.

In other instances, Western imperialism was a matter of prestige. Germany and Italy were latecomers as nation states (see 9.4.4 and 9.4.5). One way for them to assert their standing as great powers was to join the ranks of world empires. Italy took Libya and attempted to take Abyssinia too (see 9.8). Neither offered Italy much in terms of economic value. Similarly, Germany sought what Kaiser Wilhelm II (1888–1918) called its "place in the sun." Colonies of little economic use to Germany, such as German South West Africa (modern Namibia) were the result (see Map 9.2). Similarly, the United States, new as a major power beyond the Americas, bolstered its prestige by stripping Spain of the Philippines in the Spanish-American War (1898). But even well-established states, such as Britain and France, viewed imperial holdings as contributing to their standing among the great powers.

In the end, imperial conquest created a dynamic that made imperialism self-sustaining. Imperial powers began to acquire colonies to strengthen their hold on what they had or even to preempt possible rivals. Africa—especially the Congo—appeared to be a vacuum that would spark conflict among European states as they laid claim to this or that portion. The situation led Otto von Bismarck to call European powers to the Berlin Conference of 1884–1885. Bismarck's policy had been to maintain peace in Europe since Germany's unification; the scramble for Africa threatened that peace. At Berlin, Bismarck brokered the division of Africa into European colonies, setting ground rules for how Western powers could lay claim to African lands. Western powers would have actually to occupy territory militarily, not just establish commercial ties, before claiming territory in Africa. But the existence of such rules made it even more imperative for a would-be colonizer to act before others did. By 1900, European powers had carved up the continent, with the exception of Abyssinia (which fought off the Italians) and Liberia (occupied by freed slaves and their descendants from the United States). The Berlin Conference was both a symptom and an accelerant of imperial conquest resulting from imperial competition. The attitude of the French politician Jules Ferry (1832–1893) shows how concerns for prestige and the need to preempt rivals in a competitive world worked together: "Our country must place itself in a position to do what all the others are doing . . . [or be] reduced to third or fourth class."[12]

In other cases, attempts to stave off competition led Western powers actually to support non-Western ones. For most of the nineteenth century, many expected the Ottoman Empire to collapse; after all, its weak control over its Balkan provinces (see 9.4.1 and 9.4.2) had earned it the description "the sick man of Europe." For most of the nineteenth century, however, British policy was to support the empire, fearing a rush by Western powers—in particular, Russia—to seize its various territories, a competition in which Britain might not fare too well. Better to keep the empire more or less intact and exercise influence with its government. In 1898, China's government, which, as has been seen, had already made many concessions to Western countries, bowed to further pressure and surrendered more territory. A now-powerful Japan threatened to carve up large parts of the country, as did Russia, which, because it bordered China, was in a better position to deploy troops there than were other Western powers. The United States, fearful of being shut out, announced an "Open Door" policy in China in 1899: China would remain an independent country with its own government, and merchants of all countries could trade freely within it and not be blocked by other powers. This approach suited Britain as well.

---

12 Quoted in Ronald Hyam, *Understanding the British Empire* (Cambridge: Cambridge University Press, 2010), 120.

Thus, the Open Door policy saw China supported by some Western governments because of the inconvenience should it collapse.

In the eyes of many in the West, their dominance of most of the rest of the world was justified by Western superiority. Of course, most people assume the superiority of their own culture over that of others. In 1793, the Chinese emperor met demands to open up more ports to the British—barbarians, in his eyes—by commanding they desist and obey in fear. And, certainly, Western people could draw on very old Western stereotypes of the Asian East as both despotic and servile. But, in the nineteenth century, Western attitudes toward the rest of the world hardened. The British in eighteenth-century India had been fairly open to the civilization and people they ruled; they were interested in the study of classical Hindu works and mixed fairly freely with the subcontinent's population.

This relative openness changed in the nineteenth century. Several factors fed this development. The religious revival of the time was one (see 9.2). Confident Western Christians set out to convert the world. William Wilberforce (1759–1833), best known today for campaigning against slavery in the Americas as anti-Christian, saw India as a land of violence and superstition; England had a duty to introduce there not only its religion but also its law and government. Western missionaries would become very active in the non-Western world, encouraging conquest and working to Westernize as well as Christianize their inhabitants. The mere fact of Western dominance also, unsurprisingly, bolstered a sense of superiority.

The social Darwinism of the later part of the century also sharpened the assumption of Western superiority and appeared to justify Western imperialism. After all, if all peoples are in competition and if only the fit will survive, then the conquest by the fit of the less fit is only natural. Imperial rule was as natural as evolution. Such views could take various forms. The French spoke of their *mission civilisatrice*, their "civilizing mission," to bring French customs, law, and culture to the peoples they ruled. Such explicit cultural imperialism was less often official policy in other empires, but certainly the idea was to be found elsewhere. These views assumed that the defeated could, at least with time, adopt the culture of their conquerors. The superiority of the imperial power could also, however, be seen in racial—that is, biological—terms, as a case of whites versus the rest, which was also quite consistent with social Darwinist thinking. Some authorities assumed that native Americans, as an inferior people, would eventually simply die out. Some argued that Westerners should undertake the rule of others for their own good. In 1899, Rudyard Kipling (1865–1936), born and raised in British India, summoned Americans—then a white majority—to accept in their new colony of the Philippines what he believed the British had long borne in their own empire:

Take up the White Man's burden—
Send forth the best ye breed—
Go bind your sons to exile
To serve your captives' need;

To wait in heavy harness,
On fluttered folk and wild—
Your new-caught, sullen peoples,
Half-devil and half-child.[13]

Such attitudes were evident in Britain's empire when it came to colonies where white settlers were dominant. Eventual home rule was expected in territories such as Australia and Canada, and it came, although sometimes only after pressure from white settlers. Home rule was less often contemplated for the other colonies.

9.10 REFORM, STATE, AND PEOPLE

The Enlightenment's faith in the possibility of progress did not die with the eighteenth century. For if it was anything, the nineteenth century was a century of reform. In the first part of the century, nationalism and antislavery campaigns dominated. Nations without nation states directed reformist energy into movements for national unification or independence. Britain saw a flourishing antislavery movement. The British navy attempted to cut off the slave trade to the Americas in the 1830s and 40s by patrolling the coast of Africa.

Other causes gained greater prominence from ca. 1850. The midcentury saw increasing campaigns for women's equality in Britain and the United States. Both of these movements tended to draw support from the middle classes. Socialism, however, which also grew in strength later in the century, was geared to working-class interests. Socialists argued that, in one way or another, wealth should be redistributed to guarantee workers a minimal standard of living. Socialists of various stripes—from union leaders, who tended to concentrate on immediate benefits such as safer working conditions, to the radical Karl Marx, who advocated revolution (see 9.5)—met in London in 1864. There, they formed the International Working Men's Association, better known as "the Internationale," in order to work for such causes on an international basis. (Marx came to dominate the organization, just as stronger or weaker versions of Marxism came to be the common heritage of the left by the end of the century.)

These reform movements had their roots in more than one strand of Western thought. Certainly, Enlightenment notions of human equality and human rights played a significant role. But so, too, did a movement at odds with the Enlightenment, the religious revival of the later eighteenth and nineteenth centuries (see 9.2). As his Christian duty, William Wilberforce (see 9.9) fiercely campaigned against slavery; he was rewarded by learning on his deathbed that Parliament had outlawed the slave trade.

---

13 Rudyard Kipling, *Rudyard Kipling's Verse: Definitive Edition* (Garden City, NY: Doubleday, Daran, and Company, 1944), 321.

Reform movements fed each other. Susan B. Anthony (1820–1906) is best known today as a founder of America's "first wave" of feminism, which stressed the right to vote. Early in her career, she took part in the Seneca Falls Convention of 1848, which echoed Jefferson's Declaration of Independence (see 7.7): "We hold these truths to be self evident: that all men and women are created equal; that they are endowed by their Creator with certain inalienable rights; that among these rights are life, liberty, and the pursuit of happiness."[14] But Anthony first achieved prominence in the temperance movement to ban alcohol; she also vigorously supported the abolition of slavery. It was no coincidence that the same people were often active in the same movements. Both slavery and women's inability to vote offended belief in human equality. Temperance was seen as a women's issue because male drunkards often abused their wives when they did not abandon them. Orthodox Marxists favored women's equality—not to mention racial equality—arguing that women's subordination in the family was one more aspect of the evils of capitalism, and other socialists often followed suit.

Women's groups—such as the International Council of Women formed by Anthony and others in 1888—came to have a special role in reform in the later part of the century. The French Revolution had put women more firmly in the private sphere, although that goal was never, perhaps could never be, fully achieved; in their most radical phase, the eighteenth-century revolutionaries had banned women's organizations (8.5.3). But, by the middle of the nineteenth century, women's departure from the public sphere had come to give them a special moral authority. They served their families as angelic mothers and wives and, in doing so, served the nation that was increasingly important in the nineteenth century. Lacking power and their own economic interests, they were uncorrupted—unlike men. Or so the argument went. Hence, reform as promoted by women had the peculiar power that powerlessness sometimes confers. When it came to women's rights, feminists worked toward goals that varied, from the vote to entry into the universities to property rights.

As has been seen, the later century also saw the flowering of social Darwinism (see 9.6). This development took its place among the period's reform movements. For if peoples were biological groups, the argument went, then they could be improved by careful breeding, just as one improves a breed of dogs or cats. Thus was born what the era called a new science: eugenics. Persons with hereditary disabilities should be discouraged from reproducing. How far such disabilities extended was up for debate. Many eugenicists were particularly concerned that the lower classes of the nation were so because of biological inferiority. The explanation was held to account for various distinctions between the middle classes and those below them. After all, the latter generally suffered more from disease, were relatively uneducated (because presumably uneducable), and a dispropor-tionate source of crime. The eugenics movement harmonized with others. By the early twentieth century, the feminist and socialist American Margaret Sanger (1879–1966), who

---

14 Henry Steele Commager and Milton Cantor, eds., *Documents of American History* (Englewood Cliffs, NJ: Prentice-Hall, 1988), 1: 315.

advocated birth control as a way to give women more control over their lives, also did so because it offered a way to stop bad characteristics from being passed on to the next generation. Thus, the nation would be improved. The later nineteenth and early twentieth century's emphasis on competition also directed reform efforts toward strengthening society's competitiveness in other ways. The Boy Scouts originated in Britain (1908) as a means to prepare men with the skills to serve the empire and, in particular, to win the war that seemed to be coming.

As the century progressed, governments, too, embraced a reform agenda. The state attempted to shape society, an effort that greatly increased the size of government. The number of civilian government employees doubled in Germany in the last third of the nineteenth century; it quadrupled in Britain. Perhaps the most far reaching of these efforts concerned education. In 1800, most schooling was private, still in the hands of some religious denomination or other. Increasingly, however, governments sought to provide first primary and then secondary education to the entire population. Toward the end of the century, such education was not only free but mandatory. This offered several advantages. Public schools could shape attitudes. In nation states, students could be molded into better nationalists. When Italy was unified, for example, Italians spoke such varied Italian dialects that it was hard to say that all Italians spoke the same language—despite the fact that language was generally seen as a characteristic of nationhood (see 9.3). Government schools, however, taught a standard version of the language, making Italians into Italians. Governments similarly sought to inculcate good citizenship—as governments defined it.

At the same time, governments saw in education a path to economic development. Here, it should be noted, states were increasingly taking on the responsibility for actively fostering prosperity. Economic growth, it seemed, required citizens who could read, write, and compute. Free and compulsory schooling would serve this need. This drive affected higher education as well. At the beginning of the nineteenth century, the humanities and theology dominated university curricula. Aside from medicine, science was usually secondary. A university education was for gentlemen, not to prepare men—and universities accepted only men—to make a living. (The major exceptions were the study of law, medicine, and, for clergy, theology.) The second half of the century saw governments change this orientation. In part, this development was to deal with new economic demands. The age saw the emergence of a "Second Industrial Revolution." Whereas the original industrial revolution had been based on steam power, the second stressed electricity and the gasoline-fueled internal combustion engine. To the first's focus on mechanical devices such as the spinning jenny (see 8.7), the second added advances in chemistry, which now produced everything from new dyes to TNT. But the new stress on chemistry and electricity meant that science and technology were now to be closely aligned; the amateur tinkerer was becoming a relic of the (first) Industrial Revolution. Businesses set up formal research and development offices, to be staffed by trained scientists and engineers. The self-taught Thomas Alva Edison (1847–1931), who invented the first practicable electric light bulb and the phonograph, was becoming a such relic. Even Edison's General Electric Company became the home of formal research laboratories employing university-trained professionals. Universities, with government encouragement, began to offer more courses of study in the natural sciences and also in applied sciences, such as engineering and agriculture—never before university subjects. But universities are often conservative institutions; it was often easier to establish new ones than to push older ones onto new tracks. And so new universities, with a more technical and scientific focus and founded under government auspices, sprang up beginning in the middle of the nineteenth century. In the United States, the trend became evident in the passage of the Morrill Act of 1862, which sought to provide colleges to foster agriculture, engineering, and—another field of interest to the state—military science. The research of such institutions would uncover the knowledge needed for economic development (and military preparedness), while the teaching in such institutions would disseminate that knowledge. University enrollments surged. Between 1850 and 1910, the number of university students in the Austrian Empire nearly quadrupled; in France, they nearly tripled; in England and Wales, they increased twenty fold.

Universal primary education, in particular, could create controversy. Taking children out of their parents' supervision for hours a day meant that government now touched a new, intimate area of family life. The schools thus tended not just to reflect society's conflicts but even to magnify them, especially ethnic ones. In North America, conflict between black and white was played out in the question of whether black and white children would be schooled together. (In the segregated American South, they would, by law, not be.) In Hungary, newly autonomous within the Austro-Hungarian Empire, would students be taught in Hungarian or in the languages of the country's various ethnic minorities, such as Serbian? The Hungarian government, seeing an opportunity to Magyarize (i.e., "Hungarianize") non-Hungarians within the kingdom, chose Hungarian, producing a grievance for minorities. Common public schools, today taken for granted, still can set off controversy (now also taken for granted) over other matters.

In embracing reform, governments also had other targets. Those states that lacked elected assemblies generally got them in the course of the nineteenth century. And where assemblies were already elected on a limited franchise—an inheritance from the Middle Ages—that franchise was usually widened. In other words, the overall trend was toward democracy—at least, a democracy of white men, which, although not likely to be seen as democratic today, marked an enormous expansion of the political nation compared with previous practice. This development is remarkable. Even the most authoritarian governments in the later-nineteenth-century West sought the fig leaf of popular approval. (So have most governments since.) In the United States, this limited democratization came early, with the franchise extended to all free (white) men, not just those with property, by 1829. In Britain in 1832, the first of a series of "Reform Bills"—the "Great Reform Bill"—extended the electorate and made parliament more representative by, for example, eliminating "rotten boroughs" (see 7.1). Bismarck's Germany also had an imperial parliament, or Reichstag, elected by universal male suffrage. Such assemblies were a general characteristic of Western governments by the end of the nineteenth century. (Russia finally got a representative assembly—the Duma—in 1906.) Various forces account for this phenomenon. Enlightenment notions of legal equality encouraged the spread of the right to vote and encouraged people to agitate for it. Where such assemblies already had real power, political parties competed for advantage by promising to extend the right to vote, hoping that new voters would support the party that had so favored them. In this way, the British Conservative (or Tory) Party, traditionally opposed to extending the vote, passed its own Reform Bill in 1867, further extending the franchise. Governments sometimes created electoral assemblies and spread the vote because they feared the possibility of violent revolution unless they made such concessions. Here, France played a special role as an example of what could happen—in 1789, 1848, and again in 1870. The Russian tsar, it should be noted, conceded the Duma only after an abortive revolution in 1905–1906. Such democratization was also limited. The vote itself was still restricted, most notably to men. Moreover, even if assemblies were elected, that did not mean they had real power. Bismarck's Reichstag, for example, was toothless; it registered public opinion but did little else. The Latin American republics were largely oligarchies or dictatorships. Among the larger Western powers, only the elected assemblies of France, the United States, Britain, and the white-dominated "dominions" of the British Empire (e.g., Canada but not India) held powers extensive enough and had electorates wide enough to qualify as democracies of some sort in 1900.

As the nineteenth century drew to a close, governments also sometimes embraced part of the program of the socialist left in order to preempt its appeal. Germany is the classic case. Like just about everyone else in a position of political power in the nineteenth century, Bismarck was a convinced antisocialist (as well as antidemocrat). After the unification of Germany, he tried to organize an international alliance against the Internationale. Bismarck had hoped that a powerless Reichstag based on universal male suffrage would tamp down the left, including the socialist left, in Germany, leaving power in the hands of the monarch and nobility. He banned socialist parties from putting up candidates for political office, only to see socialists elected without any official party affiliation. Bismarck also legislated measures designed to show workers that a benevolent, monarchical nation state would do more for them than socialist agitation or revolution. Hence, under Bismarck, German workers began to receive government health insurance. Disability and accident insurance, limits on the employment of women and children, as well as pensions for the aged followed. Other Western states implemented some of these measures. For example, Britain and some states in the United States limited the labor of women and children, and Britain instituted old-age pensions.

But if governments in the hands of the right were nervous at the end of the century, many of their leftist opponents were becoming either less effective or less radical. There were various reasons for this. Feminists found that their movement was a largely middle-class and even aristocratic one; it was, in the language of the time, more for ladies than women. The movement attracted a minority of all women but especially few working-class women, who had concerns other than the vote and admission to universities. An alliance between feminist and workers' movements foundered on the domination of the latter by men. Labor unions, for example, were interested in limiting women's work, especially in better-paying factory jobs. Such limits cut down on the competition men faced in the labor force, especially as women were usually paid less than men. Moreover, working men were attracted to the model of the middle-class family, in which husbands earned wages and wives kept the home and children.

Furthermore, nationalism in the hands of politicians such as Bismarck was captured from the political left by the political right. And nationalism had undoubted appeal for many, including working class people.

In fact, winning elections put socialist parties in difficulties. Some socialists debated whether even to run for office. After all, their goal was not to be part of the political system, but to overthrow it. In the end, however, the lure of a legislative seat was too great. Once in office, however, socialists had to manage the system as all politicians do and make the compromises that all politicians make. In this way, electoral victory at least partly domesticated socialism. When World War I—that nationalist crusade (see 10.2)— began, all socialist parties across Europe, parties that were, of course, committed to an international community, nevertheless supported their national governments. Although the claims of socialists to define community according to class were gaining, nationalist claims were stronger.

9.11 THE CRISIS OF THE FIN DE SIÈCLE: MODERNISM AND POSTMODERNISM

Historians sometimes refer to the turn of the nineteenth and twentieth centuries (ca. 1880–1914) by the French phrase the *fin de siècle*, "the end of the century." In terms of the arts, the West entered a kind of crisis in which old traditions and attitudes no longer seemed satisfactory. It was a crisis in which Enlightenment ideas about reason and individual freedom appeared to be in conflict with each other and in which Romantic and Enlightenment concerns fused in an apparently unstable way. This crisis was largely confined to the educated: the kinds of people who usually went to the theater, art exhibitions, and concerts and read cutting-edge literature; its real impact was largely confined to a minority even of them. But, following World War I (1914–1918), the movements produced by the crisis of the fin de siècle would grow in influence: these were modernism and postmodernism.

What do these terms mean? It is necessary to begin with a terminological puzzle. It may seem odd that both modernism and postmodernism were born at the same time. After all, the "post" in postmodernism implies that modernism came first, postmodernism afterward. And, indeed, it is the case that the influence of postmodernism waxed in the decades following ca. 1960 while that of modernism waned. But, arguably, the two movements nonetheless both ran throughout the twentieth century. The "post" in postmodernism refers more to the fact that postmodernism was a kind of twist on modernism than to the time at which each emerged.

Like Romanticism, "modernism" is hard to define.[15] As the nineteenth century drew to a close, artists and writers felt that the now old, liberal ideals were not so satisfactory. Reason and observation did not seem to be the royal road to truth, although many in the sciences still followed this path, as people had during the eighteenth-century Enlightenment. In this dissatisfaction with Enlightenment ideals, the influence of the Romantic revolt against reason (see 9.2) is evident. At the same time, however, modernists broke from the nineteenth-century Romantics' attachment to tradition and the nation (see 9.2 and 9.3). How to find truth? With reason, observation, and tradition blocked, it was a very difficult question to answer. The frustrations inherent in trying to find truth under such circumstances account for the characteristic mood of modernism: *angst* (German for "anxiety"). If—to generalize—the mood of the Enlightenment was confidence and that of Romanticism was rapture, the mood of modernism was anxiety, if not downbeat sobriety. Modernists wanted to find truth, but they just did not know how.

One manifestation of the movement is evident in the first wave of what is called "modern" (i.e., modernist) art, "expressionism." Here the break with tradition is evident. Echoing Greece and Rome, Western artists since the thirteenth century had sought to render more or less realistic portrayals of the world as it really is, the world of the senses.[16] Even the impressionists of the 1870s and 80s, who had seemed artistic revolutionaries, attempted to capture the impact of the light they saw with their eyes. But could one rely on the senses? Could one rely on (artistic) tradition? The expressionists thought not. So they turned inward, using what they saw around them as a kind of language to express a different kind of truth, a truth not in the world but deep within the mind of the artist. Thus, art "expressed" (literally meaning "pushed out") something within rather than reflected the world without. Consider the *Three Women* (1907–1908) painted by Pablo Picasso (1881–1973). The work is somber and less a representation of what Picasso's senses perceived in the world than it is an application of his senses to represent what was in his head (see Figure 9.4). Such tendencies were taken further in the course of the twentieth century with "abstract expressionism," in which all reference to the world outside the artist's mind disappeared. *White Center* (1957) by Mark Rothko (1903–1970) is an example (Figure 9.5). Of course, with less and less of an external world to share, the truth such work expressed became less and less clear to any viewer other than the artist.

In architecture and design, fields in which modernism would be increasingly evident after World War I, the search for this new kind of truth and the rejection of tradition were manifested in attempts to find the "real" building and the "real" object. In other words, the aim was to create buildings and objects that were purely functional, with all embellishment stripped away. Such embellishment in the nineteenth century had usually been a way of evoking the traditional past. Nineteenth-century railway stations, for example, had been

---

15 Readers should note that "modern" is itself used variously by historians (see 7.0 and 9.1).
   Whatever those definitions, "modern*ism*" most usually refers to the developments starting ca. 1900 referred to here.

16 For an example, see Figure 6.1.

Figure 9.4 (left):
Pablo Picasso, *Three Women* (1907–1908)

Figure 9.5 (right):
Mark Rothko, *White Center* (1957)

designed to look like medieval cathedrals or classical temples. Countering these habits, Ludwig Mies van der Rohe (1886–1969), perhaps the most influential of modernist architects, worked according to the motto "less is more."[17] His Tugendhat house, completed in 1930, is a typical product of the approach: boxy, undecorated, with walls of flat glass to reveal structure as plainly as possible (Figure 9.6).

Modernism was also manifest in the rise of the philosophical school known as "existentialism." The old Enlightenment order had relied on reason and observation to identify natural laws that worked according to cause and effect. The existentialists, however, concluded that such an approach might be not only unjustifiable but, worse, a threat to something else valued by Enlightenment thinkers and Romantics too: individual freedom.

Developments in the sciences—the prime heirs to the Enlightenment's emphasis on reason and observation—help explain such fears. In the late nineteenth and early twentieth centuries, psychology was a developing field, and researchers in it sought to account for human behavior, even madness, usually by pointing to physical aspects of the brain. But if mental states are products of biology, then are human beings truly free? Even investigations of insanity that rejected a biological approach seemed to raise the question. Sigmund Freud (1856–1939) argued that people have an unconscious life as well as a conscious one. Experiences that the conscious mind forgets, and would prefer to forget,

---

17 Quoted in Edward Relph, *The Modern Urban Landscape* (Baltimore: Johns Hopkins University Press, 1987), 191.

are still remembered by the subconscious, and through it, these experiences continue to shape what we do. Crazy behavior—neurosis—is caused by such forgotten yet remembered feelings and experiences. Freud argued, for example, that a nineteen-year-old female patient had repressed from her conscious mind a sexual interest in her father. What she was aware of, however, was her bizarre effort to ensure complete silence at night so she could sleep. She feared that vases left on her bedside table would fall and break on their own, so she insisted they be moved to her desk at night. The fear of breaking vases was, in Freud's view, a worry about sexual intercourse. Thus, even neuroses and nightmares had rational explanations. And human nature—the rules by which the mind works, interacting with experience—accounts for who we are and what we do. The unconscious mind that Romantics had embraced as a source of individual freedom was itself the individual's master, operating according to rules identifiable by science. As Freud remarked, "even the delusional ideas of the insane would certainly be found to have a sense if only we understood how to translate them."[18]

Another apparent threat to individual freedom emerged in the fin de siècle: what came to be called "mass society." The mass production of goods brought by industrialization appeared to undermine the individuality represented by traditional handicrafts. The democratization of the age seemed to move in the same direction. As the number of

---

18 Sigmund Freud, *Introductory Lectures on Psychoanalysis*, trans. James Strachey (New York: Norton, 1977), 257.

voters increased, political parties were growing to enormous sizes, counted in the tens and hundreds of thousands of members and threatening to swamp decision making by individuals. Human beings were, some suspected, becoming a herd.

Existentialists produced a philosophy to counter such developments.[19] They asserted the radical freedom of the individual. We are what we choose to be by choosing to act. Not "You are what you eat" but "You are what you do" might be a good existentialist motto. Thus we are what we choose at each moment of our existence, and each moment of our existence is divorced from the moments that come before and after. To say that we are formed by earlier experiences—like Freud's patients—is to say that we are prisoners of our pasts. We are not, existentialists insisted. As Jean-Paul Sartre (1905–1980), a leading existentialist of the new century, put it, "Freedom is the human being putting his past out of play."[20] So, too, freedom put mass society out of play.

In making decisions, in making themselves, what should guide the individual? Reason? Tradition? God? The question itself was nonsensical for existentialists. The point is to be not guided by anything because being guided means surrendering freedom. There is no moral compass to direct the individual. Similarly, there is no end or goal to which individuals or, for that matter, history is moving. Like other modernists, existentialists, not surprisingly, rejected the West's traditional belief in progress, in the idea that human history has meaning (see 8.3 and 9.5). Darwin might agree (9.6). Human existence is free but, for that reason, also pointless. The sense of angst produced by such conclusions is evident in the question asked by the existentialist Albert Camus (1913–1960): why should one not commit suicide? Angst indeed.

Postmodernism, however, can be described as modernism with a happy face. Postmodern art and thought, like modernism, accepted the absence of objective truths that would hold good for all. But postmodern thinking about language took modernism further by arguing that the very idea of objective truth was a sort of accidental illusion. This position was rooted in postmodern ideas about language.

In what has been called Western civilization's "linguistic turn," postmodernists asserted that all ideas are a product of one's language rather than language being a product of one's ideas.[21] After all, if asked what a word means, one will respond with some other word or words. And if asked what those words mean, one will respond with yet more words. So a language is a system of signs, of terms that refer to other terms to create a web of meanings. Words get their meaning from how they relate to other words—that is, from the larger language—and not (crucially) from some sort of reality outside language. Hence the conclusion of Ferdinand de Saussure (1857–1913) that "without language, thought is a

---

19 The terms "existentialism" and "existentialist" would, however, be coined only in the mid-twentieth century.

20 Jean-Paul Sartre, *The Philosophy of Jean-Paul Sartre*, ed. Robert Denoon Cumming (New York: Random House, 1965), 116.

21 This was something of an echo of the nominalism of the Late Middle Ages but was not derived from it.

vague, uncharted nebula. There are no pre-existing ideas....”[22] Moreover, these thinkers argued, cultures are simply a kind of language, a system of signs in the broadest sense. Saussure himself pointed the way, noting that, when a Chinese bowed nine times to his emperor, he was using a kind of language to recognize who that enthroned figure was.

So why the happy face? Postmodernists concluded that truth was off the table, so the restless, angst-ridden, modernist search for it was pointless. Because the very concept of truth itself is simply a product of our language and culture, it is no more true than

Figure 9.7: Roy Lichtenstein, *Brushstrokes* (1965)

---

22 Ferdinand de Saussure, *Course in General Linguistics*, trans. Wade Baskin (New York: Philosophical Library, 1959), 112.

Figure 9.8: University of Houston's College of Architecture Building (1984–1986)

language or culture. The result for many postmodernists was not gloom, but relaxation. If even the idea of truth is not true, why worry about it?

For postmodernists, the mysteriousness of abstract expressionism—what exactly is being said?—could be taken to confirm the meaninglessness of the modernist quest. But, if art could not reflect some truth outside the artist (as Western artists had traditionally sought to do) and could not reveal some truth within the artist's soul (as modernists sought to do), what was left? Art could be about art, just as language was not about reality or truth, but about language. Postmodern artists produced work that aimed to remind viewers that they were looking at art and not through the window of art at the real world or into the artist's mind. One way to send that message was to produce art that simply referred to itself. An example of this self-referential approach is a 1965 painting by Roy Lichtenstein (1923–1997)—a painting of brushstrokes (Figure 9.7). Another means is quotation. In art, quotation involves artists incorporating other styles in their work so as to highlight that these *are* other styles, things brought into the work from outside. Again, Lichtenstein's *Brushstrokes* illustrates this effect. The painting uses the sort of repeated dots associated with comic books. The self-referentiality and quotation also tend to have a jokey feel.

Lichtenstein highlights this effect by quoting a cheap, popular form, comic books, in work destined for a well-heeled collector or museum. Irony and humor would be the dominant mood of postmodernism, a contrast with modernist angst. Compare the sobriety of Picasso's *Three Women* (Figure 9.4) with Lichtenstein's work.

Postmodern architects similarly turned away from purely functional buildings toward the quotation of earlier styles and decoration. Robert Venturi (1925–) replied to Mies van der Rohe's injunction with "Less is a bore,"[23] itself a joke built on the work of others—the kind of allusion so admired by postmodernists. The University of Houston's College of Architecture building (1984–1986), designed by Philip Johnson (1906–2005), shows the mood (see Figure 9.8). A building whose Roman arches and flat surface recalls the Romanesque structures of the earlier Middle Ages, it wears a reproduction of a Greek temple like a hat. The combination reinforces the fact that both are quotations. The obvious use of the "hat" as pure embellishment rejects the modernist drive for pure function.

In the years leading up to World War I, however, neither modernism nor postmodernism was characteristic of the thought of most people in the West. To them, the West, the world's dominant civilization, was on the path toward progress. Rationalism and science, the Enlightenment's legacy to the West, were now in the service of increasing technological advances and the reform of society. Romantic sensitivity to feeling was appreciated, but contained. After the war, many people, especially middle-class liberals, would look back at the fin de siècle as the "*belle époque*," the "beautiful age."

FURTHER READING

Baumer, Franklin L. *Modern European Thought: Continuity and Change in Ideas, 1600–1950*. New York: Macmillan, 1977.

Bayly, C.A. *The Birth of the Modern World, 1780–1914: Global Connections and Comparisons*. Oxford: Blackwell, 2004.

Blanning, T.C.W., ed. *The Nineteenth Century*. Oxford: Oxford University Press, 2000.

Breuilly, John. *Nationalism and the State*. Chicago: University of Chicago Press, 1994. [Theoretical as well as historical.]

Bumsted, J.M. *A History of the Canadian Peoples*. 4th ed. Oxford: Oxford University Press, 2011.

Burrow, J.W. *The Crisis of Reason: European Thought, 1848–1914*. New Haven, CT: Yale University Press, 2000. [Not for beginners.]

Burton, Orville Vernon. *The Age of Lincoln*. New York: Hill and Wang, 2007.

Bushnell, David, and Neill MacAuley. *The Emergence of Latin America in the Nineteenth Century*. 2nd ed. Oxford: Oxford University Pess, 1994.

---

23 Robert Venturi, *Complexity and Contradiction in Architecture* (New York: Museum of Modern Art, 1977), 17.

Cannadine, David. *Ornamentalism: How the British Saw Their Empire*. Oxford: Oxford University Press, 2002.

Chadwick, Owen. *The Secularization of the European Mind in the Nineteenth Century*. Cambridge: Cambridge University Press, 1975.

Chaudhuri, Nupur, and Margaret Strobel, eds. *Western Women and Imperialism: Complicity and Resistance*. Bloomington, Indianapolis: Indiana University Press, 1992.

Curtin, Philip D. *The World and the West: The European Challenge and the Overseas Response in the Age of Empire*. Cambridge: Cambridge University Press, 2000. http://dx.doi.org/10.1017/CBO9780511840098.

Diamond, Jared. *Guns, Germs, and Steel: The Fates of Human Society*. New York: W.W. Norton, 1998.

Eley, Geoff, and Ronald Grigor Suny, eds. *Becoming National: A Reader*. Oxford: Oxford University Press, 1996. [Historical and theoretical studies.]

Frederickson, George M. *Racism: A Short History*. Princeton, NJ: Princeton University Press, 2002.

Fuchs, Rachel, and Victoria Thompson. *Women in Nineteenth-Century Europe*. New York: Palgrave Macmillan, 2005.

Gaggi, Silvio. *Modern/Postmodern: A Study in Twentieth-Century Art and Ideas*. Philadelphia: University of Pennsylvania Press, 1989.

Heartney, Eleanor. *Postmodernism*. Cambridge: Cambridge University Press, 2001. [Concerned with postmodernism in art.]

Hobsbawm, Eric. *The Age of Empire, 1875–1914*. New York: Pantheon Books, 1987.

Hobsbawm, Eric. *Nations and Nationalism since 1780: Programme, Myth, Reality*. 2nd ed. Cambridge: Cambridge University Press, 1992.

Marx, Karl. *Selected Writings*. 2nd ed. Edited by David McLellan. Oxford: Oxford University Press, 2000.

Rapport, Michael. *1848: Year of Revolution*. New York: Basic Books, 2008.

Rapport, Michael. *Nineteenth-Century Europe*. New York: Palgrave Macmillan, 2005.

Steinberg, Jonathan. *Bismarck: A Life*. Oxford: Oxford University Press, 2011.

Weber, Alan S., ed. *19th Century Science: A Selection of Original Texts*. Peterborough, ON: Broadview Press, 2000.

Wills, Garry. *Lincoln at Gettysburg*. New York: Simon and Schuster, 2006.

FROM CA. 1914 TO THE PRESENT

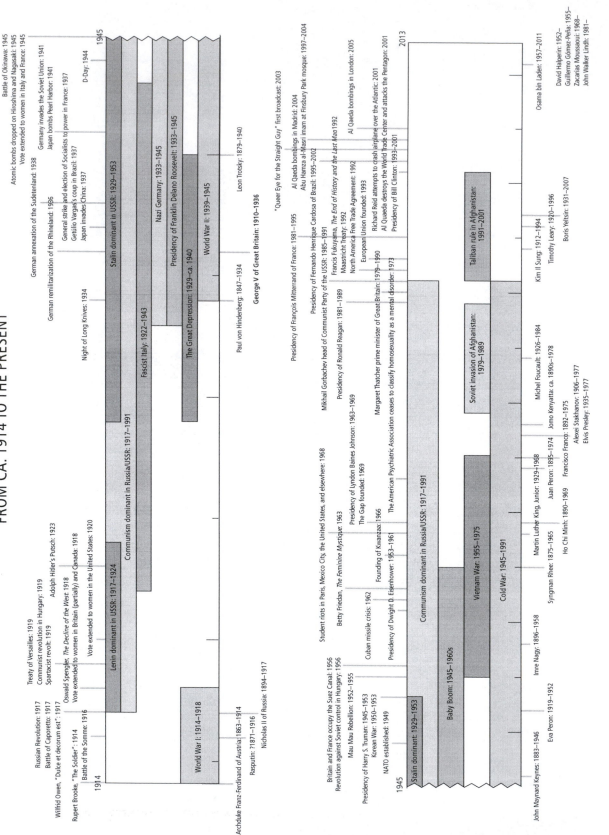

TEN

FROM CA. 1914 TO THE PRESENT: THE SEARCH FOR COMMUNITY, GLOBAL CONFLICT, AND THE HARVEST OF THE MODERN WEST

10.1 FUNDAMENTALS: STATE AND COMMUNITY

The twentieth century—and, so far, the twenty-first—harvested the fruits of the nineteenth. The question of how to find a sense of community and overcome an atomized society dominated the nineteenth century, which produced two solutions to the problem: nationalism and Marxism. Both would be major forces in the twentieth century. Nationalism led to two world wars and overcame premature death notices to survive into the twenty-first century. For much of the twentieth century, Marxism served as the official ideology of a number of states and characterized much of the political left even where it failed to take power. Moreover, these forces spread far beyond the West to influence the non-Western world; ultimately, nationalist and Marxist movements outside of the West succeeded in breaking up the Western empires that had governed the globe on the eve of World War I. The modern world still searches for a sense of community. The globalization of ca. 2000 is increasing this urgency and is making community harder to achieve.

Governments also grew more powerful. This development was not just a nineteenth-century story but one that had begun at least as early as the seventeenth century; recall the rise of absolute monarchies. The late nineteenth century, however, saw states taking on new tasks as they attempted not just to govern but to shape their societies. That trend continued in the twentieth century, most notably in fascist and communist regimes but in democracies as well. The twentieth century would also, however, see attempts to reverse such developments.

Changing technology also continued to shape society and politics. The industrialization that began in eighteenth-century Britain continued to spread. Newer weapons and methods of warfare gave the world wars of the twentieth century their distinctive characters and would influence their aftermath. Developments in communication and information technology would help shape that century and the next.

10.2 THE GREAT WAR

When I was in high school (in the 1970s), people speculated about when World War III would start. World wars seemed expected, events to be numbered. That was not so in 1914. Those who lived through World War I (1914–1918) called it the "Great War," not "great" as in grand but "great" as in big. "The big one" seemed without precedent in its destruction: nearly 10 million servicemen (and a very few servicewomen) dead, twice as many injured, many so disfigured they wore masks for the rest of their lives. The losses were so great they skewed the demography of nations. In France, for example, half the men aged 20–32 at the start of the war were dead by the end of it; young women in the 1920s found marriageable young men in short supply.

What caused the war? People disagreed about the answer even before the war ended; historians have disagreed ever since. Nationalist passions arguably played a significant role. In 1914, Europe was largely divided into two systems of alliances. On the one hand was the Triple Alliance of Germany (by far the most powerful member), Austria-Hungary, and a not very committed Italy. With the exception of Italy, which initially declared neutrality, these countries became known during the war as the Central Powers; they were joined by the Ottoman Empire and Bulgaria. Facing them was the Triple Entente. It included France, Russia, and the British Empire. With the addition of Japan, a formal ally of Britain's since 1902, and Serbia, Belgium, and Luxembourg, which were brought into the war by unfolding events, these countries (and the others who joined them after 1914) became known during the war simply as the Allies. The war would bring victory to the Allies, which managed to wear down the Central Powers before they themselves faced collapse.

How did these alliances lead to war? Nationalism in the Balkans turned out to be critical. Serbs longed for a fully realized nation state, one bringing together all Serbs, indeed, all Slavs of the Balkans (for Serbia, see 9.4.2). For that to happen, however, the provinces of Bosnia and Herzegovina, populated by many ethnic Serbs, would have to be taken from Austria-Hungary. Serbian agitation had long worried Austria-Hungary, which feared that such nationalist passions would tear its empire, a patchwork of nationalities, apart. In June of 1914, the Archduke Franz Ferdinand (1863–1914) visited Sarajevo, the Bosnian capital. Franz Ferdinand, the heir to the Austro-Hungarian throne, advocated giving Slavs, including Serbs, a larger role in the empire, then dominated by Germans and Hungarians (see 9.10). He was a perfect target for Serbian nationalists; as the future emperor, he symbolized the oppressor, and his preferred policies might reconcile Serbs to Austrian rule, threatening the creation of an enlarged Serbia. Members of the secret Serbian nationalist society called Union or Death—also known as the Black Hand—plotted to assassinate him. One succeeded, shooting the archduke as he was driven through town in an open car. The archduke cried out to his wife, also wounded, "Sophie, . . . live for our children." Neither realized that their deaths would be the first of millions.

The plot had been hatched in Serbia with the cooperation of Serbian military intelligence, although without the rest of the government's approval. The Austro-Hungarian government, still headed by the now very old Emperor Franz Joseph (see 9.4.3), saw in the incident an opportunity. A short war with little Serbia—the empire had ten times Serbia's population—would quash Serbian pretensions and firm up the empire's eroding prestige. The Austrians delivered an ultimatum: Serbia was to cooperate fully in apprehending and punishing all responsible for the archduke's death, even allowing the empire's officials to operate in Serbian territory. It was also to suppress all anti–Austro-Hungarian groups and publications. The hope was that Serbia would fail to accept all these demands—which it did—thus opening the door to war.

The danger here for Austria-Hungary was Russia. Russia had been tied to Serbia since Serbia's independence (see 9.4.2). Support for Serbia not only furthered Russian aims of countering Austro-Hungarian influence in the Balkans but also appealed to Pan-Slavic feeling (see 9.3) in Russia. Russia's Tsar Nicholas II (1894–1917) emphatically supported Serbia. The Austro-Hungarians asked their ally Germany whether they could count on support against Russia as well as Serbia. The Germans feared that their one reliable ally needed a triumph against Serbia. They also calculated that Russia's growing power would be more easily checked now than in the future. Germany guaranteed Austria-Hungary its support. A conflict between Russia and Germany naturally brought in Russia's ally, France, itching to undo the humiliation of its loss of Alsace-Lorraine in 1870–1871 (see 9.4.4). And Britain, fearing a continent united under German domination should Germany defeat France and Russia, entered the war too. In this way, the system of rival alliances, conjoined with a nationalist conflict in the Balkans, sparked war among the greater European powers, the first general war on the continent since Napoleon's defeat in 1815. This war would be fought as a nationalist crusade, and governments both encouraged and catered to nationalist passions. In Russia, the German part of the capital's name, the "burg" in Saint Petersburg ("city of Saint Peter"), was changed to the Russian "grad" to form "Petrograd" ("Peter's city"). The British royal family changed its name from the house of Hanover, of German origin, to the unimpeachably English house of Windsor.

This war was far deadlier than earlier conflicts. Since the seventeenth century, states had become increasingly powerful, able to marshal more and more resources for war (see 7.3). These efforts escalated during the Great War as governments became desperate to achieve victory. They regulated their economies and industries to serve a single aim: victory. Luxury production was curtailed by government order; exports were cut off in

ICELAND

NORWAY

SWEDEN

UNITED
KINGDOM

DENMARK

THE
NETHERLANDS

Berlin

GERMAN EMPIRE

BELGIUM

LUXEMBOURG

AUSTRIA-
HUNGARY

Munich

FRANCE

SWITZER-
LAND

BOSNIA-
HERZEGOVINA

Sarajevo

RUMANI

THE

SERBIA

PORTUGAL

ITALY

BALKANS

BULGAR

SPAIN

MONTENEGRO

ALBANIA

GREECE

TUNIS
(French)

MOROCCO
(French)

TRIPOLITANIA
(LIBYA)
(Italian)

RIO DE ORO

Map 10.1: World
War I: Allies and
Central Powers

order to keep supplies at home. Governments assumed wide powers to command resources. In Germany, for example, a shortage of the nitrogen needed to produce explosives led the government to ransack the country for the supplies, including animal manure, needed to make it. The resources commandeered by governments included people. Even Britain, which had long avoided the draft, instituted one during the war. Greater government control meant more men and more time, energy, and money devoted to war, and so greater destruction. The fighting in France consumed more ammunition in a day than had all the weapons used in the whole of the Franco-Prussian War of 1870–1871. Battlefields became so saturated with shells that live bombs are still found there.

The particular technology of war also had an impact. By the early twentieth century, the West had developed lethally effective missile weapons: powerful artillery; easy-to-reload, accurate rifles; and rapid-fire weapons, such as the machine gun. These developments, however, had outstripped the ability of soldiers to move quickly over the field of battle. Traditionally, this movement had been managed by mounting soldiers on horses. But the dashing cavalry who rode to war in 1914 were quickly mowed down by fast-firing weaponry; horses would be relegated to transport behind the lines. Moving men in a heavily armored vehicle powered by an internal combustion engine—the tank—would be possible only late in the war, and tanks were not exploited very effectively even then. Tremendous firepower coupled with the inability to move men rapidly produced "trench warfare." Soldiers could most effectively defend their positions by digging a trench, often about as deep as a man's height. The trench sheltered a man from the other side's bullets (although less so from heavy artillery, from which soldiers took refuge in the thirty-foot deep pits that pockmarked the trenches). An attacker had to "go over the top" of his own trench and hope to evade rifle fire (15 bullets per minute) and machine-gun fire (600 bullets per minute) long enough to reach the enemy trench. Battles took the form of generals sending waves of men over the top and hoping enough would survive enemy fire to cross the area between the combatants' positions, cut through barbed wire, and reach and take the opposing trench. In fact, generals had to hope their men would take at least two trenches because armies learned quickly to create back-up lines of trenches. Trench warfare heavily favored the defense, despite attempts to find weapons, such as poison gas, to overwhelm enemy lines. The battle of the Somme (1916) is a classic example. The French and especially the British attacked the German lines for four and a half months. On the first day, the British lost nearly 20,000 troops. By the time the battle was over, the British had suffered approximately 432,000 dead and wounded, the French 200,000, and the Germans perhaps 237,000. But these huge losses failed to bring the breakout victory the French and British had expected; the greatest allied gain in territory was seven miles. For the remainder of the war, the trenches—and soldiers—would remain largely where they were.

That fact helps explain the war's peculiar horror. Terrible things happen in all wars; terror and death have been common experiences of soldiers for millennia. But before World War I, armies met on a field of battle and, once the battle was over, moved on. Trench warfare was different. First, battles lasted not a day or two but, as in the battle of the Somme, weeks and months. Second, because battle lines scarcely shifted, soldiers found themselves living on the field of battle for months on end. They lived on the edge of what came to be called "No Man's Land," a cannon-made desert of churned up ground between the trenches where no soldier was likely to survive for long. No Man's Land accumulated corpses too dangerous to retrieve. And so the troops spent their time with the stench of rotting flesh, occasionally reminded again of lost comrades by the rats that sometimes invaded the trenches after feeding on corpses. With little shelter from above, the trenches themselves turned to mud when it rained. And one had always to mind the sniper from the other side, as well as the possibility of a full-scale assault at any minute.

These conditions help explain the war's long-term impact. For many, the nationalism that had initially stirred such passion had lost its savor by war's end. Consider two soldier poets. The Englishman Rupert Brooke (1887–1915) lived to see little of the war. In 1914, he was still enamored enough of the idea of sacrificing himself for his country that he could write,

> If I should die, think only this of me:
> That there's some corner of a foreign field
> That is forever England. There shall be
> In that rich earth a richer dust concealed;
> A dust whom England bore, shaped, made aware,
> Gave, once, her flowers to love, her ways to roam,
> A body of England's, breathing English air,
> Washed by the rivers, blest by suns of home.
> And think, this heart, all evil shed away,
> A pulse in the eternal mind, no less
> Gives somewhere back the thoughts by England given;
> Her sights and sounds; dreams happy as her day;
> And laughter, learnt of friends; and gentleness,
> In hearts at peace, under an English heaven.[1]

Brooke's compatriot, Wilfrid Owen (1893–1918), lived to see more of the war. On him, the trenches did their work. In a poem written in 1917, he describes a victim of a gas attack, finishing with a line from the ancient Roman Horace (65–8 BC). These words would have been familiar to educated men of his time: "*Dulce et decorum est pro patria mori*" ("It is sweet and fitting to die for one's country").

> If in some smothering dreams you too could pace
> Behind the wagon that we flung him in,
> And watch the white eyes writhing in his face,
> His hanging face, like a devil's sick of sin;

---

1   Rupert Brooke, "The Soldier," in *1914 and Other Poems* (London: Sidgwick & Jackson, Limited, 1919), 15.

If you could hear, at every jolt, the blood
Come gargling from the froth-corrupted lungs,
Obscene as cancer, bitter as the cud
Of vile, incurable sores on innocent tongues—
My friend, you would not tell with such high zest
To children ardent for some desperate glory,
The old lie: Dulce et decorum est
Pro patria mori.[2]

Many of the men who survived came to see themselves as members of a "lost generation." Revulsion against the war was not unusual among the troops, yet a number also had trouble reentering civilian life. This difficulty became most evident in defeated Germany, where the collapse of the kaiser's government at war's end threatened chaos. Some such disoriented soldiers entered the Freikorps ("Free Corps"), unofficial paramilitary units, many of which were eventually used by the government to suppress communists and socialists.

Modernism (see 9.11), still a largely marginal movement in 1914, blossomed after the war. The apparently senseless slaughter of the war made it harder to believe in an inevitable force of progress. A German scholar, Oswald Spengler (1880–1936), wrote *The Decline of the West*, published in 1918; sales were brisk. The West's confidence in its own traditions and in reason seemed to have been misplaced.

The war did, however, boost one Western intellectual tradition. If nationalism's stock fell, that of its by-now-traditional rival rose. Marxists had long argued that capitalism and the nation state were doomed and that a socialist paradise beckoned (see 9.5). Russia left the war in 1917 when a communist government came to power there (see 10.4). But communism's appeal was hardly confined to Russia. When the war ended, Austria-Hungary dissolved into Austria, Hungary, and Czechoslovakia, with a part of the empire joining Serbia to form Yugoslavia (see Map 10.2); in this way, nationalists in the Austro-Hungarian Empire got much of what they had wanted. Hungary, however, fell under the control of the Communist Béla Kun (1886–1938) in 1919 until his government was toppled later that year. Germany also witnessed some communist near successes. In January 1919, an uprising of communists known as the "Spartacists" won control of most of Berlin until it was put down by the army. Munich saw another communist uprising the following month, but it too was quickly repressed. Despite these reverses, communist parties all over took heart (not to mention direction) from the Communist Party and its triumph in Russia in 1917 (see 10.4).

The war also strengthened the hands of groups whose support governments needed. In countries that did not see a communist victory, the war still saw a strengthening of proletarian political clout, which continued after the war's end. Governments, needing the cooperation of factory workers in the management of the war economy, made

---

2   Wilfred Owen, "Dulce et decorum est," in *The Collected Poems of Wilfred Owen* (London: Chatto & Windus, 1964), 55.

concessions to labor. In 1915, representatives of Britain's Labour Party, itself a creature of the unions, entered the British cabinet for the first time. In Germany, socialists took the lead in ushering in the Weimar Republic, established as the kaiser fled the country in the wake of defeat. Governments needing support also found themselves making concessions to women as well as labor. Governments mobilized women during the war. As the armies drained men away from civilian life, women took their place. The expansion of women's suffrage was a promissory note for this support, cashed in Britain (partially) and Canada in 1918, and in the United States in 1920.

This bargaining for support took place on a global scale. The Great War started as a European war and became a world war. The United States, stung by Germany's declaration that its submarines would attack any vessels bound for allied ports and angered by the actual sinking of American ships, joined the Allies in 1917. But the war's global reach was even more a matter of the global empires that fought it. Japan, seeking Germany's holdings in Asia, declared war on Germany in 1914. The Ottoman (i.e., Turkish) Empire made the error of joining the Central Powers, bringing much of the Muslim world into the conflict (see Map 10.1). Blood was spilled in European colonies in Africa. Moreover, France, desperate for men in the main theater of war, brought African troops to Europe. Britain's resources were even greater, for it not only had troops from its non-Western colonies but drew on the loyalties of the self-governing white territories, such as Canada and Australia, as well. But exploiting these empires also weakened them. Asian and African troops who survived the trenches in France returned home less impressed by the wisdom or even the competence of the governments that sent so many young men over the top. Moreover, just as those governments had made concessions at home to workers and women, so they found themselves sometimes conceding or at least promising greater influence to non-whites in colonial governments in order to keep their support. India saw an expansion of representative assemblies and was promised eventual self-rule within the British Empire; France created an elective assembly with some authority in its colony of French Indochina (modern Vietnam). *The Decline of the West* indeed.

10.3 THE GREAT DEPRESSION

From 1929 to the start of World War II, the West—and much of the rest of the world—experienced a tremendous economic contraction: the Great Depression. Businesses went out of business; workers in huge numbers lost their jobs. Desperation bred violence. Revolution appeared imminent. The attractions of socialism, even of communism, grew. In response, governments clamped down on economic life. In doing so, they also attempted to erect defensive economic barriers around their own countries, undoing some of the economic globalization wrought by the nineteenth century.

The Great Depression was a crisis in finance and industry. But behind it was another depression, in agriculture. World War I had been a boom time for some growers of starches,

ICELAND

UNITED
KINGDOM

IRELAND

NORWAY

SWEDEN

FINLAND

Leningra

DENMARK

GERMANY
(EAST PRUSSIA)

THE NETHERLANDS

BELGIUM

POLAND

Berlin

GERMANY

SUDETENLAND
(to Germany at
Munich in 1938)

LUXEMBOURG

Rhine R.

Dresden

Ardennes

CZECHOSLOVAKIA

RHINELAND/
Demilitarized
zone

Maginot
Line

Munich

FRANCE

SWITZER
LAND

AUSTRIA

HUNGARY

RUMAN

CROATIA

YUGOSLAVIA

SERBIA

SLOVENIA

BOSNIA

BULG

PORTUGAL

SPAIN

ITALY

Rome

MONTENEGRO

ALBANIA

GREECE

MOROCCO

ALGERIA

TUNIS

LIBY

Map 10.2: Europe in the 1930s

UNION OF SOVIET SOCIALIST REPUBLICS

• Moscow

• Stalingrad

PERSIA

TURKEY

IRAQ

SYRIA

TRANSJORDAN

ARABIA

EGYPT

such as wheat and corn. The war had cut off eastern European producers from the world market, and French production fell off as the armies hammered each other in French fields. Wheat prices shot up; farmers in the New World responded by bringing more land under the plough, borrowing to do so. Moreover, agricultural output accelerated with spreading mechanization, such as the use of the combine harvester. Then the Great War ended. The price of wheat plummeted; in real terms, it fell lower than it had been in centuries. The 1920s saw farmers saddled with debt lose their land, with many more barely hanging on. Despite industrialization, a significant portion of the population of many countries still worked the land, so a significant part of the world's population lost the purchasing power that could support the economy should there be trouble.

The rest of the economy ran aground in 1929. By this time, the United States had become the West's, indeed the world's, financial titan—a position more easily achieved as the war had ground down the economies of the European powers. During the war, the Allies, borrowing for victory, had become debtors of the United States. Germany, too, handled its reparations payments to France in part by borrowing money from the United States. Many other Western countries also benefited from American investment, as America exported capital built up from the growth of its economy during the war. While agriculture suffered in much of the world, the world economy grew in the 1920s, fueled by American investors and lenders. Because of its central position in world finance, financial crisis in the United States triggered the Great Depression worldwide.

That crisis began in the stock market. Americans not only lent to foreigners, but they lent to each other too. Small investors increasingly put their money into a stock market that seemed only to go up. Many bought stock on margin—that is, they did not pay cash but borrowed up to 70 percent of the purchase price from a broker, who, in turn, might be financed by a bank. The stock itself served as collateral for all this borrowing. The market did not, however, soar forever. In October 1929, stock prices declined. The practice of buying on margin helped convert decline into collapse; investors were forced to sell their stock to repay their loans. Stocks dumped on the market drove stock prices further down, which, in turn, led more investors to sell, and so on. Stock prices fell 40 percent in a month. By 1933, the American stock market had lost three-fourths of the value it had had in 1929. Banks now faced losing the money they had loaned to brokers, and depositors rushed to withdraw their savings in case the banks failed. The fear of banks going under led to banks going under. American banks closed by the thousands in the next few years, taking many depositors' savings with them.

The precise connection between the stock market crash of 1929 and the Depression is not entirely clear, except in one sense. The crash shook confidence: confidence in growth, confidence in investment. The natural reaction was for investors to realize their investments, to keep them in cash. As Americans undid their investments and banks refused to make new loans, firms closed their doors, unable to do business without the essential lubricant of credit. White-collar workers, usually more insulated from economic slowdowns than their blue-collar cousins, found themselves out of work. Closed businesses meant unemployed workers, and unemployed workers meant less demand for the goods businesses produced and so falling prices for those goods. A death spiral resulted as more and more firms were unable to find buyers for their goods at prices that would keep their businesses in operation. Production of goods sank. In 1933, only a third as many automobiles were produced in the United States as in 1929. Tax revenues collapsed; several states defaulted on their obligations. The closure of banks—and the government's suspension of banks' operations in order to save them—made currency even more rare. Many cities resorted to issuing scrip because they lacked cash. Mexican pesos came into use in the American southwest, while Dow Chemical started to mint its own coins. By 1933, one in four American workers was unemployed.

But Americans' desire to move their investments into cash had repercussions around the world because America was creditor to the world, or at least to much of it. And so the cycle described above began to be replayed in Europe and elsewhere. The unemployment rate in Britain doubled by 1933. The Depression was to be global. One result was a decline of world trade; as countries no longer produced or consumed as much, they imported and exported less. In the first four months of 1931, the value of world trade was 42 percent of what it had been in the first four months of 1929.

People impoverished by the Depression threatened violence, as did people determined to hold onto the jobs they had, and at their previous wages. In the United States, when members of the striking Teamsters Union in Minneapolis surrounded a strikebreaking truck, the police fired. This "Bloody Friday" (July 20, 1934) saw two strikers killed and 67 wounded. In 1933, masked farmers in Iowa kidnapped a judge for refusing to block foreclosures; for fear of such incidents, several Iowa counties fell under martial law. France was hit by a nation-wide strike in 1937. With capitalism an apparent failure, socialism and communism became more attractive. In Latin America, landed oligarchies had long alternated with *caudillos* or military dictators. The Depression decisively tipped the balance in favor of the dictators. Oligarchs depended on exporting agricultural goods—a trade that had now crashed—and faced restive lower classes. A wave of military coups, promising order and the protection of property, displaced the oligarchs. In 1930, for example, the army dismissed the president of Brazil in favor of Getúlio Vargas (1883–1954), who ruled with military backing (for more on Vargas, see 10.5.3).

In securer democracies, the left gained more influence. In France, the general strike swept the socialists to power in 1937. They promptly limited the workweek to 40 hours, nationalized defense industries, and enacted price supports for agricultural products. The French case is symptomatic of the direction many governments eventually took during the Depression: increasing intervention in the economy in order to create or protect jobs, not to mention to support the jobless. In the United States, the newly elected Franklin Delano Roosevelt (1882–1945) announced a "New Deal." Farmers were subsidized—even paid not to produce—in order to bolster the prices of agricultural goods. The federal government created various make-work projects to boost employment. Steps taken long before in Bismarck's Germany and other countries, such as pensions for the elderly and welfare payments to the unemployed, were now introduced in the United States by the Social Security Act (1935). Canada's Conservative government began to provide unemployment insurance to which both employers and employees contributed. It was not always easy, at the time, to know how to read these kinds of moves. Were such measures a first step toward communism? Were they necessary to save capitalism from revolution? Would they foster a culture of dependency on government? Did they not go far enough? Agreement was hard to find. (In any case, while both sexes benefited from such state intervention, governments focused their assistance on men; if men were heads of households, their economic fortunes were central to families, and large numbers of men at loose ends probably seemed more dangerous than unemployed women.)

The Depression also encouraged governments to embrace a new theory of economic management. Economic downturns meant that tax revenues decreased because there was less to tax: less income, less buying, less selling, less importing, less exporting. Traditionally, governments, like any household faced with declining income, had responded to declining revenues by tightening their own belts, cutting spending. In the 1930s, however, the economist John Maynard Keynes (1883–1946) argued that such responses were backward. Governments needed to counteract economic contraction by spending more, even if it meant borrowing to do so. What the economy needed was greater demand for goods and services, and this demand would exist only if people had money in their pockets. If businesses were not stoking demand by employing people, then government needed to step in. People employed by the state would spend their earnings and so stimulate private firms to produce goods and services. Money spent by the state on goods and services would have the same effect. So would money doled out to the unemployed. Keynesian economics would provide the theoretical underpinning of Western government policy from the later 1930s into the 1970s at the least.

While the Depression boosted the left, it also boosted nationalism. In countries with significant foreign immigration, immigrants were easily seen as competitors for the few jobs that were left. More broadly, the Depression fostered "economic nationalism": efforts by governments to regulate trade in the national interest. In order to protect jobs at home, countries imposed tariffs to keep foreign goods from competing with domestic production. Other countries, their exports thus blocked, replied in kind. As a result, world trade, already reduced because of lower production and purchasing power, contracted further. What international trade remained was increasingly arranged by governments through bilateral agreements rather than through the open market. Britain and the self-governing territories within the British Empire—such as Canada and Australia—agreed to lower tariffs for trade with each other but to raise tariffs against the rest of the globe. Governments also constricted the flow of money beyond their borders, trying to keep capital investment at home. The multinational company Unilever illustrates the impact. Unilever, a maker of soap and margarine, found itself investing its funds trapped in Germany in, among other things, shipbuilding (even the building of whalers) and a cheese factory, all unwillingly.

One part of the world, however, appeared to be flourishing. Russia's tsar had been overthrown in 1917, and, by the end of the year, the country had a communist government. Although most countries suffered in an economic trough in the 1930s, Russia, billed as a society run by workers, appeared to be a beacon of prosperity. In 1931, 100,000 American workers applied for jobs in the Soviet Union. It is now time to discuss this alternative to the capitalist order.

10.4 COMMUNISM

At the dawn of twentieth century, most Marxists did not regard Russia as a promising center of communist revolution. Although it was industrializing fast—fast enough to alarm the Germans—Russia under the tsars was still largely an agrarian society. Peasants, not proletarians, made up most of the population. Certainly, there were tensions between peasants and aristocratic landowners. The government had freed the serfs (on whom, see 9.4.4) in 1861 in an attempt to catch up to the West in economic development; free peasants, it was hoped, might exercise more initiative than serfs, and many landowners had mortgaged so many serfs that they had little to lose by freeing them anyway. The newly freed peasants also received about half the agricultural land in the country. Yet, by 1900, peasants were eager to acquire more, which set them against large landholders. But a peasant revolution was not what orthodox Marxists were working for. A true communist revolution, they thought, would start in one of the most advanced industrialized countries, such as Germany, Britain, or the United States, and then, of course, spread to the rest of the world (see 9.5).

Russia, however, unexpectedly became the first avowedly communist state in history. To understand this, one must understand the unusual circumstances that produced the Russian Revolution of 1917. That revolution was, in fact, two revolutions: the "February Revolution" against the tsar and the "October Revolution" against capitalism.

Why did Russians rebel against the tsar? The answer is complex and much debated, but one element was surely the sheer incompetence of the tsar's government in the crisis of World War I. Russia had already experienced an abortive revolution in 1905 when its navy met humiliating defeat in the Russo-Japanese War of 1904–1905 (see 9.8). The Russian armies that marched to war in 1914 were large and, for that reason, feared, but they were not much more effective than the Russian fleet had been in 1905. Their German opponents soon discovered that size is not everything. Badly equipped and badly led— some Russian officers did not know how to read a map—Russian forces were smashed by much smaller German ones, which, in 1914 alone, took nearly a quarter of a million Russians prisoner. At home, workers, already discontent with factory conditions, faced hunger and even starvation as the government was unable to ensure the delivery of food to the cities. Transport problems also meant that fuel supplies were failing. In the capital Petrograd, temperatures in some apartments rarely topped 52–59 degrees Fahrenheit in the winter of 1917, with workplaces at 44–50 degrees Fahrenheit. At court, Tsar Nicholas II fell under the spell of Rasputin (?1871–1916), a dirty, sexually licentious priest; both the tsar and the tsar's wife—the tsarina—believed Rasputin had the power to heal their young son of hemophilia. Rasputin, not equipped to run the Russian government in peace let alone war, became the most influential figure in it. Russians read his opposition to the war as pro-German. The tsarina, herself from Germany, became widely known as "the German woman." She was rumored—falsely—to be Rasputin's lover and in treasonous collusion with him.[3] Even the tsar's traditional supporters—the nobility and the military—were alienated by Nicholas's incompetence. Senior army officers discussed the tsar's overthrow as necessary to the war effort. Moreover, by 1917, the army on the ground was disintegrating as a result of mutiny and desertion. Working conditions in the factories had deteriorated as the war strained an industrial base that had not been ready to supply millions of troops in a modern war. Every year there were more strikes, giving hope to socialists that a workers' revolution was possible. Through much of the country, councils of workers, called "soviets," were gaining more respect among the proletariat than the government.

Protests in Petrograd against the tsar and the war in March of 1917 produced the "February Revolution."[4] A cabal of nobles had assassinated Rasputin the previous December, but his death failed to quell discontent. Worse, the fact that his assassins were well known and yet at large indicated a government that could not keep order, a situation that only encouraged protest. Although soldiers sent to suppress the protests fired into the crowd, some of these men had a change of heart overnight, killed their commander, and supported the protestors the next day. The Petrograd authorities lost their nerve; Nicholas's military advisors, perhaps with relief, soon recommended that the tsar abdicate. A temporary, provisional government took control.

Insofar as anyone could take control. The provisional government, largely nationalist, was committed to keeping Russia in the war and to calling an elected constituent assembly to draw up a constitution for the country. But the army continued to disintegrate. In some units, soldiers inspired by what seemed an emerging democracy insisted on electing their own officers. The government still had trouble supplying the cities with essentials. The soviets, which generally opposed the war, continued to flourish and gained further support from soldiers who decided simply to go home. Some soviets formed their own militias and countermanded the orders of local army commanders. The provisional government did not enjoy a monopoly on the legitimate use of force, a weakness that made further revolution possible and recalls conditions in the French Revolution (see 8.5.3). Russia was developing two parallel governments: the provisional government and the soviets.

Enter Vladimir Lenin (1870–1924). Leader of the Bolsheviks, the more extreme wing of the communists, he had been in exile in Switzerland. But Germany, hoping that Lenin's presence in Russia would at least distract the provisional government from the war, returned him to Russia in 1917. Lenin had also concluded that Russia could indeed

---

3   There is no evidence of such treason or of an affair.

4   Russia, at the time, was still on the "Julian" calendar (named for the changes instituted by Julius Caesar), whereas most of the rest of world was using (and still uses) the "Gregorian" calendar (named after Pope Gregory XIII, promulgated in 1582). Thus some days as remembered in Russian history fall into the later month in the current calendar. Russia adopted the Gregorian calendar in 1918.

experience a communist revolution despite its incomplete industrialization: a revolutionary government in Russia could "build" socialism and build up the working class rather than, as Marx had predicted, be the expression of a society that had already become almost entirely working class.

Lenin's appeal to the nation was well suited to the summer of 1917. He offered "Land, Peace, and Bread": land for the peasants—the largest part of the population—who had been wanting more land ever since the end of serfdom and who were, in some places, already seizing it; peace for the majority who were sick of the war; and bread for the many who feared starvation. And, as a Marxist, Lenin naturally appealed to the soviets. "All power to the soviets!" was another Bolshevik slogan of 1917. Bolsheviks became increasingly active as members of the soviets themselves, gaining a majority in the Petrograd Soviet. In November, the Petrograd Soviet ordered its own troops to seize the headquarters of the provisional government, the former tsar's Winter Palace. Lenin and the Bolsheviks, soon renamed the "Communist Party," were in command.

Although Lenin was clearly its leader, vigorous debate was habitual within the Communist Party. It became clear, however, that the party, although determined to create a workers' society, was not prepared to tolerate dissent from those who might question the direction the party decided to take. (An exception was made, briefly, for other socialists, whose support the party needed while it consolidated power.) The "dictatorship of the proletariat" declared by Marxist theory was to mean, in practice, the dictatorship of the Communist Party, which saw itself as the proletariat's representative. The Communists quickly arrested political opponents and shut down rival newspapers. After all, they reasoned, would not even well-meaning dissent simply be exploited by capitalists? The government established a secret police, the Cheka. More effective than the tsar's old forces, the Cheka would be free of legal limits on its mission to arrest and punish. When the constituent assembly met in January 1918, the Bolsheviks had gained only 21 percent of the vote. The assembly was shut down; protests against the closure were met with bullets. Although the government insisted it acted in their name, the soviets themselves, instead of dominating the government, came to be dominated by it. Lenin implemented a self-described policy of terror against those he saw as the regime's enemies, recalling the Terror of the French Revolution (see 8.5.3). Calls for limited government, much less democracy, were merely bourgeois deceits. Yet the new government's program also enjoyed popular support. Lenin signed a treaty with Germany and Austria-Hungary at Brest-Litovsk in March of 1918, giving up large amounts of territory in Russia's west but getting Russia out of the war. Many embraced the idea of all property being held in common; the summer of 1918 saw some property nationalized even before the government decreed it. And, of course, peasants wanted land. Still, Russia experienced civil war, ultimately won by the Communist Party's new Red Army in 1921.

The new communist state has been described as "totalitarian." This form of political organization was new. Totalitarian government was a kind of absolute absolutism. The absolute governments that emerged in the seventeenth century had claimed to have no limits, to be able to override all rights of the governed, even though, in practice, they failed to do so (see 7.3). Totalitarian governments, in theory, go further, not only over-riding all rights but also regulating all spheres of human activity. Theoretically, private life in a totalitarian state does not exist, as all aspects of life become subject to govern-ment management and control. This notion of totalitarianism has been the subject of debate among historians and political scientists as applied to Russia under the Communist Party and to other twentieth-century states (for the latter, see 10.5). On the one hand, authorities in Communist Russia manipulated everything from the educational system to family life in order to achieve a new kind of man and woman. Yet, as is the case in most endeavors, ambition ultimately outstripped accomplishment. A private sphere remained despite the efforts of the party and state. No one could prevent all individual acts of initiative, even resistance. Moreover, local authorities often exercised wide latitude and were sometimes only loosely controlled by central authority; they could frustrate the central government's aims. At Magnitogorsk, the factory books were kept in dupli-cate: an accurate set for the factory managers and a false one to be sent to Moscow to show that goals were being met. Yet a totalitarian ambition was there nonetheless, and Russia under communism moved closer to a totalitarian regime than any state had ever previously done. Like "absolutism," "totalitarianism" remains a useful term, as long as appropriate caution is exercised.

The new Russia, eventually renamed the "Union of Soviet Socialist Republics," produced a new form of political organization. The Russian state's power was unlim-ited except for the kinds of limits imposed by practicality. (Lenin, for instance, found that he had to experiment with a temporary measure, his "New Economic Policy" [NEP], which allowed some economic free enterprise and private property in order to stimulate production in 1921.) But the government's direction now fell entirely into the hands of a single party, the Communist Party. Although elections were held, only Communist Party candidates were permitted to run; eventually elections would not be contested. Absolutism was, of course, an old political form (see 7.3), as those who remembered the tsar well knew. But absolute rule by a party—rather than an individual—was an inno-vation. The party's position gave many an interest in maintaining the new system. Party membership swelled. The communist revolution also meant social mobility. As business owners were displaced by government managers (increasingly party members), a new class of people, educated for their positions and immersed in party doctrine, assumed positions of influence. Such new men, and fewer new women, owed their position to the party, and supported it.

But would anyone rule the party as absolutely as the party ruled the nation? Lenin had clearly been the Communist Party's dominant figure, but he had not quashed debate within it, although a desire for conformity is evident in an ineffective party resolution in 1921 to ban party factions. Lenin, however, faded as ill health took hold of him in 1922; he died two years later. After much conflict, Josef Stalin (1879–1953) emerged as the dominant figure in the Communist Party and so in the country by the end of 1929. Stalin did not differ from Lenin in his willingness to use violence to repress opposition to the party. But, unlike Lenin, he was absolutely insistent that his word should be law, without discussion, within the party too. A related phenomenon was the development of a cult of personality—rather, two cults of personality. The first of these revolved around Lenin. His body was embalmed and put on display in a glass case in Moscow for all Russians to visit and revere. His image appeared everywhere. In publications, all under government control, Russians heard his praises—as savior of the Russian workers, as hero, as genius—over and over. Writers, from poets to chemists, claimed to derive their ideas from him. Then, increasingly, arose a cult of personality surrounding the living Stalin, one that after World War II (1939–1945) threatened to overshadow that of the deceased Lenin himself.

There was more to the cult of personality than simple extravagant praise for figures living or dead. Such cults had increasing appeal in an atomized society. If everyone felt an immediate connection to some great figure, then everyone could feel united through that person. The cult of personality offered a sense of community. And Russia was an increasingly atomized society and so in need of one. Revolution had overturned old social structures; industrialization was proceeding rapidly (more on this soon), and social mobility cut old ties to the traditional community. The Russian Orthodox Church, to which Russians had traditionally been attached, had been suppressed because the communists, being Marxists, were officially atheists. This situation gave a sense of connection to a man like Lenin greater appeal. *Pravda*, one of the two main Soviet newspapers, published this description of the deceased Lenin in the 1930s:

> It seems as though the man who lies in the tomb, in the centre of that nocturnal, deserted square, is the only person in the world who is not asleep, and who watches over everything around him, in the towns and in the fields. He is the real leader—the one of whom the workers used laughingly to say that he was master and comrade at the same time; he is the paternal brother who is really watching over everyone. Although you do not know him, he knows you and is thinking of you.[5]

A poster from 1935, "Long Live Our Happy Socialist Motherland—Long Live Our Beloved Stalin" (Figure 10.1), shows Stalin (wearing the moustache) waving from Lenin's tomb, presiding over a united people massed together. One of the planes overhead bears Lenin's name; another bears Stalin's. The distant formation of planes to the right spells "Stalin." And Russians responded to the cults of Lenin and Stalin. Hundreds of thousands of mourners turned out in Moscow on Stalin's death in 1953; the crush was so great that hundreds suffocated and thousands were trampled.

While Stalin was alive, he reshaped Soviet society in an effort to build socialism. Lenin had taken a detour from complete control of all means of production, the NEP. But, with the regime more secure, Stalin scrapped the NEP in order to finish the job of building socialism. One prong of this effort was agriculture. Russia was still largely a

---

5   Henri Barbusse, *Stalin: A New World Seen through One Man*, trans. Vyvyan Holland (New York: Macmillan Company, 1935), 282.

ДА ЗДРАВСТВУЕТ НАША СЧАСТЛИВАЯ СОЦИАЛИСТИЧЕСКАЯ РОДИНА.
ДА ЗДРАВСТВУЕТ НАШ ЛЮБИМЫЙ ВЕЛИКИЙ СТАЛИН!

Figure 10.1: Gustav Klutsis, "Long Live Our Happy Socialist Motherland—Long Live Our Beloved Stalin" (1935).

peasant society, and one of the things peasants had wanted from the revolution was land, their own land. Some peasants were more prosperous than others; these were the kulaks. But starting in 1929, all farms were to be "collectivized": consolidated under state ownership, mechanized, and organized to produce on an industrial scale. Collectivization served several aims. It eliminated private property, long a Marxist aim. It eliminated the kulaks, seen as capitalists of agriculture. It released labor from the farms, making it available for industry. Peasants, especially kulaks, resisted. Peasants killed their farm animals rather than surrender them; the number of livestock in the country fell by roughly half by 1933. Shootings of peasants and more followed. In 1932–1933, famine struck large sections of the country, as the new farms failed to produce and the government withheld food from millions of peasants believed to be "class enemies." Millions died.

Another aim was industry. In 1928, the government undertook complete regulation of industry, releasing and enforcing the first of what would be several ambitious "Five-Year Plans" that laid down how many and what goods would be produced by industry, by how many workers, at what prices, and so on. Again, several motives were behind the move. So long as the Soviet Union was primarily agrarian, it could hardly meet a Marxist definition of a proletarian society (see 9.5). Building socialism required the proletariat to be the dominant class; it required industrialization. Indeed, the Communist Party itself was a workers' party—or at least not a peasant party; fewer than 1 percent of peasant households had a party member in 1928. Moreover, such industry would produce the weapons—guns, tanks, airplanes, artillery, ships—that the Soviet Union needed in a hostile, capitalist world. Strong measures were needed to execute these plans. The government instituted internal passports to control the supply of labor; it discouraged workers from walking off with goods from the factory by making theft of state property carry the death penalty.

Yet, despite such steps, there were workers who undertook building socialism with genuine passion. The goal had real appeal, just as Marxism had appeal in the nineteenth century and still in the twentieth. Moreover, Russia's near full employment and economic growth were impressive compared with the Great Depression (see 10.3) in capitalist countries. A coalminer, Alexei Stakhanov (1906–1977), became famous for producing fourteen times as much output as required. The government fostered a Stakhanovite movement of heroic devotion to achieving or surpassing the goals of the Five-Year Plan. Stakhanov himself said that he and his imitators worked so hard because they worked for themselves, not for the capitalists. Indeed, the Five-Year Plans remade Russia. A Soviet survey, admittedly suspect, indicates that, in 1924, 10 percent of the population were workers and 77 percent peasants; in 1959, 50 percent were workers and 32 percent were peasants. And the Soviet Union did industrialize, producing, for example, four times the iron and steel in 1938 than it had when the first Five-Year Plan was launched. The Five-Year Plans, however, stressed heavy industry—such as steel, tanks, tractors—rather than consumer goods. The first Five-Year Plan limited everyone to two new pairs of shoes every three years.

Industrialization and collectivization also produced a new group: government managers and bureaucrats. Such people were required in a centrally planned economy of government-run farms and factories. The same Soviet survey of workers and peasants showed that 4 percent of Russians were white-collar workers in 1924; the figure was 18 percent in 1959. Whether from peasant or worker origins, these rising men (and sometimes women) provided the backbone of the government's support. Stalin's methods, which came to be known as Stalinism, produced enormous suffering. Stalinism also, however, produced a new managerial and technical class of people approved by the party. Called the *nomenklatura*, these individuals were still officially proletarians, but, in fact, because they had been preapproved for appointments to positions in the Soviet state apparatus, they were distinct, and owed the Communist Party a lot. Popular attitudes sometimes belied the official position that all were now workers working for the workers. One joke ran thus:

> A worker races into the Director's office and shouts, "Comrade Director, the head of personnel hanged himself in the closet!"
> "Did you cut him down yet?"
> "No, he's still alive."[6]

This class loyalty was tested, encouraged, and, sometimes, rewarded by the purges of the 1930s. Having eliminated his opponents from influence, Stalin remained deadly suspicious of rivals. So he leveled invented charges of conspiracy against members of the Communist Party, minor *nomenklatura* as well as major figures. Others took advantage of his paranoia to accuse their own enemies. Many were simply arrested and executed or sent to die in harsh prison camps, known as the "gulag." It is estimated that roughly four million lost their freedom or their lives in this way. The most public of these measures resulted in "show trials" in which the accused, after torture or threats to their families, confessed to an amazing array of crimes, such as cooperation with foreign capitalist governments to stop the progress of communism. Such trials publicized these threats and the government's ability to deal with them. The purges also persuaded many that socialism had to be

---

6 James von Geldern and Richard Stites, eds., *Mass Culture in Soviet Russia: Tales, Poems, Songs, Movies, Plays, and Folklore, 1917–1953* (Bloomington and Indianapolis: Indiana University Press, 1995), 489.

built all the more vigorously because it was endangered by so many enemies within and without—that only Stalin and his regime stood between a bright future and disaster. In addition, failures in central economic planning could be explained by sabotage carried out by conspirators. The purges also created opportunity. Many of those eliminated in these years were educated, middle-aged holdovers from before the revolution; their removal opened positions for younger technocrats of working-class origin. Often, those purged were themselves party members; in 1933 alone, about a third of the party was purged. Soon Stalin was nearly alone of the "old Bolsheviks" who had taken part in the Russian Revolution. Official history was rewritten to eliminate or demonize his old comrades and rivals. Even, or especially, Leon Trotsky (1879–1940), hero of the revolution who had led the Bolshevist Red Army to victory in the civil war, was now depicted as a traitor to the revolution and exiled. Some individuals were literally airbrushed out of old photographs. Stalin's standing was thus strengthened and the party made even more dependent on him.

Marxist theory shaped the government's goals—appropriately, given Marxism's status as the official ideology; but Lenin, Stalin and others would not acknowledge their departures from Marxism. For Marx, attempting to build socialism by planning industrialization would have been putting the cart before the horse. In a truly socialist society, according to Marx, government would fade away, not grow stronger and more coercive. A cult of personality had no role in a society supposedly dedicated to the theory that history is driven by class conflict not extraordinary individuals.

Communism was also a feminist ideology. Marx had argued that, within the family itself, women had been an exploited class. There was to be a "new Soviet woman." Indeed, in the first flush of power, the Communist Party proposed to equalize the sexes by having housework carried out by government workers. This proposal came to nothing, but, in other respects, the government worked to foster women's independence and equality by, for example, making divorce much easier to obtain by both wives and husbands. Abortion was legalized. Women's position in the Soviet Union did not, however, wholly live up to the promise of women's equality. True, education and the professions were opened to women, but this opening up was uneven. Printing, for example, remained a male occupation. Under Stalin, the pendulum in some respects began to swing against women's independence. Wanting to bolster population growth, the government encouraged a return to more traditional family life. Abortion was restricted, and men's obligation to support their children was reinforced. Women received medals for bearing children. Soviet propaganda began to stress the importance of home life, and of women's place in it. Very few women, however, were full-time homemakers. Women, particularly during World War II, worked in factories in greater numbers than before the revolution, as men were deployed to fight the Germans; the Soviet Union's heavy losses during the war meant that only some of these women were displaced by men returning from the war. The population shortage meant that the government needed women to work outside the home, but, at the same time, they were encouraged to bear and raise children. Women's additional special responsibility for domestic life remained, and men's work outside the home was assumed to take priority over that of women.

In another respect, too, communism in Russia departed from Marxist orthodoxy. This departure concerned the Soviet Union's relationship with the rest of the world. Marx had predicted a world revolution transcending nationality. As World War I came to an end, communists saw the Russian Revolution as simply the start of a worldwide movement; even anticommunists feared communism's broad appeal. Indeed, Lenin felt able to give up vast Russian territories to the Germans in 1918 because, he thought, communism would soon engulf Germany and make their loss meaningless. The (short-lived) communist rebellions and government that emerged at the close of World War I (see 10.2) seemed to confirm that conclusion. Moreover, communist parties often carried weight in Western politics even where they did not succeed in taking over. Once Russia became the world's first communist country, communists the world over naturally looked to it for leadership, which it was happy to supply. But how much support should the Soviet Union provide to global revolution? That question dominated the party at the time of Lenin's death. Stalin advocated "socialism in one country," that is, building socialism in Russia alone. The alternative, it was urged (in the days before Stalin had taken complete control), was to put Russia's resources not into forced industrialization but into world revolution; Trotsky had advocated this position. Stalin, of course, won the debate, although he continued, with some success, to attempt to direct the activities of communist parties abroad, and he did not permanently renounce the long-term goal of world revolution.

There was another departure from Marxist theory, perhaps related to the aim of "socialism in one country." At the dawn of the twentieth century, Marxism was the great rival of nationalism. To calls to heed the national spirit, Marxists replied, "Workers of the world, unite!" Marxism and nationalism offered competing definitions of community (see 9.3 and 9.5). As a Marxist state, the Soviet Union was a naturally antinationalist one. Moreover, the Russia of the tsars had been, like the Habsburg Empire (see 8.5.2), an empire of various nations and languages, albeit one in which Russians made up the majority. After the revolution, this multinational patchwork was acknowledged by forming such nationalities into individual Soviet republics, albeit under the firm direction of Moscow and dominated by Russians. The constitution gave these republics the right to secede from the Union of Soviet Socialist Republics, a propaganda point that was not seriously contemplated as a real possibility. Yet, under Stalin, the government increasingly appealed to Russian nationalism as well as to proletarian loyalties. Peter the Great was celebrated as a Russian national hero (unlikely as that may seem given Peter's career [see 7.4.4]). Russians were credited with having invented everything from the light bulb to the airplane. The trend became especially prominent during World War II (1939–1945) when Germany invaded the Soviet Union. Under pressure, the communist government resorted to nationalist appeals to keep the country together. This evidence is another indication that, profound as communism's appeal was, nationalism's appeal was at least as great in the long run. Nationalism's pull in the decades after World War I was evident also outside Russia.

10.5 FASCISM

10.5.1 General Considerations

Russia responded to the disaster of World War I with revolution, revolution that ultimately gave rise to the world's first communist government. Other countries, however—from Brazil to Poland—responded to the war and its aftermath by embracing fascism in the course of the 1920s and 1930s; still other countries saw fascist movements that failed to gain power. Yet the roots of fascism ran deeper than World War I. Fascists, facing an atomized society, continued the nationalist tradition inherited from the nineteenth century. Moreover, in their attempt to erect supreme state power, they continued a line of development traceable to the absolute monarchies of the seventeenth century (see 7.3). At the same time, in their stress on action over ideas, they drew upon some existentialist lines of thought (see 9.11). Their leaders also often adopted that cult of personality discussed already in relation to Stalin (see 10.4). Although fascism is usually associated with the 1920s and 30s, some fascist governments lasted longer. Francisco Franco (1892–1975) came to power in Spain in 1939; his regime ended only with his death in 1975. Juan (1895–1974) and Eva (1919–1952) Perón, sometimes regarded as fascists, came to power in Argentina only in 1946.

"Fascism" escapes easy definition. Various movements, most notably in Italy, Spain, and Germany, have been described as "fascist." But their ideologies were inconsistent with each other, and, at times, each variation was internally inconsistent. One can, however, identify certain common elements. "Fascist" movements are totalitarian, refusing to recognize limits on state power and vesting authority over the state in a dictator. In regard to state control, they thus resembled communism as practiced in the Soviet Union. Also, in regard to the role of the dictator, they were similar to the Soviet Union under Stalin (see 10.4). Some scholars debate whether fascism was inherently capitalist. Certainly fascist governments largely preserved private property and left private businesses to operate and make substantial profits. Yet these governments were also always ready to regulate and direct the economy as they saw fit, and they advocated and even instituted programs usually associated with socialism. Perhaps the critical point is the fascists' focus on unlimited state power rather than any particular attitude toward private enterprise itself. In this and in their opposition to liberal democracy (as practiced, for example, in France, Britain, and the United States), communists and fascists had something in common. An important element that divided fascists, usually associated with the political right, from communists, usually associated with the political left, was their attitude toward the nation. Fascists were nationalists, even hyper-nationalists, stressing the unity of the nation and its transcendence of class differences. Communists, at least officially, condemned nationalism as a capitalist trick to divide the proletariat and prevent its triumph over the bourgeoisie. Both movements, however, were heirs to the self-conscious "tough-mindedness" of the later nineteenth century (see 9.7). In one other respect communists and fascists were twins. Both saw themselves as revolutionary, as creating a new society. Although fascists and communists were, in fact, influenced by the past, both claimed to look only toward the future. In this rejection of the past, fascists may have been more influenced by modernism (9.11) than they sometimes liked to admit. Similarly, fascists often said they embraced action over ideology, that fascism was more about doing something than devising some plan. The fascist writer Giovanni Gentile (1875–1944) remarked that "Fascist philosophy is not a philosophy that is thought, it is rather one that is done."[7] Although many twentieth-century existentialists opposed fascism, in making such claims, fascists echoed the existentialists of the fin de siècle and later, who claimed that only in acting according to no design were human beings free (see 9.11).

10.5.2 Italy

The term "fascism" itself derives from an ancient Roman symbol of authority: *fasces*, bundles of sticks used to beat wrongdoers, which the first fascists adopted as their symbol in Italy in the years following World War I. Italians had won the war, having entered on the Allied side in 1915. Even more than other victor nations, however, Italians felt as though they had lost. The most notable battle in which Italy had taken part, that of Caporetto (1917), was a defeat. Moreover, although the Allies had promised Italy significant territorial gains in return for entering the war, these gains failed to materialize in the Treaty of Versailles (1919). As a result, divisions within the country grew: between, on the one hand, an energized socialist movement and, on the other, inflamed nationalists, property owners, and anyone else opposed to socialism. In 1920 alone, Italy experienced over 2,000 strikes, while the industrial city of Turin saw soviets (see 10.4) set up in factories. In various places, vigilantes, often returning soldiers, took up arms to harass or even murder their socialist opponents. These groups were the *squadristi* (squads), soon to be called the "Blackshirts." To property owners, they appeared more reliable defenders of property than the government. The Italian government appeared weak, unable to maintain that monopoly of force assumed by Western states since the seventeenth century (see 7.3). Very quickly, a former Marxist, Benito Mussolini (1883–1945), who had become a nationalist advocate of the war, brought together what had been independent Blackshirt groups under his leadership. Mussolini's frank avowal of the acceptability of violence reflected the self-conscious tough-mindedness of the last century (see 9.7). In his first speech to the Italian parliament on becoming prime minister, after his Blackshirts had filled the streets of Rome, he remarked, "I could have barred the doors of parliament and formed a government exclusively of Fascists. I could have done so, but I chose not to, at least for the present."[8]

---

7 Giovanni Gentile, *Origins and Doctrines of Fascism, with Selections from Other Works*, ed. and trans. A. James Gregor (New Brunswick, NJ: Transaction Publishers, 2002), 34.

8 Giuseppe Finaldi, *Mussolini and Italian Fascism* (New York: Pearson Longman, 2008), 141.

But despite his advocacy and use of force, Mussolini and his fascists also offered an end to conflict and, with it, a renewed sense of community. This offer of unity in community was part of their appeal. Central to the fascists' message was that both liberal democracy and socialism fed conflict and disunity. Parliamentary elections encouraged individuals to vote for their own interests, not those of the larger society; after all, multiparty systems were built for conflict (see 7.4). Socialists similarly pitted one class against another, the proletariat against the bourgeoisie. Fascists, however, held out the promise of bringing all members of the nation together—or, at least, all who wanted to be brought together. The message got through. The beekeepers around Trento, enthusiastic wearers of the Blackshirt, asked for state support on the grounds that bees were cooperative comrades, like fascists. The fascists promised that a new kind of nation would be born through revolution, a third way found between capitalism and socialism, one that brought the benefits of socialism but preserved property and, most important, centered on the nation. In 1919, Mussolini had announced, "We declare war against socialism, not because it is socialism but because it is opposed to nationalism."[9]

In 1922, Mussolini became prime minister in a coalition government with liberal politicians who saw his Blackshirts as a bulwark against socialism. Liberals also hoped that entering government would tame Mussolini. Thus, when the Blackshirts engaged in a "March on Rome" to demonstrate their support for Mussolini, the liberals were already largely prepared to make him prime minister. In Fascist propaganda, however, the March on Rome was cast as a revolutionary act, an armed seizure of power.

In political terms, it was a revolution. One way or another, the conflicts of liberal democracy would be squelched. Critics of the government were assassinated or imprisoned. In the 1930s, the police rounded up dissidents or those suspected of being dissidents at the rate of thousands of arrests per week. All political parties other than that of the fascists were banned. Mayors were appointed by the central government rather than elected locally.

Once in power, Mussolini expressed the vision of a third way in the practice of "corporatism." All economic life was to be divided into what eventually became twenty-two spheres. Each was to be guided by a "corporation," made up of representatives of labor, owners and, holding the whip hand, government. These corporations would set wages and prices and otherwise regulate their respective spheres. Cooperation and community, not conflict, was the advertised end. The corporative state promised the organic unity symbolized by the body politic of the Middle Ages: "Today there is not a single working Italian who does not seek his or her place in a corporation . . . who does not wish to become a living atom within that great, immense, living organism that is the fascist national corporate state," declared an Italian fascist.[10] In 1939, Mussolini replaced the lower house of parliament with a Chamber of Fasces and Corporations, marking the end of electoral

---

9   Charles F. Belzell, ed., *Mediterranean Fascism 1919–1945* (New York: Walker and Company, 1970), 9.

10 Jeffrey T. Schnapp, ed., *A Primer of Italian Fascism*, trans. Jeffrey T. Schnapp, Olivia Sears, and Maria G. Stamp (Lincoln: University of Nebraska Press, 2000), 67.

competition in favor of government-directed harmony. No longer would the lower house of parliament be a place where conflicts would be played out.

The corporate state gave something to both workers and employers. Strikes were outlawed and private property was protected, satisfying many of those who had supported Mussolini and the Blackshirts from the start. Workers also received something from the government. Italian socialists had long advocated a legal eight-hour limit to the workday, and Mussolini legislated this in 1925. The government sponsored the Opera Nazionale Dopolavoro, the National Leisure Association, which made inexpensive holidays, sports facilities, sewing machines, and other goods available to working-class people who, especially in impoverished Italy, were not used to such things. Such measures did not, however, mean that fascist Italy was as totalitarian as Mussolini claimed. The Italian state under Mussolini avoided biting off more than it could chew. Much of its control over the localities remained cosmetic; Mussolini was not the most effective of totalitarian rulers, despite his strut.

Mussolini's triumph indicates the power that fear of communism had for the propertied classes, as well as the impact of Blackshirted force. It also, however, points to the yearning for community that had been evident in the West for some time. The fascists' nationalism and the corporate state indicate this longing. So does the cult of personality (see 10.4) that emerged with Mussolini. Mussolini became a celebrated figure who, by dominating Italians, unified them. Although in terms of Italy's constitution he was the prime minister, such a title was colorless and no indicator of personality. Mussolini preferred the more personal "Il Duce": "the leader." Propaganda stressed his virility, on one occasion showing him jumping through flaming hoops. It stressed his wisdom; his sayings were collected under alphabetized headings, a fit sentiment to be found for all occasions. Italians often saw him referred to in print as "He" and "Him," in capitals, and they wrote Him asking for favors, many simply wanting his autographed picture.

10.5.3 Brazil

Fascism came differently to Brazil. By the 1930s, Brazil had long been dominated by a landed aristocracy whose fortunes were based on exporting commodities such as cotton and, in particular, coffee. Brazilian exporters were very open to the influence of the countries that purchased these agricultural exports, Britain, in particular. So the Brazilian government tended to be pliant when it came to dealing with Britain. Indeed, some historians have argued that, for much of the nineteenth century and the early part of the twentieth, Britain exercised an "informal empire" in Brazil and other Latin American countries. Brazilian nationalists focused criticism on the great landowners and their government because of this foreign influence.

The Great Depression (see 10.3) sharpened most economic conflicts, including that between rich and poor and, in Brazil, that between landed interests and middle-class city dwellers interested in industrialization; the cities also tended to be nationalist in outlook.

However, a fascist movement, the Integralists, advocated, as the name suggests, the unity of all classes in the nation. Its "Green Shirts" were inspired by Mussolini's Blackshirts (see 10.5.2).

The president of Brazil in 1937 was Getúlio Vargas (see 10.3). Allied with the urban middle classes, he was nonetheless a master at balancing various interests. His nationalist credentials were good; in the name of national independence, he advocated the development of Brazil's own industry rather than continuing dependence on agricultural exports. Faced with the prospect of losing office in 1937, he drew on support from the Integralists and the military and executed a coup. Triumphant, he tacked toward the fascist desire for revolution by declaring an Estado Nôvo, a "new state." The Green Shirts turned out in force to salute him upon his first public appearance after the coup. Democratic elections, Vargas stated, were simply a means for conflicting desires to run riot; he eliminated the Brazilian Congress as unnecessary. Political parties were next on the chopping block. A new law declared that no publication should undermine respect for the government. The unconvinced faced a police force created to find and arrest political opponents and critics. In this way, Vargas hoped to bring unity—and reinforce his own power. Soon after the coup, Vargas told the nation that "in the New State there will be no place for the skeptics and the hesitant, unbelieving in themselves and others."[11] Signs of a cult of personality appeared (on the attractions of this kind of cult, see 10.4); Vargas's picture was to be found in all businesses. The government bolstered its nationalist position by closing down foreign language schools and newspapers, a move against immigrants such as Italians, who, like many foreigners, had become less popular with the Depression's shortage of jobs (see 10.3).

Vargas adopted a corporatist approach to economic matters (on corporatism in Italy, see 10.5.2). Economic conflicts were to be worked out in the newly created National Economic Council rather than through operations of the market or labor strikes; economic conflict, in line with Integralists' general aims, was to be suppressed. Thus, strikes were prohibited. Borrowing from Stalin's playbook, Vargas introduced a five-year plan for the economy in 1940, one geared to the development of industry (on Stalin's Five-Year Plans, see 10.4). Although he contemplated nothing like the total abolition of private property characteristic of the Soviet Union and his five-year plan did not govern *all* economic activity, the plan indicates a move away from the conflicts of the free market and toward a managed economy. Although strikes were outlawed, the government legislated an eight-hour day, paid vacations, and other regulations favorable to workers.

Despite the Estado Nôvo, Vargas, like other dictators, still had to think in terms of his political base. In Vargas's case, the Brazilian military was critical. The military had supported Vargas's coup in 1937. So had the Integralists, but relations between them and Vargas deteriorated. Vargas suspected the Integralists of planning to replace him with their own leader, and, ultimately, he saw them as just another political faction. Moreover, although he had earlier believed that Integralists had penetrated deep into the army, he now concluded that

---

11 Robert M. Levine and John J. Crocitti, eds., *The Brazil Reader: History, Culture, Politics* (Durham, NC: Duke University Press, 1999), 189.

he had overestimated that penetration. Having assured himself of the military's support, he outlawed the Integralists in 1938. Vargas himself would remain in office until he lost the military's support and fell to a coup in 1945. He had allied Brazil with the antifascist powers during World War II. In doing so, he backed the winning side (see 10.6). But the Allies were crusading against fascism, making Vargas an awkward liability in Brazil. Yet such was Vargas's ability to manipulate alliances and reinvent himself that he would have a second career as president of Brazil. Elected to office in 1950, he refrained from reviving the anti-democratic elements of the Estado Nôvo. It was a rare second act for a fascist ruler.

10.5.4 Germany

As in Italy, fascism's triumph in Germany was fostered by the aftermath of World War I. With German armies undersupplied and in retreat in 1918 and the civilian population facing starvation, the Germany high command realized that the country was defeated. Kaiser Wilhelm II was advised to install a new government, one that would be saddled with the actual surrender. Events quickly spun out of control. Wilhelm, facing revolution, fled the country, and a democratic republic was declared at the city of Weimar. Headed by the moderate socialists who had enjoyed a majority in the German parliament, or Reichstag, the Weimar Republic was forced to accept the terms dictated by the Allies in the Treaty of Versailles. Germany lost the much-contested province of Alsace-Lorraine to France; its military was to be strictly limited; it owed enormous sums to the Allies as reparations for damage done during the war; the Rhineland, lying between the Rhine River and Germany's border with France and Belgium, was to be under allied occupation for fifteen years; German troops were prohibited from entering German territory east of the Rhine River for 50 kilometers as well as the Rhineland after the fifteen-year period had elapsed (see Map 10.2), thus making the country more vulnerable to French invasion and protecting France from a German one; and, in a "war guilt" clause, Germany accepted full responsibility for the war. Germans, especially German nationalists, found Versailles humiliating and blamed the Weimar Republic for accepting it. Adding to the new government's popularity problem was the fact that the German armies were still in France at the time of the surrender, and the Allies had not occupied any portion of German soil. The rumor circulated that Germany had not, in fact, been defeated in the field, but had been "stabbed in the back" by socialists who wanted a German defeat. For many Germans, the Weimar Republic symbolized national failure. As in Italy, the immediate aftermath of the war produced rebellion and fighting in the streets (see 10.5.2). The resort to the Freikorps (see 10.2) shows the weakness of the republic.

In this atmosphere, a former corporal joined a marginal political organization, the German Workers' Party (Deutsche Arbeiterpartei), which later changed its name to the National Socialist German Workers' Party (Nationalsozialistische Deutsche Arbeiterpartei) and became widely known as the Nazi Party ("Nazi" is a shortened version of the German word "*Nationalsozialistische*"). Adolf Hitler (1889–1945), a gifted speaker, soon became the party's dominant figure.

The Nazis claimed, like Mussolini's fascists (see 10.5.2), to represent workers' interests—hence the terms "socialist" and "workers" in the party's name—while at the same time being virulently anticommunist. Early on, the Nazis advocated government expropriation and ownership of private businesses, but the party later scuttled away from such large goals when it sought support from business interests, who would naturally not support such a program. Although the Nazis were ready, as was Mussolini, to regulate private enterprise, they did not eliminate it; large companies in particular would do well under the Nazis, and private wealth, unless it was Jewish, remained in private hands. Some moves were made in the direction of corporatism (see 10.5.2); for example, the Nazis created the Reich Food Estate to unite farmers, distributors, retailers, and consumers, to set prices, and so on. Once in power, the Nazis emasculated trade unions but also spent enormously on public works projects and armaments. With unions inactive, real wages fell under the Nazis, but employment also rose, an impressive achievement during the Great Depression. The Nazis were able to point to some evidence that class differences dividing Germans were fading. They successfully pressured the university fraternities, traditionally bastions of upper-class privilege, to close down. In 1920, more than 60 percent of German army officers hailed from the aristocracy; by 1939, after six years of Nazi rule, more than 70 percent did not.

Like other fascists, the Nazis were committed nationalists. Unlike some other fascists, such as those of Brazil or Italy, the Nazis adhered to later-nineteenth-century notions of the nation as a biologically defined race (see 9.10). Germans, along with other peoples largely of northern Europe, were the "Aryan" people: naturally stronger, more intelligent, more creative, and more attuned to all the virtues than other peoples. In line with the social Darwinism that flowed from the nineteenth century into the twentieth, the Nazis asserted that the peoples (races) of the earth were engaged in a struggle for survival. According to the Nazis, the Jews were the greatest danger to Germans in this struggle. Jews, also defined as a race, were engaged in a great conspiracy against the German (i.e., Aryan) nation; the Jews' most recent triumph was the stab in the back that many Germans believed had caused the country's defeat in World War I. Jews, diabolical, international, and given to capitalism and communism, were a particular threat because they could so easily pass as Germans, living in Germany and speaking German. But no Jew could be a true German, that is, a member of the Aryan race. A primary-school student who sent in her essay for publication in a Nazi newspaper observed that Jews were like vermin, and should be exterminated like vermin.

Central to Hitler's program was foreign conquest. Germans, as the master race, were destined to rule over all others. Indeed, Germany itself was too crowded for the Aryan people, who needed *Lebensraum* (German for "living space"). For *Lebensraum*, Hitler looked east to Poland and, in particular, Russia—both Slavic nations and so, as far as the Nazis were concerned, the homelands of people born to be enslaved, or simply eliminated. The fact that Russia was ruled by the despised communists made the idea that much more appealing. Hence, the Nazis were to usher in a new German *Reich*, or empire.

Like other fascist leaders and like Stalin, Hitler was surrounded by a cult of personality (see 10.4), which brought Germans a feeling of unity through their sense of direct connection with him. The Nazis embraced the notion that the party and nation should be governed by a single, all-powerful leader: *der Führer* (German for "the leader"). Additionally, Germany was to be run according to the "Führer principle": all institutions were to be governed by an unquestioned leader, and all leaders were ultimately subordinate to the great leader, Hitler. Hitler himself was celebrated as the nation's savior, a man of destiny who would save Germany from racial threat and the limitations of Versailles. Once Hitler was in power, his face appeared on posters everywhere. Although his formal title on taking power was "Chancellor of Germany," the same title held by other prime ministers under the Weimar Republic and Bismarck's German Empire, Hitler preferred to be known by the more personal der Führer. In 1934, all German military personnel were required to swear an oath not, as before, to an unnamed president and the German constitution but to Hitler personally. All civil servants were to include the phrase "Hail [German "Heil"] Hitler!" in their official correspondence. Most towns in Germany quickly made him one of their citizens and named their main public square for him. School children were taught to think of Hitler as another father, whom they should work to please.

Like fascists in Italy and elsewhere, the Nazis promoted a message of national unity, an important part of their appeal to an atomized and divided society seeking a sense of community. All Germans should act and work as one, regardless of class differences; Marxist class struggle was to be a thing of the past. Students bound for university, generally from middle-class backgrounds, were required to labor in camps so they would feel close to the workers and certainly not superior to them. This national unity was also to transcend regional attachments. Some Germans still felt bound to the various states that had originally come together to form a united Germany in 1871 (see 9.4.4); indeed, these states had reasserted themselves in the wake of the monarchy's fall, although Germany remained more or less a nation state. Now all Germans were to identify fully with the *Volk* (see 9.3), no matter where they lived. The thudding stress on unity—*one* nation united in a single empire and in the Führer's leadership—is evident in the Nazi slogan: "*ein Volk* [one nation], *ein Reich* [one empire], *ein Führer* [one leader]." Even those divisions reinforced by the Nazis, in particular that between "real" Germans and Jews, united the former against the latter. Struggle was to be focused on enemies of the *Volk*. Within the community, all was to be harmonious cooperation.

In their pursuit of power, the Nazis did not shrink from violence. The Brownshirts, inspired by Mussolini's Blackshirts (see 10.5.2), were the party's paramilitary organization. Known as the SA and descended from the Freikorps that had emerged at the close of World War I, the Brownshirts intimidated Jews, communists, and others regarded as enemies—and did worse. In 1923, the Nazis, relying on the Brownshirts and hoping for popular support, had attempted a putsch, or rebellion, centered on a beer hall in Munich. This "Beer Hall Putsch" failed. Hitler had hoped for something like Mussolini's March on Rome (see 10.5.2), but, unlike Mussolini, Hitler did not face a government interested in making use of him. Hitler was thrown into a comfortable prison from which to plan his next moves. He stayed there less than a year.

Hitler's plans did not get the Nazis very far until 1929 and the Great Depression. As elsewhere, in Germany, the Depression sharpened class antagonisms and whetted discontent. The Nazis' promise of unity gained greater appeal. In the election of July 1932, the Nazis took more of the vote than any other party in Germany, although the number of rival nationalist parties deprived them of a majority. At this point, the government was dominated by conservative nationalists who lacked the Nazis' popular support but who relied instead on the popularity of German President Paul von Hindenburg (1847–1934), an aged and conservative former general. The Reichstag, increasingly ineffective, was increasingly bypassed by "emergency" decrees issued by the chancellor using a loophole in the Weimar constitution. Democracy in Weimar Germany was failing, but the government still felt it needed popular support, a sign of the extent to which the expectation of such support had become embedded in Western society (see 9.10). In contrast with the time of the Beer Hall Putsch of 1923, the Nazis now had wide popular support. In January 1933, the recent German chancellor, the aristocratic conservative Franz von Papen (1879–1969), made a deal with Hitler, a deal that was somewhat reluctantly endorsed by Hindenburg: Hitler would become chancellor, heading a coalition government with other conservative parties; Papen would be vice-chancellor. The old hands expected that they would control Hitler and use his electoral strength to their own ends.

Hitler used them instead. On becoming chancellor in January 1933, he ignored his cabinet colleagues, dissolved the Reichstag, and called for new elections. The following month (February 27, 1933), the Reichstag burned to the ground, probably set aflame by the communist the Nazis said had done it. Seizing his opportunity, Hitler declared a national emergency and took control of the press. In the few weeks before the March 1933 election, Brownshirts freely intimidated political opponents. The Nazis took 44 percent of the vote; parties allied to them added another 8 percent. In the Enabling Act of March 1933, the new Reichstag approved sweeping powers for Hitler, giving the cabinet he headed the power to govern by decree.

In Germany more than in Mussolini's Italy (see 10.5.2), a fascist party was central to fascism's success. The Nazi Party, like political parties headed by other Western politicians, provided the organization that managed Hitler's electoral victories. Once in power, however, the Nazi Party enjoyed a novel position, one more similar to that of the Communist Party of the Soviet Union than to that of traditional political parties. The Nazi Party operated parallel to the state. The Hitler Youth for young people, for example, designed to inculcate Nazi principles, became compulsory, like the public schools. The Brownshirts acted as an alternate military and police force but, unlike the state army and police, were readily available for use against Hitler's political opponents. (By the end of the regime, however, all state authorities were available for use against Hitler's enemies.) Indeed, the German military establishment feared it would be displaced by the Brownshirts, who had ambitions to do just that. Hitler, in the end, sided with the army for several reasons. He gained its officers' gratitude; the relatively undisciplined Brownshirts were not the instrument he would need to embark on the conquest of *Lebensraum*; and the Brownshirts were prone to stress the more extreme socialism of the early Nazi movement, which was inconvenient given Hitler's desire to cultivate the business interests that he felt promised the fastest way to rearm Germany. In the "Night of the Long Knives" of June 30, 1934, Brownshirt leaders all over Germany were arrested and executed. Hitler announced that he had foiled a revolutionary plot to overthrow the Reich; this victory was greeted with enthusiasm. Yet a small unit of the Brownshirts, which had taken part in the Night of the Long Knives, was soon promoted to replace the purged group. This smaller and more tightly disciplined group was the SS (for the German word for "protection squad"); it had been founded, originally, as Hitler's personal bodyguard. The Brownshirt organization that had been purged (the SA) survived, but without its former influence. The rise of the SS confirms Hitler's reliance on the Nazi Party as well as the German government in ruling the country. The party also ensured that the state stayed true to party goals. At all levels of government, party minders ensured the correct political views.

As did other fascist states and the Soviet Union as well, the Nazis hoped to control all spheres of life. Central to these plans was the goal of "aligning" all organizations with the new Nazi state. Unions, schools, trade associations, religious organizations, all these and more were to have Nazi leaders or at least leaders with Nazi sympathies; to be controlled by their leaders, an instance of the "Führer principle"; and to be used to forward National Socialist aims.

Nazi Germany has been seen as a model totalitarian state (on this term and debate concerning it, see 10.4). Many have also disputed this claim, pointing to rivalries among various state and Nazi Party agencies, to the initiative often taken by local authorities, to the Nazis' willingness to co-opt rather than eliminate the army or big business, and to Hitler's own tendency to put off decisions or even issue contradictory orders. Yet an effort at totalitarian government is still evident, as the alignment policy indicates. And when it was determined to do so, the regime had real successes in quashing dissent, molding citizens, and marshaling resources.

The enemies of the German "racial community" needed to be separated from it, lest they do damage. Communists and others were subject to arrest and imprisonment in concentration camps, eventually run by the SS, where conditions (beatings, lack of medical care, and so on) were harsh and dangerous from the beginning. (Only during World War II did the camps become places of deliberate mass extermination.) In early 1933, the camps held about 45,000 prisoners; their numbers rose and fell over the years. Increasingly, however, broad criteria were applied to determine eligibility for the camps. "Asocials," people deemed by the authorities to be uncommitted to the community, became fair game. A person who shirked work could be classified as an "asocial," as could people whose attitudes might lead to asocial or actively criminal behavior.

Outside the camps, the Nazis also separated certain groups from the mass of the population. Here the Nazis aimed at the Jews. Jews had been segregated from the rest of society in the West in the course of the Middle Ages. In the eighteenth and nineteenth centuries, however, such restrictions had been relaxed and eliminated under the influence of Enlightenment ideas of equality and nationalist strivings for national integration. The Nazis, seeing Jews as a threat to Aryan purity, reversed such measures. Jews were forbidden to marry "pure" Germans. They were driven out of the professions, such as the law and medicine, a process aided by the alignment of professional associations with the Nazi state. Government positions were, of course, out of the question. Where Jewish children remained in schools, they might have to sit on a "Jewish bench" in class. Jews were forced to sell their businesses to other Germans or close. Where they could live became restricted; many German towns posted signs that Jews were not welcome. Finally came the requirement that Jews wear a yellow star on their clothing, so all Germans would know that they were Jews.

The next step was their extermination, undertaken during World War II. After the war, the term "genocide"—the deliberate and systematic killing of a people, often coordinated by the state—would be coined to describe this development. In what has become known as the Holocaust, and what Nazi authorities termed "the final solution," millions of Jews were transported to concentration camps refitted to kill on a mass scale. Many were simply deliberately worked to death, set at hard labor on insufficient calories. Outright execution was cumbersome at first. The Nazis tried to shoot them; at Borisov, about twenty Jews at a time were ordered to lie down in a deep trench, shot, and then another twenty were ordered to lie on top of them, and so on until the trench was filled. This was slow and intensive work. More efficient were the gas chambers eventually set up in concentration camps, such as those at Auschwitz and Treblinka. German control of most of Europe during much of the war meant that Jews from throughout Europe, not just from Germany, were sent to the camps. What were now death camps by design were also used to wipe out others the Nazis considered undesirable. Gypsies were a subhuman race. Homosexuals were degenerates, and so on. Along with the Jews, these other categories brought the total to some 10 million dead. The Holocaust, an enormous undertaking, especially under the pressure of war, demonstrates both the power of Nazi ideology and what powerful twentieth-century states could now accomplish.

10.6 WORLD WAR II

It is tempting to think of World War II (1939–1945) as a rematch among the major players of World War I (1914–1918) and the two decades between the wars as merely a truce. Once again, Germany went to war with Britain, France, Russia and the United States (and China), although this time Italy and Japan fought as Germany's allies rather than its opponents. Certainly, the coming of the Second World War was rooted in the experience of the First. The Nazis saw the war as an attempt to reverse the Treaty of Versailles, although their ambitions were greater than that. Britain and France, determined to avoid a repeat of their suffering during World War I, followed a policy of appeasement that arguably made the war with Germany, when it did come, a large war rather than a small one. The technology of war in World War I had made war especially dreadful; so people's experience of the horrors shaped by that technology helps explain this appeasement policy and so the coming of World War II. Changing technology also helps explain why the course of the Second World War was rather different from that of the First.

Germany in 1933 was militarily weak. It had been hobbled by the Treaty of Versailles, which had demilitarized the Rhineland, limited its army to 100,000 soldiers, prohibited Germany from having an air force, and barely allowed it a navy. The Nazis' program was to reverse all this, first as a salve to German pride but also because only a militarily strong Germany would be able to conquer *Lebensraum* in the East. And of course the Nazis believed that only the strong survive (see 10.5.4). Soon after coming to power, Hitler secretly ordered German rearmament. In 1935, he announced to the world that Germany now had an air force and would not abide by the Versailles settlement's limit on its army. Indeed, he instituted conscription. France, Britain, and Italy expressed concern, but did little else. France would not take military action without Britain, on whom it expected to rely for needed war imports. British action against Germany was, however, hampered by a sense among Britons that Germany had been unfairly punished at Versailles; the prime minister of the time had reached this conclusion even before the Versailles conference ended. Both countries preferred to avoid reliving the misery and destruction of World War I. Indeed, fear of another war was common in Germany too. In the run up to war in the 1930s, the German secret police reported great anxiety among Germans about a major war—a fear that the Nazis' control of the government meant they could largely ignore, unlike the governments of democratic Britain and France. Added to anxiety about reliving World War I was the widespread belief that advances in airplane technology rendered cities and so civilians defenseless against massive aerial bombing. Moreover, the lesson both Britain and France had imbibed from World War I was that defense was more powerful than offense. French strategy, for example, focused on the construction of the "Maginot Line," a series of fortifications—a kind of supertrench—that ran the length of France's border with Germany. Finally, war with Germany was not encouraged by the fact that politicians in both countries comforted themselves with the hope that a stronger Germany, under the ferociously anticommunist Nazis, would at least prove a military counterweight to the Soviet Union, a country still anathema to capitalists everywhere. Mussolini's Italy was also alarmed by Hitler's expansionism but was not strong enough to give France the support it sought. (Italy would eventually ally with Germany in 1936, declaring a Rome-Berlin axis along which the world would turn; thus Germany and Italy, and their eventual ally Japan, would become known as the "Axis powers.")

In March 1936, Hitler moved troops into the Rhineland, German territory in which no German soldiers had served since 1918. Indeed, since the Versailles settlement, the area had served as a buffer zone to guarantee French security. It was perhaps his greatest bluff. Germany was still weak. German forces were under orders to scurry back out of the Rhineland should French troops march to meet them; police units even accompanied German troops to make their numbers seem more threatening. Hitler announced (despite his often proclaimed goal of *Lebensraum*) that Germany had no demands for further territory in Europe. Britain and France overestimated the number of German troops in the Rhineland by a factor of ten. The French considered military action but would not move without Britain, where it was said that, by sending soldiers into the Rhineland, the Germans were simply entering their own "back garden." France's troops stayed behind the Maginot Line.

At this point, it is fair to describe French and British policy toward Germany as one of "appeasement": they made concessions to Germany in the hope that Hitler would live up to his statements that this latest concession would satisfy him. Britain embraced this approach more readily than France, but because France was unwilling to challenge Germany militarily without Britain, Britain effectively drove French decisions regarding Germany.

Austria was Hitler's next target. For nineteenth-century German nationalists, the separation of ethnically German Austria from the rest of Germany had rankled. As long as Austria had been part of the much larger Austrian (i.e., Habsburg) Empire, such a union was impossible. But that empire's collapse at the end of World War I had opened the door to union between Germany and Austria, a door that the Treaty of Versailles, aimed at weakening Germany, had slammed shut. Although the Austrian government, itself fascist, resisted German pressure to join the Reich, most Austrian political parties were for it. In March 1938, German troops entered Austria, and Hitler declared Austria annexed to Germany. France and Britain took no military action.

Most Germans now lived under the Third Reich. But not quite all. There were Germans in Alsace-Lorraine, of course, surrendered to France at the end of World War I. There were Germans in the new Polish state carved out of former territories of Germany, Russia, and the Austro-Hungarian Empire following World War I. There were smaller numbers of Germans scattered in the Balkans, the Soviet Union, and elsewhere. And there were Germans in the Sudetenland (Map 10.2), the mountainous rind of territory that separated most of Czechoslovakia, another new state cut out from the carcass of the Habsburg Empire, from Germany. The Czechs comprised Czechoslovakia's dominant national group, followed by Slovaks, followed by the three million or so Germans of the Sudetenland. So after the annexation of Austria in 1938, Hitler stepped up pressure on Czechoslovakia. The German press, firmly under government control, ran story after story about the (false or exaggerated) oppression of Germans in Czechoslovakia; rumors of impending invasion circulated. Britain made noises about defending Czechoslovakia; France had a formal alliance with Czechoslovakia. Hitler's own generals warned that if Britain and France supported Czechoslovakia, Germany would likely lose the resulting war. After all, a good number of German troops would not be available to deal with French and British forces if they had to operate in the south against Czechoslovakia. Indeed, a sign of Germany military weakness at this point was that, when Hitler showed he was determined to go ahead with the invasion of Czechoslovakia, some of his senior officers began to conspire against him. (They did so not because they disapproved of an attack but because they were convinced that Germany would not win a war against Britain, France, and Czechoslovakia.[12]) After Hitler's public threat to invade if the Sudetenland

---

12 The conspiracy came to nothing when Hitler's move against Czechoslovakia succeeded.

Germans were not granted internal self-government, Britain's Prime Minister Neville Chamberlain (1869–1940) began to meet with Hitler, who then began to demand not self-government for the Sudetenland but its union with Germany. In September 1938, representatives of Germany, Britain, France, and Italy met at the German city of Munich to resolve the crisis. Representatives of Czechoslovakia were not asked to the meeting. Britain and France agreed that Czechoslovakia was to surrender the Sudetenland, whose mountains and fortresses provided its chief defense against German attack. Returning home, Chamberlain announced that the agreement ensured "peace for our time."[13] Hitler gave assurances that Germany had acquired all the lands it wanted and would seek no more. In March 1939, Germany swallowed the rest of Czechoslovakia. French, British, and German eyes turned toward Poland.

In 1939, France already had a treaty of alliance with Poland. Days after Germany took over all of Czechoslovakia, the British government, now convinced that appeasement was failing, approached Poland for an alliance as well. Britain and France announced that a German attack on Poland would mean war with them. Given past experience, Hitler was not inclined to take this threat too seriously; the fact that Britain and France would have trouble helping the distant Poles also undermined their credibility. France and Britain, now as fearful of Germany as they had been of the Soviet Union, attempted to bring Russia into an alliance with them and Poland. But Stalin was suspicious, and the Poles, themselves suspicious of Soviet ambitions regarding their territory, did not cooperate. In August 1939, Germany and the Soviet Union stunned the world by setting aside their ideological hostility and signing a "Nazi-Soviet Non-Aggression Pact," promising to remain at peace with each other. They also, secretly, agreed to divide Poland between them. On September 1, 1939, Germany invaded Poland, and the Soviet Union soon followed, occupying Poland's eastern half. Two days after the German invasion began, Britain and France declared war on Germany in defense of Poland; the British Commonwealth—and so Australia, Canada, and South Africa followed—in part concerned that a British defeat would undermine Britain's ability to provide for their defense and in part out of deference to Britain's traditional leadership. Unwilling to take on another major power, Britain and France remained at peace, however, with the Soviet Union. Thus World War II began.

World War I had been a largely static war, especially on the Western Front, where the technology of war—trenches and rapid-fire weapons—made the defense more powerful than the offense (see 10.2). It was this kind of war for which Britain, France, and, to some extent Poland, had prepared. The Germans, however, had discovered that tanks, when massed together and supported by aerial bombardment, could punch through an enemy line and quickly spread out from behind it, effectively surrounding enemy troops and cutting them off from help. Battles in World War II would be battles of movement, not stagnation in trenches. Germany, therefore, planned for *Blitzkrieg*—lightning war—rather than a long war of attrition. The war's first years appeared to confirm the wisdom of this decision. Poland fell in a matter of weeks while French and British troops, rather

---

13 Neville Chamberlain, *The Struggle for Peace* (London: Hutchinson & Co., [1939]), 303.

than attacking Germany from the west, waited for the Germans to impale themselves on the Maginot Line, a period known in Britain as "the phony war." After gulping down Norway and Denmark in 1940, Germany turned to France the same year. Sending their tank units just to the north of the Maginot Line through the thick forests of the Ardennes (Map 10.2), the Germans raced past French lines, cutting off from their supplies French and British troops stationed in the north of France and bypassing the troops anchored in the Maginot Line. France surrendered in six weeks. Frantically, the British army and some French troops were evacuated back to Britain, leaving most of their equipment behind. Holland also surrendered to Germany. In months, Hitler had succeeded where four years of German effort in World War I had failed. Britain, disarmed except for its considerable navy and air force, stood isolated in Europe. It was, however, still supported by the self-governing dominions of the Commonwealth—Canada, Australia, South Africa—and by its empire. The Germans expected the British to sue for peace. Under Prime Minister Winston Churchill (1874–1965), who promised the country only "blood, toil, tears, and sweat" in his first speech to the House after taking the job, Britain refused.[14] That position remained unchanged even after the German air force attempted to wipe out Britain's air power and, failing that, to demoralize the British into surrender by bombing British cities. Known as "the Blitz," this effort took place between August 1940 and May 1941. Much of London was leveled—some 20,000 Londoners died—and the city of Coventry was reduced to ruins; these are simply the best known of the cities damaged in the Blitz. Civilian morale, however, did not collapse in the face of aerial bombing in the way conventional wisdom had predicted. Although Britain fought the Axis powers in North Africa, there was little it could do to strike back at Germany directly.

For Hitler, however, *Lebensraum* still beckoned. Romania, Hungary, and Bulgaria had already been pushed into alliance with Germany and Italy; the Germans had occupied Greece and Yugoslavia (Map 10.2). Encouraged by his easy victories, especially over France and Poland, and convinced that the Soviet Union was a rotten house ready to collapse once the front door was kicked in, Hitler ordered the invasion of the USSR in 1941. This perception of rot did not stem only from Hitler's own hatred of communism or from his thinking that Russian Slavs were a racially inferior people; the years 1937–1938 had seen Stalin purge more than half of his army's senior officers for political reasons (on such purges, see 10.4). The German tanks rolled up a series of successes in a matter of weeks, as surrounded Russian troops surrendered in the hundreds of thousands. German troops came within 18 miles of the Soviet capital in Moscow and began to lay siege to Russia's second city, Leningrad (formerly Saint Petersburg).

A Russian tsar had once said that his most important commanders were generals January and February (recall Napoleon's experience in Russia—see 8.6). Russian winters are fierce, and the winter of 1941 was no exception. Determined that blitzkrieg would be all but over by winter, the Germans had failed to equip their troops properly for cold and snow.

---

14 Winston Churchill, *A Churchill Anthology: Selections from the Writings and Speeches of Sir Winston Churchill*, ed. F.W. Heath (Long Acre, London: Odhams Press Limited, 1962), 664.

Soviet authorities equipped their soldiers better in that respect. The Germans had also not reckoned with the Soviets' ability to transport their armament factories beyond German reach, or their ability to draw in troops stationed in east Asia, bringing them west to face the Germans. The cold of winter, which came early that year, was also crucial to stopping the German advance. In temperatures below 0 degrees Fahrenheit, German troops short on fuel stuffed their uniforms with newspapers for warmth; 100,000 were felled by frostbite. The water pipes of German steam engines froze and burst in the cold, preventing supplies from reaching distant German armies; Russian locomotives had their pipes inside their boilers for warmth. Despite losing millions of soldiers, Soviet forces regrouped. On some occasions, German commanders asked for permission to retreat in the face of a Russian resurgence. Hitler refused. In December 1941, Russian forces rallied and attacked the Germans to the north and south of Moscow in temperatures of −15 degrees Fahrenheit, driving them back again. German forces penetrated deeper into Russia in the warm months of 1942, but they eventually would be pushed back. An instance of this dynamic is the battle of Stalingrad in 1942 (see Map 10.2). German armies penetrated deep into the Soviet Union to take the city. But they themselves were besieged there later that year, surrounded by resurgent Russian forces after Hitler denied requests to withdraw to safety. The Germans faced years of retreat before Soviet armies, equipped not only by Soviet factories beyond the Ural Mountains but by the United States. And that US support can only be explained by revisiting 1941.

In 1941, Britain was desperate to ward off invasion. For help, the British looked to the United States. The two countries had been allies in World War I and shared a common language and political culture. Moreover, the American president, Franklin Delano Roosevelt (see 10.3), was convinced that long-term US interests were against a Europe ruled by Germany. But intervention in the war was political poison. Most Americans preferred to stay out of a European fight. The furthest Roosevelt could go was to declare the United States "the arsenal of democracy," letting the British have supplies on easy terms and cooperating quietly behind the scenes.

American attention was also distracted by events in Asia. Japan, eager for rice fields and other resources, had invaded China in 1931 and expanded its invasion into the central provinces in 1937. The United States, however, did not favor Japanese dominance in China and was also concerned that growing Japanese power might threaten its own Asian possessions, in particular the Philippines (see 9.9). So the United States applied economic pressure, threatening to cut off the export to Japan of the many materials it needed to supply its industry and army; this threat was carried out in the summer of 1941. With negotiations failing in Washington, DC, the Japanese government elected to go to war with the United States, as well as with Britain and Holland. Seizing Western colonies and gaining dominance in Asia would give Japan the resources it needed. The US Pacific Fleet would be eliminated by a surprise attack, which would make that seizure possible. On December 7, 1941, Japanese planes sank much of the American navy at Pearl Harbor, and then moved in on American, British, and Dutch colonies in Asia. The United States declared war on Japan. Hitler, having earlier signed an alliance with Japan and perhaps relieved by the opportunity to have a shooting war with Britain's unofficial American ally, declared war on the United States. Now Roosevelt, at war with Japan, was also free to enter the war in Europe against Germany, as he had wished to do for some time. Indeed, he gave the war in Europe priority; American forces were essential to the invasion of Europe from Britain, "D-Day" (June 6, 1944). More than before, however, the war was a world war.[15] In the end, neither Germany nor Japan could compete with the sheer productive capacity of the US economy, which, with the stimulus of wartime demand, soared out of the Depression. American resources and much Allied blood, especially Russian blood, would defeat the Axis powers.

There would be oceans of blood. Fifteen million died in battle, many more than in World War I. The Soviet Union suffered the most, and, of the major combatants, France and the United States the least. In round figures, the numbers of military deaths came to approximately the following:

Soviet Union: 6 million or more
Germany: 3.5 million
China: 2.2 million
Japan: 1.3 million
Poland: 700,000
Britain and Commonwealth: 400,000 and more
United States: 300,000
France: 200,000

Unlike World War I, this war saw at least as many civilian deaths (but these are even harder to count); one estimate places the total number of dead at 60 million. Many died as a result of Nazi and Japanese policies toward the conquered, even leaving aside the deliberate extermination of the death camps. These policies were especially deadly in Eastern Europe, Russia, and China. Moreover, the defeated often faced deportation—such as the Germans from the German lands added to Poland at war's end—under conditions so harsh that death claimed many. Then there were the famines the war left in its wake.

Oddly, although the Second World War had been far more destructive than the First, World War II did not result in so great a revulsion against war itself, except, perhaps, among the citizens of the defeated Axis powers. True, arguably firmer steps were taken to avoid another conflagration, such as the founding of the United Nations and, later, the European Community and European Union (see 10.10), and some antiwar literature got written. But, in Russia, which had won, the war could be seen as a crusade—a successful

---

15 Indeed, although World War II is conventionally dated as starting in 1939 with the declaration of war by Britain and France against Germany, one could argue that, from an Asian perspective, the war began in 1937 or even 1931 with Japan's invasion of China, and then expanded beyond Asia with Germany's declaration of war against the United States in 1941.

one—against the Nazi invader. The other Allied powers took a similar view. Technological change also played a role. All wars produce horror as well as destruction. Yet the peculiar horror of World War I's trenches, of living on the field of battle (see 10.2), was not, by and large, repeated in World War II's war of tanks and movement. The technology of war made a difference.

One source of civilian deaths was the aerial bombardment of cities. The fears and hopes of the 1930s concerning such bombardment did not, however, entirely materialize. The experts had said that there would be no defense against bombers attacking cities and that civilians bombed from the air would give up and force their governments to surrender. Yet, as the British discovered during the Blitz, fighter planes could prevent at least some enemy bombers from getting through, especially with the help of a new instrument of war, radar; the British were further helped by the fact that they had broken the German radio code. More strikingly, civilians, when bombed, often became even more determined to see the war through. The Blitz did not break British morale as the Germans had hoped. British and American strategists would be just as disappointed. In the latter part of the war, they used their aerial superiority to bomb German cities, often with incendiaries, day and night. Germany lost some 600,000 civilians to allied bombing; the firebombing of the city of Dresden leveled the city in one night (February 14, 1945). Yet German civilians carried on, and factories were moved or rebuilt and were soon back in operation.

Near the end of the war, however, a technological breakthrough changed aerial bombardment. During the war, the United States developed the world's first atomic bomb, a weapon ready for use by the middle of 1945. Germany, bled white in Russia and invaded from the west after British and American forces landed in Europe in 1944, had surrendered in May 1945. The Nazi regime collapsed; Hitler committed suicide. But the American military, planning the invasion of Japan, still faced the problem of Japanese resistance. Aerial bombing had leveled Japanese cities; 89,000 had perished in one night in Tokyo alone. Yet the Japanese, too, did not appear ready to surrender because their cities were burning. In the spring of 1945, US forces attacked the island of Okinawa, on the approach to the Japanese home islands; 110,000 Japanese troops refused to surrender and died; 7,400 were taken prisoner. American casualties were much lighter—with some 12,500 dead—but were much heavier and at a much higher rate than in previous Pacific battles. The lesson appeared to be clear. The Japanese would fight to the death to defend their home islands; military planners were estimating American casualties at a million. But perhaps if many bombers dropping many bombs would not do the job, a single superbomb dropped by a lone airplane would make more of an impression. On August 6, 1945, the American bomber the *Enola Gay* dropped the new atomic bomb on the city of Hiroshima, killing 78,000 at a stroke. Another bomb snuffed out 25,000 at Nagasaki three days later. On August 15, Emperor Hirohito of Japan (1926–1989) announced his country's defeat. The surrender was formally accepted on September 2, 1945, ending World War II. More than conventional aerial bombing, the shocking power of the atomic bomb had changed the face of war.

10.7 COLD WAR: THE PAX AMERICANA AND COMMUNISTA

World War II left two great world powers, soon to be called "superpowers": the United States and the Soviet Union. For the first time, two states towered militarily over all others and directly competed with each other for dominance across the globe. Historians have tended to see this era of competition as one of conflict, as a "Cold War," for good reason. The United States and the Soviet Union each saw in the other its only real rival and so saw every gain by the other as its own loss. For that reason, each constantly sought to counter the other, although at times they simultaneously sought to relax tensions. Although both the United States and the Soviet Union stood ready for war, each refrained from such a war, concerned that nuclear weapons would destroy both sides—yet another example of the influence of technology on society and politics.

Yet peace, and not just peace out of fear of nuclear annihilation, is another important feature of the Cold War. The dominance of the United States and the Soviet Union also imposed peace on other states. For this reason, historians and contemporaries spoke of a *pax Americana* in the decades after World War II. For similar reasons, one can also speak of a *pax communista*, although the term never saw general use.

Pax Americana (American peace) and pax communista (communist peace): both terms are inspired by the *pax Romana*, the Roman peace. The ancient Romans subdued the frequently warring peoples around the Mediterranean Sea and, by doing so, enforced peace among them. Observers of the United States and its allies noticed a similar phenomenon. The United States led a series of alliances with smaller powers: e.g., France, Britain, Canada, West Germany, and other states in Europe (NATO—the North Atlantic Treaty Organization, established 1949), and Australia, Pakistan, Thailand, and other states in the Asian-Pacific region (SEATO—the Southeast Asia Treaty Organization, established 1954). Soon, everyone realized that the Americans so dwarfed the military resources of their allies, so dominated these alliances, that America's allies were dependent on American military support. And this dependency, in turn, made it impossible for American allies to go to war with each other. Britain and France may have entered into two wars with Germany in the first half of the twentieth century without American support, but, in the century's second half, a third such war was out of the question. Indeed, without at least the acquiescence of the United States, military adventures even outside the alliance were out of the question. Although Britain began to withdraw from Egypt in 1946—part of the British Empire's dissolution after World War II (see 10.9)—British and French interests retained ownership of Egypt's Suez Canal, which offered an easy way to ship goods between Europe and Asia. Failing to get financial support from the West for its projects, the new Egyptian government seized the canal. Britain and France responded by invading Egypt in 1956. They had not, however, consulted their American ally. The great days of European empires, and European independence, were over. The United States insisted the troops be recalled, and they were. Washington did not dictate the foreign policy of its allies. France, for example, was able to leave NATO's centralized military command structure in 1966, although it remained ultimately dependent on the United States for its defense against a Soviet invasion. But Washington did constrain its allies' foreign policies, sometimes mightily. And the United States could also, more rarely, intervene in its allies' domestic politics, for example, covertly working to eliminate the Communist Party from Italy's coalition government in 1947. Critics of the situation spoke of American imperialism.

A less noticed peace—at least in the West—was the pax communista imposed by the Soviet Union. Tension had long simmered in eastern Europe and the Balkans. Conflict between Serbia and the Austro-Hungarian Empire had sparked the First World War (see 10.2). The carving up of the Austro-Hungarian and Russian empires after World War I had simply multiplied the possibilities of conflict. The years after the war were marked by wars, some close to skirmishes, between Poland and Russia (1919–1921), Poland and Czechoslovakia (1919–1920), Hungary and Czechoslovakia (1919–1920), Romania and Hungary (1919), Greece and Turkey (1919–1922), Bulgaria and Greece (1925). World War II, however, ended differently: with Soviet armies occupying Poland, Romania, Bulgaria, Hungary, Czechoslovakia, and the eastern part of Germany. Although Stalin had told Britain and the United States that he would permit free elections in those countries, he fully intended to impose communist governments responsible to Moscow if such governments were not elected. This point was understood by at least some in the British and American governments—despite their protests—from the start. Yugoslavia, itself a collection of sometimes rival peoples (Serbians, Croats, Muslims, Albanians, and others), also found itself under a communist government modeled on that of Stalin, not because it was occupied by Soviet troops but because the communist resisters to the Germans were able to take power as Germany collapsed. All these communist states, except independent-minded Yugoslavia, were forced to become allies of the Soviet Union (an alliance eventually known as the Warsaw Pact), which also governed their foreign policies. Far more rigorously—and violently—than the United States, the Soviet Union sought to control the internal politics of its "allies." In 1956, revolution broke out in Hungary, sparked by students demanding democratic reforms and workers demanding a less repressive socialism. The Hungarian authorities installed as prime minister a reformer who had cooperated with the Soviet authorities before, thus hoping to placate opposition both at home and in Moscow. But Imre Nagy (1896–1958) proceeded to legalize noncommunist parties and withdraw from the Warsaw Pact. The Soviets invaded in force. The revolution was crushed, Nagy and others were executed, and control by the Soviet Union was reestablished. Rebellion in Czechoslovakia in 1968 was similarly defeated. No one in France feared such a result when that country left the NATO command structure ten years later, suggesting the difference in control exercised over allies by the United States and the Soviet Union.

America protected its allies with a powerful yet dangerous tool: nuclear weapons. Although the United States kept troops in Europe after World War II, eventually establishing what appeared to be permanent bases in western Germany and elsewhere, the United States soon concluded that it could not compete with the Soviets when it came to numbers of troops in Europe. (US allies themselves had already concluded that American help would be necessary for their defense; the initiative to form NATO had come from Britain, in

the face of some resistance from a US Congress hesitant about commitments overseas.[16])
Nuclear weapons covered the gap. The United States announced in 1954 that a Soviet attack
on its NATO allies would be met with nuclear arms. This "nuclear umbrella" provided
by the United States threatened to devastate Western Europe—and America itself, should
the Soviet Union, as was expected, reply in kind to American use of nuclear weapons.

The Soviet Union had tested its own atomic bomb in 1949. The United States responded
by developing even more powerful nuclear weapons, starting with the hydrogen bomb,
hundreds of times more powerful than the atomic bombs dropped on Japan. A nuclear
arms race between the United States and Soviet Union accelerated. An additional development was the invention of rockets capable of delivering such weapons anywhere in
the world. The nuclear arms of both superpowers deterred each from attacking the other
directly. The result was that both sides took care to avoid a "hot" war of the traditional
kind because it would result, according to the phrase of the time, in "mutually assured
destruction" (known by its acronym, MAD). Thus, from at least the late 1940s to the
late 1980s, the United States and the Soviet Union engaged in a Cold War, each seeking
advantage over the other, developing their nuclear arsenals to ensure the deterrence to a
nuclear first strike, yet hesitant to allow their conflicts to heat up. The technology of war
had become so destructive that it kept the peace.

But not entirely. A relatively safe way for each side to seek victory over the other was
in a "proxy war." One such war was in Korea. As World War II drew to a close, Soviet
forces, invading from the north, had occupied a portion of Korea, while United States
troops invaded from the south. The two countries agreed to what was to be a temporary
division of the country at the 38th parallel (Map 10.3). The Cold War, however, froze
that division. In the north, the Soviets supported a government set up under a Korean
communist and veteran of the Red Army, Kim Il Sung (1912–1994). In the south, the
United States sponsored the nationalist and anticommunist Syngman Rhee (1875–1965).
Tensions rose from 1948. In 1950, with an army equipped by Stalin's Soviet Union, Kim
attacked South Korea in a bid to unite the country under communist rule. The United
States saw this as communist, and therefore Soviet, aggression. The lesson of the 1930s
appeared obvious: appeasement would eventually lead to aggression on a larger scale, so
Kim's (read Stalin's) move had to be checked. The American president, Harry S. Truman
(1884–1972), ordered US troops in South Korea to defend the country and sent in more
forces. He also obtained United Nations condemnation of the attack and the military
commitment of other UN countries' forces to South Korea's defense.[17] The war lasted
until a truce was declared in 1953. No peace treaty was concluded, however, and the two
Koreas developed separately, the South as capitalist—and eventually democratic in fact as
well as in form—and the North as a highly controlled communist dictatorship. Thus, the

---

16 Indeed, the American secretary of state assured the Senate that NATO would not involve large
    numbers of boots on the ground in Europe.

17 Ordinarily, the Soviet Union would have used its veto power to prevent these UN actions, but it
    had temporarily walked out of the organization and so could not exercise its veto.

two superpowers avoided direct confrontation by helping others (proxies) fight; at least that was the official position. But the United States and the Soviet Union also worked to prevent the conflict from creating a wider war, potentially a third world war. Truman vetoed proposals to employ nuclear weapons in the war and refused to pursue Chinese forces supporting North Korea into China itself.

Another such proxy war was waged in Vietnam, at least as viewed from Moscow and Washington. As the French colony of Indochina, Vietnam experienced a communist and nationalist revolt after World War II (see more in section 10.9). The French left in 1954, but the country was divided (again, in theory, temporarily) between a communist north supported by the Soviet Union and an authoritarian but anticommunist and American-backed regime in the south (Map 10.3). In 1959, North Vietnam supported military action by its supporters in South Vietnam and civil war ensued. The United States, seeing the conflict as part of an international expansion of communism headquartered in Moscow, strengthened its military support of South Vietnam, sending its first troops in 1961. In 1964, North Vietnam sent its own forces into South Vietnam; US military intervention, including the bombing of North Vietnam, escalated. The war would end with the unification of the country under the communists in 1975. The Socialist Republic of Vietnam was proclaimed in July 1976. Yet the war was also largely contained; Soviet troops stayed out of the conflict, so American forces never fired on them. The Cold War felt hot in Southeast Asia but not in Washington or Moscow. In the Middle East, Israel, backed by the United States, faced war with various Arab states (e.g., Egypt) that were often backed by the Soviet Union. Such wars occurred in 1956, 1967, and 1973. In 1979, Nicaragua saw the overthrow of the pro–United States Samoza regime and the coming to power of the revolutionary Sandinistas, naturally supplied by the Soviet Union. The United States, in turn, supported revolutionaries who sought to oust the Sandinistas, the Contras of the 1980s.

The US government viewed the Korean and Vietnam wars as efforts to contain Soviet expansion. In Afghanistan, the United States found an opportunity to go further. Afghanistan had been in the Soviet sphere of influence in 1978, its government friendly toward the Soviet Union and dependent on its support. In 1979, however, that government's control of the country was evidently shaky; the Soviet Union responded by invading. The United States did not risk sending troops into a shooting war with the Soviet Union. Instead, it sent arms and money to those fighting the Soviets and the Afghan army. These opposition forces, known as the Mujahedin, included religiously fervent Muslims who resisted the atheistic communists. Soviet efforts to reimpose control failed, and Soviet troops returned home in 1988–1989, leaving a weak government that soon collapsed. (Among the Mujahedin, a faction eventually emerged that sought a society ordered along what it saw as rigorously Muslim lines: the Taliban. The Taliban achieved dominance in 1996.)

Nuclear weapons played a key role in preventing large-scale war between the United States and the Soviet Union. Besides keeping their hot conflicts confined to proxies, the superpowers attempted to manage their relationship to limit the danger of a nuclear war that would destroy both of them. After the Cuban missile crisis (1962), arising from Soviet

Map 10.3 (following pages): The world in the Cold War

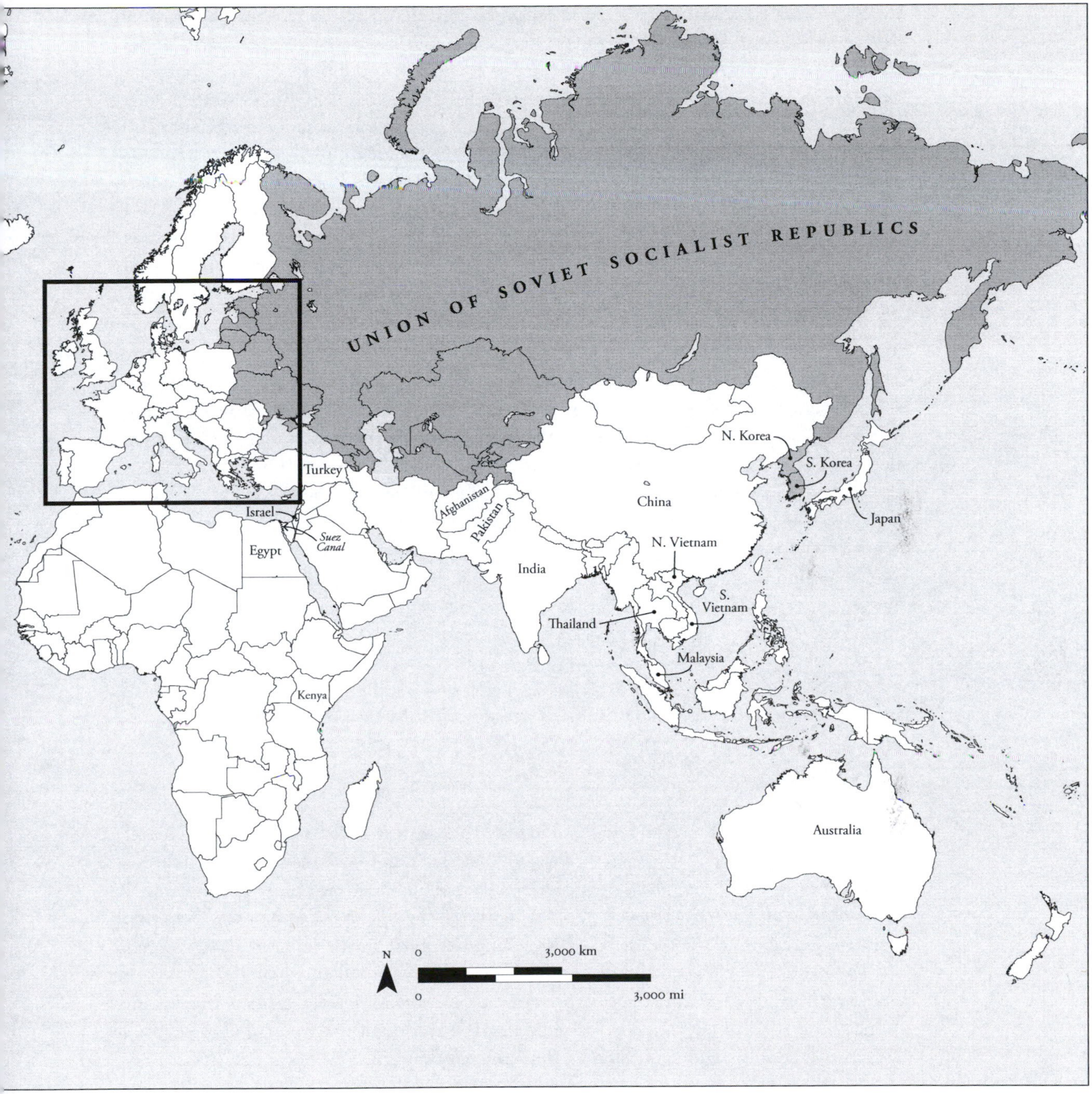
UNION OF SOVIET SOCIALIST REPUBLICS
Turkey
Israel
Suez Canal
Egypt
Kenya
Afghanistan
Pakistan
India
China
N. Korea
S. Korea
Japan
N. Vietnam
S. Vietnam
Thailand
Malaysia
Australia
N
0
3,000 km
0
3,000 mi

plans to install nuclear-equipped missiles in Cuba, a "hotline" was set up to allow immediate communication between American and Soviet heads of state. The superpowers signed agreements to limit the testing and building of nuclear weapons in the 1960s and 1970s, but the logic of MAD meant that neither seriously considered actual nuclear disarmament, despite the desire for such disarmament. Protests, sometimes vigorous, in North America and Europe against nuclear weapons little affected government policy.

The Cold War also fostered the growth of government, particularly in the United States. The 1930s had already seen an expansion of central government control in order to deal with the Great Depression (see 10.3). World War II had naturally brought an expansion of the US military. Immediately after the war, most of the boys came home, but military spending increased again once it became clear that the United States would need to be ready for war with the Soviet Union. In 1961, the outgoing American president, Dwight D. Eisenhower (1890–1969), warned of the growing influence of a "military-industrial complex" in American society and politics. Intelligence gathering and operations took on particular importance in a world in which war had to be kept cold, and their scale increased tremendously. Critics spoke, darkly, of a "national security state" aiming at the suppression of freedoms in the name of countering the Soviet Union; the Central Intelligence Agency was founded in 1947 to carry out US intelligence efforts under civilian rather than military direction, but its creation did not allay such fears. At the same time, the ideological element of the Cold War—socialists were associated with the Soviet Union and so could easily been seen as covert Soviet agents—strengthened efforts to identify a "fifth column" in Western society. This worry gained credence from the actual role of Soviet operatives in conveying nuclear secrets from the United States to the Soviet Union.

The period from 1945 to the late 1980s thus saw the world largely at peace, dominated by two superpowers reluctant to let conflict get out of hand. What would happen when one of those superpowers, the Soviet Union, collapsed?

10.8 MOVEMENTS OF LIBERATION IN THE TWENTIETH CENTURY

Despite reaction against it, the Enlightenment of the eighteenth century reverberated in the twentieth century and still does in the twenty-first. The call to equality and natural human rights is heard to this day, although now, as then, people disagree about who quite qualifies as human and in what respects people ought to be equal. At the end of the eighteenth century and again in the twentieth, these Enlightenment ideals resulted in movements of liberation in which subordinated people sought long-denied equality. Enlightenment ideology, however, was not the only force at work in these twentieth-century movements. In the second half of the century, technological innovations also encouraged them, as did a growing economy and expansion of the university system.

Moreover, the ideas driving movements of liberation underwent a shift in the latter part of the century. The influence of postmodernism (see 9.11) sapped the search for common human rights based in a common human nature. When members of oppressed groups sought liberation, they increasingly sought it in terms of identity with their own smaller subsection of society rather than with humanity at large; an interest in group rights displaced one in human rights. This development was rooted in postmodern views that culture and language divide society into groups and make some groups dominant over others. Knowledge, no longer related to some truth outside language, was simply a tool by which some people exploited others. Michel Foucault (1926–1984), echoing Nietzsche (see 9.11), observed that "the development of all those branches of knowledge [i.e., the social sciences] can in no way be dissociated from the exercise of power."[18] Hence, the influence of the Enlightenment can be said to have declined in the late twentieth century. The influence of postmodernism was not, however, only a matter of changes in intellectual fashion. As the nineteenth century had found, equality can be an atomizing force. In the nineteenth century, the result had been the search for a sense of community, to be found in the nation or class (see 9.3 and 9.5). The equality achieved through liberation fed similar demands for group identity in the late twentieth century.

Women's liberation could, of course, look to roots in the Enlightenment. Even in the eighteenth century, the essential arguments for women's equality with men were laid out, even if most people rejected them (see 8.4). Historians identify a "first wave" of feminism running from the later nineteenth century into the early twentieth (see also 9.10) but rooted in the eighteenth-century Enlightenment. This movement was firmly founded on the search for equality based in a common humanity: the same educational opportunities for women as for men, the same property rights, the same political rights. The right of women to vote became a particular focus, especially in English-speaking countries. It was achieved partially in Britain in 1918 and fully there in 1928, in federal elections in Canada in 1918, and in the United States in 1920. These were among the earlier successes in the enfranchisement of women; other Western countries would follow in their wake, e.g., France in 1945. Authoritarian Latin American governments generally did so in the 1930s through the 1950s, both in response to feminist pressure and in hopes of mobilizing women in their own support. Switzerland was the last Western state to adopt women's suffrage, in 1971.

Feminism's second wave became evident in the 1960s. With suffrage achieved, this generation of feminists continued to work for equality in education and control over property, but it focused even more on other issues: equal opportunity in employment—e.g., the elimination of discrimination in hiring and wages, as well as the elimination of sexual harassment—and the legalization of abortion. *The Feminine Mystique* (1963) by Betty Friedan (1921–2006) argued that well-educated women of the 1950s were languishing

---

18 Michel Foucault, *Politics, Philosophy, Culture: Interviews and Other Writings, 1977–1984*, trans. Alan Sheridan *et al.*, ed. Lawrence Kritzman (New York: Routledge, 1988), 106. The argument bears some resemblance to the position of the ancient sophists.

without employment outside the home. As skilled and intelligent as their husbands, they were depressed at the prospect of focusing their lives on small children and housework. (Of course, working-class women had more often worked outside the home than their better-heeled sisters.) The arguments of such feminists showed great continuity with those of feminism's first wave in that they sought equality with men as human beings, even if they now focused those arguments on new issues. In general, they sought a place for women in what had been a man's world. Increasingly in the next decades, women would achieve many of the goals of this generation of feminists. In the early twenty-first century, women in some Western countries were receiving the majority of university degrees. Even beyond the working classes, women commonly worked outside the home, even after they married or had children; Friedan's housewives were becoming rare. (This account does not mean that all agree that all of the goals of these feminists have been fully achieved, but that there has been significant change is undeniable.)

Feminists may have long criticized what they saw as male privilege, but their goal had been to extend the rights that men had to women as well. The drive was toward treating men and women the same because they had the same human nature. But, by the 1970s, feminism's second wave produced a strain of "radical feminism," sometimes described as a "third wave" of feminism, which held that women should reject the values and institutions of the larger society as simply a product of male dominance. Women, their argument ran, should identify with other women and, indeed, separate themselves from men and irredeemably masculine institutions; the term "separatist" was sometimes applied to the movement. Hence, although feminism was born out of the Enlightenment's standardizing impulse, it now began to move in the opposite direction.

Why? The rising influence of postmodernism (see 9.11) was partly responsible. Certainly radical feminists, like postmodernists, often stressed the role of language—in their case, in shaping a culture that favored men and oppressed women, the patriarchy. Radical feminists favored seizing control of language in order to gain autonomy. "Womyn," for example, was not simply a matter of getting the word "man" out of "woman" but of asserting women's control over the word applied to them. Another move was to redefine what women are by redefining the words that describe them. The Guerrilla Girls, an anonymous feminist activist group founded in 1985, note that "if the world is going to call you a Bitch for being ambitious, outspoken, and in control of your own sexuality, why not accept it and be proud? If we use it to describe ourselves, it can't be used against us."[19] Like this focus on language, the separatist tendency of radical feminism also echoed the postmodern tendency to see only culture, not some universal reality beyond it. Human rights are universal, something rooted in a universal human nature, and they need to be asserted against a culture that obscures or denies them. But if all one can really know is culture, then a search for such rights is wrongheaded. Instead, one should seek fulfillment

---

19 Guerrilla Girls, *Bitches, Bimbos and Ballbreakers: The Guerrilla Girls' Illustrated Guide to Female Stereotypes* (New York: Penguin Books, 2003), 26.

in one's own culture and shape that culture to empower oneself. Radical feminists, indeed, argued that women had a culture distinct from that of men—usually this culture was seen as stressing cooperation over conflict—a culture to be preserved and strengthened. The celebration of a distinctive culture and, with it, distinctive values went hand in hand with the rejection of a common human nature. Another impulse, however, fed radical feminism. Feminists had traditionally fought for women's freedom and equality, and achieved much. But the Achilles' heel of Western freedom and equality is that it undermines a sense of community. In the nineteenth century, nationalism and Marxism had responded to this need (see 9.3, 9.5). The very success of the atomizing drive heightened the attraction of radical feminism. In 1968, a feminist tract asserted that "Marriage, as we know it, is for women as integration is for blacks. It is the atomization of a sex...."[20] For radical feminists, women themselves were the community, a group to whom one could feel attached. "Sisterhood" not "humanity" was the rallying cry.

Those countries with significant racial minorities saw similar developments. Here, the United States was the most obvious case: a country founded on the principle that "all men are created equal" in which black Americans faced legal discrimination in favor of whites in southern states—segregated schools that were unequal in their resources, for example, and particular laws that aimed at suppressing the black vote—and de facto discrimination in other states. In the 1950s and 60s, a civil rights movement sought to change this inequality, focusing at first on the South. The goal was to make the country's founding, Enlightenment vision that "all men are created equal" a reality. In his speech on the occasion of a protest march on Washington, DC, the civil rights leader Martin Luther King Jr. (1929–1968) declared,

> When the architects of our republic wrote the magnificent words of the Constitution and the Declaration of Independence, they were signing a promissory note to which every American was to fall heir. This note was a promise that all men, yes, black men as well as white men, would be guaranteed the "unalienable rights of life, liberty, and the pursuit of happiness."... And so we've come to cash this check....[21]

Violence was minimized, although not entirely avoided, by the movement's adoption of nonviolent tactics inspired by those of Mahatma Gandhi (1869–1948) in British India (see 10.8). The sit-in, the march, and the lawsuit were the usual tools of the movement. The first two were especially suited to television—dramatic, and requiring not too large a group to fill the screen. Not surprisingly, a leading role was played in the 1950s by African American

---

20 Beverly Jones and Judith Brown, "Toward a Female Liberation Movement," in *Radical Feminism: A Documentary Reader* (New York: New York University Press, 2000), 45.

21 Martin Luther King, Jr., "I Have a Dream," in *A Call to Conscience: The Landmark Speeches of Dr. Martin Luther King, Jr.*, ed. Clayborne Carson and Kris Shepard (New York: Warner Books, Inc., 2001), 82.

veterans of World War II who had fought against the Nazis in the name of democracy and equality and returned determined to obtain these things at home.

Like feminism, however, African Americans' movement for liberation underwent a change, from an Enlightenment-based emphasis on integration and equality to a separatist one that celebrated an autonomous African American culture and values. The trend can be seen in the rise of "Afrocentrism," a movement to encourage African Americans to identify with Africa and a culture distinct from that of the white majority. Kwanzaa, for example, was created in 1966 as a holiday that would allow African Americans to have a festival of their own, as Christmas was seen as a product of a white culture and what Afrocentrists described as white values. Again, as with feminism, the movement had a rather postmodern cast, stressing the importance of language and culture: the term used to describe African Americans: "negro"? "black"? "African-American"? became a sensitive issue. And the movement offered a sense of community as equality with whites was increasingly achieved. Kwanzaa was to inculcate, among other values, *umoja* (Swahili for "unity"). By the end of the century, some of those whose parents had fought to integrate black and white schools were attempting to preserve predominantly black schools and neighborhoods.

The transition of the gay liberation movement was faster. In the middle of the century, gay people faced legal bars in most Western countries, from prohibitions against government employment to the outright banning of same-sex sexual relations. Gay people seeking liberation in the later part of twentieth century did not have the history that feminists or African Americans could look to as a movement. But they had the assumption of human equality then traditional in the West. From the 1970s, the legal disabilities of gay people began to be dismantled. In 1973, the American Psychiatric Association ceased to classify homosexuality as a mental disorder. Yet the gay rights movement also exhibited some of the characteristics of other liberation movements of the late twentieth century. Gay people asserted control over themselves by asserting control over the language used to describe them. In the 1990s, gays sought to control society's understanding of them by adopted the term "queer," traditionally a derogatory term. So widespread was this development that 2003 saw the broadcast of a popular television series, *Queer Eye for the Straight Guy*, that celebrated the idea of a special gay sensibility in matters of fashion, an idea that some gay rights proponents, in fact, rejected. Some—a minority—of gays rejected the attempt to legalize same-sex marriage as a move to integrate them into the larger society. An autonomous gay culture signified a gay community, inculcating a sense of belonging at the same time as the larger society integrated gay people. Thus, "being gay" is not simply a matter of sexual orientation but of learning a culture, a position seen in the decision of one university professor, David Halperin (1952–), to teach a course on "How to be Gay" in 2000. Indeed, Halperin has complained that equality for gay people threatens gay culture.

The stress on culture in these movements is evident in the rise of "multiculturalism" beginning in the 1980s. No culture can be said to be truer than others since postmodernists had set aside the idea that signs refer to reality (see 9.11). Therefore, cultures gain their value, so the argument runs, from the fact that people identify with them (and get a sense of community from them). Furthermore, multiculturalists argue that institutions should have within them people of various cultures, that those cultures represent various viewpoints that cannot be melded into one; fairness means each needs representation. Where commonality had been the focus, now the watchword was "diversity," in theory, cultural diversity, or multiculturalism. This encouragement of diversity became evident even in international trade; in 1993, the General Agreement on Tariffs and Trade, which sought to lower trade barriers among nations, adopted a "cultural exception" to protect countries from imports that might threaten their distinct cultures. Affirmative action programs, designed to encourage or even ensure the representation of what came to be known as "protected classes" in institutions from universities to businesses, were now justified in terms of ensuring the diversity of points of view brought by a representative of this or that culture. The United States had long absorbed multiple cultures brought to the country by immigrants from around the world, but now people spoke of the country as a mosaic of cultures rather than as a melting pot of cultures.

Another liberation movement of the later twentieth century had as short a history as gay liberation: that of young people. Here, certain other developments following World War II were critical. The postwar decades brought unprecedented prosperity in the West—at first in North America and, more slowly, in Europe. Between 1940 and 1960, the US gross domestic product more than doubled in real value. This prosperity powered "consumerism," a tendency for most people to purchase products far beyond the necessities. Goods that had been luxuries became usual. By 1960, a television set, washing machine, and refrigerator could be found in most American households. The "golden age of labor" of the Late Middle Ages was definitively surpassed. Moreover, prosperity meant that a larger portion of young people had unprecedented disposable income. If they worked, their parents were unlikely to need teenagers' income for food or shelter, and the young became even more likely to receive some sort of allowance from increasingly well-off parents. Young people with money to spend opened the door to creating and selling products aimed specifically at young people. This market was made even larger by the fact that there were more young people; the generation that returned from the war marked their hard-won prosperity with a "baby boom" into the 1960s. A "youth culture" mushroomed in the 1950s and 60s, featuring music, distinctive clothes, and other nonessentials that marked out the young from their elders. Wearing blue jeans (often more flattering to trim figures than to those of the middle aged) became a statement of youth rather than of working-class status. Rock and roll blossomed as young people's music. The emergence of the transistor radio—cheap and highly portable—increased the emancipation of the young from their parents' tastes: rather than gather around the family radio, teenagers could afford their own and so control the dial. Business, of course, responded to the new market. Two married San Francisco real-estate developers saw that department stores were not catering adequately to the demand for Levi's blue jeans, so, in 1969, they opened The Gap, a store marketing specifically to young adults. The Gap referred to the expression "generation gap," which had been coined to denote the distance between youth culture and that of older people. The store sold Levi's jeans and that other youth culture item, records, often with rock playing in the background. The store soon dropped the records and went on to open shops around the world, keeping prices low through volume. The Gap pointed to an irony of the new youth culture, which often criticized consumerism while, at the same time, being (partly) defined by it. In any case, the new generation celebrated its distance from the previous one. The rock band The Who sang, "People try put us down—*Talkin' 'bout my generation . . .* Hope I die before I get old—*Talkin' 'bout my generation.*"[22]

Small acts of liberation from the previous generation—through clothes and music—reflected larger ones. The decades after World War II saw a boom of the universities. In a move that echoed trends in the later nineteenth century (see 9.10), governments encouraged the expansion of older universities and the building of new ones as a means of investing in economic growth. The new prosperity meant that governments could subsidize university education. Tuition could be kept low, and families could more easily send children to college. University enrollments swelled, at least doubling in Western Europe and the United States in the 1960s. The result was a larger portion of young people who had greater leisure to pursue and develop the youth culture and who, with a university education, felt more distant from their parents who lacked one. With some exceptions, the young were inclined to challenge the establishment of their own times, and so veered left. If the establishment was anticommunist, they were attracted to communism, if not that of the Soviet Union, then that of Communist China. If the establishment was unsure about racial equality or was actively hostile to it, the young embraced it. If the establishment was consumerist, the young would reject materialism. And so on.

But how to rebel? The young answered this question in rather different ways. One response was a kind of withdrawal from the world, from the establishment. The hippies were a manifestation of this withdrawal, taking to heart the injunction of Timothy Leary (1920–1996) to "Turn on, tune in, and drop out" in 1967; the phrase became a slogan of the time.[23] The communes founded in the 1960s were another example. These were small communities, often agricultural and usually egalitarian, with property held in common. A different approach was activism, an attempt to change or even overthrow the established order; it took its cue from the civil rights movement's sit-ins and marches. In May 1968, university students in Paris confronted police, demanding change in the university, government, and society at large. The year saw similar developments in West Germany. In Mexico City, student protests in 1968 were so great that the army was sent to occupy the main campus of the National Autonomous University of Mexico. Students occupied several buildings at Columbia University, prompting a forced retaking of the buildings by police. (The rise of African-American separatism was evident when black students insisted on occupying their own building independently of whites.) The later 1960s and early 1970s

---

22 The Who, "My Generation," in *The Who Anthology* (Milwaukee: Hal Leonard Corporation, 1981), 64–65.

23 Timothy Leary, *Turn On, Tune In, Drop Out* (Oakland, CA: RONIN Publishing, Inc., 1999), 133. At the time, he exhorted his audience to drop out for a year or two. Leary would later say that he had not intended the disengagement from society that many had taken the phrase to mean.

saw active and loud student protests, mostly focused on ending US involvement in the Vietnam War (see 10.9) but also embracing other causes, such as student control of university governance and curricula. Although the protests subsided, a small minority decided on a violent campaign, giving rise to small Western terrorist organizations that were most active in the 1970s (the Baader-Meinhoff gang in West Germany, the Red Brigades in Italy, and the Weather Underground in the United States). A third form of rebellion was easiest and, in the end, the most attractive: embrace the music and clothing that annoyed one's elders, perhaps along with opinions that would do so as well. This form would have staying power. Generations of the young since have similarly shaped their own distinctive youth culture, with the eager help of fashion manufacturers and music producers geared toward creating new, distinctive products. The Gap lives on.

The developments described in this section marked the political left in the West. The left had traditionally been associated with the working classes, with labor and (often) labor unions. In the first half of the century, leftists had naturally tended to be Marxists and to identify with the proletariat. The decades after World War II, however, saw the birth of the "New Left." The New Left was rooted more in the liberation movements just described than in the orthodox Marxism of the Communist Party. The New Left was more interested in combatting racism and sexism (and, eventually, antigay feeling) than in the oppression of the working class. Labor union members, often culturally conservative and patriotic, were as likely to oppose the New Left as support it. Indeed, in the United States, leftists began to use the term "hard hat" as an insult for their opponents. Not surprisingly, the New Left also came to be rooted in the universities, so full of (middle-class) young people. And some of these students—as is always the case—would become the next generation of academics, which thus also became associated with the New Left.

10.9 THE FALL OF WESTERN EMPIRES

At the start of the twentieth century, Western empires governed most of Africa and Asia. By the end of the century, they did not. That transformation took place in the decades after World War II. Between 1945 and 1997—mostly in the 1960s and 70s—sixty-one independent states emerged as imperial powers went home. How did it happen? The Western empires were responsible for some of the very forces that would be their undoing.

Western conquerors had generally believed themselves culturally, or even biologically, superior to the conquered (see 9.9). That did not mean that Western imperialists always ignored the ways of non-Western peoples. Consider India, one of the older portions of the British Empire. Queen Victoria (1837–1901) of Great Britain studied Hindustani in order to better understand her subjects in India; her grandson George V (1910–1936) was sure to receive the homage of the Indian princes (on whom, see 9.8) from the back of an elephant, in traditional Indian style. More important than such royal gestures was the establishment of a school to prepare British administrators sent to India. That school sought to teach students about the society they would rule. At the same time, imperial powers worked to Westernize the peoples they ruled. The British established schools in India, which spread Western learning, even if they were not widespread enough to reach the whole population. In the other direction, Indian princes began to send their sons to Britain for their education, and British schools accepted them. English became the common language of the subcontinent.

Nevertheless, the peoples of the Western empires generally found themselves at a disadvantage with their imperial masters in matters of dignity as well as authority. In India, for example, Indians might take some first-class railway cars but not those that excluded Indians. Such conditions were especially likely to alienate wealthier and better-educated colonials—just the people empires relied upon (on indirect rule, see 9.8). The experience of several Indian princes and Lord Freeman Willingdon (1866–1941) illuminates the awkward position of the ruling Western authorities and those they ruled. Then the governor of the province of Bombay (1913–1918), Willingdon took several princes one evening to the exclusive Yacht Club of Bombay (now often known as Mumbai) for dinner. His guests were refused entrance. The club was for people of European descent only. Even his influence could not open its doors to Willingdon's Indian guests.[24]

So Western empires inculcated Western culture among many of those they ruled while holding the ruled at arm's length. At the same time, the West offered a revolutionary ideology that could be used to overthrow Western rule: nationalism. These circumstances encouraged peoples dominated by the West to reject that domination, to work for independence. After all, for an African or Asian to consider himself or herself French, British, and so on was difficult under the circumstances. But perhaps one was in fact a member of a nation. It was easy to conclude that one's nation, a *Volk*, deserved what Western nations enjoyed: a nation state. Nationalism blossomed in the colonial holdings of Western empires.

True, at times, non-Western nationalists, like Western ones, had to create a sense of *Volk* where one had not existed before. Sometimes, they had the unwitting help of imperial powers. In sub-Saharan Africa, imperial authorities had found it convenient to deal with people divided into clear tribes. So Africans were assigned to a tribal leader, even if they had not earlier identified exclusively with just one tribe. African nationalists later saw these tribes as nations. In India, British administrators underlined distinctions between Hindus and Muslims, who came to see themselves as more exclusive communities than before. A much broader form of created nationalism is evident in the Pan-Africa movement, which saw all Africans as constituting a single people, not unlike the Pan-Slavism that had preceded it (see 9.3).

Another Western invention also appealed to those who sought independence from the West: communism. Marxists had explained Western imperialism in terms of the need of Western industry for raw materials and markets for manufactured goods. Hence, Marxism provided a ready-made account of imperialism and a call to arms against it. With a common

---

24 Willingdon and his companions responded by founding the Willingdon Club, the first club to accept both Indian and British members.

enemy in imperialism, nationalism and Marxism were not seen as rivals, as they had been in the West itself. Their alliance was further encouraged by support from the Soviet Union, which proclaimed itself opposed to empire. Even in China, a theoretically sovereign country, the Chinese Communist Party under Mao Zedong (1893–1976) could appeal, in its drive to power, to feeling against foreign countries. Mao achieved power in 1949.

Given these developments, it should not be surprising that the most Westernized elements of colonial society produced the leaders for independence. Consider the career of Ho Chi Minh (1890–1969), born in the French colony of Indochina, or modern Vietnam. Ho first studied Confucius. But he also became a highly Westernized Vietnamese. While still in Indochina, he studied at a French school before leaving for the United States in 1912. He then moved to France (1919–1923), where he became a communist. There, he also railed against French writers who adopted English terminology, such as "le knock out," a measure of his own adoption of French culture. At the same time, this rather Western Vietnamese became a Vietnamese nationalist, publishing under the name Nguyen o Phap ("Nguyen who detests the French"), appealing—in vain—for Vietnam's independence at the Versailles peace talks that brought World War I to a close. For Ho, Marxism came as a revelation, an explanation of imperialism: imperial powers conquered others to gain raw materials for factories and to control new markets for products of those factories. In the 1920s, he left for the Soviet Union and, with its backing, returned to Asia to work for Vietnam's independence (see 10.7).

Other developments heightened the appeal of nationalism and Marxism in the non-Western world. To some extent, Western countries exported to their empires the very atomization that had come to characterize the West, and the need for a sense of community that went with it. How did Western conquest undermine a sense of community among the conquered? In the first place, of course, conquest itself was often disruptive. Henry Morton Stanley (see 9.9) recounted that, when Africans attacked him as he explored the Congo, he and his party fired back and chased the attackers to their villages, which he and his men then laid waste. But Western rule often struck deeper. Western powers drew borders that cut preexisting communities in two or bound disparate peoples together in the same colony; recall the Berlin Conference of 1884–1885 (see 9.9). Moreover, societies outside the West were often bound together by custom, just as the West had been (see 7.1 and 8.2). Imperialists, however, sometimes set out to weaken the traditions of the peoples they ruled, on the assumption that Western customs were superior. In India, Hindus had long been knitted together by an elaborate caste system in which all people were born into a particular caste that determined their profession and role in society—and so how they related to other people. Inequality was built into the system. In some regions, the *dalits* (or "untouchables") were considered such a source of pollution that they were barred from public roads. British imperial bureaucrats came to accept such distinctions, but with limits. Caste distinctions were not, for example, to be observed in seating on railway cars, and the British worked to make the roads open to all. Christian missionaries and their schools were, however, less tolerant, and worked to upend the system entirely. To the extent they succeeded, they atomized Hindus' sense of community.

Imperial economic policy also sometimes atomized non-Western societies. In Africa, colonial administrators often found that Africans lived largely without a cash economy, producing most of their own food in small villages where everyone knew everyone else and bartered for their unfilled needs. Yet Western commercial interests needed labor—self-sufficient farmers and herders were not people interested in building roads, bridges, or working in mines. In South Africa, Britain addressed the problem in 1894 by taxing the African population, stipulating that the tax had to be paid in cash not in kind. The idea was not to collect revenue but to force people to work for money, so they would labor in mines and for other Western businesses. African men left their villages to find work, often congregating around gold and diamond mines whose owners needed workers. Such men were thus thrown together, often living in barracks in what became mining towns: these were as atomizing as the industrial cities experienced in the West (see 8.7). Indigenous peoples were uprooted in the colonies in other ways. Britain encouraged migration from some colonies to others, attempting, for example, to develop its holdings in Malaysia by importing Indians to provide the labor for British firms and farms there. More than six million left India for other parts of the empire in the years 1834 to 1924.

World War II expanded the opportunities for national independence in various ways. The war shook Western empires. Under the slogan "Asia for the Asians," Japan occupied French, British, Dutch, and American colonies in eastern Asia during the war, suggesting the vulnerability of those empires and, as Japan fell, giving a chance for independence movements to grow before imperial rule was restored. Ho Chi Minh declared Vietnam's independence in 1945 in the wake of Japan's defeat, but he endured years of war with France before achieving it. The war also encouraged some powers to press their colonies harder for support, making independence more attractive to those who had earlier cooperated with empire. In the years 1946–1951, Britain attempted to repay debt incurred during the war by squeezing the colonies after it. It drew about £140 million from its empire in taxes while investing only about £40 million there.

American power after World War II also encouraged the independence of non-Western colonies. Itself born out of revolution against the British Empire, the United States saw the end of empires as a means of opening the world to free trade with America. In 1941, the United States called on all imperial powers to establish a timetable for granting independence to their colonies. After World War II, the failure of the Suez expedition in 1956 underlined Western European dependence on the United States (see 10.7), as well as the problems of using force to maintain empire in the face of American hostility. Here the Cold War, however, would lend some European empires a hand. Where independence movements were communist, as in Vietnam, the United States favored the continuance of colonial rule.

These conditions were opportunities to be exploited, and independence movements exploited them. Of the European empires, India and its twin, newly created Pakistan, were the first to go, in 1947. Although agitation for independence had included some terrorist activity, under the leadership of Gandhi, the movement had largely practiced nonviolent confrontation and noncooperation with British authorities. These tactics, coupled with Britain's exhaustion, worked. India would remain associated with Britain in the British

Commonwealth, on par with Canada or Australia, a condition that helped the British accept the fact of independence.

Elsewhere, independence came only as a result of violent confrontation. France fought against the Viet Minh, a communist national independence coalition, until 1954, when the French at last gave in (and the United States became the backer of a noncommunist South Vietnam). Britain did not put up such a fight, but it made the mistake of anticipating that the dissolution of the British Empire would be a very slow process. British authorities thought that the African colonies, for example, would eventually become independent, but they did not expect this to happen until ca. 2100. Colonial powers also faced a real problem: what to do about Europeans who had settled in the colonies? Britain's expectation was that they would stay and take part in a biracial partnership—with whites as the senior partner.

The Mau Mau rebellion (1952–1960) in the British colony of Kenya changed such expectations. The Kikuyu of that colony had been forced off the best land in the country by white settlers after 1945. In 1952, Kikuyu resentment produced rebellion. What began as a rebellion became a war; Britain sent in bombers, but it took years to regain control of the country. Although the Kikuyu had been more interested in land than in independence from Britain, British authorities interpreted the Mau Mau as a conspiracy by independence agitators, even imprisoning Jomo Kenyatta (ca. 1894–1978) for seven years for orchestrating a rebellion that he had in fact opposed, thinking the Kikuyu lacked the resources to succeed.[25] Kenyatta, a (Kikuyu) nationalist with Marxist sympathies, had spent time in the Soviet Union and at the University of London. He had an English wife and felt at home in English pubs. But he had returned to Kenya to work for independence from Britain. He was another example of a Westernized leader leading the charge against Western empires.

The Mau Mau rebellion persuaded the British to accelerate their timetable for decolonization. White settlers might object, but Britain concluded it could not afford to hold on to the colonies. Moreover, the British feared that communists would gain greater influence in Africa if Britain continued to resist. Better a nationalist Africa than a communist one. Kenyatta, freed from an imprisonment that bolstered his nationalist credentials, led the country to independence. In 1963, Kenya became independent. More than 55,000 whites left.

As the careers of Jomo Kenyatta and Ho Chi Minh suggest, the Western empires produced some of the forces that destroyed them.

10.10 A CONSERVATIVE TURN

Ever since the Great Depression, or even since the late nineteenth century, free-market capitalism, or economic liberalism, had been in a general retreat in the West (see 9.10 and 10.3). Governments had increasingly worked to shape the economy and to soften the blows

---

25 Kenyatta had thought peaceful agitation would work better.

that economic hardship might deal their people. Indeed, the Soviet Union presented the world a model of how far the state might direct economic life. Although the Cold War saw the United States lead the West against the Soviet Union in the name of democracy and capitalism, actual practice in the United States preserved earlier departures from laissez-faire orthodoxy, and sometimes even extended them. Upon his election in 1952, Republican President Dwight D. Eisenhower, in theory more fully committed to laissez-faire economics than members of the Democratic Party, did not roll back Roosevelt's New Deal (on which, see 10.3). In Latin America, state investment in industrialization was common into the 1970s, and governments borrowed heavily from abroad to cover resulting deficits. In Western Europe, the decades after World War II saw a consensus that capitalist economies needed guidance. On the European continent, this guidance often meant government sponsorship of deals struck between management and labor, an echo of the corporatism of the 1930s (see 10.5); these arrangements tended to depress wages lower than they might have been, allowing businesses to invest and so maintain growth. In Britain, such guidance went further. The Labour Party brought major industries, such as coal and steel, under government ownership; its rival, the Conservatives, did not undo such moves when they achieved office. In most cases, the Keynesian economics first embraced in the 1930s (see 10.3) became orthodox. Recall its basic tenets: in times of economic contraction, governments can stimulate economic growth by increasing spending, even at the cost of undertaking debt, and prevent economies from overheating by increasing taxes and cutting government expenditure. Governments usually found it more tempting to stimulate economic growth than to put on the brakes.

Most Western countries similarly embraced some version of the welfare state, extending or implementing payments to individuals who were out of work, ensuring that the poor received health care and other goods. President Lyndon Baines Johnson (1908–1973) of the United States significantly extended such principles in the 1960s with his "Great Society" programs, instituting Medicaid to provide health care for the poor and Medicare for the elderly. Canada introduced universal health care coverage in the 1960s. The 1950s and 60s saw general prosperity in the West, especially in the United States, Canada, and Europe, which appeared to justify these policies, as did Keynesian theory. And, of course, prosperity helped governments find the money to pay for the outlay required by the welfare state. Between 1960 and 1981, spending on social programs as a percentage of the national gross domestic product roughly doubled in most countries in North America and Western Europe.

The 1970s shook this confidence. Arab oil-producing countries, organized as the Organization of Petroleum Exporting Countries, raised the price of oil in 1973–1974 in order to punish the West for its support of Israel; in 1975, oil cost six times what it had before OPEC took action. Since oil supplied the energy to produce goods and transport them, OPEC's action pushed up prices generally. Government spending further spurred inflation. When raising taxes to cover spending was not palatable, governments had to borrow, and indeed they were encouraged to do so by Keynesian theory. Increasing the money supply in order to repay such debts fed inflation. In Britain, inflation was given an added boost when governments succumbed to pressure from employees of government-owned industries for wage increases. By the end of the decade, inflation in Britain reached a high of 27 percent. But the United States and other Western countries were experiencing double-digit inflation too. At the same time, the 1970s saw most Western economies slow down or enter recession. The coining of the term "stagflation," for stagnation accompanied by inflation, suggests the novelty of the combination of rising prices and economic slowdown. Traditional Keynesian prescriptions did not seem to apply.

Critics argued that government borrowing drove up interest rates. With governments effectively bidding for loans, lenders could demand higher rates of interest, thus inhibiting borrowing by businesses that needed funds to invest in new ventures and better technology. Governments were thus competing with business for loans, and winning. An alternative to government borrowing, high taxation, also took money away from private investment and, consequently, growth, so the argument ran, and also reduced incentives to work and invest. Government benefits to the unemployed also discouraged work; other government sponsored benefits, such as state-sponsored health care or higher education, similarly discouraged individuals from being responsible for their own well-being. State regulation of business hampered profitability and so investment and economic growth, and thus employment. Together, such arguments added up to a return to the laissez-faire liberal economics of the nineteenth century, itself rooted in the Enlightenment thought of Adam Smith (see 8.2 and 8.7). This revival came under the label "neoliberal" (new liberalism) or "neoclassical" economics.[26] Since such views were now identified with the political right, they were also called "conservative."

There was more to this development than a change in economic theory. The latter part of the twentieth century had seen a youth liberation movement (see 10.8). Although that movement was associated with the political left and neoliberal economics with the political right, both, in their own way, celebrated individual autonomy. Indeed, both were in this way rooted in Enlightenment thought, just as the liberation movements of the twentieth century stemmed from Enlightenment assertions of natural human equality. Whereas the New Left criticized consumerism as selfish materialism, neoliberals saw it as the exercise of individual choice. The neoliberal stress on individual autonomy was matched by a stress on individual responsibility. Society would not flourish unless individuals rather than the state looked out for their own economic well-being. Margaret Thatcher (1925–2013) enunciated such views in 1987:

I think we've been through a period where too many people have been given to understand that if they have a problem, it's the government's job to cope with it. "I have a problem,

---

26 This terminology may need some explanation given the use of the term "liberal" in later twentieth-century and early twenty-first-century America. There "liberal" came to be associated with, among other things, a belief in government intervention in the economy and government assistance to those who failed to flourish in it—the reverse of the liberalism of the earlier nineteenth century (see 8.6).

I'll get a grant." "I'm homeless, the government must house me." They're casting their problem on society. And, you know, there is no such thing as society. There are individual men and women, and there are families. And no government can do anything except through people, and people must look to themselves first. It's our duty to look after ourselves and then, also to look after our neighbour.[27]

The approach ran beyond a concern with economics. Neoliberals were more likely to insist on severe punishment for crime, asserting that crime was not caused by individuals molded by social conditions such as poverty but by individuals choosing criminal behavior. Criminals therefore deserved severe punishment and were more likely to be deterred by harsher penalties.

When it came to the state, neoliberals were thus the heirs of the atomizing tendency of the last three centuries of the West. Like Thatcher, when they thought about community, they tended to think of neighborhood or nation. Such views set neoliberals against the general drift of the left when it came to economic policy and crime, and also put them in an ambivalent relationship with those groups that had sought liberation in the late twentieth century (see 10.8). Unsurprisingly, equality was a goal that neoliberals tended to support. Policy and action based on group identity rather than individual achievement, however, met with less sympathy from neoliberals. Programs geared to ensuring racial or other kinds of diversity in terms of corporate groups, such as "affirmative action" in the United States, came under attack.

The difficulties of the Western economies in the 1970s gave neoliberals their chance. In 1979, Margaret Thatcher, as head of the Conservative Party, became prime minister of Great Britain. She broke from the policies of both her own party and that of its Labour opponents. She sold off state-owned industries to private owners. She lowered income and business taxes and reduced regulation. Ronald Reagan (1911–2004) became president of the United States in 1980 on a platform of tax reduction, deregulation, and reduction of the welfare state. Brian Mulroney (1939–) led the Conservatives to power in Canada in 1984 and worked to reduce government spending on social programs. Although the French elected a socialist president in François Mitterrand (1916–1996) in 1981, whereupon he immediately nationalized businesses, Mitterrand soon reversed course, cutting public spending and returning many firms to private hands.

These developments were merely a first volley. The neoliberal wave continued into the 1990s and beyond. Parties traditionally associated with economic regulation and the welfare state curtailed such commitments and themselves adopted neoliberal policies. In Brazil, Fernando Henrique Cardosa (1931–) had been a proponent of Brazil's traditional protection of domestic industry against foreign competition, but he won office in 1995 proposing an end to such policies; he also accelerated the privatization of publicly owned industry. In the United States, a Democratic president, Bill Clinton (1946–), promised to "end welfare

---

27 Quoted in *Contemporary Political Theorists in Context*, by Anthony M. Clohesy, Stuart Isaacs, and Chris Sparks (New York: Routledge, 2009), 129.

as we know it" and, with the cooperation of a Republican majority in Congress, did so.[28] Britain's Labour Party—now billed as "New Labour"—dropped mention of socialism and the nationalization of industry from the party platform. Following market-oriented policies in the economic sphere, it bolstered its affiliation with the left through more symbolic measures: eliminating hereditary peers from the largely powerless House of Lords in 1998 (see 7.1) or banning the traditionally upper-crust sport of fox hunting.

The 1990s saw neoliberal views on the importance of free markets shape international trade. The countries of the southern cone of South America launched a mutual free trade agreement in 1991. The United States, Canada, and Mexico agreed to lower trade barriers among themselves, signing the North American Free Trade Agreement in 1992. The European Community, an organization of several Western European states, pooled their economies into a common market (thus achieving a goal set in 1986). The European Community, at the same time, expanded its numbers to include most of Europe, becoming the European Union in 1993. The motives behind the European Union were decidedly mixed. Some saw it as a path to a "United States of Europe"—either a guarantee that the wars that had torn the continent apart would not be repeated or a counterweight to the United States and the Soviet Union—but others were attracted simply by the ease with which goods and labor would flow across the borders of its member states.

The capstone of neoliberal triumph, however, seemed to come in 1991 with the fall of the Soviet Union. The causes of that fall easily read as a vindication of neoliberal views: the failure of a state-dominated command economy. Soviet economic growth stalled in the 1970s and 80s, as did the growth of the Warsaw Pact countries. At the same time, while citizens of capitalist economies chose among a plethora of consumer goods, Soviet citizens often faced empty store shelves. Soviet economic planning had long stressed heavy industry (see 10.4), which fed military production. With the United States a constant military competitor, the Soviet Union did not have the resources to cater to consumer demand too. The Soviet Union quite visibly lagged behind the West in technological innovation, missing out on the advent of the personal computer that was increasing economic productivity in the West in the 1980s. When Mikhail Gorbachev (1931–) became head of the Communist Party in 1985, he assumed the leadership of a country in a quiet crisis. The solution, he thought, was a relaxation of central economic controls. After all, Stalin's death had been followed by the introduction of very small, privately held farms; by the early 1960s, with only 3 percent of the farmland, these farms were producing over a third of the country's crops. Such examples, as well as the neoliberal turn in the West (he consulted Margaret Thatcher regarding privatization), persuaded Gorbachev to promulgate—cautiously at first—*perestroika* ("restructuring"). This new approach to the economy allowed enterprises to cater to consumer demand once they had fulfilled government orders and, ultimately, profit or lose by their actions. Gorbachev hoped to gain the support of people at large, in the face of

---

28 Richard L. Berke, "THE 1992 CAMPAIGN: THE AD CAMPAIGN; Clinton: Getting People Off Welfare," *The New York Times*, September 10, 1992, http://www.nytimes.com/1992/09/10/us/the-1992-campaign-the-ad-campaign-clinton-getting-people-off-welfare.html.

bureaucratic resistance, through a policy of *glasnost* ("openness"), which involved relaxing government censorship and encouraging public criticism, even of the Soviet regime. He permitted more than one candidate to run for political office, a contrast with the usual Soviet practice. Convinced that the Soviet Union could no longer afford the resources to maintain its grip on the Warsaw Pact countries, he allowed them to go their own way. Under pressure from their own peoples, they quickly adopted some form of market economy and multiparty democracy, and departed the Warsaw Pact. By the end of the century, three— Poland, Hungary, and the Czech Republic that had emerged from Czechoslovakia—had become members of NATO; more followed.

Despite these policies, Gorbachev was a committed socialist. The fundamental vision of the October Revolution of 1917 (10.4), he felt, was not open for revision. He expected the state still to remain the ultimate arbiter of the economy and the Communist Party to be the ultimate arbiter of the state. His ambiguous position was evident regarding agriculture. His initial policy was to give collectivized farms more autonomy but not to abolish them; he eventually allowed private farmers to lease land from the state, but he continued to balk at private ownership of the land itself. And, in the fall of 1990, Gorbachev began to retreat from *perestroika*, which had not delivered economic growth after all.

The end came soon—and in the form of unexpected consequences of almost forgotten decisions. Legally, the Union of Soviet Socialist Republics was a voluntary union. The 1922 constitution provided that individual republics could leave the Soviet Union (see 10.4). At the time, however, this provision was a dead letter given the authoritarian, even totalitarian, nature of the Soviet state. But *glasnost* had given the republics the potential to act independently from the central state; the 1922 constitution suddenly had new life. Boris Yeltsin (1931–2007), a former party official on the outs with the Communist Party, exploited that potential in 1991, calling for independence for the republics, including the Russian Soviet Federative Socialist Republic, of which he had been elected president. Proponents of *perestroika*, frustrated with Gorbachev, turned to Yeltsin. Gorbachev, attempting a middle way, drew up a new treaty that would devolve greater power to the republics within a continuing union. This, following *perestroika* and *glasnost*, was too much for hardliners, who attempted a coup, taking Gorbachev prisoner (Gorbachev's attitude toward the coup is unclear.). The coup failed when Yeltsin took up the mantle of resistance. In the name of the Russian Republic, Russians faced down tanks in the streets. The troops, themselves unconvinced of the Soviet Union's legitimacy, largely refused to fire. A freed Gorbachev had little choice but to accept not a new constitution for the Soviet Union but its dissolution.

Democracy and economic liberalism seemed to have won the day. Latin America saw a wave of democracies replace dictatorships starting in the late 1970s. The 1980s had even seen market capitalism, although not democracy, introduced into Communist China. Now, with the fall of the Soviet Union, the Cold War was over. In a book called *The End of History and the Last Man* (1992), Francis Fukuyama (1952–) argued that the big conflicts of history were coming to an end, as (neo)liberal democracies were in the process of displacing alternatives. Despite such triumphalism, the neoliberal movement has not, however, achieved all its goals. Contrary to the fears of their opponents, even figures such as Reagan and Thatcher largely left social welfare programs in place, at most reducing their rate of expansion; their neoliberal successors have not always succeeded in going further. After being lowered, taxes were sometimes raised in order to reduce budget deficits. Although the pace of growth of Western economies had picked up by the 1990s, unemployment in Western Europe often grew; the remedy remains a matter of controversy between neoliberals and their critics. Moreover, the financial and economic crisis at the time of the writing of this book has revived faith in Keynesian policy and government economic intervention in many, although not all, quarters. And the problem of community remains.

10.11 A GLOBAL COMMUNITY?

By the dawn of the twenty-first century, the world seemed to be drawing ever closer. This development is called "globalization." It is not, in fact, unprecedented. After all, in 1914 and for decades after, most of Asia and Africa was ruled by a handful of European states. Moreover, the late nineteenth century had seen an explosion of international trade fostered by those empires and a belief that free trade was best for prosperity. But free trade declined, especially with the Great Depression and the erection of trade barriers that went with it (see 10.3). The colonial empires were dismantled in the decades after World War II (see 10.9). It might be better to say that the 1980s and subsequent decades witnessed an accelerating *re*globalization, although, arguably, a more intense one because of technological innovations. It seemed to some that a new community was emerging, an international one. But it is far from clear that a sense of community exists on a global basis. Nationalism and smaller-scale notions of community appear to give people a greater sense of connection with others than does simply belonging to global humanity.

The globalization of the second half of the twentieth century has often been perceived as Americanization. This view was closely tied to the revival of world trade after World War II and the early dominance of the United States in that trade. At the time, the American economy was easily the most productive in the world, producing half of the world's industrial goods in a world ravaged by war. Hence, purchasing consumer goods was likely to mean purchasing American-made goods, and consumerism itself was tagged as specifically American, its spread to other countries as "Americanization." This idea was arguably a trick of perception—the consequence of mistaking prosperity for Americanness. Revived economies, particularly in Europe and Japan, eventually began to produce their own consumer goods, from televisions to refrigerators, items more available in America than anywhere else in 1950 because of American wealth. Thus, the prosperity of Europe in the later 1950s and 60s, including the purchase of washing machines or Coca Cola, also seemed to bring Americanization. The triumph of rock music, an undoubtedly American invention, appeared to do the same thing. Young Europeans swooning to Elvis Presley (1935–1977) suggested the weakness of European in the face of American popular culture, just as the failure of the Suez expedition (see 10.7) suggested Western European weakness in the face of American military might. (Of course, with British groups such as the Beatles, Western Europe in the 1960s became an exporter of rock music, including to the United States.) Consumerism continued to spread. Between 1965 and 1997, the number of television sets per 1,000 people on the planet grew from 57 to 240; in Latin America alone the number of sets increased fivefold.

This rise of consumerism and the tendency to see it as Americanization would be played out in other parts of the world in subsequent decades as these regions prospered. And, as in some quarters in Europe—where a French farmer could be regarded as a national hero for vandalizing a MacDonald's restaurant—it would be resented. American leadership among its allies in the decades after World War II was not without tensions.

Particularly since the 1990s, another invention has drawn the world together more intimately: the Internet, which made use of American innovations of the 1960s. Communication by e-mail around the world became fast and inexpensive. The World Wide Web, arguably founded in December 1990, made access to information a world away easier and easier. The personal computer, ever cheaper and more powerful, had been introduced in the 1980s, setting the stage for Internet access into people's homes once the Internet came into use. Satellites and fiber-optic cable also lowered expenses. By 1980, the real cost of a transatlantic phone call had fallen to something like a twentieth of what it had been in 1950; by 2000, it was even less. These communications revolutions encouraged businesses to operate internationally, indeed, globally. Firms in the United States or Europe or anywhere could outsource back-office operations—bookkeeping, billing, technological support—to India or Singapore or anywhere. The easy flow of information, along with some deregulation of the financial industry, encouraged lending and investment across borders and continents. Such activity nearly quintupled between 1990 and 2005.

International migration also picked up. North America had long attracted immigrants from other continents and continued to do so. Western European states, however, experiencing labor shortages as their economies heated up in the 1960s (see 10.10), also were flooded with immigrants from Asia and Africa. These newcomers were often from former colonies. The trend in Europe was boosted by the European Union (see 10.10), which allowed the free flow of workers across the borders of member states. At the end of 2011, one in eight residents of Great Britain had been born elsewhere. In a manner long familiar to many in the Americas, sections of some European cities came to be dominated by immigrants or their descendants—North Africans in France, Turks in Germany, Pakistanis in Britain. Tourism also increased the movement of people across the globe. Relative to world population, the number of international tourists increased 60 percent between 1980 and 1996. To some, a globalized world means that a new community beckons, that people are at home in the world at large, that a global community now transcends attachments to a particular nation or place. At the same time, however, globalization disorients, making even home feel alien or making strange places feel like home. The phenomenon was described in 1993 by Guillermo Gómez-Peña (1955–), a native of Mexico and a frequent visitor to the United States:

I am a migrant performance artist. I write in airplanes, trains, and cafés. I travel from city to city, coast to coast, country to country.... Home is always somewhere else. Home is both "here" and "there" or somewhere in between. Sometimes it's nowhere.... We have all been uprooted to different degrees....[29]

Globalization can threaten a sense of community, even work as an atomizing force. Finding roots everywhere can mean finding them nowhere.

Indeed, the end of the twentieth century and the beginning of the next have confirmed the continuing power of nationalism rather than global identity as a source of community. The collapse of the Soviet Union brought the collapse of the pax communista (see 10.7). Nationalities were freed to pursue conflicts with each other. And they did. The former Soviet republics of Armenia and Azerbaijan went to war as ethnic Armenians sought independence from Azerbaijan; a truce was called in 1994 (Map 10.4). The collapse of the communist dictatorship in Yugoslavia in 1991 brought years of war as Serbia refused to allow first Bosnia, populated by ethnic Serbs as well Muslims, and then Kosovo, populated by Albanians as well as Serbs, to go their own way (Map 10.4).[30] Instead, Serbs attempted an "ethnic cleansing," by rape and execution, of the territories they claimed, only to see Albanians in Kosovo practice ethnic cleansing against them. Although the term was new, the idea was old. Peace in these regions remains precarious.

Some have hoped to submerge nationalism in Europe in the European Union (EU). But responses to the EU suggest that national feeling is far from dead. The Maastricht Treaty of 1992 set up the European Union, calling also for a single European currency and stronger, European-wide institutions. Danish voters at first rejected the treaty, and voters in France, one of the leading forces behind the proposal, barely ratified it. Britain insisted on opting out of the single currency. As of early 2013, it is unclear whether the European Union will survive the financial crises of several of its members, which would require some states, especially Germany, to pay the expenses of others, such as Greece. Moreover, some smaller nations have become more vigorous in pressing their claims for independence. In Britain, Scottish and Welsh nationalism led to separate Scottish and Welsh parliaments, although the British Parliament in Westminster still largely governs the United Kingdom. In Spain, Basque separatists, demanding independence for their small land in the north of the country, have planted bombs and carried out assassinations since the 1960s. All told, national identity in Europe seems stronger than a European one, much less a global one.

For others, religion rather than the nation offers a sense of community. This development has been somewhat unexpected. In Europe, religious fervor is generally muted. In the United States and to some extent in Latin America, religious identities are more vigorous but have long been accommodated to national feeling; few Americans see a

---

29 Guillermo Gómez-Peña, "The New World Border," in *The Mexico Reader*, eds. Gilbert M. Joseph and Timothy J. Henderson (Durham, NC: Duke University Press, 2002), 750–51.

30 The national, ethnic, and religious characteristics of these regions are complex. In Yugoslavia, for example, Muslims had been regarded as a distinct nationality, sometimes called "Bosnians."

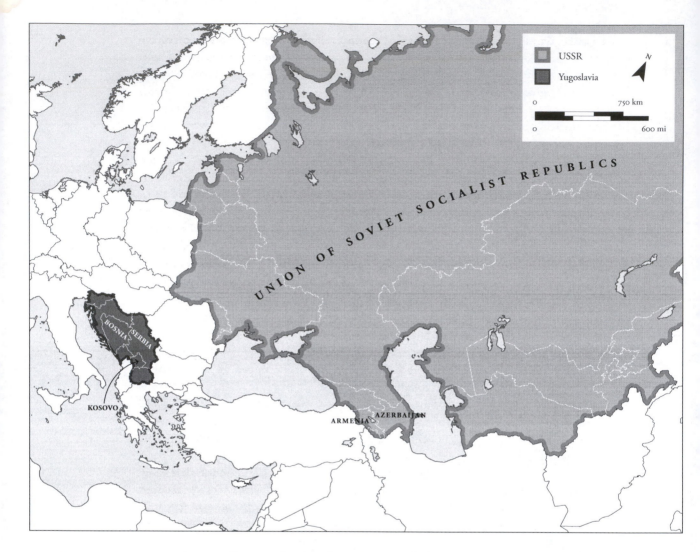

Map 10.4: The former Soviet Union and the former Yugoslavia

tension between being, say, a Southern Baptist and an American. However, Muslim immigrants in Western Europe often have had a different experience. They have not integrated so easily into the national lives of their new homes; most European countries have had little experience in assimilating immigrants and have not made vigorous attempts to do so. Furthermore, multicultural policy (see 10.8), if anything, discourages such attempts.

Nationalistic passions have long had the capacity to move national minorities to terrorism—consider the assassination of the Archduke Franz Ferdinand (see 10.2) or the Basque separatists of more recent times. Religious identity has the same capacity. A version of Islam—sometimes described as "Islamism" to distinguish it from traditional Islam—calls on all Muslims to recreate the Islamic state of the Middle Ages, which would, in turn, enforce an inflexible form of Sharia, or Muslim law, binding all Muslims into a true community. Unbelievers, even the Christians and Jews for whom traditional Islam had made a place, would have no place. What is needed is religious cleansing, a version of the ethnic cleansing rooted in nationalist passions. Ironically, this vision draws on Western Romantic criticisms of the Enlightenment and, ultimately, of the West. It sees the non-Muslim world as promoting an atomizing, selfish individualism, which is contrasted with the true Islam of Islamism (on similar criticisms, see 8.7 and 9.3). The consumerism of Western society only further sours this image of the West. Globalization, which tends to be seen as Westernization or Americanization, makes it that much more threatening. Alternatively, globalization can foster a disorienting rootlessness, the other side of the freedom celebrated by Gómez-Peña. In Muslim countries, Islamism offers a vision of community rivaling that offered by nationalism and Marxism. Much, perhaps most, of Islamist feeling has been naturally aimed against nationalist and communist regimes—both secular—in the Islamic world, which worked to suppress Islamist movements and even sometimes Islam itself. The Taliban (see 10.7) is an example of such a movement. In the West, however, a consequence of such Islamism has been terrorist attacks. The activities of Osama bin Laden (1957–2011) and his associates are an instance. After defending their version of Islam against communism following the Soviet invasion of Afghanistan (see 10.7), Bin Laden's Islamist organization, al-Qaeda, focused its attention on the United States. After bombing American embassies in Africa and the World Trade Center office towers in New York City in 1993, al-Qaeda carried out its deadliest attack to date on September 11, 2001. Its operatives hijacked several planes, flying two jets into the World Trade Center—symbol of the world commerce that seems such a threat to critics of globalization (citizens of more than 70 countries died in the attack)—and one into the Pentagon, center of the US military establishment. Nearly three thousand people died in the catastrophe. Smaller but substantial attacks followed: mass bombings in Madrid on March 11, 2004, and in London on July 7, 2005.

Islamism has it attractions in the West itself. In the years 1997–2004, London's Finsbury Park was a center for Islamist activity. Its imam, Abu Hamza al-Masri (1958–) preached revolution against the West during his tenure from 1997 to 2004. Originally from Egypt, Abu Hamza, a civil engineer by training, arrived in Britain in 1979. He praised the September 11, 2001, attacks on the United States. But such views were not confined to immigrants. Zacarias Moussaoui (1968–) was born in France, from which he moved to Britain. Although his involvement in the September 11 plot is debated, it is evident that he served as an operative of al-Qaeda. John Walker Lindh (1981–), an American convert to Islam, traveled to Afghanistan to fight for the Taliban against its rivals in Afghanistan. Richard Reid (1973–), a native of Britain, converted to Islam, quickly becoming an Islamist after attending the Finsbury Park mosque under Abu Hamza. In 2001, he unsuccessfully attempted to blow up a passenger jet bound for the United States with explosives hidden in his shoes. Three of the four London bombers of July 7, 2005, had been born and raised in Britain; the fourth had lived there since the age of five. These men found a sense of community through Islam(ism) that an atomized West did not offer.

Globalization does not appear to have created a global community. Indeed, one can argue it has made the possibility even more remote.

FURTHER READING

Betts, Raymond F. *Decolonization*. 2nd ed. New York: Routledge, 2004.

Bosworth, R.J. *Mussolini's Italy: Life Under the Dictatorship, 1915–1945*. New York: Penguin Books, 2006.

Brocheux, Pierre, and Ho Chi Minh. *A Biography*. Translated by Claire Duiker. Cambridge: Cambridge University Press, 2007.

Bumsted, J.M. *A History of the Canadian Peoples*. 4th ed. Oxford: Oxford University Press, 2011.

Buruma, Ian, and Avishai Margalit. *Occidentalism: The West in the Eyes of Its Enemies*. New York: Penguin Books, 2004.

Croucher, Sheila L. *Globalization and Belonging: The Politics of Identity in a Changing World*. Lanham, MD: Rowman & Littlefield, 2003.

Engel, Barbara Alpern, and Anastasia Posadskaya-Vanderbeck, eds. *A Revolution of Their Own: Voices of Women in Soviet History*. Boulder, CO: Westview Press, 1998. [Interviews.]

Evans, Richard J. *The Third Reich in Power*. New York: Penguin Books, 2005.

Gilbert, Felix, and David Clay Large. *The End of the European Era: 1890 to the Present*. 6th ed. New York: W.W. Norton Company, 2008.

Hunt, Michael H., ed. *The World Transformed, 1945 to the Present: A Documentary Reader*. Boston: Bedford/Saint Martin's, 2003. [Primary sources.]

Judt, Tony. *Postwar: A History of Europe since 1945*. New York: Penguin Books, 2005.

Keegan, John. *The First World War*. London: Random House, 1998.

Kennedy, David M. *Freedom from Fear: The American People in Depression and War, 1929–1945*. Oxford: Oxford University Press, 1999.

Kindleberger, Charles. *The World in Depression, 1929–1939*. Revised edition. Berkeley, Los Angeles: University of California Press, 1986.

Klein, Maury. *Rainbow's End: The Crash of 1929*. Oxford: Oxford University Press, 2001.

Kurlansky, Mark. *1968: The Year that Rocked the World*. New York: Random House, 2005. [Packed with colorful detail.]

Lyons, Michael J. *World War II: A Short History*. 5th ed. Upper Saddle River, NJ: Pearson, 2009.

Masani, Zareer. *Indian Tales of the Raj*. Berkeley, Los Angeles: University of California Press, 1987. [A secondary source, but filled with excerpts of interviews of Indians recalling British rule.]

Meredith, Martin. *The Fate of Africa: A History of Fifty Years of Independence*. New York: Public Affairs, 2005.

Mitchell , Joseph R., and Helen Buss Mitchell, eds. *The Holocaust: Readings and Interpretations*. Guilford, CT: McGraw-Hill/Dushkin, 2001.

Mittelman, James H. *The Globalization Syndrome: Transformation and Resistance*. Princeton, NJ: Princeton University Press, 2000.

Noakes, Jeremy, and Geoffrey Pridham, eds. *Nazism 1919–1945: A Documentary Reader*. 3rd ed. 4 vols. Exeter: University of Exeter Press, 2001. [Primary sources.]

Porter, Bernard. *The Lion's Share: A Short History of British Imperialism, 1850–2004*. 4th ed. London: Longman, 2004.

Service, Robert. *The Russian Revolution, 1900–1927*. 4th ed. New York: Palgrave MacMilllan, 2009.

Smith, Peter H. *Democracy in Latin America: Political Change in Comparative Perspective*. Oxford: Oxford University Press, 2005.

Snyder, Timothy. *Bloodlands: Europe between Hitler and Stalin*. New York: Basic Books, 2010.

Ward, Chris. *Stalin's Russia*. 2nd ed. London: Arnold, 2003.

ELEVEN

CODA: THE SHAPING OF WESTERN CIVILIZATION

In 1775, King Louis XVI of France's finance minister Anne-Robert-Jacques Turgot (1727–1781), himself a philosophe, explained the state of the country to his master:

> All that is necessary is to thoroughly understand and to correctly weigh the rights and the interests of men.... The rights of men gathered in society are not founded on their history as men [and so not on custom], but in their nature [and so are human rights].... The cause of the evil, Sire, lies in the fact that your nation has no constitution. It is a society composed of different orders ill-united, and of a people the members of which have between them very few social ties.... There is no public spirit, because there is no point of common interest visible and recognised.[1]

It was a classic Enlightenment statement. Turgot asserts that people's rights are not determined by custom but by nature. He sees a society made up of orders as "ill-united"; he does not see an organically unified society of orders. Turgot's complaint indicates how the West had changed since the Middle Ages, even since ca. 1600. For as late as ca. 1600, all orders were united—in the body politic. Then, the common interest was, in theory, visible to all. But in 1775, even while asserting an atomizing notion of human rights and a rejection of tradition, Turgot failed to see what those rights and that rejection of tradition entailed.

Turgot's memorandum reveals a limitation of the Enlightenment's vision of a society of free and equal citizens. The West faced an atomized society, and the path to community was unclear. From the later eighteenth century, industrialization added to the urgency,

---

1 *The Life and Writings of Turgot*, ed. W. Walker Stephens (New York, 1971), 265–68.

increasingly giving the uneducated practical experience of the atomization sensed by philosophes like Turgot. How could individuals recover a sense of connection with others?

Much of the West's later history has been the story of attempts to overcome an atomized society, to recreate that sense of community. The attractions of nationalism and Marxism, so important to the history of the nineteenth and twentieth centuries, were rooted in that desire. So, for that matter, are some of the attractions of early twenty-first-century identity politics: of a women's, or gay, or black community and, for the West the newest entrant, an Islamic (read Islamist) community. Socialists, especially since the collapse of communism, have had trouble showing a compelling basis for a sense of community, although they often assert there is one. Their neoliberal opponents, themselves the most direct heirs of Enlightenment thought, have had the same difficulty. Margaret Thatcher once famously asserted that "there is no such thing as society," arguing that we should look to neighbors for help when we really need it—to "a living tapestry of men and women," as she called such connections, rather than to the state.[2] But like Turgot's common interest, this assertion of a living tapestry is rather empty, coming with little explanation. It is not surprising, however, that, when she expressed why one should feel such ties, Thatcher was more a nationalist than a neoliberal. The West still grapples with the legacy of the Enlightenment, itself a legacy of generations who would have been appalled by it.

Ca. 1500, Western states were hobbled by their medieval legacy. A forest of orders and corporations, bristling with rights, limited the power of kings. A variety of forces had given rise to that forest in the High and Late Middle Ages, including the actions of kings, who had crystallized group rights by recognizing them (or creating them), often in courts of law. Early modern monarchies, driven to pay the increasing cost of war, did their best to cut down that forest. And, despite compromises, they met some success, fostering greater legal equality along with greater government power. The French Revolution would carry that project even further, and it would be carried further still in succeeding centuries. The modern Western state, with its enormous capacity to direct society—most strikingly evident in the ambitions of the Holocaust and of the Soviet Union's Five-Year Plans and more quietly and less dramatically evident in universal, state-sponsored education—would be the result. In Britain, however, one body successfully defended its rights against the monarchy in the seventeenth century and, indeed, radically extended them: Parliament. And it would be Britain's parliamentary government—later to be much imitated—that ultimately would be the vessel for the survival of constitutional government in the West.

Yet does examining the history of the West make sense as a means of understanding the present? There is reason to think not. I have argued that large parts of the world beyond the West have been influenced by it—in particular by Western nationalism and Marxism and by the atomization exported by the West to other parts of the world. But if people such as Gandhi can be said to have been "westernized" in this way, it is fair to say that a cultural fusion has been taking place, between the West and the rest, and has been doing so for a

---

2   Quoted in *Contemporary Political Theorists in Context*, by Anthony M. Clohesy, Stuart Isaacs, and
    Chris Sparks (New York: Routledge, 2009), 129.

couple of centuries at least. Indeed, some enthusiasts for globalization insist that a new, global, culture is emerging. After all, people like Gandhi did not, by being Westernized, cease to be Indian; they were not and are not Western clones. Instead, they became and are both. If a global culture is emerging, is it meaningful to talk about the modern West, when the West has melded with the rest of the world? Recall that the West's history is, in fact, a history of such cultural fusions: between the peoples of the ancient Near East and the Greeks, between Greeks and Romans, between Romans and Christians, and between these and Germanic peoples. Now—in the nineteenth, twentieth, and twenty-first centuries—is another one. Perhaps the history of the West now must include the history of, say, China, India, or sub-Saharan Africa—indeed, the world. Or perhaps "the West" has ceased to be a meaningful term.

The cultural fusion between the peoples of the ancient Near East and their Greek conquerors is especially suggestive when it comes to thinking about a fusion between Western and non-Western societies. That earlier fusion was the result of conquest: Alexander the Great and his followers conquered the Persian Empire and, on Alexander's death, Greeks set themselves up as a new ruling class, determined to keep themselves separate from and superior to the ruled. Yet the fusion between these groups, Hellenistic civilization, emerged without being clearly perceived by the very people who produced it. It is modern historians who can describe that fusion, and the shape of the civilization that resulted. We in the early twenty-first century may be in the midst of a grand fusion, of the creation of a global civilization. But like those ancient Greek conquerors, and those they conquered, we do not yet know what shape that civilization has. A broader history of Western civilization, or what might better be described as global civilization, will probably have to wait for centuries to be written. And so this book is about the shaping of the West, the West as most easily understood today.

This book began with R.G. Collingwood and it will end with him: "History books begin and end, but the events they describe do not."[3] Historians like to divide up the past into tidy periods. The habit is useful; it makes the preceding chapters possible. Yet, as those chapters suggest, no period is cut off from those that precede and follow it. Indeed, to reflect on the story recounted here is to reflect on the fact that history, or at least this history, is a story of unintended, unimagined consequences. Despite their (sometimes) best intentions, people in the past did not create their world according to some plan; they did not live and think entirely by design, their own or that of their predecessors. Instead, they lived in an accidental world. And so do we.

The biggest historical division felt by the living is that between the past and the present. In a fundamental sense, the past is dead; we are alive. The past is an alien world in countless ways. Ancient gods inhabited their statues. Twelfth-century juries were made up of people who were supposed to *know* what had happened rather than impartially *discover* what happened. Despite contemporary experience of feminism as the great engine prying open opportunity for women, such opportunities sometimes emerged without benefit

---

3 R.G. Collingwood, *An Autobiography* (Oxford: Oxford University Press, 1939), 98.

of a feminist movement. But if the story told here is right, one cannot expect our own time to be free of its past, even its remote past. I hope this book has shed light on change and continuity between that past and the West's present, a light to illuminate them both.

SOURCES

FIGURES

6.1: Bernini, *Ecstasy of Saint Teresa* (1647–1652). Reproduced by permission of Scala / Art Resource, NY.

7.5: Galileo's sketches of the moon seen through a telescope. Reproduced by permission of Scala / Art Resource, NY.

8.1: Jean-Baptiste Charpentier, *Duke of Penthièvre's family drinking chocolate* (ca. 1767). Copyright © RMN-Grand Palais / Art Resource, NY.

8.2: Jacques Louis David, *The Lictors Bring to Brutus the Bodies of His Sons* (1789). Copyright © RMN-Grand Palais / Art Resource, NY.

9.1: Joseph Koch *Macbeth and the Witches* (1834–5). Reproduced by permission of Snark / Art Resource, NY.

9.2: Parliament Building, Great Britain (commenced 1836). Copyright © Vanni Archive / Art Resource, NY.

9.3: Parliament Building, Hungary. Copyright © Rudy Sulgan / Corbis.

9.4: Pablo Picasso, *Three Women* (1907–8). Image courtesy of Scala / Art Resource, NY. Copyright © Picasso Estate / SODRAC (2013).

9.5: Mark Rothko, *White Center* (1957). Digital image copyright © 2013 Museum Associates / LACMA. Licensed by Art Resource, NY / Copyright © 2013 Kate Rothko Prizel & Christopher Rothko/ SODRAC.

9.6: Ludwig Mies van der Rohe, Tugendhat house (1928–1930). Digital image copyright © The Museum of Modern Art / Licensed by Scala / Art Resource, NY / © Estate of Ludwig Mies Van der Rohe / SODRAC (2013).

9.7: Roy Lichtenstein, *Brushstrokes* (1965). Image courtesy of Tate, London / Art Resource, NY / Copyright © Estate of Roy Lichtenstein / SODRAC (2013).

9.8: University of Houston's College of Architecture building (1984–1986). Reprinted by permission of Jack Chaiyakhom.

10.1: Gustav Klutsis, "Long Live Our Happy Socialist Motherland! Long Live Our Beloved Great Stalin!" (Da zdravstvuet nasha schastlivaia sotsialisticheskaia rodina. Da zdravstvuet nash liubimyi velikii Stalin!), Klutsis, G., 1935, Russian Public Library part of Stalinka, Digital Library of Staliniana, University of Pittsburgh. Reprinted by permission.

INDEX